UNEVEN DEVELOPMENT
IN SOUTHERN EUROPE

UNEVEN DEVELOPMENT IN SOUTHERN EUROPE

Studies of accumulation, class, migration and the state

Edited by
Ray Hudson and *Jim Lewis*

Methuen
LONDON and NEW YORK

First published in 1985 by
Methuen & Co. Ltd
11 New Fetter Lane, London EC4P 4EE

Published in the USA by
Methuen & Co.
in association with Methuen, Inc.
733 Third Avenue, New York, NY 10017

Typeset by
Scarborough Typesetting Services
and printed in Great Britain at
the University Press, Cambridge

British Library Cataloguing in Publication Data
Uneven development in Southern Europe: studies
  of accumulation, class, migration and the state.
  1. Europe, Southern—Economic conditions
  I. Hudson, Ray II. Lewis, Jim
  330.94   HC244.5

ISBN 0–416–32840–7

Contents

Tables

Figures

Preface

The substantive chapters which follow were all originally prepared for a conference on 'National and Regional Development in the Mediterranean Basin' that was held in St Aidan's College, University of Durham, in April 1982. It is a pleasure to acknowledge the financial assistance which we received from The British Academy, The British Council, The Centre for Middle Eastern and Islamic Studies (University of Durham), The Regional Science Association (British Section) and the Social Science Research Council, for their provision of grants or loans enabled some sixty people from twelve countries to meet and exchange ideas or information in a most stimulating environment. We are also grateful to Professor F. G. T. Holliday, Vice-Chancellor of the University of Durham, for his participation and the University's generous hospitality.

It was never our intention to publish another in the long line of volumes of conference proceedings so we have had the difficult task of selecting an integrated sample from the forty or so papers discussed in Durham. The result is a collection that reflects the emphasis of the conference on the best of current social scientific research and balances a coverage of the main themes to emerge in the debates about Southern European countries with a proportional representation of those countries. Each of the chapters has been specially revised in light of the conference discussions and the overall structure of this volume. The respective authors are grateful for the translations of all or parts of their chapters to the following: Bob Maat, Georg Stauth and Jim Lewis (Chapter 2), Ray Hudson (Chapter 5), Eleonore Kofman (Chapter 6), Chris Jensen-Butler and Jim Lewis (Chapter 9). As editors, we should like to thank the secretarial and cartographic staff of the Geography Department of Durham University for their work in transforming very difficult raw material into a high quality final product and pay a special tribute to the patience of Mary Ann Kernan who has gently reminded us of missed submission dates whether we have been in Canberra, Coimbra or Copenhagen.

1

Introduction: recent economic, social and political changes in Southern Europe[1]

Ray Hudson and Jim Lewis

The organization of the volume

This book seeks to capture the most significant of the many changes that are taking place in the economic, social and political structures of Southern European countries. Its approach, for the most part, is that of the theoretically informed case study, for we believe that there is not yet sufficient high quality social scientific research on contemporary processes of development in all parts of this region to enable the preparation of a comprehensive set of systematic studies. At present, it appears to be more useful to refine our theoretical frameworks to cope with a rapidly changing reality and collect information on comparatively new phenomena with relatively small-scale studies, in the hope that we will be able to build up comparative studies during the 1980s which will give generalizations about Southern European 'Models of Development' a closer relationship to contemporary reality than they now enjoy. While there are obviously differences between the views of the eighteen authors, the broad theoretical framework used in this volume is that of political economy, which provides a range of concepts capable of integrating local scales with international ones and placing the specific circumstances of each case in the context of more general trends. Indeed, it has been increasingly recognized within this framework that differentiation between areas is itself integral to the development of more general processes of social change (for example, see Carney *et al.*, 1980b; Harvey, 1982, especially Chapters 12 and 13). It is this framework that suggests the themes of capital accumulation, class structure and the state as the unifying concerns of the chapters for each address one (or more) of them in its analysis of the ways in which spatially uneven development occurs. Since the simplest description of the processes changing the political economy of Southern Europe would be the development of capitalism there, the theme of capital accumulation is obviously central and draws attention to the impact of spatial movements of labour – both to and from areas of rapid accumulation – and movements of capital on local, regional and national economies. As the studies by Garcia-Ramon and Pugliese show, the development of capitalism does not always involve the creation of capitalist class structures and the pattern of social change is further complicated by the presence of individuals such as returned migrants who do not fit easily into conventional categories. Thirdly, there is the theme of political change that comes to the fore in the studies of the state and its legitimacy but which is also present wherever the question of state policies towards different areas or classes is discussed.

The selectivity implied in this approach to the processes currently reshaping Southern Europe has meant that several topics are not discussed in depth. Our concern for new processes has left little room for analysis of long-established and well-studied sorts of change such as out-migration from rural areas or regional planning. At the same time, the intention of presenting investigations with a sound theoretical base has forced us to exclude some important recent phenomena such as tourism and urbanization because of the lack of appropriate research. The collection is also selective in its spatial coverage for we have concentrated on those six countries of Southern Europe that are most closely associated with Northern Europe – France, Greece, Italy, Portugal, Spain and Turkey. Since the circumstances of contemporary change in Albania and Yugoslavia are so very different, there seemed little advantage in including studies from them and we have also excluded from consideration the 'non-European' parts of countries like France and Portugal. The result of this dual selectivity is a set of studies that makes no claim to comprehensiveness but which may, through its careful examination of different parts, give a picture of the whole that is more clearly defined than many efforts to portray everything at once.

The structure of the book involves a movement from considerations of the effects of labour migration on regional and local economies, through analyses of socio-economic changes in specific areas (or firms) associated with different forms of capitalist development to considerations of the relationships between the resultant uneven development and political legitimacy. The remainder of this introduction is devoted to the setting of a context for that movement. It first summarizes the main features of the countries concerned for anyone not familiar with them all (pp. 3–16) and then outlines the sorts of socio-economic changes arising from movements of labour and capital (pp. 16–50) before reviewing the political implications of the growing disparities between people in different parts of Southern Europe.

The countries of Southern Europe: a summary of their economic, political and social features

Population

As Table 1.1 shows, there are striking contrasts between the six nations in terms of both total population and rates of demographic change. In terms of totals, France and Italy have populations that exceed those of Greece and Portugal by a factor of five, with Spain and Turkey in intermediate positions. While the range narrows in terms of densities, there are still considerable differences – especially between Italy, with 189 per sq. km, and Turkey with 58. Such basic differences in population sizes and densities both reflect and influence many other aspects of socio-economic and political structure.

In contrast to countries of Northern Europe such as Belgium, the Federal Republic of Germany and the UK which were experiencing very slow or zero population growth by the latter part of the 1970s (Commission of the European Communities, 1978), growth rates have remained generally high in Southern Europe but nevertheless with considerable variation between the Turkish rate of 2.4 per cent per annum and those of France or Italy (0.5 and 0.6 per cent respectively). These variations were very closely correlated to those in birth rates, and national differences in both of these demographic variables are quite closely associated with those in levels of economic development and performance.

Gross Domestic Product

Differences in size between national economies (measured in terms of GDP) are considerably greater than those in national populations – a difference of 27 to 1 between France and Portugal (see Table 2.2). More generally, the contrasts between France and Italy, on the one hand, and Greece, Portugal and Turkey, on the other (with Spain in an intermediate position), are very striking and indicative of qualitative as well as quantitative differences in levels of economic development. Nevertheless, much of the difference in national GDP can be accounted for simply in terms of size of population and, by implication, of labour force, for the ratio of highest to lowest *per capita* GDP (France: Turkey) falls to just over 10 to 1.

Table 1.1 *Demographic indicators*

	France	Greece	Italy	Portugal	Spain	Turkey
Population (mid-1980, millions)	53.5	9.6	56.9	9.8	37.4	44.9
Population density (per sq. km)	97.8	72.7	189.0	106.5	74.1	57.5
Population growth (annual average percentage, 1970–80)	0.5	0.9	0.6	1.3	1.0	2.4
Crude birth rate per 1000 population (1980)	14.0	16.0	14.0	18.0	15.0	32.0

Source: World Bank, 1982, Tables 1, 17 and 18.

Table 1.2 *Gross Domestic Product, 1960–80*

	France	Greece	Italy	Portugal	Spain	Turkey
GDP, 1980 ($USA, billions)	651.9	40.4	394.0	24.1	211.1	52.9
GDP *per capita*, 1980 ($USA)	12,140	4,210	6,910	2,430	5,650	1,170
Growth of GDP, 1960–70 (annual average percentage)	5.5	6.9	5.3	6.2	7.1	6.0
Growth of GDP, 1970–80 (annual average percentage)	3.5	4.9*	3.0	4.6	4.0	5.9
Percentage GDP from agriculture, 1980	4	16	6	13	8	23
Percentage GDP from industry, 1980	36	32	43	46	37	30
Percentage GDP from services, 1980	60	52	51	41	55	47

* 1970–9

Sources: OECD, 1982b; World Bank, 1982, Tables 1–3.

Bearing in mind these disparities in the magnitude of national economies – and hence very different base figures – there is a striking degree of similarity in GDP growth rates. In the 1960s they averaged between 7.1 per cent per annum in Spain and 5.3 per cent per annum in Italy, generally above the growth rates of the advanced capitalist nations of Northern Europe and North America, but below that of Japan. While growth rates in the 1970s fell in every case (although only marginally in Turkey which then had the highest rate at 5.9 per cent per annum), in general they still remained above those of the advanced capitalist world, with the exception of Japan, but tended to be below those of the newly industrializing countries of South-East Asia (Balassa, 1981).

Not only are there marked differences in the size of national economies but these also exist in the sectoral composition of GDP. Agriculture contributed 23 per cent of Turkey's GDP in 1980, with a relatively high share also originating from this sector in Greece and Portugal, whereas in Spain, Italy and, especially, France (4 per cent) it was much less significant. Industry provided between 46 per cent of GDP in Portugal and 30 per cent in Turkey, a much smaller relative and absolute range than in the case of agriculture. But the most significant source of GDP, with the exception of Portugal, is the service sector, ranging from 60 per cent in France to 41 per cent in Portugal. From this evidence of their economic structure it might be argued that all six countries have reached the same relatively advanced stage of economic development, but to do so would ignore the great heterogeneity within the service sector, which includes not only high level administrative jobs in public and private sectors, but also economically marginal activities in countries like Turkey and Greece.

External economic relationships

While there are dangers in relying too heavily on any one year's figures, given the volatility of current account net balances, the figures for 1980 (Table 1.3) show that all the countries had deficits although of varying magnitudes. However, these appear in a rather different perspective when broken down into total flows of imports and exports – both in absolute terms and relative to GDP. Thus, France's large absolute current account deficit appears in a very different light as it is also by far the largest exporter, French exports being over thirty-eight times greater than Turkish. More generally, export volume serves sharply to differentiate France and Italy from the remaining countries, particularly Greece, Portugal and Turkey. The picture in relation to imports is much the same, France having the greatest import bill, exceeding that of Turkey by a

Table 1.3 *External economic relationships*

	France	Greece	Italy	Portugal	Spain	Turkey
Current account balance ($, millions)	−7,786	−2,218	−9,958	−1,076	−4,635	−2,762
Exports, 1980 ($, millions)	111,251	5,143	77,667	4,628	20,721	2,910
Exports as a % GDP, 1980	17.1	12.7	19.7	19.2	9.8	5.5
Imports, 1980 ($, millions)	134,912	10,531	99,452	9,410	34,080	7,667
Imports as a % GDP, 1980	20.7	26.1	25.2	39.0	16.1	14.5
Tourist receipts, 1980 ($, millions)	+8,197	+1,734	+8,213	+1,149	+6,968	+327
Tourist receipts as a % merchandise exports, 1980	7.4	33.7	10.6	24.8	33.6	11.2
Migrant remittances, 1979	−4,370	+1,180	+3,017	+2,474	+1,752★	+1,735
Migrant remittances as a % merchandise exports, 1980	−3.9	22.9	3.9	53.5	8.5	59.6
External public debt, 1980 ($, millions)	n.a.	4,451	n.a.	5,610	n.a.	13,216
External public debt as % GNP	n.a.	10.9	n.a.	23.6	n.a.	22.4
Net private direct investment, 1981 ($, millions)	−2,166	520	−254	156	1,440	150

★ 1978

Sources: World Bank, 1982, Tables 8, 13, 14 and 15; OECD, 1982c; Swamy, 1981.

factor of more than seventeen. When exports and imports are considered relative to GDP then the differences between nations narrows: France, Italy and Portugal are particularly reliant upon international export markets, Greece and Spain less so, while Turkey's exports amount to only some 5 per cent of GDP (compared to almost 20 per cent for Italy and Portugal). Equally, Portugal imports by far the greatest amount relative to GDP (38.7 per cent) and Turkey the least (11.8 per cent). These differing absolute and relative degrees of dependence upon exports and imports of goods indicate the varying extent to which the six national economies are integrated and inserted into the international economy (Fuá, 1980). This, in turn, is related to the structure of, and changes in, these economies – a theme considered more fully below (pp. 25–50).

For the moment, though, some preliminary evidence can be presented in the structure of merchandise trade (Table 1.4). What is clear is the dependence of all six countries on imports of primary commodities, although there are important differences in type of commodity. Despite the often high shares of agriculture in both total employment and GDP, food figures prominently on the import bill of all but Turkey – a situation which reflects both developments in agriculture itself and in other sectors of their national economies (which are discussed below). What is more striking, however, is the extent to which fuels dominate the overall pattern of imports, an indication of dependence upon increasingly expensive imported oil for domestic and industrial energy and one which is especially marked in Turkey. Turning to manufactured goods, there is much greater dependence upon imported machinery and transport equipment in Greece, Portugal and Turkey than in the other three nations, implying in turn a considerable reliance upon foreign technology – although there is evidence that this is also marked in certain key industrial sectors in France, Italy and Spain (Granados and Aurioles, 1982).

As regards exports, an even more variable pattern is evident. With the exception of Greece, which has important mineral deposits, fuels, minerals and metals are a comparatively insignificant component of total exports. Other primary commodities (largely those of agriculture, together with fishing and forestry) are of generally more importance, and especially so in Turkey where two-thirds of mechandise exports are of this type. There are equally striking differences in the weight of manufacturing exports, ranging from 83 per cent of all exports in Italy to 28 per cent in Turkey, with the manufacturing sector also providing over 70 per cent of total exports in France, Portugal and Spain and less than 50 per cent in Greece. Not only are there variations in the overall importance of manufactured goods in total exports, but also in the type of manufactures.

Table 1.4 *Structure of merchandise trade, 1979*

	France	Greece	Italy	Portugal	Spain	Turkey
Percentage share of imports:						
Food	12	10	16	17	15	2
Fuels	22	21	24	20	30	36
Other primary commodities	9	7	15	11	13	5
Machinery and transport equipment	22	38	19	25	19	28
Other manufactures	35	24	26	27	23	29
Percentage share of exports:						
Fuel, minerals and metals	7	21	8	2	5	6
Other primary commodities	18	33	9	22	22	66
Textiles and clothing	5	17	12	31	5	19
Machinery and transport equipment	36	4	30	12	26	2
Other manufactures	34	25	41	33	42	7

Source: World Bank, 1982, Tables 9 and 10.

Textiles and clothing contribute 31 per cent of all Portuguese exports, between 12 per cent and 19 per cent of those of Italy, Greece and Turkey, but only 5 per cent of those of France and Spain.

Thus far the emphasis has remained on merchandise trade, on exports and imports of commodities and goods, but the various 'invisible' items on the current account balance sheet (notably migrant remittances and receipts from tourism) are of considerable significance in Southern Europe (Table 1.3). In absolute terms, there were considerable national differences in tourist receipts in 1980: over $8000 million in France and Italy, almost $7000 million in Spain, to as low as $327 million in Turkey. Seen in relation to merchandise exports this pattern changes dramatically and the importance to Greece, Portugal and Spain of tourist remittances – equal to between one-third and one-quarter of the value of merchandise exports – is readily apparent. The situation regarding migrant remittances is more complicated. In 1979 France had a net loss through remittances, reflecting the great inflow of migrant labour in the 1960s and early 1970s (see pp. 19–22 below) and the continuing structural dependence of the French economy on such labour. The remaining countries were all net beneficiaries of remittances, though again the contrasts are much sharper and more revealing when these are viewed relative to the value of merchandise exports. Remittances in Turkey were equivalent to almost 60 per cent of the value of exports, those in Portugal to over 53 per cent and those in Greece to almost 23 per cent; in contrast, in Spain and Italy the comparable figures were a little more than 8 per cent and less than 4 per cent, respectively. Viewed in this relative context, the great dependence of the Greek, Portuguese, Spanish and Turkish economies on either migrant remittances and/or tourist receipts is clear; to this extent the economic fortunes of those nations and the options open to their governments are heavily conditioned by changes in the labour markets of Northern Europe (and, particularly in the case of Turkey, the Gulf States) both as a source of employment for Southern European migrants and as a source of mass tourist movements to Southern Europe.

There is another sense in which the countries of Southern Europe are dependent upon events in the global economy which arises precisely because of borrowing on the international financial markets to fund development projects and offset chronic balance of payment deficits. This traps many of them in a web of international indebtedness and by 1980 external public debt was equal to about 23 per cent of GDP in both Portugal and Turkey, and 11 per cent in Greece. As events in Portugal in 1976 showed, when the IMF imposed restrictions on government policies, as a condition for granting international credit, this indebtedness can severely limit the range of policy options open to national governments in Southern Europe.

Finally, there is evidence of Southern Europe's dependence in the pattern of capital movements. The problems in using the sort of figures given for net private direct investment in 1981 in Table 1.3 are considered at length in Hudson and Lewis (1984), a review which focuses on the industrial component of such flows. Here it is thus sufficient to note the difference between France and Italy, which were net exporters of capital ($2166 million and $254 million respectively), and the remaining countries which had net inflows ranging from the substantial (Spain at $1440 million) to the relatively insignificant (Turkey at $150 million). The general results of this latter group's reliance on foreign capital for part of the national investment – often in key sectors – are the pressure on governments to pursue policies that are acceptable to the major investors and the longer-term problem of eventual profit repatriation, but there are numerous other consequences in terms of the nature and pattern of economic growth. Nikolinakos (pp. 199–209) and Murolo (1982) address some of these in the context of Greece and there are useful case studies of the other recipient countries by Eraydin (1981), Muñoz et al. (1980), Braña et al. (1982) and Matos (1973).

Employment

Given national differences in the sizes of economies and populations, there are understandable variations in numbers of civilian employees (Table 1.5).[2] What is less immediately explicable, however, are the differences in employment growth rates in the 1970s. Spain, having experienced a rapid growth of employment in the preceding decade, recorded virtually none in the 1970s, as the Spanish economy proved much more susceptible to the effects of world recession than those of the other five Southern European nations. At the other extreme, employment in Portugal rose by over 30 per cent (in part due to the extraordinary influx of population from its ex-colonies in 1975), that in Greece by 17 per cent, with both Italy and Turkey recording employment increases of the order of 12 per cent.

The continued growth in employment despite world recession in these cases can be partly explained by reference to the sectoral structure of employment and changes in this, for in 1980 there were marked differences in the relative importance of agriculture, industry and services as sources of employment. In Turkey, over 60 per cent of employment was in agriculture, compared to less than 9 per cent in France. In general,

Table 1.5 *Civilian employment, 1960–80*

	France	Greece	Italy	Portugal	Spain	Turkey
Total, 1980 (thousands)	21,142	3,347	20,572	3,951	11,254	14,610
Employment change, 1970–80 as % 1970 total	+6.2	+17.3	+12.5	+31.4	+0.5	+11.6*
Percentage employment in agriculture, 1980	8.8	29.7	14.2	28.3	18.9	60.4
Percentage employment in agriculture, 1960	22.6	49.0	31.2	46.6	44.5	74.9
Percentage employment in industry, 1980	35.9	30.0	37.8	35.7	36.1	16.3
Percentage employment in industry, 1960	40.9	23.5	39.0	30.9	32.1	9.6
Percentage employment in services, 1980	55.3	40.3	48.0	36.0	45.0	23.3
Percentage employment in services, 1960	36.5	37.5	29.8	22.5	33.4	10.3**

* Change 1973–80 only.

** In 1960 5.0% of those employed in Turkey were recorded as having 'employment unknown'.

Sources: OECD, 1982b; Hale, 1981, p. 99; Molle, 1980, calculated from data in Table 1B, p. 274.

agriculture continued to be a much more important source of employment than in the advanced capitalist nations of North-West Europe and North America, despite the considerable relative decline of employment in agriculture in the preceding two decades: in 1960, even France had over 22 per cent of its civilian labour force employed in agriculture, Turkey about 75 per cent. These declines were important in releasing labour for the other sectors within national economies, and as a source of international migrant labour.

By 1980, with the exception of Turkey, there was quite a close correspondence between the remaining five national economies in the proportion of the labour force employed in industry, from 30 per cent to 38 per cent. However, this grouping had arisen as a result of rather different national development paths. While in all cases the share of industrial employment rose between 1960 and 1970, in France, Italy, Portugal and Spain the share of industrial employment then fell between 1970 and 1980. In France and Spain, employment fell absolutely too: in this sense, symptoms of de-industrialization can be detected in this decade. In contrast, industrial employment continued to grow quite strongly in absolute terms in Greece, Portugal, Turkey and, to a lesser extent, Italy.

To a considerable degree the relative decline of the industrial sector in employment in the 1970s can be attributed to what Lipietz (1980b) has referred to as the 'tertiarization of society' and service sector expansion was marked in both absolute and relative terms in all six cases. By 1980, with the exception of Turkey, the service sector was the main source of employment in all of them.

An important component of this employment growth was an expanded incorporation of women into the wage labour force (many women having traditionally worked within family enterprises, notably in agriculture, but also in parts of the service sector). Thus several indicators (Table 1.6) make the increasing importance of women in the labour force clearly evident in all but Turkey; a tendency particularly marked in Portugal which by 1979 had emerged as the nation in which females now constitute the greatest share of the working population (38.8%).

Social and political changes

These economic changes have also had important socio-political effects. For example, the increasing importance of women in the labour force has a social significance, implying changes in attitudes towards and the roles of women in Southern European societies. These changes are indicative of a growing liberalization in traditional views and reach more deeply than

Table 1.6 *The incorporation of women into the civilian labour force, 1970–9*

	Female activity rates		Females as a % of the civilian working population		Numbers of employed females (thousands)	
	1970	1979	1970	1979	1970	1979
France	28.9	32.3	35.8	38.0	7,283	8,024
Greece	20.2*	21.1	25.5*	29.7	863*	984
Italy	21.9	25.4	28.2	31.6	5,442	6,412
Portugal	18.1	32.9	26.2	38.8	829	1,496
Spain	17.3	20.7**	24.4	29.3	2,976	3,466
Turkey	50.2	45.8***	38.4	36.1***	5,813	6,928

   * 1971
  ** 1978
*** 1980

Source: Eurostat, 1980, Table 3.4; Turkish Population Censuses, 1970 and 1980.

the superficial indicators of jeans and discothèques might suggest – although this is a far from universal process and the base-level from which it began was a low one.

Another important facet of social change with economic roots is the increasing urbanization of Southern Europe (summarized in Table 1.7). In many ways this process, associated with substantial internal rural to urban migration, is perhaps the best single indicator of a whole series of social changes which together mark the transition to 'modern' (that is, North-West European and North American) lifestyles for at least part of the population. Considerable differences in the proportion of the national population classified as urban existed in 1960: from 23 per cent in Portugal to 62 per cent in France. Such national differences persisted in 1980 and indeed widened (from 31 per cent in Portugal to 78 per cent in France), although in all cases the urban population grew over these two decades – an expansion most marked in Spain, Greece, Turkey and France (in that order). Within this general pattern of increases, some interesting developments were occurring, however. Urban primacy – the proportion of the urban population resident in the largest city – declined marginally in France and Portugal but rose in the remaining four nations. The reinforcement of the position of Athens at the head of the Greek urban hierarchy, to the extent that 35 per cent of *all* the Greek resident population lived there by 1980, is particularly striking. More generally, the proportion of the urban population living in cities of 500,000 or more

Table 1.7 Urban population, 1960–80

	France	Greece	Italy	Portugal	Spain	Turkey
Urban population as % total, 1960	62	43	59	23	57	30
Urban population as % total, 1980	78	62	69	31	74	47
% of urban population in largest city, 1960	25	51	13	47	13	18
% of urban population in largest city, 1980	23	57	17	44	17	24
% of urban population in cities over 500,000 population, 1960	34	51	46	47	37	32
% of urban population in cities over 500,000 population, 1980	34	70	52	44	44	42

Source: World Bank, 1982, Table 20.

population also rose, the exceptions being Portugal where the city of Lisbon's population declined (though the metropolitan area as a whole continued to grow rapidly), and France where it remained unchanged.

It is clear that considerable growth in large cities outside of the primate (usually capital) city was taking place over these two decades, sometimes associated with national government policies to try and counter the dominance of the capital city. For example, in France the *métropole d'équilibré* policy was associated with the growth of major urban centres outside of Paris, such as Marseilles (see Bleitrach and Chenu, 1982) while in Greece similar policies evolved to encourage growth outside Athens in centres such as Thessalonika (Stathakis, 1984). In general, though, the continuing attraction of major cities was in contrast to the spatial decentralization of both jobs and residences from such areas that characterized much of North-West Europe and North America, especially in the 1970s.

These trends towards a more individualistic and consumer-orientated society have taken place amidst substantial political changes which have affected both the internal political structures and external relations of many of these Southern European states. Without doubt, the most significant of these was the transition from dictatorship to democracy in Greece (Ioakimidis, 1984; Mouzelis, 1978), Portugal (Gallagher, 1983; Porto, 1984) and Spain (Carr, 1980; Giner and Sevilla, 1984), which at present (1983) appears for the foreseeable future to be permanent (for further discussion, see Pridham, 1984) while Turkey has recently moved in the opposite direction.

Undoubtedly, the formal political changes involved in the transition from dictatorship to democracy and the associated changes in the particular form of national states within Southern Europe have had a variety of important impacts within them. For example, democratization permitted a resurgence of left-wing politics in Greece, Portugal and Spain, and even the election of left-wing governments of various (although admittedly pale) hues of pink and red, something that has also occurred in France and Italy, giving rise to the label 'sun-belt socialists' for their prime ministers and presidents and having an important effect in strengthening the emergence of a distinctive Eurocommunism as a challenge to old Stalinist orthodoxies. Not only has a greater degree of political freedom resulted from such changes but there has also been a relaxation in social attitudes towards personal questions such as divorce and abortion. Such political changes have also had important economic ramifications, though it is important to point out that, whatever the polemical stress placed upon the socialist character of these states by the 'sun-belt socialists', their conception of economic policy remains a reformist one grounded within

an acceptance as legitimate of capitalist relations of production. Nevertheless, within these limits, there have been important changes. In part these
reflect alterations in the distribution of power between regions and the
central state (pp. 51–2) but more fundamentally the switch from dictatorship to democracy challenged the visibly close relation between the
interests of state and capital that developed within the framework of
corporatism and the extent of the deployment of state power in the
interests of capital rather than labour, not least because of the protection
offered to national capital on the domestic market via tariff and other
barriers as international political–economic relations changed.

For the Greek, Portuguese and Spanish transitions out of and into
democracy cannot be understood simply in terms of their internal political
evolution and political struggle within them. They must also be seen in
the light of the wider web of international political and economic relations
in which these nations have become entangled following the 'opening up'
of their economies in the 1950s and 1960s. In particular, having entered
into trade agreements with the European Communities (EC) and become
substantially economically integrated with the EC as a result, a condition
for the Community entering into negotiations for full political membership was that dictatorship was replaced by democracy (Tsoukalis, 1981).
The same condition would undoubtedly hold in the Turkish case if
serious negotiations about Turkey's membership were to start. Equally,
though, the increasing representation of these Southern European states
within the European Community is significantly altering – indeed
intensifying – the challenges to the coherence of the Community itself.

Movements of labour: migration and return

Before commencing this review of recent trends in labour movements,[3] a
brief theoretical discussion is necessary as it allows us to establish the
significance of such movements in relation to the broader question of the
development of capitalism in Southern Europe. One of the most distinctive features of capitalism as a social system is that its development occurs
unevenly in both time and space.[4] This results from primacy accorded to
the privatized accumulation of capital as a means of achieving economic
growth, for temporal and spatial variations in the rate of growth become
determined by relatively small changes in the conditions for profitable
accumulation between sectors and between areas. The consequent rap-
idity of changes in the location and type of productive investment is both
one of the greatest advantages of capitalism, for it ensures a continuous
revolution in types of products and in production methods, and one of its

greatest disadvantages, for decisions about which new location or type of production will be adopted are taken only by the owners of capital who generally have little interest in the effects on their labour force or the local population. To some extent the inherent instability of capitalism as a system for allocating productive resources has been reduced with the development by the state apparatus of some countries of cyclical management, location policies and a public sector which is less responsive to marginal changes in profitability. However, this sort of state intervention has not only led to new forms of crisis – such as those discussed by Vazquez Barquero and Hebbert below – but may even increase what Damette (1980) has termed the 'hypermobility of capital'. Since a greater proportion of investment costs are now socialized through state grants or infrastructure provision, private capital becomes even freer to relocate (both nationally and internationally) and/or change its production in line with ever more frequent technological developments. In the light of this enhanced mobility of capital, there has been a corresponding increase in movements of labour – both between locations and between sectors or types of job. Few people in the developed capitalist countries now expect to be able to work in a single job in the same place throughout their lifetime. The hypermobility of capital thus also involves the hypermobility of labour.

In this and the next section, the sorts of movement of labour and of capital that have recently taken place in Southern Europe in response to changing conditions for capital accumulation are summarized. Not only does this help to close the gap between the aggregate picture of national changes presented above and the more detailed studies that follow but it also provides an opportunity to pick out those research directions not represented in this volume that appear to be the most crucial for our understanding of Southern European development in the 1980s.

Internal migration

Even though there are considerable problems in comparing internal migration patterns because of data shortages, there does appear to have been a single dominant spatial pattern in Southern Europe over the past two generations. This has been an age and sex-selective rural to urban areas movement by young men in search of work and better living conditions, a migrant flow that has frequently been inter-regional rather than intra-regional. Keles presents evidence of this pattern in Turkey (pp. 57–63), as do studies of Portugal (Ferrão, 1979), Spain (Hebbert and Alonso Teixidor, 1982), Italy (King, 1984) and Greece (Drury, 1982). (See also the earlier review of trends by Fielding, 1975.) Of course, there are other important types of labour migration such as the continuing seasonal movements within rural areas and the steady flow out of the highland areas in search of better conditions for farming. Sometimes these other movements reinforce the dominant pattern − as with female migration (Majoral, 1977) − but they can also cut across or even reverse it (for example, the increasingly significant urban-urban and urban-rural flows). However, for the present, internal labour migration lies behind the growing concentration of the South European population in those major metropolitan areas, like Athens, Barcelona, Istanbul, Lisbon, Marseilles and Milan, which are perceived (often incorrectly) as offering better opportunities for regular wage labour. In practice, this has often meant that the conversion of rural under-employment into urban unemployment has given rise to serious housing shortages that have been 'solved' not by the massive blocks of workers' apartments but by a wave of illegal house building that finds its most graphic expression in the shanty towns.[5] Since the influx has generally been more rapid than the expansion of job opportunities, the presence of a surplus of labour has helped to keep wages low (though see Amin, pp. 171−80), so speeding up capital accumulation in the urban industrial and service sectors.

If the effects on the economies of the urban destination areas (although not always on individual migrants) have usually been beneficial in allowing faster rates of growth, the effects on the rural origin areas of internal (and international) migrant workers have in general not been. The selectivity of the out-migration process leads to an increasingly feminized and aged population, a decline in labour input into agriculture and a consequent fall in agricultural output and income. This, in turn, causes a deterioration in services and living standards, as well as a lack of capital for investment in creating new job opportunities. Although the precise mixture of these (and other) causes of decline have varied from one area to another, the decaying ruins of thousands of villages from Amarante to Anatolia are stark reminders of the human costs of creating the booming cities of the 1960s. However, even this devastation of rural areas has some positive possibilities. First, there is a reverse flow of remittances from urban to rural areas and, as discussed below in relation to international migration, this can maintain or raise individual levels of consumption. It may also be the case that urban migrants return to their rural roots after their working life is over, but there is little evidence of the most successful migrants doing so. When migrants do leave their villages for good, there are possibilities of rationalizing land holdings, which commentators such as Brandes (1976) regard as an important improvement, and it is also possible that their increasingly obvious role in the village economy helps women to escape from 'the shadows' (Cornelisen, 1976).

International migration

Over much of Southern Europe international migration is long established; much of it has been inter-continental (to the Americas or Australia, for example), and some of it related to the previous imperial status of three of the states, such as Portuguese or Spanish migration to Africa and Latin America (for a general review of such emigrations see Krane, 1979). Such flows continue to the present but from the latter part of the 1950s the destination, character and scale of international migration from Southern Europe began to alter significantly: the emphasis switched from relatively long-term emigration or settlement to temporary labour migration via 'managed' recruitment systems to the economies of North-West Europe (described in Böhning, 1975a; Krane, 1979; Power, 1978; and Salt, 1981). The main destinations were the Federal Republic of Germany and France – France's status as a net recipient of international migrants differentiates it from the remaining five countries – but there were also relatively important numbers of Southern European migrants in Switzerland and Luxemburg. As demand for migrant labour grew in Northern Europe and the supply from Italy decreased due to increased internal demand, then additional countries at greater distances were drawn into these international migration patterns, both from within Southern Europe (notably Yugoslavia and Turkey) and, later, from North, and even West, Africa. In addition to this general expansion in the volume of migration flows, the level of movement in any one year became greatly influenced by cyclical fluctuations in the Northern European economies (notably that of the Federal Republic of Germany). As the fluctuations in flows to 1973 (presented in Table 1.8) show, international labour migrants increasingly danced to the tune of Northern Europe's labour demands.[6]

As with internal migration, there is a considerable selectivity in international migrations from Southern Europe in terms of who moves, where they move from and to, and why they move. Internal migration itself often acts as a sifting mechanism as regards the selectivity of international migration – a point analysed below. At a national level, there is a marked selectivity in the channelling of migrants from Southern Europe: consider, for example, the concentration of Greek and Turkish migrant workers in West Germany or Portuguese in France evident in Table 1.9. This differentiation in terms of areas extends to the linking of particular national destinations to specific localities or regions within the origin

Table 1.8 *Legal emigration, 1960–80*

	Greece	Italy	Portugal	Spain	Turkey
1960	47,768	383,908	32,318	30,500	n.a.
1961	58,837	387,123	33,526	43,000	4,041
1962	84,054	365,611	33,539	65,336	8,620
1963	100,072	277,611	39,519	83,728	30,328
1964	105,569	258,482	55,646	102,146	66,176
1965	117,167	282,643	89,056	74,539	57,520
1966	86,896	296,494	120,239	56,795	34,400
1967	42,730	229,264	92,502	25,911	8,947
1968	50,866	215,713	80,452	66,699	43,204
1969	91,552	182,199	70,165	100,840	103,967
1970	92,681	151,854	66,360	97,657	129,575
1971	61,745	167,721	50,400	113,702	87,942
1972	43,397	141,852	54,084	104,134	85,229
1973	27,525	123,302	79,517	96,088	135,820
1974	24,448	112,020	43,397	50,695	20,207
1975	20,330	92,666	24,811	20,618	4,419
1976	20,374	97,247	17,493	12,124	10,558
1977	18,350	87,655	17,226	11,300	19,084
1978	14,482	85,550	18,651	11,993	18,852
1979	11,050	88,950	20,622	13,019	23,630
1980	n.a.	83,007	18,044	14,065	28,443

Sources: Greece: *Concise Statistical Yearbook 1980*, p. 42; SOPEMI, 1980.
Italy: King, 1984.
Portugal: *A Emigração Portuguesa: Dados Estatísticos Retrospectivos 1960–82*, p. 3.
Spain: King, 1984. These refer only to workers on assisted passages.
Turkey: Adler, 1981; SOPEMI, 1981.

nations in Southern Europe (Salt and Clout, 1976).[7] Indeed, selectivity also occurs in the location of migrants within the destination countries of North-West Europe; not only are they concentrated into particular regions and urban areas as a consequence of the distribution of certain types of economic activity, but they are also residentially segregated within these (for examples, see Clark, 1975; Drewe *et al.*, 1975; Mik and Verkoren-Hemelaar, 1976). As well as this spatial patterning of in- and out-migration, there is a selectivity in terms of types of migrants which, because of the managed character of these flows, is more marked than in terms of internal migration; not only is this so in terms of who is initially recruited, but there exists a further selectivity in terms of whose temporary contract is renewed. In summary, the stereotype of a migrant as

Table 1.9 *Numbers of foreign workers from Mediterranean countries in Western Europe, 1979 (thousands)*

From	Austria	Belgium	France	West Germany	Luxemburg	Netherlands	Sweden	Switzerland
Algeria	—	3.0	361.0	—	—	—	0.2	—
Greece	—	9.7	—	141.4	—	2.0	8.1	4.7
Italy	1.9	89.0	175.8	317.7	11.0	10.4	2.5	235.4
Morocco	—	31.3	181.4	16.6	—	31.0	0.5	—
Portugal	—	5.6	385.0	59.6	13.3	5.4	0.9	6.0
Spain	0.2	29.3	184.5	91.6	2.2	17.6	1.7	61.3
Tunisia	—	4.2	73.7	—	—	1.2	0.3	—
Turkey	27.3	19.0	36.3	564.9	—	45.1	5.2	18.3
Yugoslavia	117.7	2.8	43.1	372.4	0.6	8.1	24.9	27.9
Other EC countries	12.5	80.3	66.2	142.6	21.2	52.6	31.4	82.9
Other non-EC countries	15.6	36.0	135.8	318.3	2.1	23.0	155.3	54.2
Total	175.2	310.1	1,642.8	2,025.1	50.4	196.4	231.0	490.7

Source: Adapted from SOPEMI, 1980, p. 3.

young, male and single (or, if married, migrating alone) had considerably more validity in the international than in the internal case, at least until 1973, and the implications of this are summarized below.

After 1973 four important changes emerged in international migration patterns from Southern Europe (Böhning, 1979; Kayser, 1977; Salt, 1981). The effects of the November 1973 oil price rises and the international recession led to restrictions on new recruitment being imposed in 1974 in West Germany, France and Switzerland. Thus the scale of flows from Southern to Northern Europe diminished dramatically, and proportionately the 'traditional' intercontinental destinations assumed greater importance in emigration from countries like Greece and Portugal. It is important to make a distinction between Italy and the remaining nations in this context, though. An absolute decline in Italian emigration started in 1967. Because of the rights of labour mobility that Italian citizens possessed by virtue of membership of the EC, flows from Italy assumed a much greater relative significance in the overall pattern of movement from south to north in Europe. Prior to 1974, King (1976) suggests that these rights had little, if any, impact on the flow of Italian emigrants to the rest of the Community but they do now appear to be significant. A further point to note from Table 1.8 is that while flows have decreased they have by no means stopped; this was indicative of the extent to which the economies of Northern Europe remained dependent upon migrant labour from Southern Europe performing the 'socially undesirable' jobs – and not always only low wage ones (Böhning, 1975b) – that their own nationals would not do. Following from this recognition of the crucial structural role filled by Southern European and, more generally, Mediterranean migrants within North-West Europe's labour markets, an increasing proportion of migration after 1973 was of families joining husbands as both the French and West German governments sought a more stable labour force. This alone though does not account for the tendency for labour flows to increase in volume somewhat towards the end of the 1970s, as much of it was attributable to increased numbers of workers from North Africa and Turkey, rather than countries in, or hoping to join, the EC such as Italy, Portugal and Greece (SOPEMI, 1981, p. 45). However, as Lewis and Williams (1984) observe, the actual stock of migrant workers from all sources in the member states of the EC in 1979 (5.8 million) has not fallen substantially from the 1973 figure of 6.6 million, so that talk of the end of the intra-Europe part of the international labour migration system is somewhat premature.

Another important new element in international migration patterns after 1973 has been the increased flows to the oil-rich states of the Middle

East from the Mediterranean area. Of the Southern European nations considered here, only Turkey with 30,000 migrant workers (nearly all in Libya) in 1980 has become involved in these to any great extent as the demands for unskilled labour are met primarily from Egypt, the Yemens, Jordan and, increasingly, the countries of South and South-East Asia (Birks and Sinclair, 1982; Ecevit, 1981) but there are also some flows of skilled technicians and managers from the other countries associated with the design and construction of major development projects.

Finally, in relation to patterns of international labour movement, it is important to note that one effect of the mass movement of labour from Southern Europe has been to create gaps in the labour markets there which have been filled by international migrants from other areas within the Mediterranean. An obvious example of this kind of secondary labour market is the (often illegal) flows of North African migrants into Italy where they take 'marginal' jobs in agriculture, construction, domestic services, restaurants and hotels. Caldo (1982) estimates that there were 250,000–350,000 North African migrants in Southern Italy in the 1970s while SOPEMI (1981) estimated a total stock of 500,000 migrant workers in Italy in 1980 – 63 per cent concentrated in six major urban areas (Rome, Milan, Turin, Genoa, Naples, Bari). Similar movements into Greece, Spain and Portugal have added to the complexity of international labour migration patterns by making these countries both importers and exporters of labour. Kofman (p. 280) shows how this also happens in specific regions like Corsica.

Certainly there is no denying that individual migrants can significantly improve their living standards by working abroad, nor that some governments of South European countries have become heavily dependent on the inflow of migrant remittances as a source of 'hard' currencies (see Table 1.3), but there is increasing doubt that these benefits outweigh the loss of potential national production caused by emigration or represent adequate financial compensation for the education and social provision for emigrants and their families (e.g. Baučić, 1979).

Return migration

One important effect of the rapid growth of labour flows from Southern Europe on short-term contracts in the 1960s was a corresponding increase in the number of returning migrants in the late 1970s and early 1980s. Recession, racism and the introduction of schemes to encourage 'resettlement' by governments like the French may have speeded up the process somewhat, but the gradual decline in total stocks and absence of any pro-nounced peaks around 1974 in the dates of return of migrants in surveys such as Boura *et al.* (1984) suggests that most migrants returned for reasons unconnected with the growth of domestic unemployment in Northern Europe – as evident in King *et al.*'s results (Chapter 4). Of course, there have been returnees for as long as there have been emigrants and whole villages may still depend on the maintenance of close ties with a settlement in the USA or Venezuela (for a recent example of local ties between Greece and the USA, see Collins, 1983). Indeed, return flows of emigrants have been as large as the 600,000 reaching Italy in the period 1961–3 (Livi Bacci, 1972), a rate double that of any period in the 1970s. However, the nature and effects of this return have been under-researched in relation to its significance in contemporary Southern Europe. The number of studies published since King (1979) reviewed the state of our knowledge of returned migrants has helped to redress the balance some-what and permit three preliminary conclusions to be drawn about their impact.

First, it appears that returnees do not have the long-term beneficial effects on the usually rural areas from which they originated that might have been expected from the fact that those assumed to be more innovative in emigrating initially have accumulated both savings and new ideas. There are but few examples of emigrants using the industrial experience gained abroad on return and, since a large proportion of migrants have had some industrial employment, the process of emigration can reduce the industrial base of an area (for examples, see Toepfer, p. 78; Azmaz, 1980; Castillo, 1980; Lewis and Williams, 1984). Far more common is a change of occupation into the service sector – in particular the commercial parts (observed and discussed by King *et al.*, p. 111, and Toepfer, p. 85, amongst many others) – or a return to agricultural activity if the prospects for diversifying employment are considered too poor. Thus the major employment impact on the community of origin is more likely to be a proliferation of small bars or taxis run by the returnees and family than the creation of new jobs in the productive sector.

Furthermore, the effect of returnees' accumulated savings is less than might initially be expected since a large part of them (and of the remit-tances sent while abroad) are used for family consumption rather than productive investment. The purchase or construction of a new house is as common a first choice in Andalucia (Rhoades, 1979), as it is in Arakli (Toepfer, p. 87) and is likely to be followed in importance by expenditures on consumer durables ranging from cars and video recorders as well as more prosaic items such as children's education. Boura *et al.* (1984) are typical in their findings that only 28 per cent of a sample of Portuguese returnees from Northern Europe had invested savings in a business (compared with 77 per cent investing in housing or 45 per cent in a car). The fact that over one-half of these businesses were commercial and only 15 per cent industrial bears out the first general conclusion above.

Thirdly, the ability of returning emigrants to revitalize their village or small town is limited by a widespread tendency for 'urban drift'. Unger (1983) recorded some of the most extraordinary evidence of this in Greece where internal rural-urban migration is itself remarkable. Only 16 per cent of the returned migrants that he interviewed in Athens had been born there and, although the proportion who had lived in Athens before emigration rose to 49 per cent, it still means that half the returnees have moved to the city after their spell abroad. This may be exceptional, as two independent surveys in Portugal have shown that over 80 per cent of returned emigrants are now living in or near their birthplace (Lewis and Williams, 1984; Silva et al., 1984) but there can be little doubt that the dominant direction of post-return movement is townwards. If this ultimate loss of part of the population is added to the sorts of leakages of returnee investments from rural to urban areas that Toepfer has identified (pp. 96–8), the concern shown by Keleş (pp. 61–74) about international labour movements increasing the disparities between areas within a country seems well-founded.

In summary, the flow of returned emigrants is an important element in Southern Europe today but it has often involved what Cerase (1974) aptly described as a 'return of conservatism' in which cosmetic development occurs in the countryside and the few serious changes to the productive structure are concentrated in the very areas which already have the most dynamic economic environments. In these circumstances it is not surprising that the initiatives taken in the 1970s to encourage returned migrants to help develop their home areas have met with only sporadic success. Even when it has been realized that relying on individual migrants to invest in communally useful activities is not enough, schemes such as the Dutch REMPLOD one (e.g. Penninx and van Renselaar, 1978) have not been on a scale large enough to transform the very economic and social conditions that led the emigrants to leave in the first place. Until that is done, the emigrants who do return there will continue to invest outside the area and prefer to spend their savings on improving their family's welfare.

Movements of capital: economic change in agriculture, industry and services

Earlier in this chapter we noted some of the changes in the economic structures, in terms of shares of employment and GDP associated with agriculture, industry and services, of the countries of Southern Europe. Such data are indicative of the considerable economic transformation that Southern Europe – or at least a significant part of it – has undergone in recent years and reflects the changing patterns of capital accumulation emerging in response to both internal pressures and a rapidly changing international economic environment. The major features of these patterns and the reasons for their emergence are treated in turn below.

Agriculture: stasis or change?

Some sixty years ago, Newbigin (1924) characterized the Mediterranean agriculturist as a 'gardener rather than a farmer' (p. 55) referring to a polycultural system of agricultural production, carried out on small, typically fragmented plots, worked by family labour and orientated to subsistence, with any surplus sold in local or regional markets. How valid was and is this image of Southern European agriculture? While this may have described a system of production that was widespread throughout much of Southern Europe, there were even then substantial areas of large estates where agriculture was organized more on the basis of monoculture, with extensive use of wage-labour and the penetration of capitalist social relations (see Giner, p. 314). Thus, there was a dual system of agriculture, with minifundia and latifundia existing simultaneously in Italy, Portugal and Spain and this continues today. However, Newbigin's picture needs further modification if it is to capture the new position of even the small-scale units, for these have become less polycultural, with considerable specialization for markets that may be many kilometres away – and even in Northern Europe – and increasingly operated either part-time or by only part of the family.

An obvious basic cause of this change is the shrinkage of the labour force. Much of the absolute and relative decline in the agricultural work-force is associated with spatial movements of labour (pp. 17–18) and has simply involved a reduction in under-employment and concealed un-employment within this sector. This also involves a change in the structure of the labour force that remains, for the selectivity of migration means that those left behind are usually the elderly and the women, which can reduce output and innovation.

However, the scale of movement out of agricultural occupations – at least as a prime source of income – has been so great that labour shortages have been noted in recent years (Pugliese, pp. 129–31) and seasonal movements of harvesting gangs persist despite mechanization. It is important to bear in mind that some of the reduction in the agricultural labour force is due to movement between sectors within rural areas for the spread of some industries away from the urban centres has absorbed some agricultural employees, as has the expansion of services such as local government works, transport or tourism. Indeed, on many a Greek island or Algarve slope the crumbling terrace walls are due more to the demands of a job serving tourists in the local taverna or bar than to out-migration. This is one of the ways in which part-time farming has emerged as such a wide-spread phenomenon in the more densely settled areas of Southern Europe. Often males will take local jobs outside agriculture for part of the week or part of the year, leaving the bulk of the farm work to the rest of his family, but participating in some of it. Orlando (1983) reports that this was the case in about half the family farms in a sample in Marche (Italy) in 1972 and that non-agricultural activities accounted for 55 per cent of the family's income, while a 1977 survey in Friuli estimated that up to 71 per cent of all family farms under 5 ha. were run on a part-time basis (Zacchia, 1983). Jones (1984) presents further Italian evidence which shows considerable regional variation in the actual type of off-farm work undertaken – working on other farms being most common in the Mezzogiorno while the 23 per cent of farmers who have non-agricultural jobs tend to be found on the Piemonte–Venezia axis. Without such an input the resurgence of the family farm noted by Garcia-Ramon (p. 144) could not have occurred.

However, this change in the size and character of the labour force has not usually led to a shift in the size structure of farms. As Table 1.10 reveals, Southern European agriculture remains dominated by small farms: this is particularly true of Greece, Italy, Portugal and Turkey. While there were few large holdings (50 or more ha.), these were nevertheless significant in two respects. First, within Southern European states, there tends to be a marked regional pattern to the distribution of small and large farms: Portugal exemplifies this well, with average farm sizes of 2 to 5 ha. in the northern districts contrasting with those of 45 to 50 ha. in the southern Alentejo, but similar patterns can also be found in Spain and Italy. The second aspect is the concentration of land ownership. Large farms may be few in number but they control a large part of the agricultural surface. Thus in Portugal, farmers with over 50 ha. owned 51.2 per cent of the land in 1968 and comparable figures for France were 35.5 per cent (though these large farms were mostly concentrated in the north), for Spain 46.1 per cent and for Italy 30.5 per cent. The greater equality of land ownership in Greece is evident in that the equivalent figure there is only 3.1 per cent. This polarized structure persists despite various land reform programmes aimed either at breaking up large units into smaller ones (for example, in southern Portugal in 1975 and in Turkey under the

Table 1.10 *Agricultural structure and change in the 1970s*

	France	Greece	Italy	Portugal	Spain	Turkey
Percentage of agricultural holdings, 1–5 ha., 1977*	19.8	70.9	68.5	77.3	57.0	60.3
Tractors per 100 agricultural workers, 1977	67.7	8.1	37.8	6.0	19.4	3.6
Fertilizer consumption per ha. of arable land (hundred grammes)	3,008	1,342	1,707	730	810	412
Food production *per capita* index (1969–71 = 100), 1978–80	115	122	111	78	127	111

* 'Total' number of holdings excludes those under 1 ha.: such holdings accounted for 23.4% of *all* operated holdings in Greece, 25.8% in Turkey and 38.7% in Portugal.

Sources: Eurostat, 1980; FAO, 1981; Hale, 1981, pp. 175–84; World Bank, 1983, Table 6; and own calculations.

1973 Land Reform Law) or at the consolidation of small farms, either voluntarily (as in Spain from 1952) or compulsorily (as in Turkey from 1973). While such attempts at change often had some broader political significance within the individual nations and on occasion have had important localized economic and social impacts, overall they have done little to alter the basic farm size distributions or reverse the tendency towards increased fragmentation within farms (O'Flanagan, 1980).

Despite the relative lack of progress in these attempts to create a more 'modern' or equitable farming structure – and corresponding difficulties until very recently in encouraging increased mechanization or use of aids like artificial fertilizer (Aresvik, 1975) – there has been a substantial change as regards actual production. To start with, domestic food production *per capita* continued to expand almost everywhere throughout the 1970s (Table 1.10), with increases of between 11 per cent and 27 per cent over the decade. In contrast, in Portugal it fell sharply due to a combination of substantial population growth, a marked increase in part-time farming and, most of all, because of the disruption to agricultural production associated with the creation, and now the undermining, of the collective farms set up in the Alentejo during the 'spontaneous' land reform of 1975.

What is more significant than these changes in total food production is the crops grown and the pattern of changes of individual crops. The EC has defined Mediterranean agriculture as one in which citrus fruits, fruit and vegetables, olives, wine, flowers, tobacco, rice, durum wheat and sheep meat account for at least 40 per cent of total agricultural production. On this basis, the southern part of France and the remaining five Southern European states can be characterized as having a Mediterranean agriculture, although this is not to deny that significant amounts of non-Mediterranean crops are grown in them (Musto, 1982). Jones (1984) shows how this specialization in Mediterranean production, especially of fruit and vegetables, has tended to increase, often quite markedly, over the last decade or so in four of the South European countries (Table 1.11). Even in Portugal, where overall food production fell sharply, production of several citrus fruits, tobacco and sheep meat expanded significantly. Elsewhere, however, growth rates have been even higher with the result that production far outstrips domestic demand (Table 1.12). Spain, for example, produces 377 per cent of its normal consumption of mandarins, 206 per cent of the national demand for oranges and 47 per cent more olive oil than is used domestically (Jones, 1984).

Furthermore, such growth has been associated with a change in the location of production within countries, a tendency towards greater

Table 1.11 *Indices of agricultural production, 1981 (1969–71 = 100)*

	France	Greece	Italy	Portugal	Spain	Turkey
Cereals	133	154	116	63	98	140
Wheat	161	147	91	50	71	149
Rice	24	88	108	63	114	113
Barley	115	121	305	58	120	159
Potatoes	80	136	79	77	120	146
Olives	100	149	102	47	52	148
Tomatoes	156	171	125	88	123	222
Onions	66	111	112	106	52	163
Peaches	119	243	143	97	189	287
Lemons and limes	n.a.	137	92	111	384	231
Oranges	33	146	114	92	80	162
Tangerines/clementines/ mandarins	471	116	120	118	218	264
Apricots	107	281	115	85	128	173
Wine	107	124	112	87	134	89
Tobacco	102	139	156	120	158	127
Sheep ('000 head)	130	104	115	117	80	133
Beef and veal ('000 head slaughtered)	95	81	102	105	111	118
Mutton and lamb ('000 head slaughtered)	146	110	120	133	101	120

Sources: FAO Production Yearbook, 1981; own calculations.

regional specialization and the replacement of polyculture by export-orientated monoculture. Those areas with good access to the Northern European markets – either by air or by road, for speed is essential with the perishable products – have seen a proliferation of glasshouses and new irrigation works, and even in regions which are associated with traditionally local market products, like special wines or liqueurs, one or two enterprising investors will be looking to export markets. By and large, these investments have come from indigenous capital, though multi-national capital can be involved as a source of subcontracts and in marketing.

This changing pattern of agricultural production has involved a move towards specialization that cannot be understood without reference to the operation of the EC, for France and Italy are founder members, Greece, a recent arrival, and Portugal, Spain and Turkey all have trade and association agreements with it (Mishalani *et al.*, 1981). Both France and Italy have had their agricultural priorities influenced by the operation of the Common Agricultural Policy for the past two decades (with effects discussed in the Commission of the European Communities, 1975, 1980a,

Table 1.12 *Self-sufficiency in selected agricultural products*

	France	Portugal	Greece	Spain	Italy
Wheat	185	59	111	104	82
Barley	163	92	97	116	37
Maize	119	27	33	32	65
Rice	10	57	108	121	271
Sugar	183	4	120	94	93
Olive oil	—	104	107	147	—
Wine	97	122	120	125	137
Citrus fruit	2	100	156	243	114
Tomatoes	n.a.	100	100	110	—
Potatoes	99	94	107	102	100
Sheep and goat meat	74	100	66	99	64
Beef and veal	106	70	63	89	62
Pig meat	84	92	99	94	74
Eggs	98	100	101	103	95
Cows' milk (fresh)	101	99	100	99	99
Butter	112	52	79	89	69

Sources: Jones, 1984; Commission of the European Communities, 1980b.

1982; Fennell, 1979; MacKerron and Rush, 1976; Pearce 1981), while the other countries have become increasingly tied to the markets through their formal agreements. As Jones (1984) puts it in the case of four of the countries,

> agriculture like the rest of the economy witnessed a fundamental transformation from being essentially an inward-looking sector to one increasingly oriented, and ultimately incorporated within the capitalist market economy of Western Europe. An important aspect of this process has been the emergence of the EEC as a major trading partner for agricultural products.

The orientation towards the Community of the agricultural trade of three of the non-member states in Southern Europe in 1980 is graphically illustrated in Table 1.13. While the Community is heavily reliant upon these Southern European nations (especially Spain) for its imports of these five, typically Mediterranean products, this pales into insignificance in relation to their dependence upon access to the EC markets for their exports of these products: over 90 per cent of Spain's exports of oranges, potatoes and tomatoes and over 80 per cent of Greece's of olive oil and potatoes are to the Community.

Table 1.13 *Trade dependence in selected agricultural commodities between the European Community and Southern Europe*

		Oranges	Tomatoes	Potatoes	Olive oil	Wine
Spain	(a)	46.2	57.4	18.6	28.0	38.2
	(b)	92.2	96.0	93.9	38.0	34.1
Greece	(a)	1.6	0.1	7.9	13.0	9.0
	(b)	17.4	13.0	87.4	84.0	47.5
Portugal	(a)	—	—	0.1	0.2	11.6
	(b)	—	—	26.1	4.4	36.8

(a) % of EC imports from this source.
(b) % of exports taken by EC.

Source: Jones, 1984.

In the near future, most of these trading partners hope to be in the EC themselves and thus subject to the CAP, so it is worth considering its impact to date before turning to the enlargement issues. Even allowing for an increase in the total Guarantee (price support) expenditure for Mediterranean products from 12.6 per cent in 1977 to a proposed 23.1 per cent in 1983, this is still below the contribution of such products to Community agricultural output: effective price support exists only for durum wheat, olive oil, rice and tobacco, with weak support for citrus fruits, grapes, peaches, pears, tomatoes and wine and no support for other fruit and vegetables (Fennell, 1979). Italy currently dominates production of Mediterranean products within the Community, accounting for 99 per cent of its production of citrus fruits, 91 per cent of its peaches and 72 per cent of its tomatoes (Commission of the European Communities, 1981), and one effect of the bias of the CAP price-support mechanisms in favour of temperate products has been to widen regional differences in agricultural incomes between north and south (as has also happened in France, see Commission of the European Communities, 1980a). The Community's limited support for structural improvements in Mediterranean agriculture in the form of irrigation, processing, marketing and forestry is only one part of the much smaller budget allocated to the Guidance section of the CAP and has not been effective in countering the unequal regional effects of the price support mechanism of the Guarantee section (see Podbielski, 1981). Even though Italy has received about 30–35 per cent of the Guidance expenditure of the CAP (Eurostat, 1980), the absolute amounts are simply too small to make any significant impact as this is only in the order of 6–8 per cent of the total Community budget.

The question of Mediterranean production within and outside the Community has taken on a particular significance in the context of its further Southern European enlargement (see Hudson and Lewis, 1982a). This is particularly so in the case of Spain. Although Spain has had a relatively unfavourable tariff treatment, illustrated by the fact that while Greek oranges entered the EC duty free and those from the Maghreb bore a 7.2 per cent duty, those from Spain were subjected to a duty of 20 per cent (Taylor, 1980), it has made substantial inroads into the Community's agricultural markets. For this reason Mediterranean producers currently within the Community are worried about the prospects of Spanish entry for not only will trade restrictions (eventually) be removed, but additional products will be competing for the price support available within the CAP. The threat posed to Italian producers is particularly acute.

Not only will the further Southern European enlargement pose a threat to Mediterranean producers within the Community, but it will also have a potentially serious effect for other Southern European and Mediterranean states which have trade agreements with the Community: the countries of the Maghreb and Mashreq, Yugoslavia, Cyprus, Israel, Malta and Turkey (Jones, 1981). A further extension of the EC into Southern Europe will greatly increase its level of self-sufficiency – often to the point of supply exceeding demand within the Community: for example, olive oil production would rise to 109 per cent self-sufficiency on Spanish entry – so that the question of these non-members continuing to obtain privileged access to the Community market will inevitably be raised. Any reduction in access, given that they have frequently either altered their patterns of agricultural production or maintained old colonial ones on the presumption of this continuing, may have major repercussions in terms of regional and national development within these nations (Mishalani et al., 1981; Pearce, 1982).

Industrialization and the changing role of Southern Europe in the international division of labour

Earlier in this chapter, the integration of Southern Europe into the international labour market as a source of supply for North-West Europe and the Middle East was emphasized. Increasingly, however, outflows of people have been paralleled by less visible, though no less important, inflows of capital into agriculture, parts of the service sector and, above all, industry (Paine, 1979), flows which increased the penetration of capitalist social relations. Southern Europe has increasingly assumed importance as a location for production within the international division of labour as,

Table 1.14 *Indices of industrial production, 1960–80*

		France	Greece	Italy	Portugal	Spain	Turkey
		Annual average growth rate (%)					
Industry	1960–70	6.4	9.4	6.2	8.8	n.a.	9.6
	1970–80	3.1	5.3	1.5	4.5	3.9	6.6
Manufacturing	1960–70	6.6	10.2	7.1	8.9	n.a.	10.9
	1970–80	3.6	6.4	3.8	4.5	6.0	6.1
		Manufacturing output per capita *($, 1975)*					
	1970	n.a.	770	2,204	n.a.	1,704	202
	1978	4,606	1,346	2,982	1,623	2,690*	401

* 1977

Source: World Bank, 1982, Tables 2 and 6.

from the late 1950s, Southern European states actively sought entry to or association with supra-national organizations such as the EC and EFTA and changed national legislation so as to permit foreign investment and as relative rates of profitability shifted as between the older and more recently industrialized – or even unindustrialized – areas.[8] One symptom of this, demonstrated on pp. 3–5, 10–12, is the increased importance of industry in the Southern European economies in terms of its contribution to GDP and employment by the late 1970s. Although the share of industrial employment tended to fall in the 1970s, this was principally because of service sector expansion rather than because of an absolute decline in industry.

Industrial output grew quite strongly throughout the 1970s, though more slowly than in the 1960s. Nevertheless, growth rates exceeded those

Table 1.15 *Distribution of value added in manufacturing, 1979*

	France	Greece	Italy	Portugal	Spain	Turkey
Food and agriculture	16	20	10	13	12	25
Textiles and clothing	8	26	15	20	19	13
Machinery and transport equipment	32	8	26	20	17	13
Chemicals	9	8	9	10	10	11
Other	35	38	40	37	42	38

Source: World Bank, 1982, Table 6.

in most major advanced capitalist nations, particularly in manufacturing, as Southern Europe assumed greater significance within the changing international division of labour (Table 1.14).

This was, though, an essentially selective industrialization and also represented growth from a low base. Thus these nations' shares of global industrial production or exports did not increase greatly (see Hudson and Lewis, 1984, pp. 191–2) although shares of manufacturing exports tended to rise more than those of industrial production, symptomatic of the export-orientation of much of this growth (a point developed further below).

Moreover, despite this growth, great quantitative and qualitative differences continued to separate national manufacturing sectors: French manufacturing output *per capita* exceeded that in Turkey by a factor of more than 11 in 1978 (Table 1.14), while the composition of manufacturing output reflects the selective character of the industrialization process (Table 1.15), itself reflected in the selective character of exports (Table 1.4). Food processing and related agriculturally based industries are of great importance, especially in Greece and Turkey (20 per cent and 25 per cent of manufacturing output, respectively), as are textiles and clothing, which are particularly prominent in Greece, Portugal and Spain (26 per cent, 20 per cent and 19 per cent, respectively, of value added). What these figures suggest is a group of countries, with the exception of France and to a degree Italy, inserted into the international division of labour in such a way as to be specialized in these relatively simple, technically unsophisticated manufacturing industries: as these have declined in the advanced capitalist world, so they have expanded in Southern Europe (see Table 1.16). The same conclusion can be arrived at from the opposite direction: France, a relatively advanced industrial economy, has 32 per cent of value added in manufacturing arising from the machinery and transport equipment sectors, a much higher share than in the remaining five countries, particularly Greece and Turkey (which rely on imports of these from North-West Europe, especially from the FRG: Table 1.4). Clearly the reasons for these particular rates and patterns of industrial growth are of considerable significance.

In this context, industries can be categorized in terms of particular forms of industrialization (import reproducing[9]; export processing; export-platform) and different forms of organization of capital and agents of industrialization (multinational capital; state holding companies, nationalized industries, etc.; small and medium-sized local capitals). These (inter-related) issues will be considered in turn, drawing out their implications for industrial location within Southern Europe.

Table 1.16 *Employment change between Northern and Southern Europe in clothing and textiles, 1965–77 (thousands)*

	1965	1977	Absolute change	% change
Belgium	180	123	−57	−31.7
Denmark	44	24	−20	−45.5
France	660	500	−160	−24.2
West Germany	780	590	−190	−24.4
Netherlands	160	65	−95	−59.4
UK	1,086	750	−336	−30.9
Total	2,910	2,052	−858	−29.5
Greece	37	63	+26	+70.3
Italy	540	650	+110	+20.4
Portugal	116	180	+64	+55.2
Spain	225	280	+55	+24.4
Total	918	1,173	+255	+27.8

Source: Financial Times, 10 January 1980, and own calculations.

From the perspective of national governments in Southern Europe, import reproducing industries have great advantages: greater self-sufficiency cuts import bills and eases balance of payments problems. Consequently such developments have been encouraged in many industries, especially those that provide inputs into other nationally based forms of production: cement for the construction industry, and, pre-eminently, iron and steel – in turn linking to the growth of import reproducing car and other consumer durable industries, and machinery production – being good examples (Hale, 1981, pp. 191–5). With the exception of France, crude steel output continued to rise in Southern Europe throughout the 1970s (Hudson and Lewis, 1984, p. 194), despite the severe global over-production crisis (Mandel, 1978), often as a result of direct government involvement (see below). In other industrial branches, setting up import-reproducing plants has often been the only channel through which private capital could get access to the national markets of Southern Europe.

The second and third forms of industrialization are both export-orientated, encouraged by national governments to ease balance of payments problems (see Table 1.3). Export processing production takes various forms but mainly falls into one of two categories: processing minerals and other raw materials (such as Péchiney's bauxite-processing operations in Greece − see Mouzelis, 1978, pp. 121–2; Nikolinakos, pp. 204–5) or processing agricultural raw materials − canning fruit and vegetables, for example. While not all such production is export-orientated, the considerable shares of 'food and agriculture' in total value added in manufacturing (Table 1.15) is indicative of how 'traditional' food processing industries, producing for regional or national markets, may come to co-exist alongside, or be transformed to, export production for international markets.

The remaining form of production, export-platform, involves establishing factories and production complexes in Southern Europe to serve international rather than national markets. They are drawn there neither by the domestic market nor by raw materials availability but by other conditions for profitable production. Southern Europe offers various attractions and a range of industries have located there in response to these − industries as diverse as petrochemicals, cars, radios, textiles, clothing, etc. (for examples, see Balassa, 1981). For some, the attraction is large masses of cheap, pliant labour-power: in some cases, this allows cutting wages while intensifying existing work practices; in others, switching production there facilitates the introduction of new technology and changing the labour process (clothing, textiles and various component and assembly operations of a range of engineering, especially electrical, industries: for examples, see Fröbel et al., 1980). For others, the attraction is less restrictive pollution legislation (petrochemicals: for example, see Hudson 1983a). For all, the financial concessions made by national governments anxious to lure capital to provide industrial development as part of an intensifying global competition for mobile investment is, at a minimum, always a useful bonus (Hudson and Lewis, 1984). While much recent industrial expansion in Southern Europe undoubtedly has been of this export-platform type, its importance must not be over-exaggerated. Although manufactured exports from Southern Europe to the advanced capitalist world have increased, these form a relatively small share of even those of the 'newly industrializing countries' to the OECD bloc (Table 1.17). Moreover, as with their agricultural exports, Southern Europe's export-orientated manufacturing industries rely heavily on access to the European Community market via various treaty agreements: in particular, the dependence of Greece upon access to West Germany's markets, of Portugal on access to the UK's, of Spain on access to France's and of Turkey's virtually total (97.5 per cent) dependence on the EC for its, admittedly small, volume of industrial exports is marked.

Table 1.17 *Principal OECD economies' imports of selected manufactured goods, 1976 ($m)*

Country of origin	USA	Japan	EC	France	FRG	UK	Total
Greece	33	6	482 (92.6%)	44	292	17	520
Portugal	35	5	449 (63.8%)	46	103	187	703
Spain	522	27	2,049 (69.9%)	825	504	218	2,932
Turkey	—	—	154 (97.5%)	5	51	20	158
Hong Kong	2,015	140	1,917 (38.4%)	980	823	694	4,991
All NICs and developing countries	11,626 (41.1%)	2,079 (7.4%)	10,928 (38.6%)	1,915 (6.8%)	4,035 (14.3%)	2,261 (8.0%)	28,283

* Goods manufactured from plastic, glass, leather and wood; vehicle tyres, cotton fabrics, cutlery, engines, office machinery, machine tools, radio receivers, motor vehicles, clothing, footwear, toys, watches, gramophones, furniture.

Source: Edwards, 1979, Table 1.5.

The second major issue is that of the agents of industrialization, each associated with different forms of organization of capital, and the role of the first of these, multinational corporations, has already been alluded to in connection with all three forms of industrialization, for Southern Europe fits into the global production and marketing strategies of these companies in a variety of ways. Moreover, several of these corporations are larger than some of the national economies under consideration (Hamilton and Linge, 1981), and this is significant in terms of the balance between corporate and state power. It has implications for Southern European governments being able meaningfully to influence, if not control, multinationals' investment and disinvestment decisions in relation to regional and national development objectives (see Amin, pp. 155–91; Eraydin, 1981; Nikolinakos, pp. 199–208). Such potential problems have not prevented Southern European governments actively encouraging multinational capital to locate within their national territories. Industrial growth from the 1960s in Greece, Portugal, Spain and Turkey was, to varying degrees, based upon a deliberate government policy of attracting such capital, to promote industrial modernization and expansion, switching from policies of autarky to opening national economies to the influences of the wider international economy (Baklanoff, 1978; Courlet, 1980; Eraydin, 1981; Merigo, 1982; Mouzelis, 1978; Murolo, 1982).

Unlike those of multinational capital, the decisions of state holding companies and public or nationalized industries are in principle more open to domestic political control and accountability. Direct government intervention of this type is evident in all six Southern European nations. An important reason for this is that their governments see public control or direction of 'key' industries as a means to promote further industrialization or even government direction of the entire industrialization process (for example, Archibugi, 1978; Ardagh, 1982, pp. 30–122; Berberoglu, 1980; Donolo, 1980, especially pp. 170–6; Giner and Sevilla, 1980, especially pp. 212–13; Hale, 1981, pp. 141–61 and pp. 195–201).

Selective public control or ownership of 'key' industries is, in principle, a potent mechanism through which governments can influence both the overall sectoral pattern of national economic development and the intra-national spatial allocation of activities. Possibly the best-known example of this – though by no means the only one in Southern Europe – is the Italian state holding companies (IRI and ENI being the most important). From 1957 they had to locate at least 40 per cent of their total and 60 per cent of their new investment in the south (60 per cent and 80 per cent, respectively, from 1971). Although much of this investment was in iron and steel and petrochemicals complexes, the share of employment in the state holding companies in the Mezzogiorno rose from 13 per cent in 1958 to 27 per cent (of about 700,000 jobs in all) in 1978 (Ronzani, 1980, p. 138; see also Arcangeli et al., 1980; Donolo, 1980).

The third agency of industrialization in Southern Europe is indigenous small- and medium-sized firms. Such capitals are much more prevalent in Southern than in North-West Europe (Ganguly, 1982; Garofoli, 1982; Hudson and Lewis, 1984, pp. 199–201). During the 1970s, at least three-quarters of manufacturing plants had less than ten workers in Southern European countries; the comparable figure for the UK was less than 40 per cent.[10] Nevertheless, it is important to distinguish between different types of such firms: artisanal producers; independent firms; firms tied directly into wider circuits of capitalist production and the influence of multi national capital through sub-contracting arrangements (Brusco and Sabel, 1981). These differences in type of small firm have important implications for the division of labour within the firm and between it and other organizations (Solinas, 1982), the balance of self-employment, family labour and wage-labour within the firm, and the links between the social relations of the workplace and those of the surrounding community. Furthermore, these differences in types of small firm have important implications in relation to control over the production process, choice of product and technology, and access to markets. Even when formally independent, such small capitals are often heavily dependent upon exports and constrained by the imperatives of competition on international markets.

This proliferation of small manufacturing firms is intimately related to the niches that they occupy within the international division of labour. For such firms are concentrated in export-orientated 'traditional' industrial branches, often characterized by 'mature' technologies – clothing and textiles, leather, shoes, furniture and woodworking and ceramics. Nevertheless, in response to the 1970s crises and advances in micro-electronic control and communication techniques associated with the 'Third Technological Revolution', very advanced technologies began to penetrate, unevenly, into small firms in these traditional branches. In part linked to this, out-working and home-working have tended to increase. At the same time, partly in direct response to competition from other parts of the Mediterranean and South-East Asia (Balassa, 1981; Edwards, 1979), there has been a tendency to switch into higher-value added commodities. While such changes have been occurring in small firms in 'traditional' branches, related forms of decentralization became generalized over other, more 'modern' branches (such as engineering). Thus, far from being static, the small-firm sector has been heavily restructured in terms of products and technology in an attempt to retain international competitiveness.

Another crucial factor in retaining this competitiveness is where such firms locate within Southern Europe, for they have quite precise locational requirements, especially as regards labour market conditions. This has resulted in clear patterns of regional concentration of small firms in some but not all non-metropolitan regions and often to particular areas within them specializing in particular products. This spatially uneven development of small firms has been a focus of considerable research, especially in Italy (Arcangeli et al., 1980; Bagnasco, 1977, 1982; Borzaga and Goglio, 1981; Brusco, 1982; Coulet, 1978; Garofoli, 1981, 1982, 1983a; Gurisatti and Nardin, 1983; Murray, 1983; Rullani, 1983) but also elsewhere (Andrikopolou Kafkala et al., 1982; Vasquez Barquero, 1983; Granados, 1984; Kafkalas, 1984; Lewis and Williams, 1981; OECD, 1983; Turkish State Planning Organization, 1983; van Velzen, 1977).

The Italian case can be examined to exemplify the more general tendencies. Industrial growth in Italy between 1945 and 1963 was heavily dependent upon export-orientated small firms in traditional industries, locationally concentrated in the north-west, the main region of economic activity (Arcangeli *et al.*, 1980; Borzaga and Goglio, 1981; Hudson, 1983b). In 1962–3 (and at the end of the 1960s) real wages there rose sharply as a result of trade union victories following major strikes and industrial disputes. This created a serious problem for those traditional industries in which wages formed a high proportion of total production costs: operating with mature technologies (which then offered little opportunity for developments to cut the quantity of living labour required in production), these industries needed to find fresh locations with lower wage costs and more flexible labour markets. Such conditions existed in the adjacent central and north-eastern regions, especially Emilia-Romagna, Veneto and, to a lesser extent, Tuscany, not least because of the creation or persistence of numerous small farms, based on family labour. Due to agricultural underemployment, considerable labour reserves were present within them, from which workers could be drawn from and returned to the agricultural sector by small manufacturing firms as demand for their output fluctuated cyclically. This system of double-labour was, then, crucial to these firms, helping to reduce wage costs and preserving the necessary flexibility to recruit and fire wage-labour, since the general tendency among those employed on this irregular basis was to view the industrial wage as supplementary to their livelihood from agriculture and to remain non-unionized. The spatial diffusion of firms over the landscape also helped stem unionization, while dispersion of production into the existing built environment reduced the firm's fixed capital investment costs. Thus these processes of diffuse industrialization and decentralization of production resulted in particular locations within central and north-eastern Italy becoming specialized in these forms of production.

In the 1970s, however, this locational pattern also began to change in some respects in response to crises. Diffuse industrialization processes increasingly spread into non-metropolitan areas within the old industrial area of the north-west, such as Lombardia (Garofoli, 1983b). In the regions of central and north-east Italy, decentralization of production from the north-west became less important as a source of dynamism than the formation of indigenous small firms (Garofoli, 1983c). Despite these changes, as well as those in products and technology, it remains to be seen whether this 'model' of small-firm development will continue to be a viable one as competition from newly industrializing countries intensifies and as some of the initial preconditions for its success are increasingly destroyed; for example, as proletarianization increasingly becomes generalized in such areas (Borzaga, 1982).

This is merely one example of a more general feature of industrialization within Southern Europe: the distinctive spatial patterns linked with each form and agency of industrialization. These locational variations generally reflect the importance of market access and its varying connotations for different agents and forms. Existing concentrations of economic activity and population, the main domestic markets, tend to attract import reproducing industries, thereby reinforcing or exacerbating patterns of spatial uneven development associated with previous phases of economic growth. Export processing industries locate more with respect to their raw materials, commonly in rural areas or peripheral regions, whereas export-platform production tends to cluster in and around ports, themselves often existing major urban-industrial nodes (Verlaque, 1981). Within Southern Europe, Athens is the most extreme case of urban-industrial concentration (Carter, 1981; Leontidou-Emmanuel, 1981), but the trend is a general one (Gaspar, 1984). In contrast, indigenous small and medium-sized firms have tended to move from major urban-industrial concentrations to escape from their problematic labour market conditions. Nevertheless, this spontaneous (in the sense of a simple response to market forces) decentralized development is itself a selective process, both in terms of branches of industry and also of the areas in which it takes place. It has not, for example, generally spread into southern Italy or the interior of Turkey.

More generally, there are substantial areas of the national territories of the Southern European states which, for various reasons which are expressed in regional variations in profitability (Ferrão, pp. 226–43), remain excluded from or marginal to the national growth process. Governments have therefore designed and implemented regional policies and plans to try and draw such areas into the accumulation process as locations for production (and not just as sources of internal and international migrant labour). These regional policy measures can essentially be classified into major, publicly funded, infrastructure projects and programmes (to provide industrial sites, ports, roads, etc.), which have often required substantial government borrowing to fund them (pp. 9–10), or financial incentives (grants, soft loans, tax holidays, tax-free profits, etc.). Such policy packages are present in the six Southern European states (for examples, see Ardagh, 1982; Bleitrach and Chenu, 1982; Carter, 1981; Hebbert and Alonso Teixidor, 1982; Hull, 1980; Keleş, pp. 68–73; King, 1981; Naylon, 1981; Ronzani, 1980). Their availability has influenced the locational decisions of many multinationals. This is particularly so when they are in addition to measures to induce such capitals to locate within the national territory, especially in those branches such as metals production or petrochemicals which require substantial outlays of fixed capital (Amin, p. 159; Nikolinakos, pp. 204–8; Parodi, 1977).

Such industrial developments do not always coincide with the needs of the regions in which they are implanted (see Nikolinakos, this volume) – although they may have been central to national economic plans; nor was the response from private capital, in terms of type of industry and length of commitment to the location, always necessarily that assumed in regional development plans. Thus yawning gaps arise between the intentions and outcomes of plans.

Clearly, Southern European governments frequently find that managing the changing intra-national distribution of industry is problematic – yet it is something they must continue to attempt, not least because of the partial and uneven impact of past policies, and their effects on the regional distribution of employment and incomes. Furthermore, the character of the industrialization process poses parallel problems in managing the national economy. The growing influence of the economies of the advanced capitalist world on industry in Southern Europe has grave and immediate implications for national economic management – profit repatriation, technological dependence (for examples, see Cuadrado Roura et al., 1983; Giannitsis, 1983; Granados and Aurioles, 1982), dependency upon access to foreign export markets in an era of unstable currencies, international trade flows being intra-company ones, and so on.

In future such problems may intensify and new ones appear. For example, what impacts will European Community enlargement have on industries in those parts of it within Southern Europe and in those states with which it has industrial trade agreements? As with agriculture, Spanish entry will be the most problematic: in steel, shipbuilding and motor cars it will further add capacity in sectors already in severe crisis within the Community (see Hudson and Lewis, 1982a). Moreover, what will be the implications for Southern Europe of further industrial development in the newly industrializing countries of the Middle and Far East? The export-platform petrochemicals complexes which sprung up around the coasts of Southern Europe may be under serious threat when the new complexes such as Jubail currently under construction in Saudi Arabia and other Gulf states come on stream in 1984–5 (see Merrett, 1981). Small firms producing in traditional sectors will encounter further fierce competition as Far East producers, such as Hong Kong and Singapore, also restructure into higher value-added products. It remains an open question whether technological developments in micro-electronics will allow a further decentralization and fragmentation of production processes and the continuing transformation and survival of the Southern European model of decentralized production in the face of this intensifying international competition.

The tertiarization of Southern European societies?

The absolute and relative expansion of the service sector within Southern Europe in terms of employment and output (pp. 3–5, 10–12) has constituted a very profound change. Yet this sector is an extremely diverse one, encompassing a wide range of disparate and qualitatively very different industries and occupations; perhaps for this reason it remains relatively unresearched, both within Southern Europe and more generally. This is particularly so in terms of regional differences in numbers and types of service sector activities and jobs (for a very rare exception to this general trend, see Lipietz, 1980b). Rather than attempt comprehensively to cover service sector structure and change, attention will be selectively focused upon three aspects that are particularly relevant to Southern Europe: the growth of the public sector and its relation to the clientelist state (see Pugliese, pp. 123–39; Giner, pp. 328–9); the development of tourism; and the development of banking and other financial services.

Taking the latter first, there is relatively little development of specialized international banking, financial and trading services within Southern Europe (excluding Paris as non-Southern European). The one major centre for such activities is Athens, which had already begun to attract them in the early 1970s but which developed even more rapidly as a location for such operations as Beirut ceased to fulfil this role, and this does no more than confirm that the role of the 'semi-peripheral' (to borrow Wallerstein's 1979 terminology) Southern European economies within the new international division of labour is that of production rather than control. Nevertheless, domestic banking and related financial services have important effects within Southern European states. Such institutions serve to channel domestic savings selectively into particular sectors and locations, typically away from rural areas and the agricultural sector into urban areas and the industrial, property, etc., sectors (Cuadrado Roura, 1981) while their own locations can act as a powerful influence on a range of other economic activities, thereby further polarizing growth.

In contrast, growth of public sector services offers an opportunity to spread such employment more evenly within national territories – though these tend to follow the existing distribution of the population because of the types of services provided. There has been considerable growth in the public service sector in Southern Europe over the last two decades, with considerable implications for improved living conditions, as well as for

Table 1.18 *Public consumption as a percentage of Gross Domestic Product, 1960–80*

	1960	1980
France	13	15
Greece	12	16
Italy	13	16
Portugal	11	15
Spain	9	12
Turkey	11	13

Note: Public consumption is defined as 'all current expenditure for purchases of goods and service by all levels of government'.

Source: World Bank, 1982, Table 5.

employment and the growth of public expenditure. One indicator of this is the growing share of GDP taken by public consumption (Table 1.18), particularly when the growth of GDP itself is taken into account (Table 1.2). Such figures are in a sense deceptive, however. For the public sector provision of many basic educational, health and social services commonly began from a very low level, part of the inheritance of right-wing dictatorships; despite continuing increases in central government expenditure, very significant differences in *per capita* expenditure remain (Table 1.19). The gap between France (and to a lesser degree Italy) and Spain and

Table 1.19 *Central government expenditure* per capita *on health and education, 1972–9 ($)*

	Education		Health	
	1972	1979	1972	1979
France	n.a.	255	n.a.	406
Greece	54	88	44	76
Italy	178	n.a.	150	n.a.
Portugal	n.a.	n.a.	n.a.	n.a.
Spain	43	65	5	7
Turkey	32	49	6	8

Source: World Bank, 1982, Table 24.

Table 1.20 *Indicators of provision in education and health, 1960–77*

	Secondary school enrolment, as % of age group		Population per physician		Population per nursing person	
	1960	1979	1960	1977	1960	1977
France	46	84	930	610	530	170
Greece	37	81	800	460	800	600
Italy	34	73	640	490	1,330	330
Portugal	n.a.	55	1,250	700	1,420	470
Spain	23	78	850	560	1,290	900
Turkey	14	34	3,000	1,760	n.a.	920

Source: World Bank, 1982, Tables 22 and 23.

Turkey, particularly in central government expenditure on health, is massive: in excess of 50 to 1. Nevertheless, despite such differences remaining – with very real implications for the quality of educational and health services – it is equally clear that the numbers employed in such services have risen sharply in all six nations. While populations have been growing, those in employment to serve them have been increasing even more sharply (Table 1.20). While this has increased employment opportunities nationally within the public service sector, it has also tended to exacerbate uneven spatial development by encouraging intra-regional and rural to urban migrations, such employment typically being located in urban areas.

There is another aspect to public service sector growth, however: expansion of employment in public administration, particularly in so far as this is related to the distribution of welfare payments to and within peripheral regions. A characteristic feature of peripheral regions within Southern European countries has been the growing dependence of people resident within them on transfer payments from national states (and, in the case of France, Greece and Italy, the supra-national European Community). This process of 'welfarization' has recently been both highlighted and reinforced as flows of alternative sources of income, notably migrant remittances, have been reduced in volume while levels of unemployment and under-employment within them have risen as the level of net out-migration from them has been reduced or even for a time reversed in regions such as Andalusia, the Mezzogiorno and Thraki (pp. 19–25).

Furthermore, as Pugliese (pp. 123–39) emphasizes, increasing 'welfarization' also can be associated with profound changes in class structure and
pose considerable problems for a class analysis of social structure in such
areas. He poses the question as to whether farm workers in Italy are
members of an agricultural working class, landless peasants, or clients of
the welfare state. Growing 'welfarization' also raises other important
issues: is the expansion of welfare payments to be interpreted as part of a
conscious strategy of social control pursued by the state, providing a
minimal floor to consumption levels, while possibly also reinforcing long-
established patterns of patronage and clientelistic social structures (Giner,
p. 317) so as to defuse potentially explosive political challenges to the
dominant pattern of social relationships, the existing distribution of
power within society, and the unequally distributed costs of uneven
development? Clearly the answers that one gives to such questions have
deep implications in terms of political strategies in and for such areas.

Leaving aside this question of interpretation for the moment, what is
undeniable is that such expenditures can be considerable – social security
payments in the order of £500 million per annum in the Italian Mezzogiorno alone, for example (Ronzani, 1980, p. 153). The growth of
public administration to manage the distribution of these payments itself
provides a source of employment, albeit relatively poorly qualified, in
areas such as the Mezzogiorno characterized by chronic under-
employment and unemployment. Such jobs are again typically located in
urban centres and so encourage short-distance, intra-regional, rural to
urban migration; as with similar migration in response to the availability
of public sector jobs in education and medical care, this in turn has a
multiplier effect in stimulating some employment growth in locally based
consumer-orientated services. Furthermore, the growth of employment in
public administration to administer and allocate public expenditures for
regional planning and policy purposes, whether through the normal
channels of local and central government departments or special agencies
such as the Cassa per il Mezzogiorno serves to reinforce the clientelistic
social structure of such areas.

But the service sector – indeed *the* – activity which for many people is
synonymous with Southern Europe is the tourist industry, in particular
that part of it that caters for the mass tourist market. There has been a
considerable growth in hotel capacity (Table 1.21), as well as in the transport and service infrastructure needed to sustain modern mass tourism.
Such growth has typically been encouraged by national governments as a
way of utilizing natural environmental advantages of sand, sea and sun in
attracting foreign capital and foreign currency via tourist receipts to offset

Table 1.21 *Number of tourists (thousands), hotel capacity (thousands) and financial receipts (US$M), 1981*

	France	Greece	Italy	Portugal	Spain	Turkey
Number of tourist arrivals	30,471	5,094	43,506	2,566	40,129	1,405
% change 1980–1	+1.1	+6.2	–8.9	–5.2	+5.5	+9.1
of which: from Europe*	25,967 (85.2%)	3,327 (65.3%)	36,031 (82.8%)	2,271 (88.5%)	35,540 (88.6%)	641 (45.6%)
from major source	7,733 (West Germany)	968 (UK)	9,340 (West Germany)	1,120 (Spain)	10,659 (France)	155 (West Germany)
Capacity of hotels (and similar establishments)	1,578	296	1,577	99	982	51
% change 1970–81	+30.2	+148.7	+18.3	+35.6	+44.0	n.a.
Financial receipts	7,193	1,881	7,554	1,023	6,716	381
as % of value of exports	4.5	18.7	7.5	16.1	18.9	11.2**
% change 1980–1	–12.2	+8.5	–8.0	–10.9	–3.6	+16.7

* European members of OECD (excluding Yugoslavia)
** 1980

Source: OECD, 1982c.

visible trade deficits (Table 1.3; Boissevain, 1977, 1979). With the exception of Turkey, the attainment of such aims has met with some success (Table 1.21) though inflows of tourist receipts must be offset against increased import bills to cater for tourists (such as those from imports of food: Table 1.4); equally, the attraction of foreign capital into tourism must be seen in relation to profit repatriation and the often considerable public expenditure and borrowing costs involved in providing sufficiently attractive environments to entice it in the first place (see, for example, the study of the development of Languedoc-Roussillon summarized in Pearce, 1981). While such tourist developments have resulted in the generation of employment (Ciaccio, 1978; Dumas, 1982, and Loukissas, 1977), often in areas where jobs are at a premium, this has often been on a smaller scale than was originally anticipated or planned (see Kielstra, pp. 256–7; Kofman, pp. 278–80), while the jobs themselves are often seasonal, unskilled and poorly paid; indeed, they may be filled not by the indigenous population of the area in which tourist investments are implanted but by international migrant labour from other Mediterranean states, such as those of North Africa (see p. 23). Furthermore, if such jobs are filled by the indigenous population, they typically involve further intra-regional migration (even if only on a seasonal basis) from inland, rural agricultural regions to coastal tourist complexes, further exacerbating polarized development within typically peripheral regions.

Clearly, this form of integration between the Northern and Southern European economies has brought certain macro-economic benefits but also numerous problems, both at macro-economic level and by exacerbating internal uneven development (de Kadt, 1981). Yet perhaps the most fundamental problem of national economic management that it poses for the states of Southern Europe is that their economies become doubly dependent upon the performance of those of the advanced capitalist world: firstly, as a source of capital to finance tourist development and, secondly, as a source of revenue, via workers' wages, to sustain mass tourist flows from Northern to Southern Europe. In addition, the continuation of such flows depends upon particular locations in Southern Europe continuing to be perceived favourably as holiday destinations within Northern Europe and as events such as the Portuguese revolution graphically show, these are perceptions that are susceptible to rapid change in the light of internal changes within Southern Europe, with dramatic effects upon tourist flows and receipts. Despite the attendant changes, the one Southern European nation under consideration here not to have become deeply entangled in the international mass tourist industry is currently making this one of its main national development priorities –

indicative of the fact that for Turkey, as for Greece, Portugal and Spain in particular, there seems little choice but to set out down this particularly hazardous route towards desired national and regional development aims.

Concluding comments: heightened regional and national uneven development

In the preceding two sections we have commented upon the impact of labour migration and capital movements in increasingly differentiating the nations and regions of Southern Europe, in both qualitative and quantitative terms. At national level, their effect has been to widen the gap between France at one extreme and Turkey at the other, so that these various nations occupy qualitatively different roles within the new international economic order. At regional level, their effect has been to differentiate increasingly between particular economies and societies, as capital movements and economic change lead to new forms of export-orientated regional specialization in agriculture and industry, or to new forms of mass tourist development orientated to the international market. While the differential incorporation of regions into internal and international labour migration systems has likewise had the effect of increasing regional differences in levels of economic development and human welfare.[11] Kielstra (pp. 246–62) and Kofman (pp. 263–83) consider some of the implications for peripheral southern French regions of these processes.

   What then of political responses to such increasingly spatially differentiated and polarized development within Southern Europe? To a considerable degree, especially in the agriculture sector in Greece, Portugal, Spain and Turkey, increasing regional specialization has reflected a domestic political choice to seek economic links with the European Community, while in France and Italy it cannot be understood without reference to the internal policies of the European Community. The further Southern European enlargement of the Community will lead not simply to a heightening of this process of increasing regional specialization, but also to potential regional crises as the new Community's productive capacity exceeds its continued internal and export demand across a range of both agricultural and industrial commodities. This tendency to over-production within an enlarged Community will also have serious repercussions on regional (and national) development strategies in those Southern European and North African Mediterranean nations that will remain outside the Community but linked to it in various ways by trade and aid treaties.

Table 1.22 *Indices of regional polarization within Southern Europe*

Nation	Dominant region(s)	% national area	% population	% GDP
France	Île de France	2	19	27
Greece	Athens	3	32	47
Italy	Lombardia, Piemonte	16	24	30
Portugal	Lisbon-Setúbal-Oporto	11	46	56
Spain	Viscaya, Madrid, Guipuzcoa, Barcelona	4	30	37
Turkey	Istanbul, Ankara, Izmir	6	21	41*

* % manufacturing labour force; regional GDP data do not exist.

Sources: Hudson and Lewis, 1982a; Eurostat, 1983; Turkish Population Census, 1980.

But if this points to future deepening and broadening of national and regional differentiation within Southern Europe as a direct result of a deliberate political choice on the part of the European Community and some Southern European nations, what have been the political responses within the latter to the existing processes of spatial differentiation? One response at national level has been the formulation of development plans and strategies to try to close the gap between poorer and richer nations within Southern Europe (for example, by heavy government borrowing to fund such programmes, by the attraction of foreign capital, by entering into trade treaties to guarantee access to export markets), but implementing such strategies in a way that guarantees the realization of their intended national developmental objectives is fraught with difficulties precisely because of the location of these nations within the new international economic order, and in practice has not been attained. Giner (this volume) further elaborates upon the political issues surrounding the formation of such policies and the domestic political implications (for example, in relation to the transition from dictatorship to democracy) of attempts at national economic modernization and growth.

These internal political implications take on an added dimension in that even when there has been a limited degree of success in meeting national economic growth objectives, this has often been achieved at the price of widening inter- and intra-regional differences within countries (Table 1.22). Polarization is particularly marked in France, Greece and Spain. This pattern of sharp inter- and intra-regional differentiation has on occasion provoked regionalist and nationalist political movements within

Southern Europe, although these are rarely simply a response to economic differentiation but rather an interaction of this with cultural, linguistic, political or social dimensions (see Nairn, 1977). In some cases, regionalist demands and political movements have been most prominent in the peripheral regions within Southern European nations: those in Corsica (Kofman, 1981; 1982; this volume), Friuli and Alto-Adige in north-east Italy (Geipel, 1982), Andalucia and Galicia (Vazquez Barquero and Hebbert, this volume) are representative of this type. In other cases, the strongest regionalist and nationalist separatist movements are not found in those peripheral regions which in some sense see themselves exploited by the core areas of the state, but by those economic core areas themselves which see the character of the state – or even membership of the state itself – as a brake upon their further economic and social development. The outstanding example of this sort of movement is that in the Basque and Catalan regions of Spain (see Giner, 1980; Medhurst, 1977). An important effect of these regionalist and nationalist political movements, one related to the general leftward swing in Southern European politics often associated with a return to democratic government, has been an increase in the degree of political autonomy granted to such areas, in part in response to fears of the break-up of the existing nation state. The most far-reaching example of such decentralization and devolution of power is the Spanish one, which is analysed by Vazquez Barquero and Hebbert (pp. 292–308), but similar tendencies towards granting a greater degree of regional autonomy are present in France (Ardagh, 1982, pp. 187–205), Italy (Slater, 1984), Greece and Portugal. Will further devolution be the model for the future in Southern Europe (Hudson and Lewis, 1982b) or will the political tensions generated by uneven development prove too great for democratic governments to survive in Southern Europe?

Notes

1 Although written specifically as an introduction to this book, the chapter contains both information and ideas that were first used in teaching under-graduate and postgraduate courses on Southern Europe in the University of Durham. We should thus like to thank those students who have taken these courses for their help in clarifying our thoughts and those colleagues in the Department of Geography who have shared their knowledge of these countries with us. We are particularly indebted to Michael Drury, not only for making the joint teaching of most of the courses an enjoyable as well as an educational experience, but also for all the discussions of South European issues which have made Tuesday lunchtimes in the New Inn a highlight of each week in term. In writing this chapter, we have drawn upon the results of

several years of research in Southern Europe and gratefully acknowledge the financial support that we have received from the Comissão de Coordenãçao de Região Centro, Commission of the EC, Gulbenkian Foundation, Nuffield Foundation and University of Durham.

2 Because problems of different national definitions compound those of non-registration and under-employment, no attempt is made to compare levels of unemployment.

3 A fuller discussion of these trends in four of the six countries is provided in the excellent survey by King (1984).

4 For a fuller discussion of the relationships between capitalist development and uneven spatial development, see Carney (1980), Lipietz (1980) and Läpple and van Hoogstraten (1980).

5 The character of urbanization in Greece, Italy, Portugal and Spain is summarized in Gaspar (1984) while case studies of the housing crisis in such countries can be found in Wynn (1984).

6 It should be noted that there are considerable variations in national practice in recording international migrants so that the figures in Table 1.8 are not directly comparable. Furthermore, these fail to capture much of the illegal emigration from countries like Portugal and Turkey and so should be regarded as understatements of the true position.

7 This selectivity is not confined to the Southern European countries under consideration, as it is also demonstrated in studies such as Baučić (1974).

8 For an extended discussion of capital movements and industrialization in Southern Europe, on which this section draws, see Hudson and Lewis, 1984.

9 'Import reproducing' seems more appropriate than 'import substituting' as the new products are generally similar to those previously imported, often being made by the same firm.

10 There are clear dangers in using 'small' (and 'large') as adjectives to describe firm size without further qualification: it is clear that the meaning of 'small' varies between industrial branches, for example. Nevertheless, such qualifications would not alter the basic point as to the importance of small firms in Southern Europe.

11 Although for a rather more optimistic view of the extent of national and regional socio-economic convergence, see Giner, especially p. 343.

2
The effects of external migration on regional development in Turkey

Ruşen Keleş

Introduction

The bulk of the international labour migration from Southern Europe during the last two decades has been regulated more by the demand for labour of Northern European countries than by 'push' factors in the countries of emigration (Kindleberger *et al.*, 1978). Of course, domestic socio-economic conditions have had a role in pushing labour to leave, so the present picture is a product of 'pull' and 'push' factors which Newland (1979) described as being 'like positive and negative charges on a battery, each pole without the other is powerless' to induce the current of 'economic refugees'. The relative importance of these factors depends on the level of development of sending countries and the level of labour demand in receiving countries. However, whatever the dominant factors involved, the process and effects of international labour migration are usually examined from two essentially different theoretical standpoints which can be summarized as follows:

Balanced growth approach

According to this approach (illustrated by Griffin, 1976; Lutz, 1961; Kindleberger, 1965; and Rist, 1978) the emigration of surplus labour from an underdeveloped or peripheral region paves the way for a new balance between labour and capital which furthers development. This optimistic model presupposes a positive influence upon the national balance of trade, an increase in domestic investment and therefore an accelerated growth rate of the economy. It assumes that the relief of pressure on the job market involves no loss of production as it is partially or entirely unemployed workers who leave. Finally, it is believed that on their return, migrants will have the opportunity to apply the industrial training and experience acquired abroad to the development of their homeland. All these benefits, of course, can be obtained only so long as such a training occurs and it is appropriate to the developmental needs of the country of emigration. Furthermore, the returning emigrants should be able to continue in their own land the occupation for which they were trained (van Velzen and Penninx, 1977, p. 12). A number of studies (e.g. OECD, 1967; Trebous, 1970; Kayser, 1970) designed to test the balanced growth hypothesis have only partially confirmed it, as the main arguments of the model concerning the flow of money, regional development, and the industrial training of workers were not supported by the empirical findings of field surveys.

Asymmetric growth approach

The main assumption behind the asymmetric growth model is that a close connection exists between continuing underdevelopment in one region of the world and development in another and that inequalities, dependence and imperialism are just the manifestations of the same uneven nature of the world economic system. Not only the displacement of capital and labour from underdeveloped to industrialized countries, but also the transfer of capital from agriculture to industry, and from one geographical region to another in a single country are inescapable results of domination relationships between the core regions and the periphery (Galtung, 1971; Nikolinakos, 1974; Paine, 1974). It is remarkable, as observed by Portes, that through this process, 'power and capital flow in one direction, economic surplus and labour to another. After a while, it is not clear what is left in the periphery or how such places can survive' (Portes, 1978).

What the asymmetric growth approach hypothesizes seems to be underlined in the cumulative causation theory developed by Gunnar Myrdal in the 1950s (Myrdal, 1957). This was further elaborated by Paul Baran and other Marxist scholars or by dependency writers in Latin America (Baran, 1957; Furtado, 1971; Frank, 1970; Cockcroft *et al.*, 1972). This model has also been widely utilized in explaining the interrelationships between regional differentiation in one country and the dependence of Third World countries on industrialized nations (Santos, 1975, 1977).

Cinanni's analysis of the effects of labour migration from southern Italy and the studies of Marios Nikolinakos on Southern Europe support the main arguments of the asymmetric development hypothesis. G. Schiller, A. Aker and N. Abadan-Unat *et al.* have provided detailed empirical research findings that also prove the validity of this approach (Cinanni,

1979; Nikolinakos, 1973; Schiller, 1972; Aker, 1972; Abadan-Unat *et al.*, 1976).

Migration and regional disparities

Assumptions of the international migration theory relate to changes in socio-economic structures of both sending and receiving countries. What interests us here is to see to what extent emigration helps the development of backward regions. Or, in G. Myrdal's words, whether the under-developed regions are affected more by the 'spread effects' (positive ones) than by the 'backwash effects' (negative ones) of the migration process? Although migration takes away part of the surplus population and helps in this way to increase the marginal productivity of those left behind, the logic of growth itself may operate to enlarge the differences between developed and backward regions. Tapinos (1974) draws attention to the probability of three kinds of settlement decision upon return home, namely: rural to rural, urban to urban and finally rural to urban, and he concludes that in the absence of infrastructure and a suitable professional environment, return to the region of origin is practically impossible. Choosing to settle in a region other than the one lived in prior to departure is usually explained more by psychological factors than the attraction of the urban regions. In fact, the reasons for international migration are almost exactly the same as those causing internal migration, mainly the lack of employment opportunities and inadequate income in the regions of origin. Economic conditions pushing people away from their native land to domestic metropolitan centres or to the cities and towns of industrial-ized countries operate, in turn, to influence the decisions of migrants upon their return to stay away from rural areas. Thus, external migration usually means a complete loss of population in the villages, and is also an indirect first step in rural depopulation in the labour-exporting countries.

The experience of Southern European countries like Turkey and Greece (Abadan-Unat, 1976; Penninx and van Renselaar, 1978; Papa-georgious, 1973; Krane, 1975; Toepfer, 1980, 1981) – and also of some North African countries (Koelstra, 1978; Koelstra and Tieleman, 1977; Heinemeijer *et al.*, 1977) – generally fit this pattern. Kayser (1970), for instance, believes that

> Unless migrants are attracted to the region from which they originate, emigration is in the long run nothing but a factor of impoverishment. At the outset, it relieves congestion but little by little it becomes erosive. As there can be no qualitative control over the departing emigrants, the

cream is bound to be skimmed off. In this way, a community loses structure while its economic system disintegrates.

Similarly, Cinanni (1979) talking about Calabria, Italy, found that 'emigration caused a decline through unemployment and further migration in a chain reaction leading ultimately to total abandonment of the region'.

Geographical characteristics of labour migration

Modern Turkey is a rapidly urbanizing country. During the past quarter century, its urban population has increased from 18.7 per cent in 1950 to 47 per cent in 1980. This rapid growth brought an additional sixteen million people into urban centres. Before the Second World War Turkey's rate of urbanization was very low, ranging between 1 and 2 per cent annually. Only after the War did urbanization develop the remarkable momentum that increased annual growth to as much as 7 per cent. Since 1950, localities with 10,000 or more inhabitants have had an average annual rate of increase of 7.1 per cent, compared with 1.4 per cent for rural areas and 2.8 per cent for the nation as a whole. Large cities have grown even faster, experiencing an average rate of increase of 9.1 per cent during the same period.

Although the annual growth rate of the Turkish population has been above 2.5 per cent since 1950, only a very small portion of urban population increase stems from natural growth. The major factors underlying accelerated migration have been low agricultural productivity, inadequacy of agricultural income, disparities in the distribution of land ownership, mechanization and the fragmentation of agricultural land holdings. The share of the agricultural sector in the GNP has decreased from 42.4 per cent in 1950 to 23.0 per cent in 1979, and the downward trend seems likely to continue.

Heavy investment in highway construction made possible as a result of the Marshall Aid Programme has further contributed to the acceleration of migratory movement by enlarging the road network connecting small towns and the rural periphery with growing urban centres. The underemployed who moved to the city have probably caused a *per capita* increase in agricultural income, but this was not adequate to retain people on the land (Keleş, 1973). Recent attempts to reform the land distribution pattern have had only a minimal effect in keeping the farmers on the land.

The last three decades have greatly increased the mobility of the population. The proportion of the population living away from their birthplaces rose from 9.3 per cent in 1945 to 10.3 per cent in 1955, to 21.0 per

Table 2.1 *Urban population and the number of cities by city-size categories, 1960–80*

Size categories		1960	1965	1970	1975	1980
10,000–20,000	%	15.8	12.9	12.7	12.5	10.8
	(number	69	92	117	154	160)
20,000–50,000	%	21.9	23.1	19.0	16.5	15.2
	(number	51	74	72	89	99)
50,000–100,000	%	17.0	13.3	11.6	9.5	10.7
	(number	18	18	20	24	32)
100,000 and over	%	45.3	50.7	56.7	61.5	63.3
	(number	9	14	20	25	29)

Source: Population censuses.

cent in 1970 and to 24.0 per cent in 1980. The masses who rushed to the cities from rural areas in the last twenty-five years have not all been gain-fully employed. The ratio of labour supply in the services sector of the large cities has increased at a much higher rate than in manufacturing industries. In metropolitan centres a significant number of economically active people work in marginal, low-productivity service jobs as street vendors, waiters, porters, janitors, street sweepers, and shoeshiners. Thus, rural migrants to cities are by no means all absorbed by industry (Munro, 1974).

Internal migration was almost unidirectional until the late 1960s, in that the flow of population was directed mainly to the largest centres and small towns were steadily losing population. Similarly, migration was, and still is, from eastern to western provinces of Turkey. However, during the period from 1960 to 1980 some growth centres in the central, southern, eastern and south-eastern provinces of Anatolia have flourished and have begun to attract population from their surrounding underdeveloped provinces. For instance, nine out of the twenty-nine cities of over 100,000 inhabitants are located now in Eastern and South-eastern Anatolia, while there were none in that region until 1960.

Differences in their degrees of urbanization between geographical regions are apparent and vary between 24.0 per cent and 68.7 per cent according to the provisional results of the 1980 Population Census. Almost half of all large industrial establishments are concentrated in the province of Istanbul, and only 3 per cent are located in Eastern Anatolia According to a survey of the State Planning Organization which used a composite index of socio-economic development, the most developed

Table 2.2 *Regions by degree of urbanization, 1970–80*

Regions	Urban population 1970		Urban population 1980	
	%	Rank	%	Rank
Marmara	50.4	1	68.7	1
Southern	39.7	2	48.8	2
Central	36.5	3	47.4	4
Aegean	34.2	4	48.6	3
South-east	25.8	5	36.5	5
East	20.3	6	27.2	6
Black Sea	17.8	7	24.0	7

Source: Population censuses.

provinces scored between 100 and 250 and the least developed ones scored between 27 and 47, the national average being 100 (Tolan, 1972). A recent income distribution study indicated that the index of average income in the less developed regions was less than half of that of the developed ones (Danielson and Keleş, 1980).

Labour exporting provinces

Similarities between internal and international migration with respect to the factors accelerating them make it possible for us to look at both processes together. The principal source for migration studies in Turkey is the quinquennial population censuses. Census figures concerning the population living outside their birthplaces give a rough idea about the mobility of people and especially about the extent of in-migration province by province. Since the results of the 1975 and 1980 censuses are not fully published yet, we will confine ourselves to showing the general characteristics of out-migration by utilizing the data that are available.

First of all, it is generally observed that the number of persons living outside the province where they were born has almost tripled during the last thirty-five years. Their percentage increased from 6.8 in 1935 to 21.0 in 1970 and reached 24.0 in 1980. Two other characteristics of internal migration merit mentioning: first, males predominate in the process of migration as 65 per cent of the migrant population are males, and secondly, the whole of Eastern and South-eastern Anatolia, the Black Sea region, and some Central Anatolian provinces (excluding Anakara) are Turkey's principal out-migration areas. Where net population loss is high, out-migration accounts for the decline. There is no considerable out-migration from places where the net population has risen. According to the census results, two-thirds of Turkey's sixty-seven provinces feature out-migration. The further west one progresses, the fewer such provinces are encountered (Figure 2.1 on p. 71 shows the location of the provinces).

Using the figures of the 1965 Census, E. Tümertekin (1968) found that the provinces exporting labour included Rize, Erzincan, Trabzon, Gümüşhane, Çankırı, Kastamonu, Bilecik and Tekirdağ. Most of them are in the Black Sea region (see also Sanli et al., 1976). It is interesting to note that these out-migration provinces are also ones with little or no population increases. According to the provisional results of the 1980 Census, the provinces with less than a 9 per cent increase of population during the previous five years were Trabzon, Tokat, Urfa, Çorum, Yozgat, Kastamonu, Sinop, Nevşehir, Kırşehir, Kars, Erzincan, Gümüşhane, Çankırı and Tunceli. It should also be noted that all of these provinces, except Trabzon, are grouped as underdeveloped by the State Planning Organization (SPO) and so benefit from investment priorities. Finally, with few exceptions, the out-migration provinces are located in the eastern and south-eastern regions. The Black Sea region (excluding Samsun and Zonguldak) and Central Anatolia (excluding Ankara and several large growth centres) may be added to the list.

As explained elsewhere, relatively well-developed regions of the country are at the same time centres of out-migration abroad (Abadan-Unat, 1964; Keleş, 1976; Kudat et al., 1975). Figures pertaining to the place of origin of emigrant workers throughout the period 1963–78 show a constant pattern in the sense that relatively underdeveloped central Anatolia is second to the well-developed Marmara region in sending workers abroad.

Since both the internal and international migrations take place under the same economic circumstances that may be briefly called under-development, one might normally expect the regions of emigration to be the poorest ones. How then can the complex picture in Table 2.3 be explained? If the expected relationship is not visible in the above table, it is because emigration is to a great extent a two-step phenomenon in Turkey.[1] As a result, people leaving the land come and settle in one of the large cities of developed regions for a certain period, where they acquire necessary means and experiences to enable them to live abroad.

Another reason for this paradox is that the Employment Service is better organized in the metropolitan centres and potential migrants prefer to make their applications through these offices. Therefore, the migrants

Table 2.3 *Regions of origin of migrants abroad, 1963–78*

Regions of origin	Migrants abroad	%	Applicants on the waiting list	%	Average rank of socio-economic development of the provinces in the region
Marmara	247,839	31.1	250,182	23.7	20
Aegean	87,089	10.9	104,270	9.9	22
Central Anatolia	217,123	27.2	276,687	26.2	28
Black Sea	128,444	16.1	182,956	17.4	39
South	58,210	7.3	95,758	9.1	18
Eastern and south-eastern	59,132	7.4	144,543	13.7	51
Total	797,837	100.0	1,054,396	100.0	

Source: Gitmez, 1979, p. 285; DPT, 1973.

who left the country from these points seem over-represented when compared with migrants who left from other localities. In fact İstanbul (20.7) per cent of the total), Ankara (7.8 per cent), İzmir (5.2 per cent) and Konya (3 per cent) seem to be the main export centres of migrant workers (Gitmez, 1979).

This is in line with the figures concerning the urban-rural background of the migrants which indicate that 53.8 per cent of around one million migrants were of urban origin, and only 46.2 per cent were coming from rural areas (Aker, 1972). However, one should be careful not to regard the total urban based migrants as a loss to the large cities and to developed regions. Since most of them were originally inhabitants of rural areas, their emigration causes an absolute depopulation of rural areas and contributes to the sharpening of regional disparities.

This is an inverse correlation between the level of development of emigration provinces and the number of migrants if one looks at the number of potential emigrants rather than the guest workers that actually migrated. As Table 2.3 shows, the share of the three relatively backward regions (Black Sea, East and South-east) in the total applications made for emigration (40.2 per cent) is much greater than the share of the same regions in actual migration (only 30.8 per cent). An income distribution study made in 1973–4 also revealed that there was a correlation between the average income of rural families in various agricultural regions and the rate of out-migration of these provinces (State Institute of Statistics, 1979).

Receiving provinces

One-third of the sixty-seven provinces seem to be receiving population in all censuses. However, only a small fraction of them are rapidly growing provinces; they are Ankara, İstanbul, İzmir, Hatay, Adana, Zonguldak and Samsun. All of the in-migrant provinces are located west of the line that can be drawn between Samsun and Hatay. In these fast growing provinces, the percentage of the population born elsewhere is higher than the national average. These figures for İstanbul, Ankara, İzmir, Kocaeli are 63.3, 42.2, 38.9 and 36.1 respectively and they are followed by Eskişehir, Tekirdağ, Sakarya, Kırklareli, Edirne, Bursa, Manisa and Adana.[2]

The attraction of the cities located in the centre of these provinces has undoubtedly had a great role to play in the movement of population, for the first five metropolises of Turkey are included in the above list. Among these five, the size of the smallest is over half a million and their annual growth rates vary between 1.7 and 5.0 per cent (State Institute of Statistics, 1977). They are also highly developed, and located to the west of the Samsun-Hatay line.

The high proportion of population born elsewhere in such provinces of Thrace as Edirne, Tekirdağ and Kırklareli may be explained by the great number of refugees from the Balkan countries following the proclamation of the Turkish Republic in 1923. Likewise the cases of Bursa and Eskişehir may also be better understood by the reference to immigration. In-migration centres attract population more from the provinces in their immediate surroundings than from all over the country. This is especially true for the newly flourishing metropolises in Anatolia. For instance, the percentage of population born elsewhere in Adana was 19.3 per cent in 1970, and 22.2 per cent in 1975. This included those born in Maraş (17.9 per cent), Urfa (15.0 per cent), Malatya (14.2 per cent), Adıyaman (10.5 per cent) and İçel (10.4 per cent). In other words, 68 per cent of the in-migrants were coming from the provinces whose centres were located at a distance varying between 68 and 423 kilometres from the metropolis. Similarly, 62.8 per cent of the population born elsewhere in Gaziantep came from the nearby provinces like Adana, Adıyaman, Malatya, K. Maraş and Urfa.

Another striking point is that as the size of the growth centre increases, the percentage of population migrating from the nearby provinces gets lower. In other words, the metropolis gradually loses its character of a regional centre and becomes a national focus.

External migration and regional disparities

Patterns of return migration

Studies on international labour migration in Turkey have produced different estimates as to the number of returning emigrants. Abadan-Unat *et al.* (1976) concluded in their monograph on Boğazlıyan that returning migrants were only about 13 per cent of the total. According to a recent study by Gitmez (1977) on return migration, the number of returned migrants who applied for the return of their social welfare premiums was 59,479 in 1975, or only 7.4 per cent of the total. This does not correctly reflect the number of returnees because it is not obligatory to apply for premiums, and it can be assumed that a great number of returned migrants have not had a chance to make their applications for various reasons. Gökdere (1978) estimated that average annual returns were about 20,000–25,000 during 1962–74. Based on his estimate, one can assume that 250,000–300,000 Turkish workers returned home by 1975. The economic crisis of the early 1970s in Europe may have encouraged at least some of the workers to accelerate their return. Taking this factor into consideration, one would not be far wrong in estimating that the total number of returnees is around 400,000 – nearly 40 per cent of the total number of guest workers still in European countries.

It is not easy to determine where these migrants settle on their return and to what extent they contribute to rural-urban imbalances and regional disparities. One hypothesis is that they prefer to choose urban centres where they can practise what they have learned abroad. Our own Boğazlıyan study has shown that 32 per cent of all migrants who invested in housing had a house built outside their original village (Abadan-Unat, *et al.*, 1976). Small provincial towns like Boğazlıyan do not offer much attraction for the returning migrants because of the inadequacy of infrastructure. They do not even serve as stop-overs for migrants on their way to or from Europe and have far less drawing power than nearby growth centres like Ankara, Kayseri and Adana.

Similarly, Toepfer (Chapter 3) found in some small towns on the Black Sea that returnees had a tendency to choose growing urban centres for settlement. The percentage of those living in the villages decreased from 76.6 per cent to 56.0 per cent after return. According to Gitmez (1977), 63.7 per cent of those returned migrants who applied for the return of their social welfare premiums were living in the centres of provinces or sub-provinces (which are regarded urban by official definition) and only 37.3 per cent were settled in the villages.

A second hypothesis is that there is a counter-movement going from the town centres towards the villages, which has increasingly characterized return migration during the last few years. It is based on the difficulties encountered in the cities as a result of the impact of skyrocketing inflation and worsening living conditions. No empirical data have yet been produced to justify this hypothesis. In short, it may not be wrong to assume that both villages and urban areas are chosen for settlement upon return home, but the propensity to live in urban centres is far higher.

Another crucial point is to know how migration affects regional disparities. The fact that the majority of out-migration provinces are already the most developed may convey the impression that the imbalances in favour of large centres will be diminished to a certain extent. However, the decision of most returning migrants to settle in the metropolises acts as a countervailing factor, increasing imbalances. Since the location of the largest metropolises are west of a line between Samsun and Hatay, the negative impact of international migration upon regional disparities is evident. A brief look at the chosen residences of migrants after their return sheds more light on this point.

What is striking in the table is that the western regions like Marmara and Aegean plus Central Anatolia attract most of the return migrants (69.7

Table 2.4 *Distribution of returned migrants by region, 1977*

Regions	Migrants	%
Marmara	16,685	28.0
Central	16,552	27.8
Aegean	8,757	14.7
Southern	4,586	7.7
Eastern	2,825	4.7
Black Sea	9,360	16.2
South-eastern	520	0.9
Total	59,535*	100.0

* Number of returned migrants who applied for the return of social welfare premiums.

Source: Gitmez, 1977.

per cent). East and South-east together get the lowest share of the migrants.

Distribution of workers' investments

Another way to identify the likely location of return migrants is to look at their investments. Their decision to invest in a particular place is not only an indication of their intention to settle there, but also it can affect the distribution of population. For instance, according to Bovenkerk (1974a) funds transferred by migrant labourers are usually invested in industrial activities which frequently take place in regions that are already developed to a certain extent.

From the late 1960s, the Turkish government has supported the establishment of workers' joint stock companies that would invest in Turkey and especially in the less developed regions. This attempt to facilitate the reabsorption of returning migrant workers in the national economy was supported by the feelings of workers' regional chauvinism coupled with hopes of securing work upon return home, and nearly 500 workers' companies have thus been created with varying capital and numbers of shareholders.

A survey of the Turkish Industry and Workers' Investment Bank of 200 companies with 100 or more shareholders revealed that about 90 per cent of all the companies were located in the regions of central Anatolia, Black Sea, Aegean and Marmara (İşletmeler Bakanliği, 1979; Bulutoğlu, 1980). Unpublished data of the same bank confirm the findings of this survey. Although the workers' companies aim at achieving a certain social goal by developing the backward regions in general, they are unable to get away from the economic considerations that matter considerably as far as the productive operation of the enterprises is concerned. The concentration in these four regions is 91.5 per cent of the number of shareholders, 89.9 per cent of the employment created, 92.6 per cent of the total capital and 90.2 per cent of the amount invested. With the exception of the Black Sea region, these are the most developed and urbanized regions of Turkey. Only 26 per cent of the workers' companies are established in the provinces that are regarded by the SPO as regions for priority development. In other words, in fifteen out of forty provinces for priority development, there exists no workers' company. On the other hand, particular provinces in the above-mentioned regions seem to have got a considerably higher share of the workers' companies. Although their numbers vary from one region to another, Balıkesir and İstanbul in Marmara, Trabzon and Zonguldak in the Black Sea, Denizli and Aydın in the Aegean, and

Table 2.5 *Workers' companies by geographical regions, 1979*

Regions	Com- panies	%	Number of shareholders	%	Employment	%	Capital (thousand TL)	%	Investments (thousand TL)	%
1 Marmara	43	19.6	37,772	17.1	6,720	24.6	1,157,600	14.1	5,096,600	22.6
2 Aegean	40	18.3	57,672	26.0	7,630	28.0	2,405,300	29.3	4,093,300	18.2
3 Central Anatolia	67	30.6	69,204	31.3	6,226	22.8	2,543,100	31.0	8,001,500	35.5
4 Black Sea	42	19.2	37,843	17.1	3,949	14.5	1,490,100	18.2	3,137,500	13.9
5 Southern	12	5.5	8,740	3.9	1,346	4.9	295,100	3.6	910,000	4.0
6 Eastern	11	5.0	8,859	4.0	1,180	4.3	250,000	3.1	1,101,200	4.9
7 South-eastern	4	1.8	1,360	0.6	242	0.9	54,500	0.7	2,121,200	0.9
Total	219	100.0	221,407	100.0	27,293	100.0	8,195,700	100.0	22,552,300	100.0

TL = Turkish pounds

Source: State Industry and Workers' Investment Bank (unpublished data).

Ankara, Kayseri, Konya, Yozgat, Sivas and Niğde in central Anatolia are the most obvious examples.

This picture is almost identical with that which Toepfer (p. 93) found in Trabzon. He indicated that the villages do not profit from the investments of re-migrants: while 17 per cent of the invested capital flowed into the villages, the remaining capital goes to the cities in his survey and to Istanbul.

Policies for the reintegration of returning migrants

The first policy of the government to assist the reintegration of the returning migrants was to support the creation of Village Development Co-operatives. There were about half a million such co-operatives, though only 110,000 were registered in 1973, most of them seeking to secure jobs for their members rather than to realize productive investments in the villages through remittances (Abadan-Unat *et al.*, 1976). Devoid of any kind of administrative and technical guidance, they were left to the imagination and initiative of uninformed villagers, and most village development co-operatives were really just used as a vehicle to facilitate migration.

A second method for attracting the savings of the migrant workers was to induce them to establish joint stock companies. Investments of these companies would provide job opportunities to returning migrants, and at the same time they would serve as a device for the economical use of their savings. This was regarded as an efficient way of industrializing the regions of origin. The creation of workers' companies was supported from the beginning by some of the receiving countries through special funds in order to facilitate the reabsorption of returning workers within the national economy (van Renselaar and van Velzen, 1976). Following the shift of interest of West Germany from the reintegration to the assimilation of guest labourers, workers' companies have become deprived of one of their financial resources. Despite the determination of the government to back them by all means, workers' companies have run into various problems like project identification, financial and technical planning and management, and inadequacy of communications. Hence their role in fostering the development of less developed regions has been minimal, although their numbers approached 250 by 1980.

As an implication of the official policy of attracting workers' savings to put them to productive use, a public bank, the State Industry and Workers' Investment Bank, was created in 1975. It advocated mixed enterprises organized by the state with the participation of the private capital. According to the organic law of the bank, its goals are:

(1) to consolidate the savings . . . of citizens working abroad and to put them to productive use, [and]
(2) to channel these savings into country-wide enterprises, especially industrial investments in accordance with the aims of national development.

The aims of the National Development Plan envisage a harmony between the social and economic targets. Since the major social goal is to reduce regional disparities in Turkey, at least 75 per cent of the funds to be invested by this bank has to be used for the projects in areas identified as underdeveloped by the SPO in its Annual Programmes according to the law. Those investors receiving loans for underdeveloped regions receive more favorable interest rates than accorded elsewhere and they benefit from a period of fifteen years for the repayment of the capital that they borrow.

The last six years' experience in implementation shows that DESİYAB (State Industry and Workers' Investment Bank) has not been able to channel its investment resources into the less developed regions. The observation that the entrance of workers' enterprises into Turkey's economic system has not contributed to the reduction of serious regional disparities as was originally hoped (Abadan-Unat et al., 1976) is confirmed six years after the creation of a special-purpose state bank. Despite all kinds of public incentives, workers' enterprises have concentrated in already developed regions, thus contributing to the persistence of the present inequalities. This means that the reintegration methods used for the last several years have not been very successful.

Policies for balanced regional development

Turkey's policies for regional development were shaped at the beginning of the planned development period. The aim of the First Five Year Development Plan (1963–7) was to increase overall productivity by giving priority to the allocation of resources to regions with high social and economic potential in order to eliminate regional imbalances. Studies were undertaken by the SPO in co-operation with the Ministry of Reconstruction and Resettlement to identify promising growth centres and backward regions. One of these studies has shown that among sixty-seven provinces ranked by their level of socio-economic development, only the first twelve were above the average figure. These most developed provinces had at least 100,000 inhabitants and almost all of them were located

Table 2.6 *Geographical distribution of manufacturing industries (those enterprises with ten or more workers), 1977*

Regions	Private enterprises		Public enterprises		Total	
	Number	%	Number	%	Number	%
Marmara	757	13.6	55	13.5	812	13.6
Aegean	332	6.0	21	5.2	353	5.9
Southern	342	6.1	42	10.3	384	6.4
South-eastern	114	2.1	17	4.2	131	2.3
Eastern	56	1.0	31	7.6	87	1.5
Central Anatolia	284	5.1	44	10.8	328	5.5
Black Sea	356	6.4	100	24.6	456	7.6
İstanbul	2,346	42.2	34	8.4	2,736	45.8
İzmir	563	10.1	17	4.2	580	9.7
Ankara	415	7.4	46	11.2	461	7.7
Total	5,565	100.0	407	100.0	5,972	100.0

Source: DPT, 1979, p. 73.

in the western part of Turkey (the list was İstanbul, Ankara, Kocaeli, İzmir, Zonguldak, Adana, Içel, Aydın, Eskişehir, Bursa, Sakarya and Rize). On the other hand, the fifteen least developed provinces were located in eastern Anatolia (Tolan, 1972).

Location decisions of the firms and of public enterprises were utilized in the hope of closing gaps of regional development and tax incentives were increased for the enterprises that invested in less developed regions. Despite all the efforts made, however, the distribution of public service investments among geographic regions remained all but unchanged throughout the planned development period, and the lack of adequate infrastructure continued to deter private enterprise from setting up factories in the east. For instance, in the late 1970s, the geographical distribution of manufacturing industries was far from reflecting a balanced picture (Table 2.6). Marmara and Aegean regions (including İstanbul and İzmir) represent 75 per cent of the country's industrial base as measured by the number of industrial establishments with ten or more workers.

The Second Five Year Development Plan (1968–72) reiterated the regional development policy of the First. Special attention was devoted in the Second Plan to regionalizing sectoral investment programmes around selected growth centres. A balanced distribution of service investments among regions was also emphasized. However, the establishment of a regional development authority, as envisaged, during the plan period did not occur. Priority for development for target regions has remained on paper, except for the refinement and continuation of minor incentives for choosing sites of operation in underdeveloped areas.

The Third Five Year Plan (1973–7) approached the problem of regional development in a considerably different way. In it, concern for a balanced geographical development of public services has assumed secondary importance to the use of economic criteria to govern the allocation of productive investment. However, one new department was created in the SPO in order to identify better the less developed areas and to make appropriate recommendations to the government to reduce regional imbalances. It was called the Department of Priority Development Regions, and the annual implementation programmes have continued to provide incentives for private business willing to invest in underdeveloped regions. These included customs tax exemption for the import of machinery and materials, the possibility of meeting the custom taxes in instalment payments, income tax reductions and availability of medium term credits. Annual implementation programmes enumerate the sectors and industries to be supported for the development of backward regions and they designate the priority development provinces which are shown in Figures 2.1 and 2.2.[3]

In the Fourth Five Year Development Plan (1979–83), the principle of balanced development is stressed again and the State Industry and Workers' Investment Bank is responsible for financing the industrial projects designed to be located in central, eastern and south-eastern Anatolia using a special fund established for financing these projects

Table 2.7 *Geographical distribution of the loans given by state and private banks, 1962, 1974 and 1980*

	Share of the region in total loans (%)		
Regions	1962	1974	1980
The most developed regions	79.3	74.2	60.4
Moderately developed regions	15.4	19.2	35.5
The least developed regions	5.3	6.6	4.1
Total	100.0	100.0	100.0

Source: Ertuna, 1976, p. 49; Union of Turkish Banks (unpublished data).

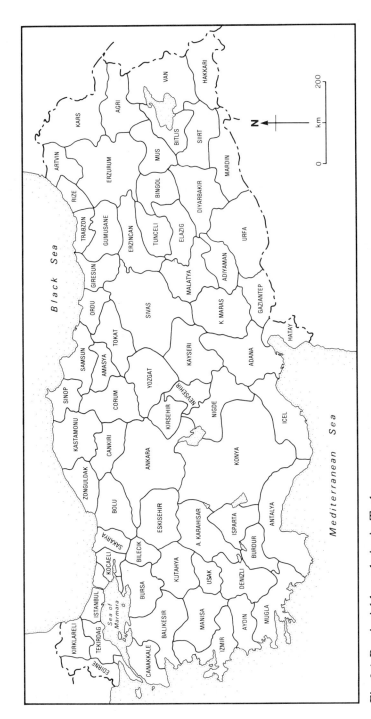

Fig. 2.1 Provincial boundaries in Turkey

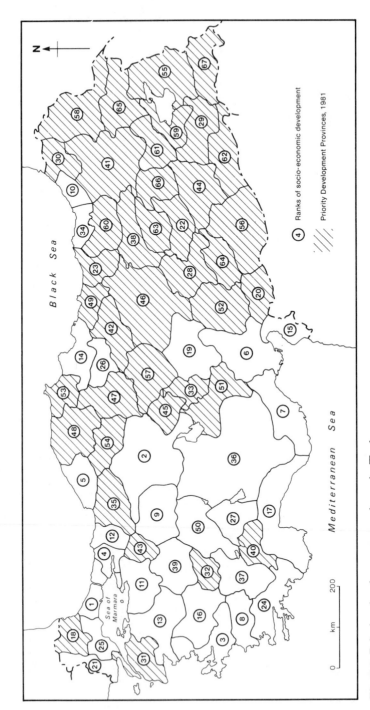

Fig. 2.2 Priority development provinces in Turkey

Ranks of socio-economic development

Priority Development Provinces, 1981

Black Sea

Mediterranean Sea

Sea of Marmara

Table 2.8 *Share of the regions of total bank deposits, 1963, 1970 and 1980*

Regions	1963	1970	1980
Marmara	39.6	43.2	44.9
Central	26.2	23.4	24.5
Aegean	13.3	11.2	12.9
Eastern	3.0	3.5	3.7
South-eastern	1.3	1.0	1.2
Black Sea	9.1	10.9	5.6
South	7.5	6.8	7.2
Total	100.0	100.0	100.0

Source: Tolan, 1972; Union of Turkish Banks (unpublished data).

(DPT, 1979). Despite all the efforts made, there has been considerable inconsistency in the implementation of regional development policies. For instance, the distribution of public credits was geographically quite uneven until very recently. Perhaps these and similar factors reflecting the inconsistencies between policies and their implementation have been added to structural characteristics of the economy to make the regional imbalances last longer. In fact, if the total of bank deposits is taken as an indicator of capital accumulation in a certain locality, one can see a widening gap between the level of development of some regions in favour of already prosperous regions in Turkey. Table 2.8 is illustrative of this uneven distribution, and the tendencies in it over time, suggesting that workers' investments, even if they were distributed evenly all over the country, remain too small to help to promote the development of less developed regions.

The policies outlined above regarding the re-integration of migrants and that of using them to reduce regional inequalities are the responsibility of numerous central departments. The Ministries of Labour, Social Welfare, Finance, Education, Industry and the State Planning Organization, an advisory institution to the government, all have to act in concert with each other in order to achieve the unified policy objectives in matters concerning both of the above-mentioned questions. This has not been possible so far simply because of the lack of a concrete and unified set of policies and because of inadequate co-ordination (Akre, 1975).

Conclusions

The experience of Turkey with regard to emigration is one which is better explained by the asymmetric growth model. Over half of the migrants and their families are preparing themselves to settle in the central countries of Europe forever. Indeed, they have been warned by the Mayor of West Berlin that those who do not wish to go back to their countries must be prepared to become German citizens. As stated in a report to the German Government by Herr Heinz Kuhn, migrants are no longer regarded as 'guest labourers', but as settled migrant workers.

The assimilation policy of Western countries contributes not only to stopping return migration but also to the persistence of rural-urban and regional differences by freezing the present unbalanced structure of population distribution. This fear is strengthened by the findings of a recent survey which proved that migrants of rural origins changed their residences to urban centres of provinces and sub-provinces upon their return after having worked for an extended period in Europe (Gitmez, 1981). Thus, the relative relief of the overpopulated rural sector as advocated by the balanced growth model is counterbalanced by over-concentration of returning migrants in large urban centres located in the western half of Turkey.

Furthermore, workers' remittances, despite their positive impact upon the balance of trade, tend to be invested in already developed regions, thus increasing regional imbalances. Investments by several workers' companies in such relatively less developed regions as the Black Sea and central Anatolia may be regarded as exceptional cases because investment in the metropolises in the western half of the country is the prevailing pattern. Measures taken by the government so far have perhaps helped the workers' companies to select the right economic sectors in which to invest, but they have not complied very well with the principle of balanced development of the Plans as far as the location of their undertakings is concerned.

Notes

1 It has also been argued by Tümertekin (1970–1) that internal migration has the same character, but I do not share his view.
2 The role of the central city is more apparent if one makes the calculations for urban areas only (i.e. for those settlements of 10,000 inhabitants or more). Using this method the percentages of the population born elsewhere in large cities are the following: Ankara (56.9 per cent), Edirne (41.0 per cent), Eskişehir (40.1 per cent), İstanbul (63.6 per cent), İzmir (50.1 per cent), Kırklareli (44.7 per cent), Kocaeli (51.6 per cent), Zonguldak (40.4 per cent).

3 The number of priority development provinces grew from 23 (1968–71) through 32 (1972) and 36 (1973–6) to 40 (1977–81). In 1981 the total was reduced to 25, with 20 first priority provinces and 5 of second priority.

3

The economic impact of returned emigrants in Trabzon, Turkey

Helmuth Toepfer

Introduction

Between 1970 and 1979, 922,681 non-Germans moved from the Federal Republic of Germany (including West Berlin) to Turkey (*Statistisches Bundesamt*, 1973 onwards). This movement is largely a reflection of the return of Turkish workers and their families but there are no exact figures available on their movement from Western Europe as a whole since the Turkish authorities do not officially register returnees – except at the customs. Some further idea of the magnitude of this return movement may be gained from the social security office (*Sosyal Sigorta Kurumu*) in Ankara, as returnees must register here if they wish to transfer pension rights from abroad to Turkey. However, not all returning emigrants have foreign pension rights and not all that do so advise this office, so the total flow can again only be estimated. Keleş (p. 63) has considered these and other estimates and opts for a total figure of about 400,000 returned migrant workers by the end of 1981. Together with their families and their capital, these emigrants represent an enormous potential for innovation in Turkey for they can fundamentally change the occupational, social and economic structures – especially in areas outside the big cities. In this chapter, the extent and nature of such changes are analysed in depth by focusing attention on a part of Trabzon province (see Fig. 2.1).

In 1975 the province of Trabzon, with 159 persons per sq. km (*Statistiches Bundesamt*, 1979, p. 4), had the second highest population density in Turkey (after İstanbul) and the population of Trabzon, its capital city, had risen some 54 per cent to 81,528 over the period 1960 to 1970 (*Statistiches Bundesamt*, 1973, p. 102). However, even at this time, the province had the highest loss through migration of all provinces. The main destinations of the migrants were, in descending order of importance, İstanbul,

Samsun, 'other destinations' (especially abroad), Ankara and Zonguldak (cf. Ritter, 1972). In rural areas, the small size of peasant holdings and high population density meant that labour migration had characterized the province for decades (Karpat, 1976, p. 48) so that, once started nationally, the guest worker movement to Western Europe became established rapidly here. During the survey reported below, it was estimated that about 30 per cent of the village households had relatives in Western Europe and that these emigrants constituted 6.5 per cent of the village population (a similar proportion to that noted in the district of Boğazlıyan, Yozgat province by Abadan-Unat et al., 1976, p. 165). However, for every six emigrants there is already one returned migrant and 320 of these were interviewed by Mr Vural Suicmez and the author in March and April 1979.[1]

The survey concentrated on the socio-economic position and occupation of these former guest workers before their departure from Turkey, during their work abroad and since their final return, providing data on eighty-seven variables which could be examined for statistical inter-relationships using chi[2] tests. Since no complete list of returnees could be obtained, standardized interviews were conducted with all those who would be found in the area of the small towns of Arakli and Sürmene – on the Black Sea coast some 30 km and 38 km respectively east of Trabzon – and the surrounding villages. Those who had originated in the area but who had migrated within Turkey after their return (an estimated 17 per cent) were not interviewed. In addition to the 320 interviews of returnees, persons who had sold building plots, agricultural land, buildings, houses or business premises to returnees were interviewed. These interviews were intended to trace the money invested by the re-migrants and were in part group interviews, often lasting several hours. The objective was to record, as accurately as possible, the extent to which invested capital remains in or flows out of the location in question but it is clear that this survey has not resulted in complete information nor 100 per cent accuracy.

The returned migrants before their departure

About one-quarter (23.4 per cent) of the interviewed former guest workers came from the two small towns of Arakli and Sürmene and the remainder (76.6 per cent) from the surrounding villages. About two-thirds (67.5 per cent) first left in the period 1962 to 1967, the remaining one-third (32.5 per cent) in the period 1968 to 1973. They had an average age on departure of 29.7 years with the youngest being 20 years of age and the oldest 42. They came from families in which an average of 6.1 persons lived (in

Table 3.1 *School attendance of returned migrants by date of birth (C = 0.52), origin (C = 0.49) and occupation before departure (C = 0.64)*

Duration of schooling (years)	0	1–4	5	6–9	Total
Year of birth (%)					
1925–9	12	46	39	3	100
1930–4	11	37	45	7	100
1935–9	11	17	65	7	100
1940–4	12	10	72	6	100
1945–9	0	0	48	52	100
Original residence (%)					
Village	14	28	53	5	100
Town	0	4	71	25	100
Pre-migration occupation (%)					
Agriculture	17	20	63	0	100
Industry	0	9	52	39	100
Handicraft	0	49	44	7	100
Construction	4	36	46	14	100
Retailing	14	14	72	0	100
Services	0	7	21	72	100
Total					
Absolute	34	72	184	30	320
%	11	23	57	9	100

addition to the migrant and spouse) and two-thirds (66 per cent) of those interviewed had completed five or more years of formal education (i.e. finished primary school). Educational background tends to improve with decreasing age (Table 3.1), so of those born after 1945 more than 50 per cent had one to four years' education beyond primary school. However, since a relatively large number were born before 1945 and as there were no schools in some (39 per cent) of the villages, the share of those with less than five years of education (34 per cent) is very high (cf. Gor, 1976, p. 28, who reports a figure of 22 per cent). Table 3.1 also reflects the fact that, especially in the past, the availability of education in small towns has been considerably greater than that in the surrounding villages. Furthermore, it indicates that those who did not attend school at all were mainly employed in agriculture and commerce, while the level of education was much higher for those who had formerly been employed in industry and the service sector.

The migrants abroad

Almost half (48 per cent) were mainly employed in industry abroad (Table 3.2). However, 31 per cent shifted from one economic sector to another, the shift from the industrial to the service sector being the most common. Those who had previously been employed in handicraft or in the service sector and who had found a job abroad in industry were especially prone to such shifts. Likewise, those from the agricultural sector frequently did not remain in their first jobs in industry as 25 per cent of them changed economic sector, while those who came from the building trade remained in this sector abroad to a much greater extent (71 per cent).

Although only about one-third of those employed abroad decided to change economic sector, regional mobility was considerably higher (52 per cent). Of those interviewed, 41 per cent had worked continuously in only one place in West Germany (FRG) and 46 per cent had shifted working place within the FRG, while another 6 per cent were employed in one place in other Western European countries and 1 per cent had shifted working place within them. Finally, 6 per cent changed country within Western Europe. Change of working place was particularly frequent (73 per cent) for those who had also shifted from one economic sector to another.

The emigrants earned an average monthly pay of about DM 1,400 net abroad. Of those who worked in agriculture abroad, 75 per cent did not earn this average income, however, nor did 62 per cent of those employed in industry. On the other hand, those employed in the building trade or in the service sector very frequently (77 per cent and 100 per cent respectively) earned more than this average sum. Furthermore, a majority of those who had shifted from one economic sector to another reached at least this average income level (Table 3.3).

Table 3.3 also demonstrates that net income and average monthly savings were positively correlated (r = 0.93). On average, DM 676.69 were saved out of the average net income and, during an average period of stay abroad of 92.8 months, mean net earnings amounted to DM 132,606, of which on an average DM 62,796 were saved (this represented 47 per cent, identical to the rate found by Paine, 1974, p. 103). The high rate of savings is not surprising when it is borne in mind that the main motive for migration for the majority has been the wish to accumulate some capital (cf. Özkan, 1975, p. 196; Abadan-Unat, 1974, p. 386).

Table 3.2 Occupations before departure and abroad (C = 0.71)

Occupation abroad	Pre-migration occupation (%)						Total	
	Agriculture	Industry	Handicraft	Construction	Retail	Services	Absolute	%
Agriculture	13	0	0	0	0	0	20	6
Industry	56	49	12	29	66	43	152	48
Construction	6	27	9	71	0	0	43	13
Services	0	0	0	0	16	0	7	2
Mixture of sectors	25	14	79	0	18	57	98	31
Total	100	100	100	100	100	100	320	100

Table 3.3 Average income by occupation abroad (C = 0.49) and savings (C = 0.80)

Monthly income abroad (DM)	Occupation abroad (%)					Average monthly savings (DM)			Total	
	Agriculture	Industry	Construction	Services	Mixture of sectors	1–599	600–899	900–1199	Absolute	%
700–1099	0	20	7	0	1	25	0	0	35	11
1100–1399	75	42	16	0	39	69	25	0	124	39
1400–1699	25	31	47	100	38	6	66	46	116	36
1700–2204	0	7	30	0	22	0	9	54	45	14
Total	100	100	100	100	100	100	100	100	320	100

The regional and sectoral mobility of the migrants

With the exception of one divorcee, all those interviewed were married on return (before departure it was 95.6 per cent) and the average number of children, 4.9 children per household, is very high. In spite of the large numbers of children the size of households has decreased since the number of persons apart from the nuclear family who lived in the household of the interviewees has fallen markedly – from 6.1 persons (s = 4.8) to 0.9 (with only a moderate standard deviation of s = 1.4). This value is also similar to that in Paine (1974, p. 191) of 0.7 persons.

Since Turkish guestworkers abroad frequently express the wish to return to their native communities (e.g. Kallweit and Kudat, 1976, p. 75: 63 per cent; or Atalay, 1976, p. 111: 74.8 per cent) a question of particular interest has been whether return migrants had actually returned to their native communities or had shifted their place of residence. Table 3.4 and Figure 3.1 present the results of a comparison of previous and current residence, controlling for pre-migration occupation and education. Of those interviewed, 74 (23.1 per cent) did not return to their native communities. Apart from four respondents who migrated from towns to country, the direction of spatial mobility was clearly towards the two small towns, so the proportion of the sample who lived in towns rose from 23.4 per cent before departure to 44.0 per cent after return.

The majority of those who had been occupied in agriculture before departure had lived in a village, and the vast majority (72 per cent) of these returned there, while of those who had lived in town before departure all returned to urban areas. Of those who had been employed in industry, on the other hand, the majority originated from the small towns of Arakli and Sürmene and had returned to them. However, among those there have been numerous cases of changing location (more than one-third of the total) both from village to town and, less frequently, from town to village. The return migrants who had worked in the handicraft sector showed little spatial mobility, returning, with one exception, to the village or town from which they had come, but for those who originally had been occupied in the building trade or retailing the situation is different. Here a very large number has migrated from village areas to the towns (39 per cent and 32 per cent respectively). Even though only a few were in the service sector before departure, they have clearly either returned to towns (43 per cent) or migrated to them (50 per cent).

It has already been noted that those who came from the small towns were, on average, already better educated before departure (i.e. had attended school for a longer period of time than the village inhabitants)

Table 3.4 Place of residence in Turkey and activity before departure (C = 0.60) and school attendance (C = 0.56)

Residence before migration and after return	Pre-migration occupation (%)						Years of schooling (%)				Total	
	Agriculture	Industry	Handicraft	Construction	Retail	Services	0	1–4	5	6–9	Absolute	%
Same village	72	0	65	50	41	7	91	74	47	13	175	55
Same town	11	61	33	11	27	43	0	4	29	50	71	22
From village to town	17	27	2	39	32	50	9	22	24	23	70	22
From town to village	0	12	0	0	0	0	0	0	0	14	4	1
Total	100	100	100	100	100	100	100	100	100	100	320	100

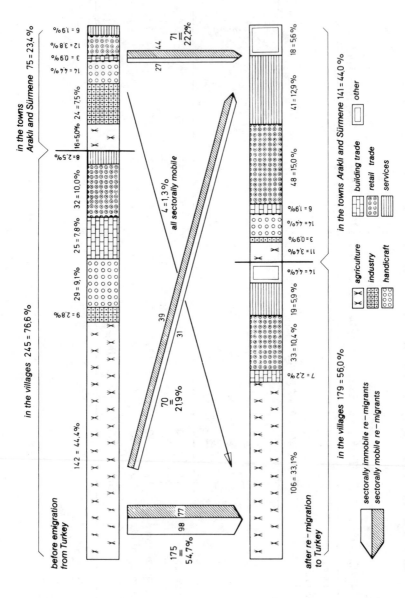

Fig. 3.1 Residential location and occupation prior to migration and on return

but Table 3.4 reveals 'educational erosion' in the village areas after the return of the migrants. While almost one-quarter of the better educated have moved from their village to a town, those without school education have nearly all (91 per cent) returned to their village. Table 3.4 also makes it clear that returnees have either returned to their native communities or shifted from one village to town or vice versa; no one has left one village and gone to another upon return or, coming from one small town, migrated to another.

As Table 3.5 and Figure 3.1 show, changes in location and occupation are linked for while a total of 125 (39.1 per cent) remained faithful both to their native communities and their former economic sector, 43 (13.4 per cent) changed both their place of residence and economic sector and the remainder changed either their place of residence (10 per cent) or economic sector (38 per cent). The frequent shift from one economic sector to another in rural areas results from the fact that there is less demand for employment in agriculture and the building trade after return and that labouring jobs in industry and handicrafts are not taken at all by those who have not previously had them. In contrast, the proportion employed in the retail and service sector rises substantially. (Under the heading 'other' are included both pensioners and those who designate themselves as 'unemployed', which means that they live on their savings and invested capital.)

In the urban areas, the share of service employment has also risen considerably – largely due to movement out of agriculture and industry. This is the more surprising since such a high proportion of the returnees (48 per cent) had worked in industry abroad – and implies that the experience gained abroad is not utilized at home. In this respect, migrants do not seem to exercise a significant innovative effect on the economies of the areas to which they return. Given the intensified building activities in the towns which were largely financed by current and former guest-workers (see below), the share of those employed in this sector has grown, although the absolute figures remain small. Again, the reason for this is that the migrants do not wish to be employed as wage-labourers, and there are few opportunities to become independent in this sector. The major sectors of those moving into urban areas are, as in rural areas, mainly commerce and services.

As regards occupational position, in the sample as a whole, 23 (7.2 per cent) are workers or employees and the bulk of the migrants have either become independent (82.8 per cent) or live on their interest or invested capital (10.0 per cent).

When the relations between the various types of mobility (immobile,

Table 3.5 Types of mobility and occupation before departure (C = 0.60), occupation abroad (C = 0.58) and location of residence abroad (C = 0.63)

Type of mobility	Pre-migration occupation (%)						Occupation abroad (%)					Residence abroad		Total	
	Agriculture	Industry	Handicraft	Construction	Retail	Services	Agriculture	Industry	Construction	Services	Change of sector	One place	Several places	Absolute	%
Immobile	53	9	14	14	50	43	100	43	0	100	34	44	34	125	39
Sectorally mobile	29	52	84	47	18	7	0	24	63	0	59	34	41	121	38
Regionally mobile	7	0	0	21	16	50	0	12	14	0	7	7	12	31	10
Doubly mobile	11	39	2	18	16	0	0	21	23	0	0	15	13	43	13
Total	100	100	100	100	100	100	100	100	100	100	100	100	100	320	100

sectorally mobile, doubly mobile) and other variables are examined, the following points emerge as significant:

(a) Sectoral mobility is more common (64 per cent) among those originating from small towns than for those who lived in a village before departure (47.3 per cent).

(b) A large proportion of the 'non-movers' is found among migrants who were either self-employed or assisting relatives in agriculture, in commerce or in the service sector before migrating. On the other hand, former workers in handicraft, in the building trade and in industry are frequently sectorally mobile – the latter group very frequently (39 per cent) being doubly mobile. A strong spatial mobility is shown by those who were formerly employed in the building trade, in commerce and, particularly, in the service sector.

(c) Many of those classified as immobile were not only employed in agriculture or in the service sector before and after but also during their stay abroad. In contrast, a high degree of mobility (especially sectoral) is evident for those who were in the building trade abroad (0 per cent immobile) and for those who were sectorally mobile during their stay abroad (34 per cent immobile). Also, as Table 3.5 shows, those who were regionally mobile abroad show a higher mobility after their return than those who did not shift from one town to another whilst abroad.

(d) Much of the difference between those who have changed location and/or job and those who have not can be explained in terms of their attitudes whilst in the FRG. Whilst 57.6 per cent of the 'non-movers' bought machinery or tools abroad, only 19.5 per cent of the others did so, which clearly indicates the former's goal of accumulating capital to improve their position within their original activities. (For further discussion see Toepfer and Sviçmez, 1979.)

Capital investments of the migrants

The 320 returned migrants had invested approximately DM 21 million by the second year after their return. Table 3.6 reveals that 59 per cent of this went into housing and building sectors together, followed by agricultural land (11 per cent), vehicles and industrial equipment (9 per cent each) and business premises (7 per cent). The remaining 5 per cent was used for miscellaneous expenses – of which the largest share covers acquisition of objects for household purposes but which also covers the (1 per cent) DM 119,000 spent on shares (cf. Hümmer and Soysal, 1979, p. 316, who identified two share-holders in their sample of seventy return migrants).

Table 3.6 Investments by returning emigrants, classified according to rate of saving, place of residence after return and occupation after return

Sector of investment	Amount of investment		Percentage of investment in each sector									
	Absolute (1000 DM)	%	Amount of savings (1000 DMs)			Location		Post-migration occupation				
			10–49	50–89	>89	Village	Town	Agriculture	Industry, handicraft, construction	Retail	Services	Other
Housing	8,841	42	32	48	39	35	49	38	22	57	41	60
Building sites	3,554	17	16	17	18	23	11	32	15	7	10	2
Agricultural land	2,405	11	14	9	14	16	6	16	6	4	11	21
Vehicles	1,862	9	16	4	11	4	14	0	7	8	26	13
Industrial equipment	1,795	9	2	13	5	6	12	0	47	2	0	0
Shops and workshops	1,445	7	12	5	7	10	3	7	0	15	7	0
Other	1,154	5	8	4	6	6	5	7	3	7	5	4
Total	21,056	100	100	100	100	100	100	100	100	100	100	100
Number of interviewees	320	–	121	147	52	175	145	117	30	81	60	32
Investment per interviewee (in 1000 DMs)	66	–	36	70	123	63	70	61	118	56	62	64

No further comment on this small category will be made here. When attempts are made to reveal the relations between the sectoral distribution of capital investments and other variables, the influence of three factors becomes evident: the amount of savings, occupation after return and place of residence of the interviewed (both before departure and after return). These are examined in turn.

When the returnee has only a modest amount of capital at his disposal (up to DM 49,000), the usual preference is for investments which are expected to give rapid returns and which directly serve to provide an occupation (e.g. land for agricultural usage, business premises, vehicles), and such people invest less than average in the partly speculative housing and building sectors. However, when the migrants have a capital of between DM 50,000 and DM 89,000 at their disposal, they are more likely to invest in the rented flat sector and they also spend more on the purchase of tools and machinery for their activities in the fields of industry, handicraft or the building trade (13 per cent of their investments rather than the 9 per cent average). When the migrants have even larger amounts of capital at their disposal, the speculative purchase of land is more evident, as is the purchase of vehicles – which are often not used by the migrants themselves, but rather are hired to others (as a rule, relatives) who wish to be taxi-drivers and who are not in a position to finance a taxi by themselves.

The influence of post-migration occupation is also quite complex. In the simplest case, there is a marked emphasis on land by those employed in agriculture after their return, shown by the expected high share of investments in the purchase of land, which either serves the purpose of providing migrants with their own agricultural holdings or shows an unambiguous speculative character since the building sites purchased are in urban areas. The small group of 30 who became employed in industry, handicraft and the building trade is the only one with a large investment in tools and machinery: 47 per cent of their investment was used for this purpose, and special attention should be paid to the fact that this group had the highest average investments per interviewee at DM 118,000. Those employed in commerce tend to invest in the housing and building sector as well as in the purchases of business premises, while those who live on their capital often support themselves on incomes originating from letting flats. Further incomes also originate from the renting out of purchased land for agricultural usage and from placing of vehicles at the disposal of taxi-drivers. However, the majority of the taxi-drivers are independent, and this is reflected in the large share of investments in vehicles (26 per cent) made by those in the service sector.

Thirdly, there is the influence of residential location which is best considered by distinguishing two groups of returnees:

(a) those (175) who have returned to their village of origin, hereafter designated as village-returnees; and

(b) those (145) who, after their return, have settled in one of the two small towns in the survey area – including the four who lived in one of them before departure and who have since migrated to neighbouring villages but whose major economic activity remains in one of the small towns – hereafter referred to as town-returnees.

When we look at the three main spheres of investment – houses, building sites and land for agricultural usage, it becomes clear from Table 3.7 and Figure 3.2 that average investment in those cases where returnees

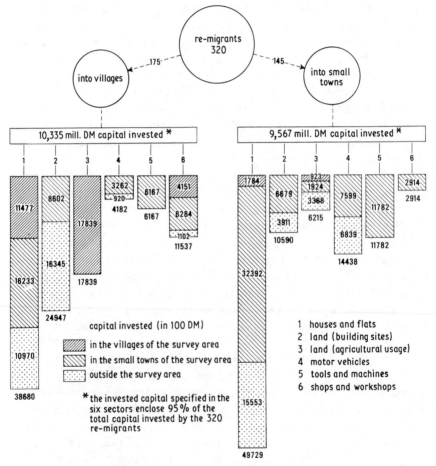

Fig. 3.2 Locational and sectoral distribution of investments by returned migrants

Table 3.7 Type and location of investment by location of returned migrants

	Sector of investment														
	Housing					Building sites					Land for agricultural use				
Location of returned migrants	None	Village	Small town	Outside area	Total	None	Village	Small town	Outside area	Total	None	Village	Small town	Outside area	Total
Village re-migrants															
Number of investments	78	48	35	14	175	69	—	59	47	175	71	104	—	—	175
%	44.3	27.6	20.1	8.0	100	39.4	—	33.7	26.9	100	40.6	59.4	—	—	100
Amount of investments (1000 DM)	—	23.9	46.4	78.4	—	—	—	14.6	34.8	—	—	17.2	—	—	—
Town re-migrants															
Number of investments	27	5	91	22	145	65	—	67	13	145	111	6	17	11	145
%	18.6	3.4	62.8	15.2	100	44.8	—	46.2	9.0	100	76.6	4.1	11.7	7.6	100
Amount of investments (1000 DM)	—	35.7	35.6	70.7	—	—	—	10.0	30.1	—	—	15.4	11.3	30.6	—

invest outside their places of residence is much greater. This is especially so for capital investments outside the survey area. As far as the building site and housing sectors are concerned, this can be explained by the fact that these investments are almost exclusively made in Trabzon, İstanbul and Ankara, where housing is considerably more expensive and the price of land is far higher than that in the survey area, so that such investments absorb considerably larger amounts of money than they would within the survey area. A further expense is incurred due to the building society system. Following acquisition of building sites in one of the big cities, the building on the plot is normally taken care of by a building society which carries out the project and which gives the owner one-third of the resultant buildings in exchange for the building site. Thus attempts are made to acquire building sites large enough for at least three houses to be erected there. It goes without saying that this requires great financial resources.

The village-returnees are heavily involved in investment in building sites in the big cities – 78.3 per cent of these investors are from villages but only 21.7 per cent from towns – in order to obtain a second source of income to add to the meagre income possibilities available within the village economy. In this way, returned migrants contribute to the general tendency for agricultural activities to become marginal to household incomes. The initial expectation that involvement in the building site sector of the big cities would increase with the magnitude of savings was not supported by the data of Table 3.8. While involvement in the building site sector increases with increased savings, the largest investments are mainly in small towns of the survey area, not the big cities. The 'export' of investment is more common among the village returnees – particularly in the building site sector – while the town-returnees limit themselves more to investing in building sites in their places of origin.

A similar picture emerges with respect to the investments in the housing sector: 42 per cent of capital investments of the village-returnees in this sector are into the small towns of the survey area and 28 per cent of them go outside it (primarily to Trabzon, İstanbul and Ankara). However, 65 per cent of investments in this sector made by the town-returnees are in their place of residence.

Since very little land for agricultural usage is available in both small towns (and this is often sold only when it has been officially designated for building), the limited number of purchases of land for agricultural usage by town-returnees is necessarily directed to areas outside the survey area. These purchases are spread over a large part of the country so when returnees have acquired land for agricultural usage in a distant district, the fields are usually worked or managed by their relatives – in contrast,

Table 3.8 *Amount of savings and investment in building sites*

Investment in building sites	Amount of savings (1000 DM) as %		
	1–49	*50–89*	*90–159*
None	53.7	41.8	13.5
In small towns of the survey area	26.4	39.7	69.2
Outside the survey area	19.8	18.5	17.3
Total	100	100	100

village-returnees attempt to buy any plot of land offered for sale in their districts of origin, since they basically see only three investment possibilities there: housing, land for agricultural usage or business premises, and workshops. It is in the latter sectors that some capital could be fixed in the villages, since the extent of business activities in the past has been insufficient. However, investments by village-returnees in business premises and workshops are greater outside their villages, so that it is business and handicraft in the small towns which receives the greater stimulus.

With respect to the villages, it is initially surprising that no capital was invested in motor vehicles and machinery. However, the limited size and steep slopes of the agricultural plots, as well as the predominance of hazelnuts as a crop, mean that no agricultural machinery could be introduced in the villages. Furthermore, the roads to and in the villages of the sparsely populated areas can only be used with great difficulty at the best of times and, for part of the year, not at all. For this reason, the motor vehicles (taxis, small buses, trucks) and machinery (especially for handicraft and building trade purposes) acquired by the returnees are to be found either in the small towns or – especially for motor vehicles – in the big cities of Trabzon, Istanbul and Ankara.

When the total amount of capital invested of approximately DM 20 million is considered (as in Figure 3.3), it is evident that this has only partially been located in the places of residence of the returnees: for the village-returnees 32.4 per cent; for the town-returnees, 66.2 per cent.

It is clear from these figures that the town-returnees concentrate on the possibilities of securing their existence in their towns whereas the village-returnees clearly see that a considerable share of their capital can only be invested meaningfully in the neighbouring small towns or more distant

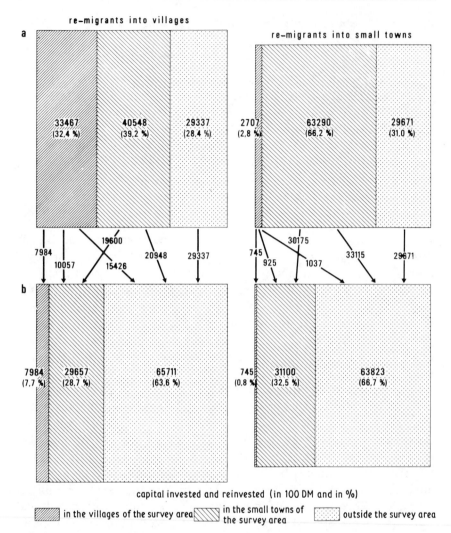

Fig. 3.3 Relationships between residential location of returned migrants and the location of their investments

big cities. Thus, 39.2 per cent of the value of their investments was located in the small towns and 28.4 per cent outside the survey area altogether.

During the interviews the returnees were asked if they regarded their economic future as secure. From their replies four further comments on the question of capital investments can be made. First, no statistical

relationship could be ascertained between the magnitude of capital investments and the number who considered their economic existence to be
secure.

Secondly, only 24.1 per cent of all returnees considered their economic
future to be secure. However, there were significant deviations from this
percentage shown by the investors in motor vehicles and in business
premises: 39.1 per cent of the former group and 55.7 per cent of the latter
did consider their future secure.

Thirdly, when the capital investments of the seventy-seven who considered their economic existence secure are examined more closely, two
types can be discerned:

Type 1: return migrants to the small towns with investments in building
sites and in housing as well as in a third sector, e.g. motor vehicles or
workshops (24.7 per cent of the group).

Type 2: returnees who distribute their capital widely regionally and
sectorally, since they become active both in the villages and in the big
cities (27.7 per cent of the group). Some of them have acquired building
sites in the big cities and at the same time acquired or built a house, dwelling, business premises or workshop in the villages. The others had
acquired land for agricultural usage in the villages and additional incomes
from a motor vehicle, business premises or a workshop in one of the big
cities. Among both types, who together account for 62.4 per cent of those
who consider themselves economically secure, there are both village and
town-returnees. Even though the remaining 37.6 per cent could not be
classified more precisely, it may be concluded that the economic situation
of the returnees depends to a great extent on the regional and sectoral
structure of their capital investments, rather than on the magnitude of
these investments.

Fourthly, similarly, there is no relationship between the magnitude of
capital investments and the subsequent social situation of the re-migrants.
The social situation seems to be determined by other variables. With
respect to the social situation of the re-migrants inquiries were made as to
the extent to which:

(a) the activities of the returnees have resulted in the displacement of
    others;
(b) the returnees are looked upon as models by the inhabitants of a com-
    munity;
(c) the relations of the returnees with the dignitaries of the survey area
    have improved;
(d) the returned migrants have been asked for advice; and
(e) the returnees give information about their experiences.

There were clear relationships with school education (a negative correlation in all five cases), the age of the returnees (a positive correlation with (c)) and the duration of stay abroad (a negative correlation with (d) and a positive one with (e)) although the exact reasons for these cannot be discussed more fully here. However, in none of the cases could a statistically significant relationship with the magnitude of capital investments be ascertained. In other words, the fact that the former guestworkers have capital at their disposal which enables them to undertake further activities does not give them any special social position.

Further employment of invested capital

In this section, the flow of returnees' investments through the local and regional economies is traced, considering each sphere of investment in turn.

First, investments in houses and dwellings. Talks with builders in the villages revealed that about 30 per cent of building costs is wage expenditure, and, as a rule, manpower originates from the village itself. Some 90 per cent of these remain in the villages, the remaining 10 per cent being spent in both small towns. About 70 per cent of the building costs are materials: of this about 10 per cent remains in the villages, 55 per cent flows into the small towns and 35 per cent flows outside the study area. Builders in both small towns calculate wage costs at approximately 40 per cent of building costs and material costs as 60 per cent. Whereas wages largely remain in the small towns, about 35 per cent of material costs flow outside. In the big cities a 50 : 50 relationship holds between wage and material costs in construction. Manpower and materials for the construction of the building project as a rule originate from outside the survey area so the amounts of money spent on building there are entirely 'leakages'.

Secondly, investments in building sites. Inquiries with the sellers of building sites in the small towns suggest that approximately 25 per cent of the sale price is re-invested in the small towns but some 75 per cent flows out of the survey area into the big cities. As sellers of building sites outside the survey area could not be interviewed, it can only be assumed that they re-invest their sales revenue outside the Arakli/Sürmene economy.

Investments in land for agricultural usage come next. Statements made by the sellers of land for agricultural usage in the villages lead to the conclusion that about 15 per cent of the sales revenue is re-invested in the villages, 20 per cent invested in both of the small towns while 65 per cent leaks to the big cities. Inquiries with sellers of land for agricultural usage in both small towns revealed that an estimated 40 per cent of the revenue is re-invested in the small towns and 60 per cent flows out. Again, there is no reason to expect that the proceeds of transactions outside the local area are ever invested in it.

Fourthly, investments in motor vehicles and tools and machinery. All of these were purchased outside the survey area.

Last, investments in business premises and workshops. The pattern for construction of business premises and workshops in the villages follows that of the construction of houses there. In the small towns, 10 per cent of the premises were purchased (and the re-investment of money is the same as that noted for the sale of building sites there) and 90 per cent newly constructed (giving capital flows the same as for the construction of houses in the small towns). Capital which was raised for the business premises and workshops purchased outside the survey area is no doubt re-invested there by the sellers.

The initial location and eventual impact of these capital flows are illustrated by Figure 3.3. Since 56.1 per cent of capital investments in the villages is for the acquisition of land for agricultural use and the sellers of land for agricultural use do not re-invest a high percentage of the sales revenue there, the bulk (58 per cent) of capital outflow from the villages must be attributed to this process. Since this capital to a large extent flows into the big cities outside the survey area it is also clear that the local small towns are often ignored in the process of economic decision-making (as observed with the second of the types of economically secure returnee above).

First and foremost, the small towns profit from the building trade in the villages since many suppliers of building materials reside in the small towns. Since a large share of capital investments of the town-returnees is concentrated in the building trade, the supplying firms have good opportunities for profit-making. This is also true of the building contractors there (in part, returnees with investments in building machinery). However, a considerable part of the building materials (such as cement) is not manufactured locally so that there is again a large capital outflow via the building activities (18.9 per cent of the outflow from the small towns if machine and motor vehicle purchases for the building are excluded).

In addition to these capital outflows for machinery, motor vehicles and building materials (72.2 per cent of the outflow), the small towns lose another 21.2 per cent of invested returnee capital due to the fact that the sellers of small-town building sites do not re-invest all their sales revenues in Arakli and Sürmene.

Thus, the initial capital flow into the survey area shows only a short-term beneficial impact in the local economies, particularly in the villages.

The facts that village-returnees frequently also invested capital in the small towns and big cities and that nearly one-third of the capital investment by the town-returnees took place outside the survey area raises questions as to the extent to which there is a return flow of income from the outward capital investments into the small towns and villages respectively. Unfortunately precise comments on this point cannot be made yet. However, discussions in the survey area revealed that incomes from outward capital investments tend to be re-invested there or used to take care of relatives who have migrated rather than flowing back into the village or small town economy.

Conclusions

It was originally believed that international labour migration would have two beneficial effects on the Turkish economy:

(1) the emigrants would gather knowledge and skills in the various industrial areas in Northern European countries which could help domestic industry after their return to Turkey; and

(2) their accumulation of capital would give a strong boost to the industrialization of Turkey.

We have been able to show, however, that very few returnees are absorbed by industry (0.9 per cent) and an indication of the disinclination to seek an occupation in industry after return is apparent during the stay abroad: only one of those interviewed had accepted the offer of further industrial training within the framework of the Labour Support Act in the FRG.

Since the returned migrants in earlier years very quickly realized that initiatives by one single individual in the industrial sector nearly always turned out to be unsuccessful, from the late 1960s they embarked on establishing capital associations – mostly on a co-operative basis – in order to be able to build industrial enterprises on a broader basis and later secure the investor a job in his home country (Ileri, 1975, p. 139). This was a very promising development supported both by domestic and foreign state institutions (such as the Ministry of Economic Co-operation of the FRG). However, experiences with dishonest enterprises and the numerous business failures have shaken their faith in such capital associations. The fact that the Turkish State Planning Organization has since 1973 offered 'feasibility studies' for such projects free of charge has been of little help: those interviewed in the present study used only 1 per cent of their investments for shares and other forms of participation in such economic enterprises.

Furthermore, these participations were as a rule only on a modest scale, involving amounts of about DM 3000.

The difficulty in finding a job after return, as well as the high rates of inward migration to the towns, leads to a concentration of investments in the building trade by the returnees, especially in the towns. They are freed from paying rent themselves, and in a situation of a strong demand for dwellings it is possible to live off rents without having a job. Under such conditions, no great boost to the economy of the state will be generated. The fact that these conditions are not exclusively applicable to Turkish returned migrants has been demonstrated by studies in other Southern European countries (e.g. Baučić, 1972; Böhning, 1976; Lienau, 1977; Schrettenbrunner, 1970).

Even though the labour emigrants left with the objective of improving their position, they still feel economically insecure after their return. The fact that going abroad once more is considered the only way of reducing this insecurity does suggest that chances for building a better future at home with money already earned have not been recognized or been wasted. Certainly the present economic situation in Northern Europe suggests that few will have a second chance of migrating. In these circumstances it is necessary to consider measures which do not depend on making a lot of money relatively quickly. Rather, if returnees are to act as economic innovators in their home communities they must be presented with a better picture of the real opportunities (through vocational training, further training in the field of management and in other fields of business economics, and information about possibilities of investing capital in the rural areas of Turkey and keeping it there).

In these ways it might be possible to reduce the gap between the migrants' clear intentions of accumulating capital and their vague ideas about what to do with it. Interviews with migrant workers in the FRG revealed that shortly before return about 40 per cent of these were not able to say in which field they would seek an occupation on their return to Turkey (Aker, 1972, p. 43 and p. 61; Kallweit and Kudat, 1976, p. 65). The only clearly defined wish is to become independent and the present study has shown that the majority of the re-migrants do realize this wish. However, the chances of being able to establish oneself permanently in the tertiary sector are becoming poorer. It is not surprising, then, that the majority of guestworkers in Western Europe in the meantime must be characterized as semi-permanent migrants who have no fixed period of stay and that the policies in the Western European countries have been transformed from their original emphasis on the principle of rotation to ones based on the principle of integration (Abadan-Unat, 1979, p. 18).

Note

1 I should like to express my thanks to all those interviewed for their patience and their willingness to give information. I should also gratefully acknowledge the support of Turkish institutions and personnel – especially Osmar Cebi and Ali Karaderiz, the Mayors of Arakli and Sürmene.

4

Return migration and rural economic change: a south Italian case study[1]

Russell King, Jill Mortimer,
Alan Strachan and Anna Trono

Introduction

Migration is undoubtedly one of the main features of the human geography of Southern Europe. Although details differ between countries – indeed every village probably has its own unique migration profile – there is a certain communality of experience, particularly in rural areas, from Portugal in the west to Turkey in the east. Starting in some places from quite modest flows in the 1950s and early 1960s, and in other places continuing migration streams dating back to the late nineteenth century, the post-war period has seen an emigration boom, dictated largely by the labour requirements of Europe's main industrial powers. From the Italian Mezzogiorno, as from Trás-os-Montes, Andalucia, Croatia, Macedonia and a dozen other South European regions, farm labourers and other workers have emigrated in droves to the industrial and service sectors of the north where, in the 1950s, 1960s and early 1970s, jobs – of a certain range of types – were available in abundance.

For the last ten years, however, this trend has been reversed in the sense that counterstreams of returning migrants, for most South European countries, now outweigh the much reduced outflows. Three reasons may be advanced to account for this turnabout. One is the temporary nature of European labour migration in the first place, with most migrants intending to return home at some stage, or being encouraged to do so by the 'labour rotation' policy of receiving countries. Second are national and international economic factors, such as the economic crisis and reduced availability of jobs in receiving countries since 1973, and the way in which these economic trends have affected bilateral quota arrangements with non-EEC sending countries. Third, and more insidious, are problems of mounting racial disharmony which have also made governments like the

Swiss and the French look carefully at their migration and repatriation policies. The mounting tide of returnees has caught South European governments unaware. Whilst policy statements abound about 'a healthy re-entry', re-integration, return of innovation, use of returnee capital, etc., in reality governments are rather ignorant about the precise economic behaviour of their returning migrants.

This chapter examines the economic behaviour of returned migrants and the economic and physical transformations they have contributed to in one village in southern Italy. The village is called Leverano and it is in the province of Lecce, which is the southernmost province of the region of Puglia (Figure 4.1). Although we acknowledge that village-scale studies may not be very geographically fashionable at the present time, we believe that fieldwork at this scale is necessary to document and understand processes that return migration gives rise to in rural areas, not only in southern Italy but in other 'migration regions' of Southern Europe and the Mediterranean basin.

There were particular reasons for choosing Leverano. Most field-based studies on the socio-economic impact of return migration in southern Italy have looked at remote interior or highland villages; examples are Lopreato's portrait of a Calabrian hill-village and Reyneri's work in central Sicily (Lopreato, 1967; Reyneri, 1979). Although such settlements have been most heavily affected by emigration in the past and currently have large numbers of returned migrants, the returnees are returning to an economic environment which still holds little promise: agriculture is still poor, industrial potential is still minimal and physical isolation is still extreme. Small wonder, therefore, that such studies frequently conclude that returning migrants have little developmental impact, since the prospects for development are so low anyway!

We decided that, in order to test the hypothesis of return migration as an agent of rural economic change more rigorously, a settlement should be chosen which was in an area where some economic progress – chiefly agricultural development – was being experienced. A previous spatial analysis of socio-economic and migration data for southern Italy revealed that most of Puglia was a relatively rich and progressive area with prosperous agriculture, a buoyant pattern of agricultural employment and a relatively high rate of return migration compared to outflows of migrants (Strachan and King, 1982). Leverano is situated in this Puglian zone of agricultural prosperity and intensification. In this particular part of Puglia, the western flank of the Salentine peninsula, a traditional pattern of farming, based on vines, olives, wheat and pasture, is being modified by the addition of market gardening, vegetables and floriculture. The irrigated

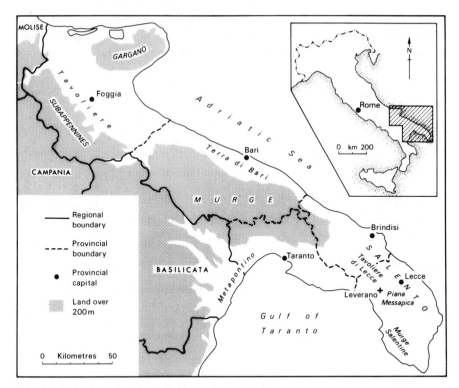

Fig. 4.1 Location of Leverano in south-east Italy

area in Leverano's territory tripled between 1968 and 1978, reaching 424 ha. of which 229 ha. are used for vegetables and 52 ha. for flowers; 239 Leverano farmers belong to the local irrigation consortium. Olives and vines still predominate in the local farm landscape, accounting for 39.6 per cent and 33.6 per cent of the village agricultural land respectively; 11.8 per cent of the land is devoted to the new specialized crops, including 50 ha. of glasshouses. New agricultural co-operatives are replacing private chains of middlemen. The first were the *cantina sociale* or wine co-operative, founded in 1959, and the olive oil co-operative founded by the local land reform agency in 1962. More recent, and more interesting, are two important co-operatives founded in the early 1970s: the 'La Salentina' tomato-processing plant, and the 'San Rocco' flower co-operative, the latter founded by 22 returnees from Liguria where they had gained experience of working on the flower-terraces of the Italian Riviera.

Thus Leverano presented interesting developments in agriculture, both economically and from the point of view of the social organization of production, processing and marketing. One of our central questions in selecting this settlement was the role that the recent wave of return migration in the 1970s had played in these aspects of rural development.

Leverano and emigration

Like so many other villages in southern Italy, Leverano was hit by emigration fever in the 1950s and 1960s. During the 1970s, however, return migration was dominant (Figure 4.2). In spite of its size (population in 1979: 13,028) and relative closeness to the provincial capital, it is an overwhelmingly rural community with, according to the 1971 census, 70.4 per cent of its working population engaged in farming. Flattish topography and an inherently fertile soil enabled a steady intensification of land use since the nineteenth century, a process which has accelerated in recent years. However, the realization of a fully efficient farm economy, with benefits widely distributed to all concerned, was hampered by an outmoded landholding structure. Large landholdings, often cultivated below capacity in spite of a large reservoir of underemployed rural labour, dominated over peasant smallholdings. Many large and medium-sized estates were leased out on old-fashioned and burdensome renting and share-cropping contracts. Emigration of surplus rural labour was virtually inevitable in this system, given the opportunities available in industrial Europe after the war. Some of the larger estates were dismantled by the 1950 land reform, but the new smallholdings created by the reform were mostly too small to be economically viable (King, 1973).

Figure 4.2 records annual in and out movements for the period 1951–79, taken from village records. Out-migration has generally fluctuated within the range 100–150 per year, but with much higher peaks in 1952, 1967 and 1971. For migrants going abroad, the available data are more limited. France was the main destination during the 1950s, Germany and Switzerland thereafter. Both for internal and external migration, annual returns exceeded outmovers for the period 1972–8. During this period about 50–90 migrants returned each year from abroad. It is, however, almost certain that, especially for migrants going and returning from abroad, these official figures underestimate the size of the movements, for many migrants move without bothering to inform the local authorities.

According to village records for returnees coming back to Leverano from abroad between 1971 and 1980, 61.9 per cent were from Germany and 28.7 per cent were from Switzerland. Much smaller numbers were from France and Belgium as most of these returns, the result of emigrations during the 1950s, had already taken place before 1971. Local

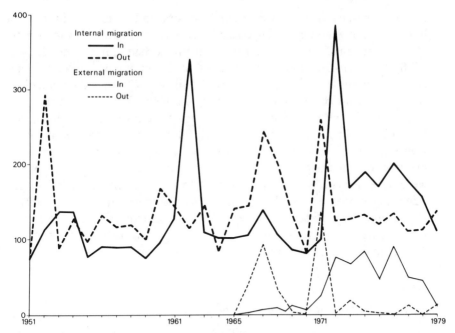

Fig. 4.2 Official data on annual migration for Leverano, 1951–79

records also provide skeletal data on returnees' occupational and educational characteristics. For males returning between 1971 and 1980
occupations were overwhelmingly of an unskilled or semi-skilled nature:
38.0 per cent were farm labourers, 25.6 per cent were construction
workers and 5.4 per cent were artisans working as carpenters, joiners, etc.
Female occupations comprised 64.2 per cent farm workers, 24.8 per cent
housewives and 6.4 per cent tobacco workers (tobacco is an important
local crop in Lecce province). Educational levels were low: only 5.9 per
cent of returnees over 20 years of age had a secondary school leaving certificate, and 24.1 per cent had no school certificate of any kind. Again,
however, it must be stressed that these village statistics are based only on
those returnees who recorded their movements with the local *municipio*.

The questionnaire survey

The main focus of the interview survey of returned migrants was on
economic aspects, including employment, income, remittance and investment patterns, participation of returning migrants in the various processes
of economic change in southern Italy such as industrial development, rural

co-operatives, tourism and the retailing sectors, and the geographic moves linked to these economic processes. In Leverano we aimed to interview 100 respondents who had returned from abroad during the decade 1970–80. A returnee was considered eligible for interview if he or she had been abroad for at least one year, returned since 1970 and had remained in Italy for at least one year at the time of interview. The interviewing was carried out in the second half of 1981, using a questionnaire which had been piloted in the area in April 1981. Names and addresses of interviewees were selected at random from the town hall's list of returning migrants during the period 1970–80. Where possible, entire family nuclei were interviewed. We felt it important to get women's perspectives on migratory movements as their experiences and their influences on household migration are frequently overlooked. We also interviewed children of working age who had spent part of their lives abroad. Each interview lasted, on average, one hour.

Basic demographic and migration profile data

Interviews consisted of 95 individuals, comprising 55 family nuclei or part-nuclei. The sample consisted of 57 males and 38 females; 92 were married, one was single, one widowed and one divorced. Their average age was 38 years. The earliest year of departure was 1951 and the latest 1975, but three-quarters of the sample departed during the decade 1960–70. Their countries of destination were Germany (54 emigrants), Switzerland (22), France (12) and Belgium (2). Five migrants had migrated to two countries, in most cases France initially followed by a transfer or a re-emigration to Germany. The mean age at departure was 22 years with 78, or 82 per cent, in the age band 17–29 years. The mean duration of absence was 6.7 years. Although absences ranged from 1 to 27 years most (70 or 74 per cent) had been abroad for 4–15 years, thus confirming Böhning's characterization of 'polyannual' migrants (Böhning, 1974, p. 48). All respondents had returned during the period 1970–80. The mean age of return was just under 29 years. Most returned in the age band 25–34 (52 or 55 per cent); only 12 were aged over 40 at the time of their return. This indicates the young age of Leverano's migrants who left during the 1960s and the fact that very few of them have yet reached retirement age. Of the 95 respondents, 36 left when single, 31 emigrated with their spouses, 20 emigrated to join their spouses already abroad (normally this was wives joining husbands), 4 married men emigrated alone leaving their wives behind and 4 migrated as children with their parents. Upon return 75 (79 per cent) came back as family nuclei or part-nuclei, indicating that some migrants had married during their migration period, either to another Italian abroad, or during a visit home, or (in three cases) to a foreign national. Of the 87 interviewees who had children before emigrating, most (68) took them with them abroad, but 19 left all or some of their children with relatives in Leverano, a decision taken largely to increase the earning power of the wife abroad. Of course, some children were actually born abroad. Children initially taken with their parents were sometimes sent back before their parents' return. Conversely, a few of the older returned migrants had left grown-up children working, studying or married abroad.

Before emigration

Most interviewees (84 out of the 95) had worked before emigrating, 1 had never worked but had been looking for work, 8 were housewives with no other work experience and 2 were school pupils. Of those who had worked prior to departure, 40 were in agriculture, 13 were employed in the building sector, 10 worked in industries employing at least five workers, 6 were artisans or craftsmen, 7 classed themselves as general labourers and 8 were so-called *figure miste* ('mixed figures') doing two or more jobs simultaneously (e.g. combining farming with labouring on construction sites). Most were classed as employees; only a few were self-employed (6) or worked in family-owned enterprises (5). Only 9 interviewees owned any land before emigrating; in all cases these were very small amounts of less than one hectare. Whilst the respondent was abroad, this land was mostly cultivated by the remaining family or by relatives. Formal educational achievements amongst respondents were generally low: 76 (80 per cent) had had no more than some elementary school education and 2 had had no formal education at all. Few had received any kind of specialized secondary or further education. Summarizing thus far, we may say that the typical Leverano migrant was in his or her early twenties, poorly or semi-educated with work experience limited to low-grade farming or labouring employment. Some women worked, as they still do, on embroidery in the home on an 'outwork' basis: this is called *lavoro nero* or 'black work'. Notable was the lack of any migrants with medium or large landholdings, any kind of clerical or professional employment, or even skilled, secure manual jobs. This picture is reflected in the declared motives for departure abroad, where 76 (80 per cent) explicitly mentioned the primary economic function of their migration – to get a job, earn more money, etc. The remaining 20 per cent who went for family-linked reasons were mostly women moving with, or joining, their husbands or children moving with their parents.

Experience abroad

Of the 95 interviewees, 90 worked whilst abroad (though, if children or housewives, not necessarily all the time), whilst 5 remained as full-time housewives/mothers, etc. Twenty-five had a work contract arranged before going, either by relatives, friends, or some official agency. Obviously, some migrants will have had two or more jobs during this period abroad – perhaps several if they were abroad for an extended period – but, basing ourselves just on the main job (i.e. that held for the longest time), the principal employment types were industrial (65 respondents, mostly in factories employing at least 50 people), building sector (11), commerce (3) and other types of manual labour (9). Virtually all working migrants had employee status; only one was self-employed – he worked as a builder in France. Thirteen had reached positions such as foreman or leader of a factory work-team where they had some responsibility for or control over other workers, and the same number (though not necessarily the same individuals) said that they had obtained some form of qualification whilst abroad. Of the 90 working migrants, 70 claimed that they were 'much better off' and 17 that they were 'better off' economically when abroad than in Italy. The rest were unable to say, but significantly none judged that they were economically worse off as individuals when abroad.

Remittances and savings

Reflecting the primary economic motivation of emigration from the Italian Mezzogiorno, 70 emigrant *Leveranesi* of our sample had been able to send money back to Leverano in the form of more or less regular remittances. In 52 cases these were sent to parents, in 8 cases to a brother or sister and in 10 cases to combinations of these people or other relatives. Forty-seven respondents remitted regularly every month; the rest were more irregular or occasional remitters. Only 49 were willing to estimate for us the proportion of their earnings remitted. Of these, 13 reckoned that they remitted over 75 per cent of their earnings, 20 remitted 50–75 per cent, 15 remitted 25–50 per cent and 1 10–25 per cent. Half the respondents (48) also managed to accumulate savings whilst abroad; 21 reckoned the savings to have been 25–50 per cent of earnings, 3 saved 10–25 per cent and 2 saved less than 10 per cent; the rest refused to answer, did not know, or gave only vague indications. The distinction between savings and remittances is actually rather blurred, for some remittance cash is banked in addition to that used to support family members back home.

Eighty-nine migrants had invested their foreign-earned savings and remittances in something specific upon return or whilst abroad. Seventeen had bought agricultural land (this included 5 couples buying together);[2] 53 (including 21 couples) had bought plots for building (generally this building land was purchased prior to the actual return); 75 (including 30 couples) had invested money in a new house (nearly always of brand new construction and built to the migrant's specification); and a further 16 respondents (including 4 couples) had spent money on modernizing a house already possessed before migration. It is worth emphasizing again that much of this house-related investment took place whilst the migrant was still abroad. Decisions on buying land and building a house can be taken during annual visits home, and parents and other relatives are often on hand to supervise building activity whilst the purchaser is abroad. The decision to sink money in a new dwelling seems to be the principal justification of many *Leveranesi* migration decisions in the first place. But the *casa nuova* has a further symbolic meaning. The decision to build a new house whilst abroad indicates the strength of the ties to the home village. Visible for all to see, it is also the status symbol *par excellence* of the returnee – indeed 16 respondents (including 7 couples) had built more than one house, the extra dwellings being for renting out or for their children.

Turning now to what may be regarded as more strictly economically productive forms of investment, only three people (including one couple) had actually invested in farming (beyond just buying agricultural land), 19 (8 couples) had invested in some form of commercial activity (mainly shops), 8 (3 couples) had invested in some other service sector enterprise, and 7 (2 couples) in some form of craft or building activity. Other outlets for migrant spending included a car or other form of four-wheeled transport (76 interviewees), paying off debts and loans (11 respondents), and a dowry (12 respondents). Twelve interviewees had migrant savings as yet unspent; 5 of these were planning on spending this money on their housing.

Return

Decisions to return home appeared to be undertaken for a more complex set of reasons than the motives which underlaid the initial emigration. The return decision is a difficult and often emotive time, surrounded by great uncertainty as to what the future may hold. The original emigration

Table 4.1 *Motives for return to Leverano*

	Number	%
Primarily economic	12	12.6
Primarily family-related	31	32.6
Nostalgia, homesickness, ill-health	13	13.7
Combination of economic and family reasons	25	26.3
Other combinations and reasons	14	14.8

Source: Questionnaire survey.

decision, although it involves in one sense a tremendous step into the unknown, is often fairly clear-cut; it is to be a temporary move, a job is often fixed up before departure, and there are relatives and friends already established at the destination who can help and provide support in an alien environment. The return may have few of these circumstances and there is the additional pressure of wanting to be seen to have succeeded and prospered and to have moved up the social ladder. Rarely are return movements attributable to a single reason; often a combination of motives and circumstances are intertwined. As with all interview data that elicit explanatory responses for events that happened some time ago, there is the additional danger of false and possibly unrealized *post hoc* rationalizations.

Return migration motives were classified and distributed as follows (see Table 4.1). Economic motives mentioned included the increasing difficulty of finding enough work abroad, the threat of unemployment abroad, the inability to save, the expectation of finding a job back in Italy and the achievement of a target amount of savings to be invested in a particular project or enterprise. This list involves both 'push' factors propelling the migrant away from his destination country, and 'pull' factors attracting him or her back home. Secondly, and more often cited by Leverano returnees, are family-related motives which include the desire of the spouse to return, the need to return to look after ageing parents, the return to get married, and reasons related to children – their education and the fear of them becoming too 'German' (or whatever) if the family were to remain abroad. The third broad category of motives for return is related to various aspects of physical and mental well-being and includes ill-health, nostalgia, homesickness and general discomfort. Table 4.1 shows that the most important group of reasons for return are family reasons, often linked to some form of economic consideration as well.

One of the most important aspects of the economic impact of return migration is the employment characteristics of returnees. The data here are not completely clear-cut, however, for the south Italian rural employment picture is a miasma of part-time work, hobby jobs, 'mixed figures', underemployment and semi-fraudulent benefit claims. Questionnaire answers in this field undoubtedly contain errors of imprecision and ambiguity, not to say misinformation. One source of inconsistency was a few women who at one point in the interview said that they were not in paid employment and at another claimed that they were agricultural workers (an agricultural labourer working at least 51 days per year is eligible for unemployment benefit) or admitted that they did *lavoro nero*. Not to recognize these shortcomings is to claim a falsely detailed accuracy of the research data, but we do believe that the information we have is substantially correct and therefore has, at the very least, general indicative value.

Of the sample of 95, 74 had worked since return, 10 were not looking for paid employment (mostly housewives), 3 were pensioners and the rest (8) gave unclear answers about their current work status. Most of those who had worked (61) had done just one job since return, although some, particularly those returning in the early 1970s, had done different jobs, up to six. Taking the job currently done, the sectoral distribution was as follows: agriculture 29, industry 18, commerce 15, building 14, other manual labour 8, artisan crafts 3. This pattern is quite similar to the range of employment performed by migrants before departure, although there has been some movement out of agriculture and craft trades and into industry and commerce. Migration also leads to a significant increase in the self-employed: 6 were self-employed before migrating, 19 after return. Nevertheless, the post-return activities are almost all relatively low-grade and unqualified types of work, the distribution of which probably reflects the limited educational and skill levels of the migrant population and the restricted availability of job types locally. As mentioned earlier, Leverano is still overwhelmingly an agricultural village and there are few industries in adjacent communes. Lecce has received little of the new industry that has settled in Puglia since the late 1950s; the town remains a centre of residence for landowners and commercial bourgeoisie, reflected in the baroque elegance of its large *centro storico*. Tourism in the local area is as yet embryonic. Access to the large number of newly created public service clerical posts in the commune offices may be largely denied to the returnees because of their limited educational qualifications and lack of local patronage.

So far, the Leverano results seem to fit fairly closely with the other studies of return migration employment in southern Italy and other parts

Table 4.2 *Post-return employment experiences and attitudes*

	Current employment	Employment desired at moment of return	'Ideal' employment
Agriculture	29	7	2
Artisan trades	3	5	5
Industry	18	30	15
Commerce	15	11	11
Building sector	14	10	5
Other manual work	8	12	25
Clerical and professional	0	0	3
Total responses	87	75	66

Source: Questionnaire survey.

of Southern Europe in which the conservative, house-building, self-employed, semi-retired or hobby-job returnee predominates (cf. King, 1979, pp. 17–22). Looking at the post-return jobs actually done, however, is only part of the story; it assumes that migrants are doing jobs that they want to do and ignores the very severe choice constraints in rural employment. Accordingly we asked, in different parts of the interview, what type of employment the returnee *wanted* immediately upon return and what was the *ideal* type of job for him or her at the time of interview. We also tried to explore job-finding mechanisms and the knowledge and use made of regional government incentives for returned migrants.

Table 4.2 compares actual employment with that sought at the point of return and that considered as ideal. Although the numbers of total responses are not strictly comparable, the data reveal some interesting tendencies. Upon return there seems to be a desire on the part of around 40 per cent (30 out of 75) of the migrants for industrial work. Migrants are attracted to this type of job because of its regularity and security, with fixed hours and guaranteed pay. In some cases this type of desired employment was related to the foreign work experience; other respondents said it was the type of work they had always wanted, even before emigrating. The 'ideal' type of job was a question respondents found more difficult to answer – hence the lower number of responses – but notable about this column in the table is the generally negative feeling towards farming and construction work, both of which are casual, insecure and poorly paid, and the stronger desire for other types of manual work (often specified as service sector or public employment) which are lighter forms of labour, more secure and better paid. When asked why they favoured their particular types of ideal job, respondents' comments mostly focused on the nature of the work involved (17 cases) and on security and pay aspects (19 cases), but many could not really articulate their feelings towards the ideal job very clearly in terms of specific reasons. Experience abroad as a factor in nominating an ideal job was mentioned by only two respondents.

A question was asked about help sought from various institutions and individuals during the job-finding process. Two-thirds of those who answered this question (45 out of 68) applied directly to the enterprise or employer concerned (30) or to the local labour exchange (15), but whilst 12 got their jobs from application direct to the employer, none succeeded through the labour exchange! Other media and contacts used included a local trade union, the commune, a political party, an 'influential person', a relative or friend, and a priest. Less than half the returnees who used these intermediaries reported that they had been of any use in getting employment.

The issue of the economic reintegration of returnees has been much debated in Puglia (Signorelli, 1980) and a special regional statute was passed in October 1979 which made available certain grants and incentives to returnees coming back to Puglia after a spell of work abroad. Two broad categories of help are offered under this scheme: grants for housing and aid for the establishment and improvement of economic enterprises such as farms, industries, and hotels. Both individually and co-operatively run enterprises are eligible. Requests for these aids are not made direct to the regional government in Bari but must be submitted via the local commune office of the town or village of residence of the returnee. According to the regional government office responsible for administering the returnee law the proportion of applications for aid from communes in Lecce province has been much higher than those from the other Puglian provinces of Bari, Brindisi, Foggia and Taranto, a fact that is explained as being due to the greater level of political awareness and organization of commune authorities in the province of Lecce. However, of our 95 respondents, only 21 knew about the regional measures for house construction, including 6 who had learnt of this facility from the Italian consular authorities abroad. And only two had actually applied for the house grant −both were still waiting to hear if their applications were successful. The main reason why so little use is made of the house grant is that most houses in Leverano, as elsewhere in the rural Mezzogiorno, are built without proper planning permission and in defiance of local planning guidelines. Other reasons given by returnees for not applying for the housing aids included not knowing how to go about it, lack of eligibility, lack of faith in the outcome and fear of, or unwillingness to tangle in, the bureaucracy. Seven returnees, mostly self-employed in the commerce sector, had heard of the regional aids for economic activities. Two of these had applied, one was successful (he was a building entrepreneur who used the grant to buy machinery) and the other was still waiting to hear. Such findings would appear to verify the widely felt gap in information, communication and credibility between the Italian bureaucracy, with its multifarious levels, departments, procedures and forms to be filled in, and the ordinary working population.

Discussion

The account of the questionnaire results presented so far has been packed with figures and with very little interpretation. In this section we try to draw out the broader themes of return migration's impact on Leverano, looking at various sectors of the village's economic activity in turn.

Agriculture

For a commune whose reliance on agriculture is so strong, returnees have had remarkably little impact on the farm sector. Forty of our sample had been employed in farming before emigrating; 29 came back to a job in agriculture, but most of these would prefer not to work in farming (Table 4.2). Of the 29 whose main post-return job is agricultural, all but two are agricultural labourers with little or no land of their own. Many of these labourers work on privately owned vine estates of 50–200 ha. Evidence from the interviews suggests that work as agricultural day-labourers holds few attractions for returnees. Very few respondents said that this was the job they wanted on return and these all qualified their answer by the observation that there was no other alternative work available locally. All stressed that the work was hard and insecure and the pay derisory. None indicated farm labouring as their 'ideal' work. Thus despite some investment in land by returnees and the general intensification of agriculture evident in Leverano, work as an employee in agriculture still offers few redeeming features; returnees opt out of it if other alternatives arise.

Of the two self-employed farmers, one grew tobacco and the second was a semi-retired 'hobby-farmer' who lived mainly off a foreign pension. Rather more interesting, in terms of the innovative impact of return migration, was the case of a day-labourer who worked for most of the year on other farmers' land but who was also building up his own enterprise for growing flowers under glass, on a small plot of his own. But the real significance of this case, however, is that he is the *only* example of a returnee having a positive impact in the field of local agricultural development. A good deal of the land owned by other returnees (in all, land was possessed by 24 returnee units, including 14 couples) had been inherited, although, as we have seen, some had bought small amounts with migrant savings. No returnees owned amounts of land greater than 5 ha., and indeed most were small plots of less than 0.5 ha. growing mostly vines, olives, wheat and vegetables for family consumption rather than for the market.

Building

It has been amply documented in virtually all studies of return that one of its most conspicuous effects is on housing, at least in rural areas of sending societies (cf. the cases reviewed in Bovenkerk, 1974b; Gmelch, 1980; and King, 1979). Leverano is no exception to this. Nearly all the family nuclei interviewed had constructed or bought their own houses in the village. This pattern was already in evidence in the 1960s and continues into the 1980s, sustaining the post-war building boom more or less unchecked over three decades.

A proportion of the male returnees also participates in this boom as employees and entrepreneurs. In fact, the building sector provides the biggest single category of adult male returnees with 13 respondents currently working in construction. Building is also the sector which provides the biggest overlap between jobs done before, during and after migration: 14 were construction labourers before leaving, 11 did this work as their main job abroad, and 13 are currently builders in the post-return phase. Many of these individuals have stayed in the building sector right through their migration profiles. Nearly all the building sector returnee workers in Leverano were unqualified labourers. The major exception was one man employing a workforce of 20 men, with an office in Lecce.

By their frenzy of new building, returnees are instrumental in changing the physical appearance of Leverano. New residential development, financed partly if not largely by migrant money, has enlarged the settlement well beyond the medieval compactness of the *centro storico* and its modest nineteenth-century additions (Figure 4.3). Most of the newly built homes of returnees are found to the west and south-west of the village centre, particularly in the Pozzolungo district where limestone outcrops provide good dry foundations for house construction. Open countryside until a few years ago, Pozzolungo is now a well-developed residential suburb. With its pastel-painted villas, patios and gardens it has a character

very different from the stone-built terraced compactness of the traditional
village. The Pozzolungo district is expanding southwards to link up with
Tenuta Diana, a zone scheduled by local planners for Leverano's further
residential expansion. At present this zone to the south of the village is
being gradually filled in with new, migrant-financed villas but it does not
yet have the density to form part of the continuous built-up area of
Leverano (Figure 4.3).

What is happening in Leverano is typical of thousands of other villages
in Southern Europe.[3] Like microcosms of Western cities, their inner areas
decay through migration and abandonment, whilst upon return these

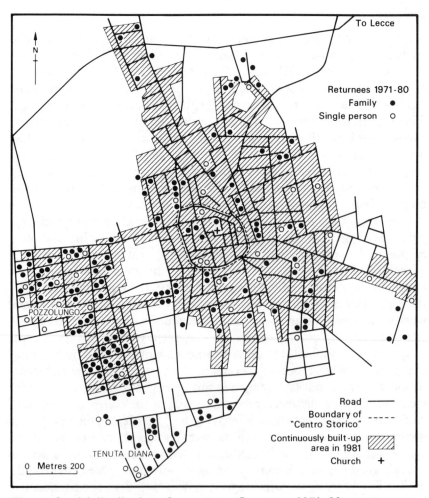

Fig. 4.3 Spatial distribution of returnees to Leverano, 1971–80

same migrants transfer the vitality of the village to the peripheral estates of villas and apartments. In Leverano this change in residential values, adhered to increasingly by the non-migrant population too, has weakened the prestige of the old village nucleus. Many central place functions – the police station, the town hall, the post office and several commercial outlets – have moved out of the *centro storico*. Most have moved to a location between the *centro storico* and Pozzolungo where a new piazza, parish church and market-place have just been built. This spatial shift in the centre of gravity of economic activity is reinforced by new shops opened by returnees outside the *centro storico*. There is something very symbolic about these micro-geographical changes, for they represent a challenge to the established hegemony of church, town hall and piazza traditionally clustered at the social centre, and the spatial centre, of village life.

Shops and services

Commercial enterprises prove to be the main focus of economically directed investments made by returnees. Fifteen respondents were involved in this sector; all were self-employed and they employed little other labour outside family help. The main types of enterprise were food, clothing or haberdashery shops, bars and barbers/hairdressers. All were geared to the local market of Leverano and adjacent villages. Although in one case – a female owner of a hairdressing salon – the business was owned before departure, in other cases migration had permitted a change in status from employee to self-employed. It is also worth noting an interesting two-stage *sectoral* migration of returnees in this category who started off as agricultural labourers, went abroad to work in industry and then returned to run self-employed service activities: such migrants move from primary to secondary to tertiary sector as they progress through their migration profiles.

For the service sector group of returnees, migration provided the means to the end of setting up a small independent enterprise. Whilst most respondents reacted positively to the notion of working in this sector, in two cases it was regarded as the only alternative available, indicating by implication that they would have preferred to do something else. Few reported any direct influence other than capital that their experience of living abroad had had on their setting up a shop. Overall, it seems that this is seen as a means of securing a reasonably respectable living on return. Although some claimed to have been amongst the first to introduce their particular type of merchandise to Leverano, attempts to bring in other innovations had not always been successful: one barber who had trained abroad had to abandon his attempts to use new styles of cutting and tinting and return to more traditional styles to satisfy his local clientele.

Although shops and small-scale service enterprises are clearly an expanding part of Leverano's economy and can profit from the general post-war boom in consumer spending in southern Italy as well as afford their owners the dubious prestige (nevertheless important locally) of being their own bosses, such activities rarely prosper. Hardly any respondents had concrete plans for reinvestment and expansion of their enterprises beyond token repairs and improvements; problems of supplies from wholesalers were often complained about; and such small enterprises face competition from supermarkets and co-operatives. Saturation of the market is occurring, and this affects not just returnee enterprises but also traditional, long-established shops run by non-migrants, many of which are located in the decaying *centro storico* whereas the returnee shops tend to be situated in or near the expanding suburbs.

Crafts and industry

One of the most marked trends of village economic life in southern Italy is the decline of artisan trades over the past twenty-five years. Trades such as tailor, blacksmith and basket-weaver have disappeared from village streets as mechanization takes over the rural sector and as mass-produced factory goods undercut local wares. Only trades connected with the building industry, such as carpenter, survive and prosper. Small wonder, then, that only three returnees had settled in the artisan or craft sector, two as carpenters making doors, door-frames and furniture and one as a specialist in garden sculpture. Also to be counted as possible members of the craft sector are those women employed in black market embroidery on an out-work basis. Apart from one woman working seasonally in the local tomato processing plant, most of the rest of the 18 returnees recorded as being industrial workers were more genuine factory operatives working mostly in metal-working and engineering industries in and around Lecce. Manu-facturing industry was, therefore, able to absorb about one-fifth of the returnees interviewed.

However, in terms of potential impact, industrial employment is an area where migrants' experience abroad seems to have the most influential effect, for 40 per cent of the individuals interviewed who wanted to work on return wanted an industrial job. They reasoned that work in industry tended to be cleaner and lighter than work in either farming or construc-tion. In their experience of industrial work in Europe, they generally had worked regular hours and been paid for any overtime done, and they all had had some kind of contract which gave at least a measure of security and predictability in their lives.

The theme of returnee employment in industry in southern Italy has yet to be properly studied. Small-scale studies made ten to fifteen years ago indicated that very few returning migrants were getting employed in the then mushrooming industries of Puglia and other parts of the south (Cassinis, 1963 and 1968; Vigorelli, 1969; Zingaro, 1969). The Taranto steelworks, for example, 70 km from Leverano, employs 5,000 workers but no indications exist as to the proportion of the payroll made up of ex-migrants. It may be that migrants have continued to fail to get jobs in large numbers in the south's new industries: employers are unwilling to hire them because of their familiarity with union practices or their high wage expectations, or perhaps migrants lack the local political connections and patronage that are often still necessary to secure factory jobs under the prevailing *raccomandazione* system of job allocation. These are hypotheses that have yet to be tested. Of course, it is also very likely that by interviewing returnees in Leverano we are missing the more industrially orientated returnees who may settle in urban areas like Taranto or the regional capital, Bari.[4]

Conclusion

These results tend to go somewhat against the commonly held picture of an emigrant workforce, gritting its teeth and suffering in degrading work and living conditions in North-west Europe, attracted solely by the possibility of saving to return and make themselves a position in their home area. Whilst this description still has a grain of truth in it, it was more characteristic of an earlier phase of Italian emigration, in the 1950s and early 1960s, than it is of the 1970s and 1980s. Compared to the Turkish, Balkan, Iberian and Maghrebian groups the Italians are to some extent an élite amongst European immigrants. This position has been forged by the longer experience of migration, permitting a certain amount of occupational mobility, and a relatively stronger legal position due to EC regulations.[5]

Conditions of emigration and return migration have also changed in respect of their significance for the sending area. Continuity certainly exists in so far as emigration still presents an attractive option for some sectors of the population. However, the conditions underpinning this kind of labour movement have altered. First, differences in wage levels between southern Italy and industrial Europe are not so marked now as they were in the 1950s and 1960s. This change is linked to the changes in the south itself with the regional development effort, the operation – even if somewhat distorted – of a welfare state and the secondary effects of early return. Secondly, return is no longer new: it has been part of the socio-economic structure of southern villages for more than twenty years (considerably longer in the case of those villages which developed nineteenth-century links to the Americas). Returnees in the 1970s and 1980s therefore have less possibility of making a 'large splash' in their home economy and society. Any cultural changes, such as fashions in dress and modes of behaviour, have already been incorporated and diffused, a process aided not only by return migration but also by the spread of mass media culture and tourism. And not only has the cultural distance between Leverano and Northern Europe shrunk, so too has the actual distance. Long, uncomfortable train journeys have been replaced by fast motorways and charter flights. Notions of 'emigration', 'absence' and 'return' therefore become less fixed. The modern migrant worker has become more like a long-distance commuter. This condition has also been reinforced over the past ten to fifteen years by the increasing precariousness of the labour migrant as migrant job opportunities become saturated and as recession eats into the economic fabric of all European countries (Cerase, 1979).

In addition, southern Italy is no longer a 'peasant society' in any real sense of the term. Economically the significance of agriculture has declined, especially in terms of the overall sectoral distribution of income. Small-scale craft industries such as tailors, shoemakers and smiths have been squeezed out of existence by more competitively priced industrially produced goods brought in from northern Italy and abroad. The sale of these imports in conjunction with real increases in consumer power have stimulated the expansion of the commercial and service sectors, a 'tertiarization' process in which the returnees themselves have played no small part . The south Italian economy can now be defined as one of 'capitalism without production', reflecting a process of increasing consumerism and a decreasing productive base. Migration and return migration appear to hasten this trend, lessening the productive base and increasing consumerism.

If the context of migration has changed in the last decade, both in terms of international economics and the nature of the sending area, the migrants still retain the possibility of more liquid capital and some qualifications or important work experience from their time spent abroad.

As regards the capital, the first priority in Leverano is usually the house. Inflation in both land and construction prices coupled with decreasing real savings from abroad in recent years have meant that the house itself takes up a larger proportion of this capital than previously. The almost complete lack of rented accommodation in Leverano means that the house is a primary necessity for the returnee, quite apart from questions of social prestige and personal satisfaction. Knowledge of regional housing grants for returnees is not widespread but applications for these measures are further limited by the fact that most new building contravenes Leverano's *piano regolatore*.

Some returnees, either through staying abroad longer or saving a greater proportion of their earnings, have capital left over to invest in an enterprise. In the main, this capital is directed towards shops and services, contributing to the commercial expansion of the economy. This, together with the funding of the building boom, has been the main impact of return in Leverano in the 1970s. Investment in farming has been minimal, despite the fact that Leverano's agriculture is relatively rich and intensifying (indeed this was the reason for choosing this village in the first place).

Whilst the Leverano returnees sampled had acquired very little in the way of formal qualifications whilst abroad, they had accumulated a certain amount of industrial training and work experience which appears to have affected their attitudes towards certain types of job, especially factory work. The problem is that there are very few areas of coincidence between the two economies such that the industrial skills acquired can be put to use upon return. Industrial skills go to waste, not because of the lack of volition amongst returnees, but because of the lack of an appropriate industrial structure in the south and in this part of southern Puglia in particular. Building work and crafts like carpentry, plumbing and plastering do offer some possibilities, as do services such as car repairing and servicing, but the fairly widespread desire recorded in our interviews for larger-scale factory work goes largely unsatisfied.

We feel, therefore, that the almost unanimous condemnation of returnees as uneconomic, bourgeois petty traders interested only in big, villa-style houses is too sweeping. The recent or current returnee who came back during the last ten years is of a different generation to those returning in earlier decades, most of whom were born before the war. The current returnee, in his or her 30s or late 20s, is part of the post-war generation, growing up and experiencing part of the post-war Italian boom in socio-economic well-being and mass media influences, influenced by these new trends but also disappointed by them – for example, frustrated by the *existence* of industrial jobs and yet their *insufficiency* for all, especially in the south. The current returnee is therefore a different type from those studied in the well-known essays of Cerase (1967 and 1974) and Lopreato (1967) who revealed the experiences of a dying breed, returnees from the

USA. The world of those over 60 is a different world, one which is less relevant to labour migrants in the 1980s.

Notes

1 This chapter presents some results of the first fieldwork phase of a two-year research project on 'The Economic Impact of Return Migration in Southern Italy', financed by the Social Science Research Council, Grant No. HR 6977. The project is based in the Department of Geography, Leicester University. Russell King and Alan Strachan are co-directors of the project and Jill Mortimer, an anthropologist, is the project's research assistant. Anna Trono is a geographer at the University of Lecce who collaborated in the project's early fieldwork. Leverano, the village featured in this chapter, was the first of seven carefully selected rural, semi-urban and urban settlements in southern Italy in which interviews of returned migrants were carried out in 1981 and 1982. We are grateful to Professor Luigi Di Comite who gave the project valuable office space in his department, the Institute of Economics and Finance of the University of Bari. We also wish to acknowledge the help and valuable discussions we had with Professor Cosimo Perrotta, Professor Luigi Za and Dr Franco Merico, all of the University of Lecce. Our greatest debt, however, is to Lucia Albano, Lucia Carlino, Cosimo Di Mastrogiovanni and Danilo Muci who carried out most of the interviews in Leverano.

2 Since part of the sample was made up of people from the same family, usually married couples and occasionally adult children, certain categories of information are duplicated in the responses. Investment behaviour is one of these, so we give the number of couples included in each total response figure here.

3 Twenty years ago Mori (1961) wrote about the *case americane* built around the edges of Sicilian villages by returned migrants from the USA. The development of new village suburbs by returnees is also described by Rhoades (1978 and 1979) in Spain, Brettell (1979) in Portugal, King (1980) and King and Strachan (1980) in Malta, and Baučić (1972) and Bennett (1979) in Yugoslavia.

4 A later phase of research involved a programme of 200 interviews of returnees in the city of Bari. These interviews, only just completed, have yet to be analysed; the results will be written up by King, Mortimer and Strachan.

5 However, Mottura and Pugliese (1972, pp. 10–12) suggest that these EC regulations are far from effective and that in practice they actually work to the disadvantage of Italian workers in other EC countries because employers pass Italians over in favour of the less protected and more manipulable non-EC migrants from Turkey, North Africa, etc.

5

Farm workers in Italy: agricultural working class, landless peasants, or clients of the welfare state?

Enrico Pugliese

Introduction

Social, political and economic changes in the rural areas of Italy – and, indeed, most Southern European countries – have been remarkable in the past three decades. The combination of a general rural exodus in search of jobs and better living conditions with the regionally selective increase in the availability of employment in the industrial and service sectors has exacerbated the already large disparities between north and south, plain and highland, accessible and remote areas. At the same time, and related to the effects of migration and industrialization, there have been important changes in agriculture, both in terms of methods and social relations of production (see also Garcia-Ramon, pp. 140–54). These interrelated processes of agricultural change, industrialization and migration have been associated with profound changes in the class structure of rural areas. Their effects have varied as between rural areas, however, serving to differentiate them in important respects. This differentiation in terms of class structure, class de-composition and re-composition has had important implications for the forms of organization and practices of trade unions and other organizations seeking to advance the interests of those working in agriculture or, more generally, resident in such areas. Moreover, in so far as these interrelated changes have tended to reproduce a burgeoning surplus population in rural areas, they have been important in the emergence of state welfare policies (such as those of income transfer to such areas), though these must not be interpreted in functionalist terms as simply a mechanistic response by the state to the needs of capital but rather as contingently produced in relation to class struggles and the demands articulated by people in such areas and the requirements of the state for legitimation.

It is one aspect of these latter changes that is considered in this chapter, as it addresses the questions of the contradictory class positions of farm workers today and the interaction between their political structures and the forms of state intervention to subsidize agricultural enterprises, while controlling a relative surplus population.

Any attempt to locate the Italian farm worker in the framework of a dualistic labour market encounters serious difficulties. In the first place, this occupational group (defined as *lavoratori dipendenti*, 'dependent farm workers', by the Istituto centrale di statistica) is made up of people who differ widely as regards security of employment, real wage levels, skill specialization and union strength; but more significant than this internal heterogeneity is the fact that this category of workers as a whole possesses certain general characteristics that make it difficult to place in one market segment or another. In the model proposed by Edwards *et al.* (1975 and 1982), the Italian farm worker would apparently be considered part of the secondary segment of the labour market. The proportion of workers regularly employed in large enterprises is very modest and occupational instability is high, features that are both characteristic of their location in the secondary segment. However, one of the key attributes of the primary segment of the labour market, the level of unionization, is extremely high among Italian farm workers – in fact, they are the most highly unionized group of dependent workers in the country. This introduces another paradox for, notwithstanding the generally high rates of unionization, the group clearly has little control over the conditions of its employment.

To explain this situation, along with the complex of contradictions that characterize the condition of the Italian farm worker, one must refer to the historical processes and political practices that have shaped it. In the Mezzogiorno, at least, these have caused the farm worker's position to become increasingly similar to that of a worker on state benefit, a precarious client of the welfare state, revealing a method of managing the unemployment problem that is spreading to other nations of Southern Europe. It is perhaps worth emphasizing that this is not characteristic – nor seems likely to be – of some sorts of agricultural workers (in particular, most of the workers in the capitalist agricultural enterprises of the Po Valley and of some limited areas in the south). It is equally true that the term 'agricultural working class' can only be applied to a limited proportion of the national farm labour force.

At present, Italian farm workers (or rather, all those persons who, in one way or another, are engaged in agricultural activity more or less regularly as dependent workers) waver between the two class poles – 'clients of the welfare state' and 'agricultural working class'. In the past, this group wavered between two other poles – those of 'agricultural working class' and 'landless peasant'. The fluctuation between these two pairs of poles, and the different interpretations of reality that follow reflect neither simply a structural determination nor a purely ideological one. These two aspects are deeply intertwined and one or the other predominates according to historical and economic circumstances and according to the extent of agricultural development.

In Italy, the predominance of the first or the second image of the agricultural labour force has been closely linked with labour union strategies and each of these images has been related in a different manner to the structural realities and production relations in the two principal areas of the nation (north and south). To attempt a schematization, one might say that from a historical point of view the concept of the farm labourer as an agricultural worker was dominant in the tradition of the first, strongest and most widespread farm workers' union, the *Federterra* (Zangheri, 1959). The concept of the farm worker as a landless peasant existed, but was not predominant, in the thinking of the *Federbraccianti-CGIL* (the main farm workers' union reconstituted after a complex series of events in the post-1945 period) and it prevailed in the political organizations of the workers' movement, especially in the Italian Communist Party. Naturally, the development of the *Federterra* from the beginning of this century up to the 1920s, when it was banned following the advent of Fascism, took place in the northern regions (especially in the Po Plain), where a capitalist form of agriculture was being established and an agricultural proletariat had been formed. Hence the *Federterra*'s political and union policies reflected the structural reality of the northern regions, although they were not applicable nationally. Instead, in the south, as we shall see in more detail, in the majority of cases the image of the landless peasant corresponded more closely to the real position of farm workers.

Farm workers and poor peasants

This type of question is not restricted to the Italian situation as it relates to the general attitude of the organized workers' unions to the 'agrarian question' and poses problems of a theoretical and general nature, signalling a marked deficiency in the traditional analyses. Giovanni Mottura (1980) observed that in the literature on the 'agrarian question' and on the general analysis of social classes in Italy, the definition of 'dependent workers' in the primary sector as 'agricultural proletariat' usually meets with no objections, adding that

this manner of conceiving the question seems to be quite common in the theoretical texts of the Left: inasmuch as they are part of the proletariat, farm workers represent a known entity within that group, while peasant agriculture – to use Kautsky's term,[1] which reappears in later literature – seems to the workers' movement to be a 'mysterious' area of social activity that presents difficulties of interpretation to Marxists on both practical and theoretical levels.

One cannot help but agree with Mottura's conclusion that a radical distinction between farm workers and peasants unquestionably exists in texts on the 'agrarian question', while the question of class location of the peasants remains open. Instead,

> limiting ourselves to Italy between 1940 and 1950, we must say that today the distinction appears to be much less evident in reality than it does in the texts, and above all that the hypothetical line that should distinguish the figure of the farm worker from that of the peasant in 'qualitative' terms seems to be very indistinct.   (ibid., p. 15)

This uncertainty as to the class location of these workers of the land is the basis of differences in the strategies of the Left. On one hand, the view of the farm workers as peasant farmers and landless peasants inevitably led to a policy based substantially on a demand for agrarian reform. On the other hand, the straightforward *operaist* image of a large component of the farm workers' union met with a series of difficulties both because of its inadequacy when applied to various aspects of the south of Italy and because the supporters of this policy were isolated and faced adamant opposition within the workers' movement itself (Di Leo, 1959, 1976).

The most interesting, and in some respects paradoxical, aspect of the mobilization of farm workers in favour of agrarian reform is that they were engaged in a struggle that would eventually lead to the negation and abolition of their role as farm workers. In joining the struggle for land reform, the farm worker did not see himself as a proletarian but as a potential farmer – an owner or manager of a plot of land – who would come into being after approval of the agrarian reform. It should also be remembered that this type of struggle was to continue even after the image of the farm worker as a poor peasant had been eliminated from the social reality of the south as a result of the mass exodus that took place in the subsequent decade. It is understandable that this type of struggle made sense in those areas in which land tenure was characterized by absentee land ownership on a vast scale but it was not particularly relevant to the more limited group of farm workers, those in the Po Plain and in such areas of intense capitalist development in the south as Apulia. In the south in the 1940s and 1950s 'land to the peasant farmers' was the cry chiefly of the *non-*peasant farmers. In the same way, forty years earlier, peasant farmers belonging (as they could) to the *Federterra* had fostered a policy that made no significant claims relative to their status as peasant farmers because they looked upon themselves as a prospective proletariat, no longer peasants but dependent workers.

As a result of the Land Reform in the post-war period, only a small number of farm workers became peasant farmers. As for the others, the evolution of the Italian productive system and the speed of capitalist transformation of agriculture brought about changes in their class positions and reduced the extent to which the farm workers could still be regarded as peasant farmers. During these years the farm worker in the south, peasant *manqué*, experienced a profound proletarianization, for migration and emigration transformed him and a majority of his kind into an industrial worker. Thus, one of the two class poles disappeared as a result of a wave of population migration in which the number of peasant farmers decreased from nine to two and a half million, and the number of farm workers from two and a half to one million (for further information on the regional distribution of different types of agricultural worker, see Figures 5.1–5.4).

It is beyond the scope of this chapter fully to discuss all the structural transformations and changes in the labour market that took place in Italian agriculture, especially in the south, during the 1950s and 1960s, since these subjects have been amply studied and documented elsewhere (e.g. Bartolini and Meloni, 1978; Mottura and Pugliese, 1975; Stefanelli, 1969). Nevertheless, it is important to note the broad-scale structural transformation of a large sector of agriculture on the plains of the south, which became very rich and formed the basis of a network of capitalist enterprises. On the labour market, there was a drastic reduction of the farm labour force while, as regards the union, there was a defeat on work conditions (in particular, on the issue of *imponibili di mano d'opera*), a victory in the campaign on social security issues and, finally, a decline in the national importance of the farm workers' union.

An important factor in this context was the veritable boom in wage levels that began in the early 1960s, in the period immediately following the peak of the great wave of emigration from the south (1959–62). At the end of the 1950s, with wages that were little more than 1000 lire per day (women at times earned even less), there was talk of a campaign for a minimum legal wage. Four years later, in 1963, daily wages for the grape harvest in Apulia amounted to 7000 lire. Even before the beginning of the inflationary trend, towards the end of the 1960s, the amount rose to

10,000 lire. At the end of the 1970s in some cases this had risen to 40,000 lire (although then as now considerable wage inequalities existed and some workers rarely earn more than 10,000–15,000 lire). No longer subjected to those historical forms of oppression and extortion that arose from a lack of alternatives, the farm worker thus acquired and used greater bargaining

Fig. 5.1 Regional boundaries in Italy

power. However, this new power did not express itself in comprehensive political and union action but simply reflected the law of supply and demand. Daily wages increased because the labour supply had progressively decreased as a result of the vast out-migration. The reduced

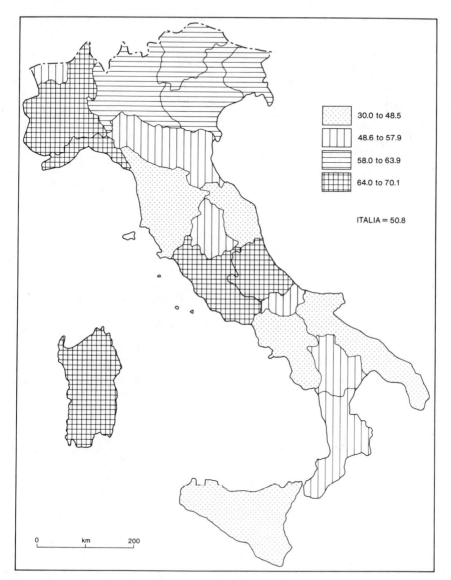

(dotted)	30.0 to 48.5
(vertical lines)	48.6 to 57.9
(horizontal lines)	58.0 to 63.9
(cross-hatch)	64.0 to 70.1

ITALIA = 50.8

Fig. 5.2 Casual employees as a percentage of the regional agricultural workforce, 1975

number of workers on the labour market also opened up the possibility of achieving higher skilled jobs for those who remained. But the objectives of past campaigns, which aimed at linking occupational improvements to transformations in production (especially the *imponibili di mano d'opera*

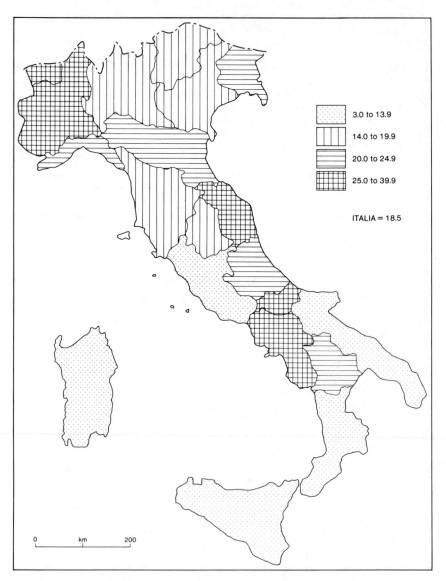

Fig. 5.3 Family workers as a percentage of the regional agricultural workforce, 1975

which sought to encourage labour-intensive methods), definitively disappear from union practice. Management was now free to make autonomous, uncontested decisions, proceeding with its policy of transforming production, intensively or extensively, in response to price-regulating systems and the open market.

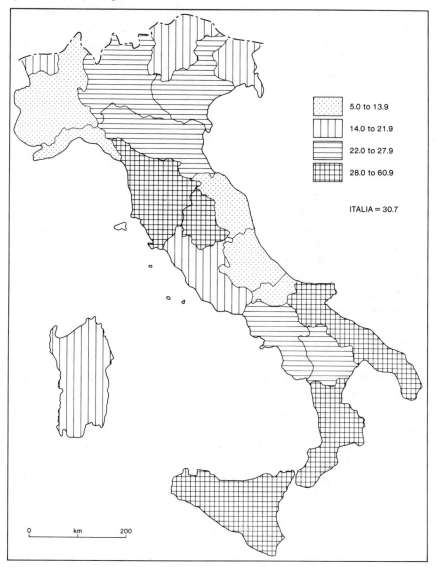

5.0 to 13.9

14.0 to 21.9

22.0 to 27.9

28.0 to 60.9

ITALIA = 30.7

0   km   200

Fig. 5.4 Full-time and part-time employees as a percentage of the regional agricultural workforce, 1975

In those northern regions where a modern type of farm workers' class already existed and possessed the characteristics of an agricultural working class, the process of restructuring of agriculture had begun at the end of the 1940s and took a less drastic form. As far as the agricultural proletariat was concerned, the combination of the 'pull effect', of local industrial development, and the 'push effect', due to the processes of mechanization and restructuring, had no traumatic results. Local opportunities for extra-agricultural employment led to a relatively painless shrinking of the labour supply – a feature of the processes of reorganization and rationalization typical of modern agrarian capitalism. In this, farm workers do not change their class position; they simply diminish in number.

The farm worker in the welfare state

As was noted above, union failures on the issues of working conditions and wages were compensated by a victory regarding social security. The union managed to make its strength felt mainly on the welfare question. The INCA-CGIL, the welfare organization of the union, was extremely active in administering both the health and unemployment benefits won in the struggle. It is noteworthy that these union campaigns and their early victories came about in an era when the guaranteed income typical of the present welfare state could certainly not be taken for granted. For this reason, union mobilization was strong and resistance to the idea marked. Of course this has always been true of the overall policy of welfare for workers in the welfare state, for these benefits have only been achieved through the struggles of the working class (see O'Connor, 1973; Gough, 1979).

The most interesting aspect of this is a kind of 'protection' that the state has gradually come to grant to agricultural enterprises. As a result of a curious compromise, these enterprises were free to expand, unfettered by the demands of their labour force (above all in terms of maintaining employment levels), while the state assumed the burden of guaranteeing a minimum income in order to maintain some social stability. As a matter of course, as is customary in the welfare state, corruption immediately began to thrive (see Boccella, 1982; Collidá, 1978).

The first important negative aspect of this change concerns the discretionary element in the distribution of welfare. In order to obtain welfare benefits, including unemployment compensation for those who were entitled to it, it is necessary to register with the *Servizio Contributi Agricoli Unificati*, the social security agency for farm workers. Registrations were determined by those who were able to make them in a highly discretionary manner. The union began to find itself in a difficult situation for, on one hand, it risked losing the support of its potential members if it exercised too strict a control over enrolments (and in a rural environment it is always difficult to determine who really is an agricultural worker). On the other hand, a more open policy resulted in the inflating of the social security rolls which thus became a means of providing a subsidy to any low-income residents in rural areas (and, in some cases of corruption, to undeserving people who had managed to wangle a place on the rolls). Control of the social security rolls became one of the first elements of social control exercised by the welfare state over the rural masses in the south.

For the farm workers' union, the expansion of the scope and amount of welfare entailed both an increase in its size and, at the same time, a loss of its identity. It was no longer the union of the landless peasants struggling for land reform, and no longer the union of agricultural workers but rather a force that represented a variety of people, temporary workers of all types who sought to obtain social security. Furthermore, there is cause for concern in this intermingling of welfare dealings with the union activity of the *Federbraccianti*. Each of the three main unions operating in agriculture (*Federbraccianti*-CGIL, FISBA-CISL, UISBA-UIL) devote much of their time to handling social security issues through their social security departments (INCA-CGIL, etc.). In Italy, enrolment in the union is totally voluntary and is wholly independent of use of the services provided by the unions, with union patronage offered regardless of enrolment. Nevertheless, union enrolment has become a way for obtaining assistance with social security matters. Therefore, present and former farm workers and other members of the rural population who have managed to become part of the farm-workers' lists join the union just in order to obtain welfare and pension benefits.

This is not the only aspect of welfare policy to affect farm workers, however. The administration of both public works and reforestation projects, which have become increasingly important, have also become a means of providing income for part of the rural proletariat.

During the 1960s and especially during the 1970s, agricultural employment in Italy became increasingly concentrated in the south (Furnari, 1977) as the proportion of southern workers in the total of all farm workers grew considerably. At the same time, there was a decrease in the number of permanent farm workers enrolled in both the welfare lists and the union itself (Fonte and Furnari, 1975). Statistics show that the greatest number of farm workers is concentrated in the southern regions and that their proportion among agricultural workers is on the increase. In short, the farm worker characterizes agriculture in the south and is evident to a greater degree than in other regions. This suggests that, in the southern regions, part of the rural population identifies itself socially with the role of farm worker, while in practice it lives mainly on welfare – they are really clients of the welfare state. This image of them as clients is accurate in so far as the individual's income is made up principally of subsidies (whether unemployment compensation or disability pensions); it is, how-ever, incorrect in that the welfare state also provides him with a means of making a living by employing him in public works, mainly in reforestation (thereby constructing a form of social control). These activities are not dictated by ecological concern for land conservation or by plans for economic development of forest resources but by the contingent needs for legitimation in those regions where the reforestation activity is carried on. The response of the union to this situation is highly ambiguous.

The union declares itself against a policy of discretionary labour market management on the part of agencies in charge of forest resource conser-vation and development but when the rank and file movements call for the opening of new projects in order to relieve unemployment, the union does not dissociate itself from them. Naturally, the union pays dearly for this ambiguity, revealing its inability to offer a credible alternative and to oppose the generally clientelistic management of reforestation works. The advantages are reaped by the local state-bourgeoisie and the local political machine since the legitimation which they derive from the administration of public funds and from the discretionary criteria used in opening and closing reforestation projects reinforces their existing clientelistic desig-nation of the individuals to be employed on them. This absolute dis-cretionary power becomes institutionalized when, as happened in Calabria in 1981, legislation changes the basis of the recruitment of workers from a numerical one (in which it was not supposed to be possible to call up a specific individual from the ranks of unemployed farm workers) to a nominal one (which makes it possible to call up one person instead of another).

Thus, in the hilly and mountainous interior of the south, the former farm worker has become a forestry worker. From being a temporary and irregular employee of private agricultural enterprises, who rounded out his income with public works jobs (such as the soil conservation or refores-tation projects of the 1950s and 1960s), he has now changed not so much from one profession to another but merely from agriculture to forestry. However, his social position has changed with his passage from the employ of private enterprise to that of the state. He no longer has to commute 40 km to the plain below in transport belonging to the *caporale* for a daily wage of 15,000–20,000 lire but now finds himself working in his local area for a daily wage of 40,000 lire. Furthermore, it might be added that work on the local forestry projects is much less strenuous than agricultural work on the farms. Naturally, not everyone gets this opportunity, for the administration of funds in the welfare state is discretionary and funds are limited.

There is a division between workers employed in public reforestation works and those who work as commuting labourers which reflects the difference between productive workers in a sector of capitalist industry (in this case in the agricultural sector) and people supported by the welfare state, occupied in activities conducted at government expense. This differentiation becomes less marked and more ambiguous if one considers that at times it appears in the same individual, who for some months manages to be supported as a client by the welfare state and for another period of the year must work as a commuting labourer. In other cases, as a result of age and, above all, sexual discrimination, commuting labourers are more frequently young people and women.

Social transformations among farm workers and shifts in political relations have also changed the union situation. The *Federbraccianti-CGIL* has seen its almost exclusive representative role diminish and has had to enter into competition with the FISBA-CSIL (commonly known to be linked with the local clientelistic machine) which has become predominant in those parts of the south in which the welfare functions dominate individual and union activities.

Italy in context: some international comparisons

This chapter has dealt primarily with agriculture in the south of Italy for that is where the largest number of farm workers are found. This situation reflects the nature of the labour market in an impoverished area in the context of the welfare state. The characteristics indicated are less evident in areas that have a more flourishing agriculture and are richer in other types of activities. In these areas the labour force is handled differently by the welfare state but still in such a way that agricultural enterprises may make their decisions autonomously.

Some comparisons on an international level may help explain how this process of 'welfarization' of the farm labour force fits into the more general picture of the capitalist development of agriculture. First of all, it should be remembered that Italian farm workers, and especially those in the south, are settled as regards their residence (no matter how temporary they may be in their employment). In this respect, there is a marked difference from the situation in France. The current tendency in France of reducing the number of permanent farm workers and replacing them with casual labourers, in an indiscriminate mechanization of agriculture (Bourquelot, 1976), corresponds to the Italian agrarian and labour policies that protect the enterprise from conditions imposed by the labour force. However, this does not imply the formation in France of an unemployed labour force of indigenous workers to whom the state must guarantee income or welfare payments. Recourse to a foreign labour force (Spanish and African, for the most part) protects the firms and offers no guarantee to the workers, while posing no serious problems of legitimation to the state, so presenting considerable political and economic advantages.

In the USA the farm worker is a client of the welfare state *par excellence*. However, since these people are mainly foreign labourers or members of subordinate ethnic groups (blacks, for example), they really are welfare clients *senso strictu*. In America, there is no policy of guaranteeing income by supplementary occupation (as in public works, etc.) for farm workers. Those who receive welfare payments do so because they are 'poor', not because they are 'farm workers'. In this lies one of the principal differences from the situation in Italy. Another arises from the fact that in the USA a large number of workers are non-resident foreigners, *braceros*, who are often illegally in the country (see McWilliams, 1972; Friedland and Nelkin, 1981; Friedland, Barton and Tomas, 1980). Nowhere is an enterprise afforded so much protection as in the USA, where traditional forms of protection are reinforced by the fact that (at least until a short while ago) union legislation completely ignored farm workers.

Whether in France, the USA or Italy, some form of protection for agricultural enterprises is common. Furthermore, it gradually becomes more evident as the processes of multinational capitalist integration take place. As far as the EC is concerned, current policy, which tends to favour 'efficient and competitive farms', has the effect of consolidating present trends in technological development that produce labour-saving methods, with very serious effects on farm workers' employment. The problem is of little importance in areas where there is a strong demand for workers in sectors other than agriculture. It has, in contrast, tragic implications for Southern European agriculture, especially in southern Italy and southern Spain, where the supply of jobs outside agriculture is limited and where the employment of peasants and workers in agriculture plays an important role.

A trend towards organizing Southern European farming into large-scale enterprises, with small labour forces and a high degree of mechanization,

would perhaps render agriculture more competitive in terms of production costs, but it would leave unsolved grave problems of agricultural
unemployment. As a result of this kind of choice, farm workers end up
depending heavily on state-paid jobs – reforestation in Italy and road
maintenance (that is, weeding the edges of roads) in Spain (Perez Yruela
and Sanchez, 1981). In Spain the situation is aggravated by the fact that
some of its migrant seasonal workers, employed in subordinate agricultural jobs in France during part of the year, return to spend several
months a year in their native country. There they become peasants or join
the ranks of the unemployed, thus becoming a burden on the agrarian or
welfare policies.

In short, one thing seems certain; capitalist agriculture tends to develop
and become consolidated along industrial lines, but this does not, in turn,
result in the formation of a modern agricultural working class. The risks
that this would entail are avoided, on one hand, by processes of mechanization and the general replacement of living labour with dead labour and,
on the other, by broadening of the socio-professional base from which
manual labour is drawn. Periods of demand for manual labour tend to
become shorter and the demand is met by a labour force that very often is
unskilled. There are also the old methods of piece-work surviving, bol-
stered by job insecurity among agricultural workers and by their need to
augment their daily income, even at the cost of disproportionate increases
in productivity. In all cases, recourse to 'imported' workers seems to be
the norm; 'imported' either in the form of foreigners and migrants, as in
France and the USA, or 'imported' in the form of seasonal workers
engaged in other activities during the rest of the year, as in Italy, the USA
and sometimes also in France.

Conclusions: contradictions in the Italian situation

In Italy the situation of agricultural workers seems to be complicated by
the historical tradition of labour struggles and by the traditional organization of farm workers into unions. Italian agricultural enterprises are
totally free in their management decisions while agricultural policy has
followed the directions of the EC and favoured a process of agricultural
industrialization by developing labour-saving technology. None the less,
some defences remain for the farm worker – and to his status as a member
of the working class. His ability to exert pressure on the state reflects the
organizational force that is inherent in his status as a worker. The
comparisons with the situation in other nations (especially in the USA)
precisely underline this aspect. In Italy, union campaigns have made farm

workers into welfare clients and for this reason welfare assumes such particular forms as workmen's compensation and provision of supplementary work, while it does not appear in the form of guaranteed income for the poor as in the USA.

It is the traditional organizational strengths that have permitted this kind of outcome, its defeats notwithstanding. The same historical fact explains the contradictory situation as regards the farm worker's location in the labour market. For example, in France or the USA, the agricultural working class belongs unquestionably to the secondary segment of the labour force and it is no accident that the class is only slightly unionized or that residential stability is totally irrelevant. In Italy, on the contrary, while farm workers are certainly not a strong force, they retain some elements of union strength and bargaining power in certain areas and situations. Indeed, in some cases, farm workers even command relatively high wages. What is notable in Italy, rather, is a growing internal segmentation of the agricultural working class and increasingly differentiated wage levels on the basis of geographical area, sex, age, skills and degree of effective union protection. Instances of daily wages of no more than 10,000 lire (from which the *caporale*'s share must be deducted) are common, but so are daily wages of 30,000 lire, with no deduction, given local shortages of manual labour and the necessity to take what is available on the market. In addition, some traditional skills not yet made obsolete by modern technology (such as pruning or grafting) call for even higher wages. Then there are also the forestry workers mentioned above, with their high daily revenue.

Because of a lack of solidarity, the majority of the agricultural working class in the end comes to depend mainly on the welfare state. This dependence has its origin in two different routes. On one hand, there is the case analysed above of the agricultural worker who is progressively distanced from productive activity but obtains income either through a direct subsidy or through public works. In this latter case it is a question of a contraction of the occupational base and the consequent intervention of the state to guarantee an 'integrative' income, aimed at ensuring legitimation by demonstrating the social integration of the individuals. This intervention increases proportionately to the decrease in occupational opportunities in the productive sector and to the increase in the ability of the masses involved to bring pressure. In these cases, the 'welfare payment' becomes both a means of reducing the total labour costs borne by the enterprises and also a way of managing a relative surplus population.

The second route occurs where there is an advanced capitalist agriculture – where the nature of technological development and the evolution of the labour process give rise to a strong demand for unskilled or only slightly skilled manual labour. In this case, the type of labour force needed does not have to be of agricultural origin and, indeed, in practice it tends not to be. The enterprise does not need skilled workers but rather people who are willing to take on hard, unskilled jobs for short periods of time, probably being paid on a piece-work basis. The new agricultural work force in this case is composed of students and even pensioners, along with seasonal part-time workers, all of whom usually live directly or indirectly on welfare payments. As is evident, in this second case, it is not the former farm worker who becomes a client of the welfare state, but rather that part of the population already on welfare (the classic example in Italy being that of the retired worker) is retained to become part of the agricultural labour force.

This second model applies better to the northern regions, where the labour market is more active and where the local rural labour force is more restricted; it is also more like the situation in most other nations. However, it presupposes the existence of socially marginal groups or, at least, of an area of marginal proletariat. In short, it appears when the labour market is already greatly segmented with some weak and peripheral sectors, and when the state provides welfare payments for their subsistence. With reference to the USA, Harrison (1979) demonstrates that welfare payments are a form of 'integrative' income for workers in small firms in the competitive sector. Thus, the state intervenes in these cases so as to diminish labour costs for business (whether agrarian or industrial), while guaranteeing the availability of the required quantity and type of manual labour. The 'welfarization' of the labour force is the mechanism that makes this possible and is thus likely to become an ever more widespread phenomenon in the countries of Southern Europe.

Note

1 The reference to Kautsky is to the preface to the French edition of *The Agrarian Question*.

6

Agricultural change in an industrializing area: the case of the Tarragona area

M. Dolores Garcia-Ramon

Introduction

At the well-known conference *Problèmes du développement dans les pays méditerranéens* held in Naples in 1962, it was specifically recognized that 'si dans l'ordre économique, l'aire culturelle méditerranéenne a quelque consistance, c'est à l'analogie des problèmes et à l'affinité des situations seulement qu'elle se doit' (Cuisenier, 1963, p. 13). It would not be amiss to include amongst these common problems and situations the economic importance, until a few years ago, of a traditional agriculture, one which was under-capitalized and with a low level of technical input; similarly this was so for a frequently dependent industrialization, which was suddenly 'imported' into the region. It is precisely the relationship between the transformation of a traditional agricultural system, based on the family holding, and, at the same time, the coastal industrial development at Tarragona (the *comarca* of Baix Camp) which we will discuss in this chapter. In particular, attention will be focused on the extent of relationships between the growth of large-scale, modern industrialization, the transformation of traditional to more modern, more specialized market-orientated production – both in terms of crops produced and of the dominant social relations of production – and the limits imposed upon this process by industrial growth. These relationships are not defined simply in quantitative terms of physical input-output relations between industry and agriculture, or in terms of the changing patterns of demand for agricultural commodities engendered by higher industrial wages, but rather in qualitative terms of the extent of the introduction into agriculture of capitalist relations of production that have become most fully developed within the industrial sector. The implications of the penetration of capitalist social relations and the creation of an agricultural wage-labour force in areas previously dominated by petty commodity production and production systems heavily reliant upon family labour for the changing class composition of such areas are considerable (see also Pugliese, pp. 123–39). In these respects, the particular area analysed in this chapter can be seen as exemplifying some aspects of much more generalized processes of social and economic change in Southern Europe associated with the penetration of capitalist social relations into agriculture and the changing character of agricultural production.

The timing of the Spanish industrial take-off in the 1950s and the consolidation of this process after the radical change in 1959 and all the consequences this implied for the political economy is generally agreed. Leal *et al.* (1975) have shown the contribution of the agricultural sector to this industrial sector, firstly as an exporter of goods and capital in the 1940s and early 1950s, and later of labour in the 1950s and 1960s. The latter function has taken place during a period of crisis in the traditional means of production and has, consequently, reinforced the role of agriculture as a market for industry. Such a situation suggests, without any doubt, a close connection between the transformation of a traditional agricultural and industrial development. However, when looking at it on a more local level, the relationship needs to be much more subtly examined. This results as much from the great variety of Spanish agricultural systems (Benelbas, 1981, p. 17), transformed by the rapid rate of industrialization, as from the highly unequal spatial distribution of the effect of this process upon agricultural structures. The relationship appears very clearly in the example of the coastal belt of Tarragona where a sudden and massive industrialization has occurred simultaneously with a major transformation of the agricultural sector without the links between the two being as direct as might at first seem.

Baix Camp (see Figure 6.1) is one of thirty-eight Catalan *comarcas* drawn up by the Autonomous Government in Catalonia in 1932–3; in this work only the plain was studied; that is, the area below 300 m., which is agriculturally the most dynamic. The region in question extends over 300 sq. km and includes eighteen municipalities with a rural population estimated at about 25,000 inhabitants during the period we are studying. It is a typical Mediterranean plain bordered by the sea where, until the end of the 1950s, the agricultural landscape was dominated by two of the three well-known Mediterranean crops – the olive and the vine – and by other very Mediterranean ones such as the carob and almond trees. To these was added the hazelnut in the nineteenth century which originated from more humid areas. It was grown in the area bordering the mountains and only ventured on to the plain with the initial introduction of irrigation in the first half of the twentieth century.

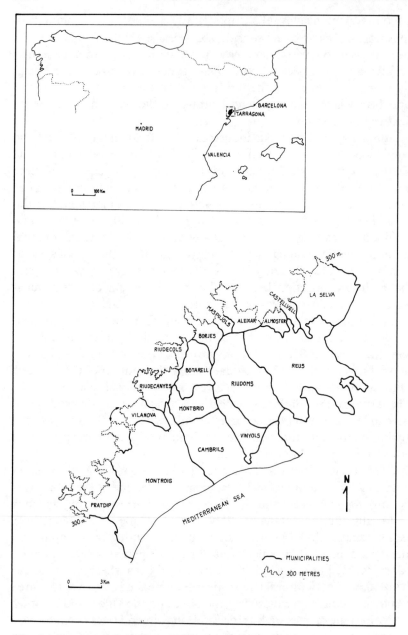

Fig. 6.1 Location of the Baix Camp in north-east Spain

In this chapter I will study the process of 'rationalization', by which I mean the introduction of capitalist relations of production, into the traditional agriculture of a *comarca* adjacent to the provincial capital of Tarragona, an area of recent and expanding industrialization. A priori, one might expect that industrialization has had a very direct influence on the enormous changes in agriculture. Nevertheless, a detailed study of the productive forces and the relations of production will show that the role played by industry in these changes has been practically nil. It has, notwithstanding, acted indirectly as a factor raising salaries in the area. The crucial period for observing the interrelationship between them started in 1955 before the beginning of industrialization, until 1975, by when one was able to record the potential effects of industrialization, which basically dated from 1964–5.

We cannot effectively speak of an agricultural system which has not undergone change in a zone where production varied in 36 per cent of the cultivated area in a short period between 1955 and 1971. Furthermore, irrigated land increased relatively by a spectacular 40 per cent, which basically occurred at the expense of non-irrigated land. Equally, two of the most traditional crops in terms of the land under cultivation, the vine and the olive, lost 50 per cent and 35 per cent respectively of their area in the period from 1955, while other new crops increased relatively rapidly. For example, the land under early potatoes grew by 290 per cent, and that of fruit trees, essentially peach trees, by 95 per cent. It is therefore clear that farmers made considerable efforts to adapt to the fluctuations of demand and that the agricultural activity of this zone was undergoing major changes.

Likewise it should be noted that Tarragona and its surrounding area was in the process of becoming, during the last fifteen years, the second Catalan industrial zone. The city of Tarragona (101,000 population in 1975) gew only by 15,000 inhabitants from the beginning of the twentieth century to 1960, but by 60,000 from 1960 to 1975, with more than half this growth a consequence of immigration from other regions in Spain. The major reason for this expansion was industrial growth, in particular the chemical industry which contributed more than 80 per cent of the total industrial growth and has come to absorb 95 per cent of the total industrial investment of the area (Margalef, 1979). Clearly, the chemical industry has exerted a certain local multiplier effect, but this influence has not been direct since we are dealing with a capital-intensive sector in which the local technical contribution is limited to the installation of totally foreign equipment. This multiplier has operated indirectly through its impact on salaries, though this sector creates little industrial employment. Apart from its impact on the agricultural sector, this type of industrial structure is, in fact, completely independent of the human and physical resources of the neighbouring comarcas. Its effect has been rather to raise the level of demand for horticultural products and the salaries in this zone, thus reducing the available labour which has forced a greater rationalization of the agricultural holdings. Furthermore, and especially since 1979, the enormous water consumption by the petrochemical industry, particularly the Enpetrol refinery and the nearby nuclear plant at Vandellós, have posed very serious problems for the supply of water to Tarragona and its surrounding area, and have lowered to critical levels the reservoirs and water table, upon which the irrigated land of Baix Camp depends. The Catalan Parliament has passed as a priority measure the 'Minitrasvase' Project for carrying water from the Ebro basin to the Tarragona area. This will benefit industrial users of water much more than agricultural users.

Two aspects of this process of modernization should be noted. On the one hand, there is the stability and persistence of the family holding; on the other hand, the self-financing of the agricultural innovations which has not come from the industrial sector. The financing has been made possible through other activities undertaken by the farmers, such as small poultry farms or the sale and leasing of plots to the tourist sector, or even small savings derived from these agricultural activities during the years in question. All this is yet another indication that family labour has played a crucial and decisive role in the transformation of agriculture.

As mentioned before, the process of change in the Baix Camp is not an isolated aspect but is closely related to the introduction of a capitalist mode of production in the Spanish countryside. The approach of some French writers (Servolin, 1972), as well as the work of the Russian agronomist Chayanov (1966), have provided us with a very useful theoretical perspective for analysing the introduction of capitalist relations in Baix Camp. It has been a particularly important line of argument, since the dependence on the family for labour has been the key element in understanding the logic of the rural economy (Harrison, 1977). Obviously there is not a closed and stable economy here as in Russian society at the beginning of the century when the only sources of change were demographic. However, in the Baix Camp there are many other sources of change such as the very severe frosts of 1956, the introduction of poultry in 1957, the upsurge of tourism from 1960 on the Costa Dorada and, lastly, the rapid industrialization, mentioned above, in the Tarragona area.

Thus, using this theoretical perspective, the basic problem will be to study empirically changes in the use of land, capital and labour within the family holding in Baix Camp between 1955 and 1975. Most of the data used in this study were collected by fieldwork and using an areal sample (Garcia-Ramon, 1975). Other data, such as prices, hours of work, etc. were also obtained personally through visits to technicians, but above all, in long communication with some farmers who had for some time kept a rational and modern system of accounts for their holdings.

Land ownership and size of farm units

System of land ownership

An examination of the percentages (see Table 6.1) shows the dominance of direct ownership, a system which was also totally stable. However, there has been a significant decrease in the percentage of sharecropping, some increase in tenancy and no change at all in other categories which, in the context of this survey, means the management of the agricultural property by salaried technical staff. Nevertheless, the lack of change in these two cases is not the result of complete immutability but due to the fact that certain internal changes have produced similar outcomes in both these years, as can be seen in Figure 6.2, where the area within the squares is proportional to the percentage of land in each of the systems of land ownership; the arrows indicate the direction of change.

Table 6.1 *System of land ownership (%)*

	No answer	*Direct owner*	*Sharecropping*	*Tenant*	*Other*
1955	0.0	77.4	17.4	0.9	4.3
1971	1.8	77.4	14.3	2.2	4.3

Acquisition of land

Given the diversity and range in the survey on this issue, I have been able to construct a diagram, Figure 6.3, summarizing the patterns of acquisition. All the percentages refer to the 1971 population, and the sum of the inputs is obviously equal to those of the outputs. It is, however based on assumptions gained from personal knowledge of the area; that is, that the acquisition of property which comes from the family is considered as inheritance, while that which comes from outside the family is bought.

Several conclusions can be drawn from this: (a) most of the changes in property have occurred through purchase; (b) of the changes in plots between 1955 and 1971, most took place before 1962; and (c) there are

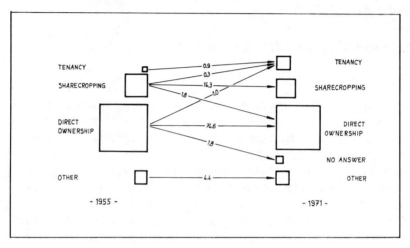

Fig. 6.2 Changes in land ownership, 1955–71

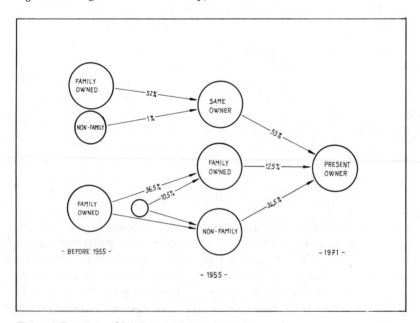

Fig. 6.3 Patterns of land acquisition, 1955–71

certain parcels of land which are more susceptible to transactions of buying and selling, while others only change hands through inheritance.

It is interesting to compare the numbers of cases in which there has been a purchase and a change of ownership in the period between 1955 and 1971. For the whole area there was no change in 53.1 per cent of cases, but amongst this percentage of properties, 24.7 per cent changed hands as a result of a purchase. The percentage indicates significantly the existence of an active land market.

Size of holding

We should emphasize the fact that the average size of the holdings was rather less in the second instance than in the first and that already in 1971 it had decreased to 14.4 ha. This trend is somewhat unexpected and unusual, for it is commonly held that the size of a holding increases as modernization takes place in agriculture. However, the total irrigated area in each holding shows a slight upward trend from 4.1 to 4.5 ha. in the whole area, while an examination of the distribution of irrigated land by municipalities, reveals a concentration of irrigated land in certain municipalities.

Other aspects which could throw some light on this trend are the evolution of income from irrigated land in relation to the total agricultural revenue and the number of plots per holding. In 1955 the average revenue from irrigated land formed about 30 per cent of sales; by 1974 this had risen considerably to 50 per cent. On the other hand, the average number of plots on a holding had decreased from 5.7 in 1955 to 5.2, a figure which I consider high. If we accept that this distribution of plots helps one to gain access to good land and diminishes the risk of losses, we should not forget the technical disadvantages of this situation, especially when the size of the holding is not large.

In conclusion, then, the stability of the family unit should not surprise us; certain apparent aspects of change, such as the transaction in plots, have had the effect of reinforcing and assuring the stability of the holding within a system of direct ownership. The virtual lack of change in the size of the family holding should not be considered as unusual although, clearly, the slight increase in the average numbers of hectares under irrigation in a few municipalities indicates that we are witnessing more a concentration in labour power than a simple spatial concentration (Kautsky, 1970).

Capital inputs

Sources of water

In the survey we look at three possible sources of water supply and their combination as primary and secondary sources. They are the *qanat*, in which a shaft is dug down and along to the water table, the well (*pozo*) and the reservoir (*pantano*).

The three possibilities and their different combinations refer to different degrees of capitalization. The *qanat* assumes a very large investment in labour at the beginning, but at the moment the costs of running it are practically nil. However, an abundant supply of water is not always certain and problems of repairing it are enormous. The well requires a risky, yet considerable, investment, given the costs of drilling and equipment, but it offers a sure supply when water is needed. The initial cost of procuring water rights in the *pantano* is very high, especially if one wants to guarantee a given supply when levels are low, but for some well-off farmers it assures an abundant supply and a safe way of investing some of their savings.

In 1955 as in 1971, the land irrigated by *qanat* predominated in the peripheral mountain municipalities, a situation even more marked in 1971. Water from reservoirs therefore increased in their neighbouring municipalities, such as Reus and Riudoms. The increase in well irrigation is clear especially in the municipalities with some agricultural capitalization arising from the accumulation of small capitals at the time of the poultry boom. In 1971, *qanat* irrigation was mainly relegated to second place, if used at all.

Combining different variables of the survey yields some interesting results. In 1955 as in 1971, *qanat* irrigation was popular amongst the older group while well irrigation dominated amongst the young. In 1955 50 per cent of farmers relied on water from two sources, but this percentage had decreased by 1971, suggesting that there was a more assured water supply. In 1955 most of those who used water from reservoirs also had a second type of water supply, probably because their share in the water rights could not guarantee a sufficient supply. On the other hand, those who used the *qanat* as their principal source did not need a secondary supply, since these were small capitalized holdings. The situation had changed by 1971 for while, on the one hand, the reservoir capacity increased, the opposite occurred with the *qanat* which was relegated to second place. In this way the plots which were supplied by reservoirs began to use wells as a second source of supply, the surest and most efficient combination, although one that requires a significant initial investment. This trend has become more marked since the water crisis in 1979 so that more wells have been drilled and the existing ones deepened. In general, we can state that there exists a significant relationship between expansion of irrigated land and whether the water comes from wells or reservoirs (Garcia-Ramon, 1979).

Degree of mechanization

Another variable which is related to the capitalization of the holding is the use of tractors. In 1955 only 8.9 per cent of people used them, but by 1971 the situation had radically changed and the degree of tractor utilization reached 72.1 per cent in the whole area and, in some municipalities, rose to practically 100 per cent, indicating a considerable investment.

Calculation of cost per crop and per hectare

Apart from the increasing cost of almost all young fruit trees, overall the greatest increase is without any doubt the cost of machinery. The increase in the cost of chemical fertilizers is also very important for all types of crops, although the highest increase was borne by irrigated cultivation. The situation reflected in Table 6.2 shows a significant and growing investment by the farmer but, above all, an increasing integration into the market economy with all the consequences this implies for unequal interchange between agricultural products and those of the secondary sector. The farmer is forced constantly to consume more from the secondary sector due to technical progress. Thus with the worsening price relationship for the farmer, which has accompanied the industrialization of agriculture, the farmer has constantly to improve his productivity if he wants to remain in this sector. Such an increase in investment can only be financed by loans and, hence, progressive indebtedness has come to be the normal way of life for the farmer, as has happened elsewhere (FAO, 1977).

Labour relationships on the family farm

These relationships constitute the key element for the understanding of the survival and competitiveness of the family type of agriculture. The variables available for its analysis are the following: whether agriculture is the primary or secondary activity, the level of salaried workers and, lastly, the hours of work necessary per hectare and type of crops.

Table 6.2 *Costs per hectare per year (pesetas)*

Crop		Machinery		Nursery	Irrigation	Fertilizers
Carob tree	1955		576*			765
	1974		720			900
Almond	1955		1,680			1,250
	1974		2,100			2,500
Irrigated	1955		9,000		1,500	6,463
hazelnuts	1974		12,485		6,000	7,182
Non-irrigated	1955		5,800			1,500
hazelnuts	1974		7,360			2,702
Irrigated cereals	1955	4,000		1,050	450	2,000
	1974	8,000		1,050	1,500	3,300
Non-irrigated	1955	5,600		1,050		2,380
cereals	1974	7,000		1,050		2,380
Fruit trees	1955		10,100		1,200	34,650
	1974		10,100		4,000	38,500
Horticulture	1955	15,300		15,200	2,400	16,770
	1974	15,300		15,200	8,000	25,800
Corn	1955	1,600		750	1,245	4,320
	1974	3,200		750	4,150	7,200
Olives	1955		1,752			2,747
	1974		2,190			3,925
Early potato	1955	10,500		10,500	1,200	19,950
	1974	10,500		8,750	4,000	21,000
Vine	1955		4,868			2,246
	1974		6,085			2,246

* Figures in this column indicate the average of the machinery and nursery columns.

Source: Data gathered and elaborated by the author.

Agriculture as primary or secondary activity

In 1955 the percentage of rural dwellers whose primary activity was agriculture rose to 67.5 per cent, a percentage which had decreased to 54.7 per cent in 1971, a not surprising decline considering the other possible alternative activities during this period in question – agriculture, tourism, industry.

Combining these variables gives us an idea of the very high percentage of farmers in 1955 whose main activity was their own agriculture and who, by 1971, had adopted other activities. There is no example of the opposite happening. Only 40 per cent had kept up agriculture as their sole activity between 1955 and 1971. The rest had turned to other activities, either as their principal or their complementary source of income.

The group which has decreased most clearly in the survey is that which appears as the category of 'other farmers'; that is, sharecroppers and tenants. In 1971 all this group had some other activity of a secondary nature. It is worth stressing that between these dates agriculture lost its importance as a secondary activity. This is really surprising and suggests an uncertainty associated with part-time agriculture. In general, we can speak of a tendency to intensification of labour and partly the need for family farms to turn to outside sources of income to maintain their livelihood.

Salaried labour force

From the survey we could only deduce the existence, or not, of permanent or seasonal workers, but it was impossible to say exactly how many there were due to the reluctance to declare the number for fiscal reasons. In 1955, 54.9 per cent of farmers employed a seasonal worker at some time or another, while in 1971 this had risen to 55.9 per cent. In 1955 there were 34.6 per cent of farmers with permanent workers and there was a decrease from 1955 to 1971 of 2.6 per cent due to the constant growth of wages and the increase in agricultural mechanization.

In 1955 as in 1971 the farmers who owned their land employed fewer seasonal workers. Those who were in poultry farming had the highest percentage of seasonal workers in 1971. As for the permanent labourers the highest proportion was found amongst the older owners, especially in 1971; the same happened with the seasonal workers, although there was less difference between the two dates.

It is important to differentiate between what was happening in the irrigated and non-irrigated sections. In 1955 farms with irrigation employed a much higher percentage of permanent workers and this persisted, though to a lesser degree, in 1971. The same applied to seasonal workers, but we can note a tendency for salaried workers, permanent and seasonal, to decrease as the area of irrigation and new crops increased, including those in which investment in machinery and fertilizers was substantial. This aspect is, of course, symptomatic of the dependence of agriculture on other sectors of the economy.

Salaries and hours of labour per hectare

This section deals with salary costs or the calculation of hours of labour

Table 6.3 *Hours of labour required per crop per hectare*

		Hours of labour	Percentage of labour cost in relation to total cost
Carob tree	1955	2,650	64.5
	1974	2,650	60.9
Almond	1955	5,200	63.2
	1974	5,200	52.3
*Irrigated hazelnuts	1955	22,240	57.8
	1974	22,240	47.1
Non-irrigated hazelnuts	1955	9,520	58.5
	1974	9,520	48.0
Irrigated cereals	1955	14,640	66.4
	1974	12,200	46.8
Non-irrigated cereals	1955	960	9.5
	1974	800	7.1
*Fruit trees	1955	23,650	33.6
	1974	23,500	30.7
*Horticulture	1955	80,000	59.1
	1974	80,000	53.4
*Corn	1955	13,000	60.8
	1974	6,500	29.5
Olives	1955	12,150	72.1
	1974	12,150	65.9
*Early potato	1955	17,500	29.1
	1974	10,175	18.5
Vine	1955	9,975	55.1
	1974	6,650	42.9

* New crop in the area.

Source: Data gathered and elaborated by the author.

required per crop, irrespective of whether the cost is in the form of salary paid to a worker or is the result of family labour (Table 6.3).

Between 1955 and 1974 the number of hours worked is fairly similar for seven crops and decreases markedly for five of them. Now, if we distinguish between the new and the traditional crops, the percentage in hours worked per hectare increased for the new crops by 15.4 per cent and decreased for the traditional by 6.2 per cent, with an overall decrease of 5.1 per cent.

If we add the increase in hours of the new crops to the decrease in permanent workers, which has already been mentioned, we see the considerable increase in the hours worked by the owner and his family. We can also see that, in the percentage column, all crops, at least in relative terms, have shown a fall in the number of hours required per hectare, a situation that could be interpreted as a desire to modernize production. However, the marked relative decrease in salary costs is due to the effective rise in other costs.

One can deduce from all this that labour does not constitute for most of the crops the most decisive factor in the choice made by farmers, because the farmer already uses a fair amount of machinery and his holding is not very large. The family can cover the labour requirements for most of the year and they do not calculate their salaries as such, seeing that they do not differentiate between the concepts of salaries and profits. However, the farmers do not work a normal eight-hour day, but vary according to the season; the same would apply to the members of the family who help them.

Conclusion

We have noted the stability and persistence of the family holding during a period of significant agricultural change. Obviously, family labour has played a crucial and decisive role in the agricultural transformation of the Baix Camp as it has elsewhere in Catalonia (Brunet *et al.*, 1980, p. 272).

An examination of the statistical data has shown the dominance of direct ownership and its total stability between the two dates. The virtual lack of change in the size of family holding needs to be emphasized. Furthermore, the slight increase in the average number of irrigated hectares and their concentration in a few municipalities are signs of a concentration of production in these farms rather than a tendency towards the concentration of ownership.

The capital invested in machinery, irrigation equipment, crops and chemical fertilizers has increased considerably during the period studied, so that the farm is constantly forced to improve its productivity due to the increasingly unfavourable relative prices for agricultural products. Thus, although the farm remains as such, its internal structure bears no resemblance to what it was. So the farmer's holding yields neither rent nor profit as it only remunerates his labour force.

The percentage of workers fell between 1955 and 1971, while that of seasonal workers remained more or less the same. There was also a decline in the numbers of salaried workers as the area under irrigation increased, as well as an increase in the hours worked by the owner and his family in the plots under new crops. The labour force does not, therefore, constitute the decisive factor in the choice of new crops made by the farmer. This is due to the fact that the farms are not very large and that family labour attempts each time to cover more of the required labour input.

This family type of agriculture has become the most 'rational', convenient and cheap way of integrating the agriculture of the Baix Camp into the capitalist economy. Family labour makes up, to a great extent, for the insufficient amount of land and capital and helps to offset the deterioration in the relative price of agricultural products. Hence the intensification of family labour comprises a key element in understanding the self-financing of agricultural innovations.

Tourism and local poultry raising have also contributed to this self-financing, though this has not happened with the petrochemical industry of Tarragona. An industry which transformed agricultural products could have undoubtedly combined with agriculture, but the industry of the area is structured in such a way that it has practically no links with resources of the neighbouring comarcas. Nevertheless, it has acted as a factor raising the level of salaries and, thus, in reducing the availability of labour, has indirectly led to the transformation of the farms, which has mainly taken the form of an intensification of family labour.

Furthermore, since 1979 the enormous water demands of the petrochemical industry have had serious consequences for the agriculture of the surrounding area by lowering to critical levels the water table and the reservoirs upon which the development of irrigation in the Baix Camp totally depend for the moment.

The process of change described above is not limited to the Baix Camp. Of course, similar developments occur in areas of specialized agricultural production elsewhere in Southern Europe and these are deemed to be 'functional' in terms of the strategy of capital at a specific stage. However, this process has its limits and it is likely that we are now witnessing in Baix Camp the swan-song of its agricultural system, precipitated in this case by the constantly rising costs of providing water due to competition from large industrial concerns. The sole hope for survival for this agricultural landscape rests perhaps in Spain's entry into the European Community, although the prospects for Baix Camp are less promising than those for the more southerly agricultural areas which are endowed with better resources.

7

Restructuring in Fiat and the decentralization of production into southern Italy[1]

Ash Amin

Introduction

Traditionally, descriptions of 'uneven' or 'dependent' industrial growth in southern Italy have tended to point to the progressive decline of endogenous, small-scale and low organic composition manufacturing industries (textiles, leather, wood or food processing) and to the emergence of exogenously owned, high organic composition production goods industries (chemicals, petrochemicals and iron and steel) during the 1960s. It is now commonly accepted that investments made by the private and state companies which dominated these latter industries were located in the south because of the availability of state financial and tax incentives which reduced substantially the enormous fixed capital costs of new investments in these sectors. It is also agreed that several of these investments were made simply for clientelistic purposes and that, in the case of some corporations, government funds were used for speculation in the financial market. Whatever may have been the reasons for these investments, their presence in the south not only transformed the industrial structure of this region but also gave it a new role within the national economy. Graziani (in Graziani and Pugliese, 1979) makes two important observations concerning the nature of the south's productive integration into the national accumulation process. First, in providing a significant proportion of production goods (destined predominantly for consumer good producing industries in the north), areas of the south began to participate, for the first time, in the *national* process of industrial accumulation. However, in so doing, they also came to have a very restricted sectoral role (production goods only) in the spatial division of industrial activity in the whole economy. Secondly, the employment and growth impact of these investments has been disappointing, owing to the high capital intensity and vertical integration of production in these industries. Accordingly, the south is described as having experienced, in the 1960s, 'dependent (since the investments were exogenous) industrialization without growth' (Hytten and Marchioni, 1970).

During the early 1970s, however, another, very different, pattern of industrialization occurred in the south. The years between 1969 and 1974 constituted a period of intensive industrial investments in the south, by private corporations traditionally based in the 'industrial triangle' of the north-west and by the state. Giannola (1982) has shown that the majority of private investments in this period, unlike previously, were in highly competitive consumer goods manufacturing sectors, such as automobiles, mechanical and electrical engineering and electronics (Del Monte and Giannola, 1978). Indeed, even the state sector, which had begun to extend its productive interests into high profit commodity sectors, such as electronics and mechanical engineering, chose to locate its new investments in the south. Clearly then, in the light of this change in both the industrial composition of the south and thus in the form of the south's productive integration into the national industrial apparatus, the above-mentioned, traditional view of the industrial role of the south can no longer be sustained. This is because areas of the south have come to be integrated into the production cycles of some of the dominant durable commodity manufacturers in Italy (e.g. Fiat, Olivetti, Pirelli) (Accornero and Andriani, 1979).

A closer inspection of the labour processes of, above all, the new private sector investments, reveals two important aspects of this most recent process of industrialization in the south. The first aspect concerns the nature of this new form of productive integration of the south into the national economy, whilst the second concerns the growth impact of these investments upon the south. As far as 'integration' is concerned, it would be inaccurate to say that the problem of 'dependency' which characterized the previous phase of investment has been overcome. On the contrary, it persists but in a different form. These new investments are branch plants which are owned and controlled by those corporations of the north-west which were responsible for the 'economic miracle' of the 1950s and 1960s. They were located in the south as part of a process of productive restructuring and spatial fragmentation of the production cycle that began to take place in the factories of the north-west during the late 1960s. As a result of the spatial decentralization of certain functions of the production cycle away from the industrial triangle, the new investments in the south continue to be entirely dependent upon their 'parent' firms in the north. Hence, it cannot be said that the areas of the south which received the new investments have come to occupy an independent position in a sector or industry-based spatial division of labour within the Italian economy. Instead, they have become integrated into a new type of spatial division of labour that began to emerge in the early 1970s, namely the geographical separation of different processes of the production cycle *within* a single firm. What is more important is that they occupy a subordinate position within the productive hierarchy of the firm, since it is usually only semi-skilled, assembly work that has been decentralized to these areas.

As far as the growth impact of these investments is concerned, measurements of aggregate, area-based growth indicators such as 'value added' or 'type of industry', tend to suggest growth in these areas. Indeed, it is these measurements which have allowed orthodox, and often even radical, *meridionalisti* and regional planners, to form the opinion that the early 1970s were a 'golden era' for industrial and employment growth in the south. Moreover, this view has been reinforced by the fact that industrial intervention in the south, in high organic composition sectors, has declined substantially since 1974. However, growth measurements based upon the labour, technical and supply requirements of the investments themselves, show that this view cannot be sustained. The plants, which do not contain the full production cycle, are predominantly small, high-technology assembly units which receive most of their components either from other plants which belong to the 'parent' company, or from the traditional suppliers of the company which have always been based in the north. This means that only a limited volume of predominantly semi-skilled or unskilled jobs has been created within the plants, and that very little productive growth in the local economy has been generated directly by the investments (Ferraris, 1978).[2]

Fiat as a case study of recent private investments in the south

The principal concern of this chapter is to account for the decentralization, from the north-west to the south, of branch plants which belong to some of the largest, private Italian manufacturing corporations, and to assess the employment and growth impact of these investments in their areas of location. This will be done by using the case of Fiat as an appropriate and representative example of this process of spatial decentralization of production.

The analysis of decentralization of production in Fiat is restricted to the company's car manufacturing plants in southern Italy. The empirical material for the discussion of decentralization will be drawn from three Fiat branch plants, two of which are located on the southern mainland

(Termoli and Cassino) and one at Termini Imerese, in Sicily (see Figure
7.1). It is beyond the scope of this chapter to examine another important
pattern of decentralization that Fiat pursued increasingly during the
1970s – the internationalization of car production, principally into Latin
American countries and socialist countries in Europe. The quantitative

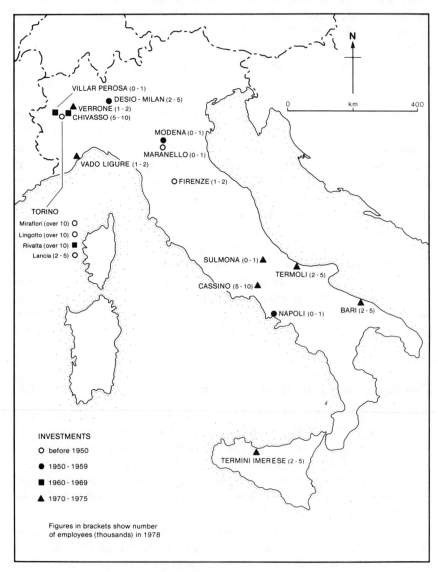

Fig. 7.1 Locations of Fiat production facilities in Italy

relevance of this strategy is shown in Table 7.1, which shows that the proportion of production abroad has risen from 28 per cent to 42 per cent in just seven years. However, the discussion here will only consider four features of Fiat's investments in the Italian south during the early 1970s.

The first concerns Fiat's decision to make its new investments away from Turin. It will be argued that by 1970 it was no longer profitable for Fiat to expand its productive apparatus in Turin. This was because the labour relations which had come to prevail in the Turin factories no longer corresponded to the labour requirements for profitable production that were demanded by the existing technical and organizational conditions in the factories. Within the factories, Fiat was faced with an organized and militant labour force, whilst outside the factories it was presented with all the problems of urban congestion that two decades of heavy migration to Turin had created.

The second issue is Fiat's reasons for locating production units in the south and, above all, in rural areas. One obvious reason was the availability of government incentives for investments in the south. Another reason, which explains why it was possible – and indeed desirable – for Fiat to locate its plants in rural areas, is to be found in the product and technical characteristics of the labour process in these plants and in their labour requirements. Fiat's response to labour problems in Turin was not simply to decentralize a technically unchanged labour process (the mechanized and fully integrated cycle of production) into areas offering a nonmilitant workforce. Instead, it chose to locate a *restructured* and technically more flexible labour process in these areas. As highly automated units engaged predominantly in assembly work, they were only marginally dependent upon a skilled labour market, and therefore could be located in depressed rural areas of the south which offered an abundant supply of semi-skilled and unskilled labour.

The third feature concerns the profitability of these plants. It will be argued that they have been profitable investments and the reasons for their productive efficiency will be sought both in the technical organization of the labour process and in the socio-demographic characteristics of the labour force.

Finally, the chapter assesses the growth impact of these investments. It will be argued that the high growth expectations associated with the production cycle in the car industry have not been met as far as Fiat's investments in the south are concerned. This is because of the nature of the work they carry out and their subordinate position in the division of labour within the company.

It is clear from the above summary that the restructuring of production

Table 7.1 *Internationalization of production of Fiat automobiles in the 1970s (thousands)*

	1973	1974	1975	1976	1977	1978	1979
Italy*	1,628.1	1,417.3	1,182.2	1,326.5	1,277.3	1,325.3	1,322.6
Argentina (Fiat Concord)	73.1	78.6	57.8	44.7	49.2	26.5	41.3
Brazil (Fiat Automovels)	—	—	—	10.0	61.0	98.0	129.3
Total Fiat holdings	1,701.2	1,495.9	1,240.0	1,381.2	1,387.5	1,449.8	1,493.7
Spain (Seat)	355.0	364.6	332.0	347.0	353.0	292.0	299.0
Turkey (Tofas)	24.0	28.8	29.7	26.0	19.1	20.4	22.0
Yugoslavia (Zcs)	95.0	112.6	120.8	134.8	147.5	157.0	161.6
Poland (Fso-Fsm)	70.2	121.8	157.0	205.0	260.0	310.0	315.0
Total under Fiat licence	544.2	627.8	639.5	712.8	779.6	779.4	797.6
Overall total	2,245.4	2,123.7	1,879.5	2,094.0	2,167.1	2,229.4	2,291.3
% production in Italy	72.5	66.7	62.9	63.3	58.9	59.4	57.7
% production abroad	27.5	33.3	37.1	36.7	41.1	40.6	42.3

* The data for Italy include Fiat, Autobianchi, Lancia and others.

Source: Fiat, 1980a.

in Fiat's factories in Turin constitutes the basis for explaining the process of productive decentralization into the south and thus the growth impact of this process. The location of branch plants in the south was an important part of Fiat's strategy to restructure the labour process, in response to new labour relations which had come to threaten the productive viability of the spatially centralized and technically integrated cycle of production. However, restructuring did not mean only a change in the company's locational pattern. It also meant changes in the technical organization and in the use of labour in the production process. One example of the latter changes was the duplication and decentralization of assembly functions away from Turin, in order to guarantee continuous product output. The intention was also to eliminate one important area of worker resistance, namely the capacity to prevent given output requirements being met.

Since the spatial decentralization of production is an integral part of the restructuring of the labour process in Fiat, it is appropriate that this chapter should begin with an analysis of the latter. The analysis will not be restricted to events which led to the location of plants in the south, but will also consider the major changes which have taken place in the technical and social (remuneration, use and control of labour) relations of production during the 1970s. One reason for doing this is to place the role of decentralization within a broader strategy of productive restructuring and to demonstrate that, in the case of Fiat, changes in the geographical distribution of labour are part of an attempt to reorganize fundamentally the form of the capitalist labour process (Del Monte and Roffa, 1977).

For the purposes of this study, which is concerned with changes in the technical and social organization of work at a plant level, the analysis will not be directly concerned with product, financial, marketing or research and design innovations at the level of corporate management. The section on restructuring begins with a description of the causes and nature of labour process innovations in Fiat during the 1970s. This is followed by an assessment of the impact of these innovations upon both plant flexibility and labour flexibility (changes in the nature, use and control of labour). The empirical material for this analysis will be drawn principally from the Mirafiori plant in Turin – one of Fiat's older and larger investments. The factory employs a large labour force, contains the full production cycle and has experienced important technological and organizational changes so it is an appropriate example for the study of restructuring. The section ends with an evaluation of the extent to which these innovations are radically transforming the labour process in which commodities for mass consumption are produced. The question posed is whether a new principle of work (automation) is emerging in which production for profit no longer depends

Table 7.2 *World and home market shares of the Italian car industry, 1970–81 (%)*

Year	Italy in national market	Fiat* in Italian market	Fiat in Europe**	Italy in EEC market	Italy in OECD market
1970	71.7	63.1	6.5	18.2	6.9
1973	73.1	61.4	5.8	17.4	5.9
1974	71.6	61.6	5.9	18.3	6.0
1975	68.4	56.3	6.1	16.2	6.7
1976	62.6	53.5	5.8	15.2	5.7
1977	63.0	54.7	5.7	14.4	5.2
1978	63.7	53.9	5.3	15.0	n.a.
1979	60.5	50.2	5.4	14.7	n.a.
1980	60.1	51.5	n.a.	n.a.	n.a.
1981	59.1	51.4	n.a.	n.a.	n.a.

* Including Lancia and Autobianchi.
** Spain and Italy excluded.

Sources: Ward's Automative Yearbook, 1980; Financial Times, 10 February 1982.

Table 7.3 *Demand for new cars (%) in total demand, 1960–90*

	1960	1970	1980	1990
OECD	49.7	47.2	29.1	15.2
North America	43.6	33.2	20.0	12.2
EC	75.6	53.7	28.9	10.7
Japan	79.1	77.1	41.9	15.7
World	52.1	50.9	35.5	25.0

Source: Elaborations of OECD data.

upon the mechanized and integrated assembly line which requires the manual operation of certain productive functions.

Methodological and theoretical considerations

Explaining variations in the economic performance of Fiat

During the Italian 'economic miracle' of the 1960s, Fiat emerged as a leading volume producer of small cars and came to occupy a dominant position in the domestic and European markets. However, during the 1970s, its dominance was increasingly threatened, initially by productive constraints in the factories of the north and, since 1973, by intensive competition in the domestic and European markets (see Table 7.2) from the French, German and Japanese producers. There is a wide range of economic literature on the various factors which have influenced changes

Table 7.4 *The car industry: indices for production, employment and productivity, 1972–7*

	Production, 1972 = 100					
	1972	*1973*	*1974*	*1975*	*1976*	*1977*
Great Britain	100	102	93	86	87	92
France	100	108	102	100	127	131
Germany	100	109	95	99	111	121
Italy	100	109	101	83	94	99
Sweden	100	109	125	124	112	110
Japan	100	115	108	116	136	149
United States	100	101	87	76	96	109

	Total employment of operatives, 1972 = 100					
Great Britain	100	104	102	93	91	99
France	100	105	101	100	108	106
Germany	100	102	92	86	93	96
Italy	100	114	108	100	105	112
Sweden	100	102	107	114	115	110
Japan	100	109	111	108	108	110
United States	100	110	99	89	99	101

	Labour productivity (cars per person), 1972 = 100					
Great Britain	100	98	91	92	96	93
France	100	103	101	100	120	124
Germany	100	107	103	112	119	126
Italy	100	95	93	83	89	88
Sweden	100	107	117	109	97	100
Japan	100	106	97	107	126	135
United States	100	92	88	85	97	109

Source: Istituto di Studi sulle Relazioni Industriali, 1980.

Table 7.5 *The car industry: productivity (cars/manual worker/ annum) and ratio of labour cost to value added (%) (average values 1977–8)*

	Productivity	Labour cost: value added
Opel	28.9	70.4
Nissan	28.1	n.a.
GM	15.2	n.a.
Volvo	15.0	81.0
VW	13.6	71.9
Ford Germany	n.a.	68.1
Renault	n.a.	78.8
Citroën	13.1	62.9
Peugeot	12.6	55.8
Audi	12.5	78.8
Fiat	11.2	99.2
Alfa Romeo	7.2	100.5

Source: Ministero Industria, Commercio e Artigianato, 1980a.

in Fiat's profitability and in its market position. Opinions are often conflicting, which is hardly surprising, given the choice of variables which can influence profitability. In the case of Fiat, the major variables identified include: decline in the demand for new cars, especially in the EC countries (Table 7.3); low product output and productivity in comparison to other countries (Table 7.4) and other manufacturers (Table 7.5); overmanning (Table 7.4) and lower returns on labour cost in comparison to other European manufacturers (Table 7.5); insufficient capital investments in the mid-1970s (Table 7.6); lower plant and labour utilization in comparison to Fiat's French and German competitors (Tables 7.7 and 7.8); high price of product and unfavourable terms of exchange in the late 1970s; insufficient product and design innovations in the early 1970s (Ciborra, 1979; Pennacchi, 1979; Pescetto *et al.*, 1980; Prodi, 1980; Silva and Grillo, 1980).

This chapter seeks to avoid an analysis of this nature, that is, one in which the identification of separate economic variables constitutes a sufficient explanation for changes in Fiat's profitability. Instead, the aim here is to approach the problem by focusing on the nature and form of the social and technical organization of the process of *production* that made it *possible* for Fiat to be profitable in an expanding market. Similarly, its profit 'decline' is also explained in terms of changes in the form of the

Table 7.6 *The car industry: value added per operative and fixed capital per employee (average values 1976–8)*

Firm	Value added per operative		Fixed capital per employee	
	$ × 10³	*Index*	*$ × 10³*	*Index*
Fiat (Italy)	12.5	100	20.0	100
Renault (France)	19.7	158	24.0	120
Peugeot (France)	21.5	172	24.4	122
BL (UK)	8.1	65	8.4	42
Ford (UK)	15.8	126	13.4	67
VW (Germany)	27.7	222	43.2	216
Opel (Germany)	27.7	222	n.a.	n.a.
Daimler Benz (Germany)	29.6	237	n.a.	n.a.
Ford (Germany)	30.0	240	34.9	174.5
Volvo (Sweden)	21.7	174	28.6	143
GM (USA)	32.9	263	26.3	131.5
Ford (USA)	28.1	225	26.3	131.5
Nissan (Japan)	24.9*	199	n.a.	n.a.
Alfa Romeo (Italy)	13.0	104	27.9	139.5

* Only 1977.

Source: Fiat, 1979a.

Table 7.7 *Indices for labour time, work intensity and labour costs in the European car industry, 1979*

	Actual labour time* (man hours/ annum)	Line speed (hours/car)	Work intensity (man hours/ annum/car)	Labour cost
Fiat	100	100	100	100
Peugeot	113	109	123	122.2
Renault	118	126	148	n.a.
VW	117	116	136	153.6
Ford (Germany)	126	114	143	n.a.
Mercedes	124	116	144	155.0
BMW	130	109	142	145.6

* Calculated by subtracting total paid labour time lost in production (due to absenteeism, meal breaks, pauses and fatigue) from total expected paid labour time and overtime.

Source: Ministero Industria, Commercio e Artigianato, 1980b.

Table 7.8 Labour time per employee in the European car industry, 1979

	Fiat	VW	Ford (Germany)	Mercedes	BMW	Peugeot	Renault	BL
Labour time per day (hours)								
per shift workers								
Attendance	8.00	8.30	8.30			Morning 8.00 / Evening 8.40	8.30	9.00
Meal break	0.30	0.30	0.30			0.30	0.20	1.00
Meal time paid	0.30			—		0.30	0.20	—
Total – time paid	8.00	8.00	8.00	8.00	8.00	8.20 (av.)	8.30	8.00
Total labour time	7.30	8.00	8.00	8.00	8.00	Morning 7.30 / Evening 8.10	8.10	8.00
Labour time per week								
No. of working days	5	5	5	5	5	5	5	5
Total labour time	37.50	40	40	40	40	39.10 (av.)	40.50	40
Labour time per annum								
No. of working days	229	224	223	223	222	233	230	233
Expected labour time (hours)	1,731	1,792	1,784	1,784	1,776	1,806	1,876	1,864
Absenteeism (hours lost)	251	242	178	227	243	249	189	143
Overtime (hours gained)	41	35	70	70	152	40	70	126
Actual labour time	1,521	1,585	1,676	1,627	1,635	1,597	1,757	1,847
Index: Fiat = 100	100	104.2	110.2	107.0	110.3	105.0	115.0	121.4

Source: Ministero Industria, Commercio e Artigianato, 1980a.

labour process. More specifically, changes had occurred in the social relations of production which had come to be incompatible with the technical organization of production and work practices which had prevailed in the Turin factories, a change which prevented the possibility of producing commodities *in a certain way*.

The overall concern, then, is first to identify structural and general reasons which can explain this change in Fiat's market performance and, indeed, which can also provide a framework in which the individual explanatory variables above can be inserted. The second concern is to recognize the importance of social relations within capitalist production, which determine profitability. The production of commodities for profit depends upon the extraction of surplus value from labour and is therefore a process which is underpinned by a relationship of domination and subordination between different social actors (management and workers). Hence this form of production is not merely a *technical* process in which commodities are produced only for consumption but it is also a *social* process which permits the production of commodities for profit. The third concern is to stress that a change in market performance often involves radical changes in the technological and social form of the labour process. An approach restricted to micro-economic specificities often fails to explain – or even acknowledge – these transformations. For example, during the 1960s production in Fiat's Turin plants was organized according to the technical principles of the Fordist labour process (mechanized continuous flow line) and Taylorist principles of 'scientific management' (time and motion studies).

Accordingly, profitable production depended upon the availability and flexible use of a large supply of semi-skilled labour, a condition which was fulfilled during this period. The labour struggles of 1968–72 and the legislative gains made by workers during this period endangered the basis of the Fordist regime of production and led to a series of changes both in labour use and control and in the technical organization of assembly work. Hence it is important to note that this change in the conditions for profitable production and Fiat's response to it have also meant a transformation of the Fordist regime of production.

The causes and role of process innovations (restructuring)

It has already been pointed out that the term 'process innovation' is not restricted to technological changes. Innovations are stimulated by change in the conditions of accumulation, which can include a series of 'external' factors (e.g. the labour market; the socio-political situation, legislation;

trade union practices; quantitative and qualitative demand for products; new models; offer of other product technologies and methods of production) or 'internal' factors (e.g. costs and economies of production; quality of the product and the means of production; the structure, composition and skills of the workforce). In the case of Fiat, two major changes in the conditions of accumulation can be identified, each of which influenced different process innovations. The first concerned changes in the cost, flexibility, control and organization of workers engendered by the labour struggles of 1968–72. The combined influence of worker and trade union demands, new labour legislation and weakened management control led to innovations in labour deployment such as job rotation, production groups and fixed position work. The second change concerned the market. Until the mid-1970s, despite Fiat's productive problems due to the fall in productivity and output in its Turin factories, its market position remained more or less intact. There was still sufficient demand for Fiat cars in the domestic and foreign markets to offset rising costs of production. Since the mid-1970s, however, the 'product-profit' cycle of the car industry, stimulated by the oil crises of 1974 and 1978, has rapidly shown signs of being in a 'mature' stage. This stage is characterized by increased concentration and intensified competition in a declining market (due to insufficient demand in low-income countries and saturation in the advanced economies). 'Maturity' has also meant that in the industry as a whole, the average rate of profit has been lowered and has tended towards equalization – except for the oligopolies which can sustain higher than average profits. In such market conditions, producers have sought to make appropriate process innovations (e.g. automation) in order to raise productivity and reduce production costs (Catalano, 1980; Graziosi, 1979).

The impact of different process innovations is not merely techno-economic (i.e. lowered costs of production, economies of scale, increased productivity, saturation of working times, capacity utilization of the plant, etc.). Their impact is also to transform the nature, organization and control of work practices. Indeed, even the aim of strictly technological innovations such as automation is not simply to raise the profitability of an enterprise by technical means (as many 'technological determinists' would argue) but also to restructure social relations and work practices in such a way as to allow profitable production to take place. Consequently, the form of the entire labour process may change. It will be suggested that automation in Fiat, at least in the areas of assembly work, does represent a system of work that is different from the principles of Fordism. However, no firm conclusions will be drawn since the full implications of automation, a new and evolving principle, are as yet unknown.

The Fordist labour process

Historically, it would seem that market requirements in the 'competitive' stage of a product cycle (rising demand, high individual rates of profit) were met by the revolutionary system of production that was developed by Henry Ford in the 1920s. The possibility of rapid, mass production of low-price commodities was provided by a form of technical, social and hierarchical division of labour which allowed the maximum reduction of unit time and costs. In other words, a system which could secure high rates of labour productivity and a high volume of output at minimum labour costs. Ford has replaced the individual piece-worker who was paid in accordance with the volume of goods that he/she produced with the 'collective' worker who, for a fixed daily wage, was made to work at an intensive pace which was not determined by himself/herself (hence the notion of the labourer who works for the machine and not vice versa). Technically, all this was made possible by the fully integrated and mechanized system of flow line production, with individual workers in fixed positions along the production line (one person: one job). Fordism also involved a rigid and hierarchical division of labour not only between mental (white-collar) and manual (blue-collar) labour, but also within the latter category (skilled and unskilled). The assembly line workers, dispossessed of all their skills and know-how, came to be required only for their capacity to work – to perform simple, repetitive tasks. The function of mental labour increasingly became one of organization, control and discipline, to ensure the smooth operation of the whole system. Into this system Ford incorporated Taylor's principle of 'scientific management', whereby the flow of the line and the expected rate of work per unit time were carefully established by time and motion studies (Braverman, 1974; Taylor, 1911).

The Fordist labour process is thus a highly integrated and rigid system which operates profitably as long as the flow of the line and its pace are not interrupted. It is 'efficient' as long as plant rigidities and diseconomies can be minimized and as long as maximum labour flexibility and control can be guaranteed. In Italy, until the mid-1960s, such conditions did prevail owing to the availability of a large supply of labour which permitted firms like Fiat to exercise strict discipline in their factories so as to ensure high rates of productivity and continuous output.

Regimes of production, restructuring and spatial location

During different regimes of commodity production (machinofacture, mechanization, automation) and realization ('free' competition, integration, monopoly domination, etc.) in the cycle of a given sector, the requirements for profitable production also differ. For example, the mechanized labour process may have required a continuous supply of cheap and unskilled labour, whilst automation may do away with this necessity. The transition from one regime to another occurs when the nature, availability or form of these requirements change and, in so doing, bring about a transformation of the technical, social and spatial organization of the production process (Aglietta, 1979).

In a given historical period, the requirements for profitable production (e.g. raw materials, infrastructure or labour) are unevenly distributed in space, so the pattern of spatial location will be determined by the spatial distribution of these specific requirements of accumulation. This means that the spatial distribution of production units is *uneven*, that the spatial pattern of location *changes* historically, and that these changes are determined by changes in the regime of production. Hence the restructuring of a particular labour process may also restructure the spatial pattern of location. For example, the use of numerically controlled communications systems allows the spatial dispersion of production units, while process automation allows the location of assembly work away from the central plants.

In the Italian car sector, a new spatial division of labour is beginning to emerge as a result of historical changes in both the requirements of production and the form of the labour process. That is, while 'agglomeration' was an inevitable outcome of the pattern of accumulation that dominated the 1950s and the 1960s (mass production in large, centralized and integrated units of production), the social effects of agglomeration (e.g. labour militancy, urban congestion) served to act as 'diseconomies' for this system of production. The combination of these social changes with new technological developments led to the location of branch plants in the Italian south. That is, the 'new' spatial division of labour is the outcome of 'crisis' and restructuring in a particular system of production and in a particular type of industry. The 'new' spatial distribution is *defined* by the changed form of production.

Restructuring of the labour process in Fiat

Three different production phases, characterized by different work practices and market performance, can be distinguished:
  (1) pre-1968 – Fordism, factory despotism and market dominance
  (2) 1969–1977 – Fordism, 'weak' management control and falling profits

(3) 1978–1981 – automation, 'centralized' management and rising profits.

The major features of each period will be summarized in turn:

Pre-1968 – Fordism, factory despotism and market dominance

The market, both within Italy and in Europe was characterized by high demand for small-volume cars. High rates of profit were possible for Fiat because of the availability of a continual supply of unskilled workers from the Italian south and the absence of legislation on the length of the working day, overtime or wages (determined by the firm on a piece-work basis). Furthermore, the management had the ability to exercise sufficient control over labour to ensure maximum flexibility and production output (with strict disciplinary measures and a high turn-over of labour).[3] Fiat plants operated a fully mechanized and integrated cycle of production with a full saturation of labour time, capacity utilization of plant and high line speed fixed by Taylorist time and motion studies, to allow high productivity.

1969–77 – Fordism, weak management and falling profits

During 1968, a spontaneous movement of worker representation independent of national trade unions emerged in the Turin plants. These 'factory councils' (consigli di fabbrica) were the outcome of factory despotism, intensive exploitation and low wages. They were largely organized by young, southern migrants and later, when incorporated into the national trade union structure, were influenced by radical intellectuals, the communist party and the trade unions. After all the long and bitter struggles of 1969, a series of worker demands concerning work conditions, wages, job content and unionization, were met by Fiat and the 1970 'labour statute'. These reforms included:

– the 40-hour, 5-day week, with restricted use of overtime (the effects of which can be seen in the comparison of car industry labour times in 1979 in Table 7.8); the reduction of the number of wage categories and incorporation of both white-collar and blue-collar workers into one professional hierarchy, which led to the promotion of a large number of workers into higher wage categories; agreements with individual firms on a basic wage rate. The net effect of these concessions was that a high basic wage was guaranteed and was no longer dependent upon productivity or output. However, a collective bonus system still existed.

- recognition of union representation on the shop-floor, the right to strike and guarantees on job protection (workers could not be made redundant but only laid off temporarily and were then to receive 80 per cent of their wage from a pool of funds consisting of industry and government money). It should be noted, however, that the rate of unionization in Fiat has remained low.
- greater job control and job enrichment for assembly line workers.
- improvement of work conditions and health and safety standards.

With these reforms the essentials of Fordism collapsed. A strong, militant and organized workforce no longer allowed Fiat to maintain despotic control in the factories. Additionally, the changed system of work practices and labour legislation no longer allowed Fiat to raise profit margins by reducing wage costs or by increasing productivity on the basis of intensified work rhythms or speed-ups (as is still evident in the comparisons of line velocity and work intensity between Fiat and other firms for 1979 given in Table 7.7). Productive output could not be guaranteed since Fiat could not take any action against stoppages, 'wild cat' strikes or absenteeism. The relations of production had changed and prevented Fiat from relying upon traditional mechanisms to restore profitability. They had also come to question the viability of the technical and social organization of Fordist production.

As far as the structure of management is concerned, Fiat did not respond to the new labour rigidity in any positive way. In contrast to other countries where labour militancy heralded the end of factory despotism and its replacement by a system of collective bargaining with the labour aristocracy, Fiat refused to 'liberalize' its management practices. It maintained its traditional vertical hierarchy of control even though it had ceased to function in the way Fiat wanted, and it continued to maintain a conflict-based relationship with worker representatives. Fiat rather sought to regain flexibility by innovating in two other areas of the labour process – labour deployment in assembly work (with work 'islands' and production gangs), and later, automation in some areas of assembly work.

It should be noted that both interventions met with the approval of the unions, who envisaged that these innovations would improve work conditions by eliminating noxious and dangerous work and would 'reconstitute' the alienated assembly worker by bringing him/her greater job control and professional enrichment. Many union activists now acknowledge the fact that the first innovation did not really enrich the job content of the worker nor give greater control over the pace of work. In the early 1970s, Fiat introduced the notion of the rotating work group in areas of assembly work which were characterized by a high number of stoppages and conflict. Fiat's aims were quite different to those of the unions. Their aim was to reduce the occurrence of stoppages by creating a collective of workers who were paid a bonus for the volume of output. This meant that the individual workers were no longer responsible to management (shop foreman) but to their colleagues since a refusal to co-operate affected the wages of their colleagues. As far as control went, although the volume of output was regulated by the group, its pace of work was still linked to the speed of the production line. Finally, with respect to 'job enrichment', although workers could alternate their specific tasks, the nature of the work itself was such that skilled work was excluded from the group's collective activity. In Fiat's terms the notion of the production gang was a useful innovation that allowed a greater mobility and flexibility in the deployment of the unskilled worker without engendering a loss of control. In this sense, it can be considered a significant alteration of the 'one person: one job' principle as envisaged by the Taylorist system of labour use. Of course, the net effect on profitability was not substantial, since this form of work organization was only applied in a very small part of the production process (Bonazzi, 1975; Butera, 1980; Fiat, 1979b).

1978–1981 Automation, 'centralized' management and rising profits

The second, and more important innovation is in the automation of certain areas of the assembly line, both in Turin and in the south.[4] Although Fiat began to introduce automated processes in the mid-1970s (e.g. fully automated lines for floor panel, body and roof assembly, 1975; robotized paint spraying 'arms' in various years; automatic presses for external panels in 1975), its most recent innovations have radically altered the technological and social organization of Fordism. There are three technological innovations which have been at the heart of this change:
(1) *'Robogate'* – an electronically controlled multi-headed welding system, used for body assembly and introduced in the Rivalta and Cassino plants in 1978.
This is an extremely flexible system which can be used for a number of different models. It raises productivity enormously by reducing unit job times and has an infinitely long 'life-cycle'. The main 'social' impact is that the numerically controlled welding robot effectively displaces skilled manual labour (welders). Several workers are replaced by one highly skilled engineer/operator who is trained in computer science and by multipurpose maintenance personnel. As a result, the necessity for control over living labour is no longer necessary, since the manual worker has been

eliminated. Thus, in addition to raising plant efficiency, this innovation has also had the effect of transforming the social composition of the workforce. The 'new' computer technicians often identify themselves as white-collar workers and not with the workforce. Moreover, electronic control also means the elimination of any possibility of job control on the part of the operator.

(2) *'Digitron'* – a magnetic machine transfer system used for final assembly of the body to an already assembled sub-frame and mechanical parts. Magnetic carriers ('Robocarriers') transport mechanical parts to fixed stations, over which passes an overhead line which brings the shell of the car. At each station, the body is joined on to the mechanical parts by an automatic multiple rivet-head system. It was introduced in 1978 at Mirafiori.

The automatic machine transfer system replaces a number of mechanical operations and eliminates the assembly chain by replacing it with the magnetic carrier. The effect is to make the flow line much more flexible. For example, it prevents problems of over-stocking and also offers a different network of 'routes', in case of blockages in the main transfer line. It has influenced changes in the organization of work – a collection of workers who control the movement of the 'robocarrier' have replaced the single worker who has to work at the pace of the flow line. As far as 'mental' labour is concerned, the work of planning and control has been appropriated by a central computer. Thus the function of control of the labour force and of production has been appropriated, both horizontally and vertically, by the computer.

This form of robotization, then, allows a great deal of plant flexibility and also allows control functions to be automated, thereby replacing the necessity for several 'social actors' – the foreman, unskilled labour (where the jobs have been automized), and skilled welders. Malfunctions and technical hitches are immediately recorded by the central computer, and rapidly rectified by adapting to a different route of machine transfer or intensifying work in those stations which continue to function. The social composition also changes in favour of an increased number of indirect workers – such as electricians and maintenance workers. Perhaps the most revolutionary aspect of Digitron lies in the possibility of eliminating the assembly line and its replacement by a 'modular' system of production, where work on different models can be carried out in different modules. At present, each assembly line can only work on one model and a break-down in any one part can bring the whole line to a halt.

(3) *'LAM'* – an automated engine assembly unit in which electronically controlled magnetic trolleys transport engine components

for final assembly to fixed stations where 'islands' of workers assemble the engine. LAM was first used at Mirafiori in 1980.

The logic that lies behind the automated engine assembly unit is similar to that which lies behind 'Digitron'. With the use of 'LAM' different engines can be assembled at the same time; the time of transport and the number of mechanical jobs is reduced; the rejection rate of finished engines has been halved; 20 per cent fewer workers are now each producing 4.3 engines per shift, against 3 previously and direct labour time per engine has been reduced by 25 per cent. In addition, 'LAM' can be adapted to produce a number of different types of engine. For example, at Mirafiori, where 110 different engine specifications exist, it is of crucial importance to be able to respond quickly to changes in demand for specific engines (Comito, 1980).

Technological change is not the only factor that has allowed Fiat to regain its competitive position in the market. Fiat claims that, in the last two years, productivity has risen by 20 per cent to equal that of its French and German competitors, while absenteeism has dropped from an average of 17 per cent to 5 per cent (equal to the Japanese producers). This 'miraculous' recovery has been helped by Fiat's unprecedented victory over the trade unions in September 1980, when 40,000 white-collar and skilled manual workers went on a return-to-work march against a trade union decision to remain on strike over Fiat's plan to lay-off 24,000 workers for an indefinite period. As a result of the march, the trade unions were forced to ratify Fiat's decisions. Many commentators argue that Fiat's ability to resolve its long-standing 'impasse' with the unions, by way of returning to its pre-1968 hard-line approach, can be explained by a change in the relationship between trade unions and the workplace that had come about in the mid-1970s. In that period, the trade union executive decided to increase its participation at a national political level and sought to influence the government into passing a series of reforms in the direction of indicative economic planning. This led not only to a relaxation of trade union support for day-to-day struggles in the workplace, but also to an agreement with employers not to press for a rise in wages, over and above the index-linked increase. It is argued that the emergence of this gap between trade union objectives on a national scale and economic demands in the workplace (in particular those of white-collar workers) had the effect of weakening labour solidarity within Fiat and allowed the resurgence of uni-directional, centralized management practices (Ciafaloni, 1981).

Of the reasons that have been put forward for Fiat's historic victory over its workers and the trade unions, the one given above is among the more obvious but is perhaps simplistic in that it only identifies an external factor, namely a change in the relationship between unions and workers. A thought-provoking essay by Revelli (1982), written within the *operaist* (worker-oriented) tradition, attempts to explain the defeat of October 1980 in terms of an important change in working class culture and identity that was engendered during the 1970s in the face of a qualitative alteration in the relations of production. He argues that the introduction of new technologies has transformed the labour process. This transformation has meant not only a change in the social composition of the workforce but also a weakening of the culture and political strength associated with the Fordist 'mass-worker'. In addition, he explains the actions of middle management during the strike in terms of their political and economic subordination to Fiat in a climate of job and representational insecurity.

Finally, of course, the importance that the economic crisis, growing unemployment and chronic inflation have had in fostering job insecurity and divisions within the working class should not be underestimated in explaining the events of October 1980. Unfortunately, it is beyond the scope of this chapter to assess the relevance of the different factors which explain the recent return to strict management practices in Fiat. The main concern here is to point out that Fiat has succeeded in reversing some of the major gains which were achieved by the workers' struggles of the late 1960s. As a result, for the first time in over a decade, Fiat has succeeded in raising its profitability on the basis of a direct attack on workers, which has involved mass redundancies, the intensification of work rhythms and despotic control on the shop-floor (Dina, 1980a, b; Ferraris, 1981; Gigliobianco and Salvati, 1980).

The decentralization of Fiat branch plants into southern Italy

One of Fiat's principal responses to growing urban congestion in Turin and to labour rigidities which had been created within the factories in Turin by the workers' struggles of 1968–72 was to decentralize some of the functions of the production cycle into the south. The quantitative significance of this process of decentralization into the south is revealed in a recent report concerning investments in the latter region (Fiat, 1981). The report claims that in 1979, 62.5 per cent of employees in all firms located in the south with a labour force of over 500 were in externally owned firms. In the same year, 21.3 per cent (40,700) of the total number of employees (190,980) working for the major private and public investors in the south were employed by the Fiat group and 11.3 per cent (21,500) worked for Fiat's automobile industries. This made Fiat the largest single employer within this group of firms.

Decentralization of production from Turin as a form of restructuring of the labour process

In the late 1960s, market conditions were sufficiently favourable for Fiat to make new investments in order to meet the high demand for small and medium-capacity cars. However, there were three major reasons why Fiat felt it could not invest again in Turin. First, Turin had become a heavily congested city as a result of more than a decade of continuous and massive migration of workers (especially from the south) into the city. This congestion had been exacerbated by another huge Fiat investment in Turin, the Rivalta plant which opened in 1967 and had a workforce of over 10,000 employees by 1969. For Fiat, urban congestion, which manifested itself in the form of insufficient and often poor quality housing, poor transportation and other public service facilities, meant added costs and inefficiencies in the output of the workforce (Alquati, 1975).

The second reason for not investing in Turin concerns the quantity and social composition of skilled and semi-skilled workers in the urban labour market. Rapid and extensive industrialization in the north-west during the 1950s and 1960s had progressively reduced the supply of skilled workers in the local labour market and in so doing has raised the bargaining strength of these workers. Fiat knew only too well that many of the protagonists involved in organizing the factory councils of 1968 were skilled and technical workers, and it had no wish to further consolidate their strength by investing in Turin. It was also Fiat's intention to avoid the recruitment of young male workers, because this group had shown itself to be the most militant during the 'hot autumn' (Pizzorno, 1974–8).

The third, and most important, reason for decentralizing production away from Turin concerns Fiat's strategy to restructure the Fordist labour process in order to eliminate the plant and labour rigidities which had become apparent through labour gains and labour legislation made after the 'hot autumn'. The way in which the new labour gains challenged the technical and social adequacy of the system of production has already been discussed and in the face of these problems Fiat's aim in decentralizing production was to achieve two things: first, to invest in areas which offered different and more attractive labour conditions, and secondly, to restructure the form of the cycle of production.

It is important to understand that decentralization did not mean simply relocating the Fordist labour process in areas of low labour militancy. It meant the reorganization and fragmentation of work in the integrated production cycle and the relocation of only certain functions into the latter areas. This objective was clearly understood by Agnelli, the president of Fiat, when he said in an interview (quoted in Guidi *et al.*, 1974).

> The labour conflicts in the factories have taught Fiat management an elementary truth: large plants like Mirafiori can no longer be governed and therefore the Fiat system must be reformed – that is, to create factories in the south, but in a certain way . . . one does not create a Mirafiori in the south, but several small plants. What these plants have in common is that they are independent from each other.   (p. 116)

Decentralization then, like automation, was part of an effort to restructure the labour process and to achieve greater labour and plant flexibilities in the production cycle. Fiat's strategy was to build vast chains of small- to medium-size production units in which simple productive tasks were duplicated, in order to guarantee the continual supply of parts and finished cars in case of output failures (due to stoppages, breakdowns, or strikes) in Fiat's older factories. The technical possibility of spatially fragmenting the production cycle was produced by a computerized administrative system which allowed full control over production in branch plants separated from Turin.

Elasticity in the production cycle was to be achieved by duplicating and 'dislocating' two types of function from the integrated cycle of production. The two functions were assembly work and the production of particular mechanical parts such as brake systems and engines. Each function was to be carried out in more than one branch plant. The duplication of assembly work in different plants aimed to alleviate one major rigidity of the Fordist labour process, namely the possibility of bringing the whole production cycle to a halt in the event of output failure in one area of the cycle. The multi-sourcing of assembled products was one way of preventing this problem, because the product could be obtained from different plants. For example, in the mid-1970s the Fiat 126 was assembled at Cassino, Turin and Termini Imerese. This seemingly 'harmless' technical decision also fulfilled an important social function as some of the most bitter struggles which were fought in the Turin factories involved the mass worker on the assembly line. Decentralization would geographically fragment worker solidarity in these traditionally militant areas of work, whilst duplication would weaken worker resistance by removing the dependency of the firm on one set of workers for a given product. Finally, of course, the location of a plant in a labour market characterized by very different social and cultural practices and attitudes to work would serve to fragment the solidarity of Fiat workers as a whole.

The second 'type' of production unit that was to be decentralized from the main production cycle was the small- to medium-size plant with its own independently run cycle. These 'independent sub-cycles' would not perform all the functions required to produce a car (production and assembly of mechanical parts and the car-shell) but would supply only one or two parts for other Fiat plants. The Termoli plant was conceived in this fashion and produces engines and gearboxes. The advantages offered by this kind of production unit, as far as the profitability of the firm is concerned, are two-fold. First, the plant can act as an independent supply source for a number of different plants. Secondly, in possessing its own production 'sub-cycle', the volume of output produced is not bound to other phases in the production cycle. Therefore, the volume of output can be varied in accordance with the demand for the product from other plants. In this way, the firm can avoid costs incurred from over-production or storage costs. However, as far as the branch plant is concerned, it suffers from the disadvantage of being only a supply unit which can be subjected to constant variations in demand. For example, in the mid-1970s, the Termoli plant produced engines for the 126 model which were destined for the Fiat factory in Poland. The Polish plant, however, also produced the same engines which, for reasons of over-capacity, were sent to the Cassino plant!

Decentralization, as a form of productive restructuring, has also allowed Fiat to experiment with new production techniques in order to reduce intra-plant rigidities in the aftermath of the 'hot autumn'. On the basis of their success in the new plants of the south, these innovations were later to be introduced in the Turin factories. For example, the Cassino plant was installed with four independently run assembly lines, all of which produced one model. This overcame mechanical and labour problems associated with the traditional single assembly 'serpent' which produced only one model. The plants at Cassino and Termoli were also used to experiment with the principle of production 'islands' which has been discussed. Finally, numerically controlled machines were also introduced, during the mid-1970s, in some of the plants at Cassino and Termini Imerese.

Hence, the investments which were to be made away from Turin were to be of a specific form and in accordance with the essential reason for productive decentralization, namely the restructuring of the social and technical composition of the labour process. The specific labour requirements which were appropriate for the new type of production units were found by Fiat in the rural areas of the south.

The location of the new branch plants and the labour market

Fiat's car investments in the south are small- to medium-sized branch plants (except Cassino, which has 10,000 employees) which are engaged either in assembly work or in the production of specific mechanical parts. The plants are 'disseminated' in five provinces of the south, principally in agricultural zones (the Naples and Bari plants are an exception) which are well endowed with civic and industrial infrastructures. The plants also tend to be located in the vicinity of small provincial towns and the main features of three typical plants and localities are summarized in Table 7.9.

In addition to the availability of regional development grants for construction and infrastructure costs and also of financial loans at minimum lending rates, labour conditions in the south were a major influence on Fiat's decision to decentralize production into this region. Having experienced the militancy of young workers in the factories of Turin during the late 1960s, Fiat's preference was for a male labour force of an average age of over 30. It was not so much regional wage differentials that interested Fiat – as regional variations of wage levels in the same branch of production were declared illegal after 1971 – but the 'quality' of labour. Fiat's policy was to invest in depopulated areas of the south which were characterized by small-scale production in agriculture. These were also high unemployment areas so for the kind of work which was being brought to the south, namely semi-skilled and unskilled jobs, Fiat's intentions were to draw upon an abundant and politically conservative labour supply composed of workers from heterogeneous professional backgrounds (small farmers, agricultural workers, employees in commercial and service activities). The aim was to create a new type of manual worker in whom the industrial and political militancy of the urban worker was absent. In this way, Fiat could obtain from the outset a workforce which could be 'moulded' to fit the social requirements of repetitive work. The existence of a professionally heterogeneous workforce, which was also characterized by a high percentage of workers with second jobs, was, contrary to expectations, a benefit for Fiat, in so far as it prevented the development of a collective identity among the workers. The existence of these two phenomena was illustrated by a union official, whose reply when asked to comment on the kind of worker taken on in Fiat's southern plants, was, 'Well, all types really. There are agricultural day labourers, barbers, unemployed workers, carpenters and a lot of small farmers (20 per cent) . . . 60 per cent of the manual workers have another job.'

It would seem that, although dual labour presented Fiat with the disadvantage of having a higher than average rate of absenteeism, a 'cultural'

Table 7.9 *Plant and locational features of three Fiat branch plants in southern Italy*

Plant Characteristics	Cassino	Termoli	Termini Imerese
The plant			
Employees	Production began in 1972 with 1300 employees. Presently 10,000.	Production began in 1973. Presently 2400 employees, all taken on in 1972/3.	Production started in 1971. 32,000 employees in 1979.
Technology and product	Body works (plate pressing, paint shop and assembly). 'Robogate' for welding four assembly lines. Paint shop robotized in 1981. Production 'islands' used.	Engine assembly and, later, gearbox assembly to allow saturation of worktime.	Final assembly using three shifts. Robotized paint shop and body welding.
Productive efficiency	'Vulnerable' due to very rapid growth of workforce during mid-1970s.	Better than average for both north and south.	The most efficient of Fiat's car plant.

(continued)

Table 7.9—continued

Characteristics \ Plant	Cassino	Termoli	Termini Imerese
Location			
The commune	Officially designated development zone. Cassino is the only town (population 30,000).	Development zone. Termoli is the only town (population 20,000).	Development zone, 40 km from Palermo. Small town of Termini Imerese (26,000).
Economy	De-populated area due to mass emigration prior to 1971. Mainly subsistence farming and tertiary activities. A few industries but not locally owned.	Fiat was the first industrial investment but otherwise largely small-scale agriculture and fishing.	Subsistence and small-scale agricultural industries other than Fiat employ a total of 600 workers.
Political vote	Christian Democratic.	Christian Democratic.	Christian Democratic.
Employees			
Absenteeism	High due to wide area of recruitment. Same as Turin plants (17% 1975–8)	25% lower than Fiat's average.	50% lower than Fiat's average.
Militancy	64% of Fiat's average for strike action.	19% lower than Fiat's average.	28% lower than Fiat's average.
Unionization	Higher than Fiat's national average.	Lower than Cassino.	One of the highest of Fiat plants.

advantage that outweighed this was that it generated a certain detachment on the part of workers towards collective demands made in the workplace and within the broader labour movement. Often the dual labourer perceived his work in Fiat as a means of elevating his low total family income and was, therefore, less susceptible to involvement in non-wage related workers' struggles.

What has been said above is a more accurate description of working class 'culture' in the southern plants in the earlier stages of their development. A decade of industrial experience in plants which are characterized by a very low labour turn-over (6.4 per cent of the total workforce between 1978 and 1980 as compared to 13.1 per cent in the northern plants – Fiat, 1981) has consolidated a collective worker identity that resembles its counterpart in Turin. This is clearly indicated by the figures for strike activity as shown in Table 7.10. Strike activity in the southern plants is now not much lower than in Turin. However, the important point to be made here is that decentralization of production into the south involved a qualitative change in the socio-cultural composition of the Fiat workforce.

Finally, one other labour factor which influenced Fiat's decision to locate in the rural south can be mentioned. After its experience in Turin, Fiat wished to avoid locating plants in areas where workers would have had to migrate to their place of work. Therefore, in order to prevent problems of housing shortage and congestion from arising, Fiat decided to locate its plants in areas in which workers would not have to transfer residence. The depopulated rural areas which were selected by Fiat offered a large stock of unused housing. In addition to this advantage, there was another factor which reduced the proportion of workers who could migrate to the factory. Those workers who were also economically 'tied' to their homes (e.g. small farmers, artisans) preferred to commute to the factory.

Labour efficiency and profitability in Fiat's investments in the south

Often, during periods of heightened strike activity or production problems in Fiat plants in the south, journalistic claims are made, both by Fiat management and by independent observers, concerning the poor economic viability of these plants. The reasons given for this usually unsubstantiated claim concern the quality of labour in the south. References are usually made to high absenteeism, lack of union 'control' over the workers, the absence of an 'industrial culture' among the workers, the high frequency of 'wild-cat' strikes, and so on. This chapter, however, has suggested the opposite. It has been argued above that one of the main

Table 7.10 *Losses in production time in different Fiat plants in Italy*

	Plant	Location	Number of employees *av. 1978/9*	Absenteeism (% hours lost in total expected labour time) *av. 1978/9*	Shop-floor strikes (% hours lost in total expected labour time) *av. 1978/9*	Absenteeism and strikes *av. 1978/9*	Plant failures, breakdowns and faults (% hours lost in total actual labour time) *av. 1978/9*
Engine and transmission shops	Mirafiori	Turin	13,444	15.4	3.1	18.1	14.0
	Rivalta	Turin	3,456	15.3	2.4	17.7	7.5
	Sulmena	South	870	13.9	3.2	17.1	5.3
	Termoli	South	2,494	12.6	2.1	14.7	9.5
Body assembly shops	Mirafiori	Turin	17,118	17.0	3.9	20.9	23.6
	Cassino	South	8,147	17.3	—	19.7	33.8
	Desio	Milan	3,909	11.1	3.5	14.6	8.15
	Termini	South	2,591	9.8	3.8	13.6	11.7
	Rivalta	Turin	11,809	17.3	3.0	20.3	30.6

Source: Fiat, 1980b.

Table 7.11 *Hours of expected time of attendance lost in Fiat, 1978–80*

		Absenteeism (%)	Strikes (%)
South	Manual	13.78	3.02
	Non-manual	8.38	0.15
North	Manual	15.01	4.31
	Non-manual	7.80	0.15

Source: Fiat, 1981.

reasons for locating in the south was precisely the 'quality' of labour it offered. In fact there are documents (e.g. Fiat, 1980b, 1981) prepared by Fiat itself, which show that labour 'efficiency' in the south is, if anything, better than in Turin. Fiat's most recent survey of its plants in the south (Fiat, 1981) concludes in its analysis of labour quality that, 'The level of efficiency of human resources in Fiat's car plants in the south . . . tends to be similar to that in the northern plants' (p. 87).

Furthermore, the same document shows that the average percentage of expected labour time lost due to absenteeism or strike activity, between 1978 and 1980, was lower in the south than in the north. This is confirmed by the data of Table 7.11. However, among Fiat's investments in the south, there is one exception as far as absenteeism is concerned (the Cassino plant). Table 7.10 shows that, in this plant, between 1978 and 1979, an average of 17.3 per cent of total expected labour time was lost due to absenteeism. None of the other Fiat plants in Italy, except the Rivalta plant, had such high figures. It would seem, however that high absenteeism in the Cassino plant is caused by higher than average travel-to-work distances, rather than other factors. It can be said in conclusion, that labour efficiency in the southern plants is not 'abnormal', and therefore a negative assessment of the quality of labour in these plants cannot be sustained (Castellano *et al.*, 1978; D'Aloia, 1980).

Indeed, there is also evidence to show that these plants are economically viable. Unfortunately, owing to company restrictions, it has not been possible to obtain directed data on productivity or production output in individual Fiat plants. However, in Fiat's report to a government inquiry on the Italian car industry (Fiat, 1980b), individual plant efficiencies are compared on the basis of measurements of the number of hours of production time lost in each plant due to absenteeism, strike activity and technical failures. Relevant data for the years 1978 and 1979 has been extracted from the report and are shown in Table 7.10. The comparison of losses in production time for identical productive functions in different Fiat plants in Italy, shows that both plant and labour efficiency in all the plants in the south – with the exception of Cassino – is higher than in the Turin factories. Plant efficiency, if measured in terms of the volume of 'actual' (or 'activated') labour time lost due to mechanical failures of faulty products, is often almost 50 per cent higher in the south. For example, in the assembly shop at Termini Imerese, plant failures constitute 11.7 per cent of lost labour time, whilst the figure for the same shop in Mirafiori is 23.6 per cent. Similarly, in the engine and transmission shop at Termoli, plant failures amount to 9.5 per cent of labour time, whilst in Mirafiori they amount to 14.0 per cent. According to Fiat management, high plant efficiency in the south is explained by the type of technological and organizational innovations that have been made in the labour process, in order to reduce plant rigidity. In addition to this, Fiat maintains that the size of the plant also plays an important role, in so far as production in the small- and medium-sized plants is more easily managed. According to the firm, the latter factor explains why Cassino suffers from a very high rate of plant failures (see Table 7.11). It has an extremely large workforce in its assembly shop which, according to Fiat, makes it more difficult to maintain quality controls over the product and the plant equipment. Table 7.10 also suggests that 'labour efficiency', if measured in terms of loss in production time due to absenteeism and shop-floor strikes, is often slightly higher in the southern plants. Hence Fiat's own calculations tend to confirm that the firm's strategy to restructure the labour process (in terms of both its technical and social composition and its organization) when it decentralized production units to the south has been successful as far as profitability is concerned.

The growth impact of Fiat's branch plants

The Fiat report (1981) claims that Fiat has been responsible for initiating a process of industrialization in the areas in which its plants have been located and for reversing the historic trend of mass emigration from these areas. The report also claims that Fiat has raised the total income (wages and value added) of these areas by a significant margin. If the meaning of the term industrialization is taken to be the arrival of an industry in a non-industrial area, then Fiat's claims are correct. If, however, this term also conjures up some notion of productive growth or the type of industrial employment created, then Fiat's claims cannot be sustained.

At the outset, it was suggested that an analysis of the nature and volume of productive employment generated by the branch plants in the south shows that the process that firms like Fiat have initiated can be more appropriately described as 'industrialization without growth'. An assessment of the real growth impact of Fiat's investments can be obtained from an analysis of the direct and indirect productive employment generated by the investments as follows.

Direct employment

In being small- to medium-sized plants, the volume of jobs which have been created is fairly limited, except in the case of Cassino which now employs about 10,000. However, the wages of those workers who are employed by Fiat are significantly higher than the regional average for industry. The latter advantage is somewhat reduced when the quality of employment is taken into consideration. Since these plants are engaged predominantly in assembly work, the bulk of the labour demand is for semi-skilled and unskilled work. It is interesting to note that one of the examples that Fiat gives to show its 'commitment' to the south is its expenditure on training schemes for workers. The scope of these schemes is to acclimatize newly recruited workers to 'factory life' and to ameliorate their 'professional' qualifications. The irony is that after being retrained and supposedly endowed with certain skills, these workers return to the factory to carry out repetitive and unskilled work!

In addition to the high volume of unskilled work in these plants, there exists the problem of deskilling associated with automation. Several of the plants now use numerically controlled machine tools which have replaced skilled (and unskilled) workers.

It is thus clear that the combination of Fiat's labour recruitment preferences and the nature of work demanded by the branch plants served to generate predominantly unskilled jobs which did not deplete demand in the surplus labour market.

Indirect employment

Usually in the south, the location of an industrial investment has tended to generate significant employment in the housing construction industry. In the case of Fiat, since most of the investments were made in areas which provided a large housing stock and since a substantial proportion of workers remained in their own homes, the new plants did not create much employment in housing construction.

An assessment of the product and technical characteristics of Fiat's branch plants in the south would suggest that the number of locally owned supply industries which have been induced by Fiat's investments is low. Both types of plant which have been located in the south only perform a specific task (assembly or production of specific parts) within the production cycle of a car. Moreover, these plants are integrated into the supply and decision-making structure of the whole company. One consequence of this is that the individual plants cannot choose their suppliers as they are incorporated within the network of Fiat's traditional suppliers. Given the low rate of industrial growth in the areas of the south into which Fiat chose to decentralize production, it is unlikely that large, locally owned firms grew as a result of the Fiat investment. If anything, one would possibly expect the emergence of small firms which are totally dependent upon Fiat's custom, since they are too small to produce several commodities and since there is insufficient demand for their product from other sources. It is also very likely that the latter firms are characterized by poor working conditions, low wages and a high rate of exploitation within production and limited guarantees in the market (owing to the dependence upon one receiving firm). Another factor which leads one to expect that only a few production goods' suppliers could have been induced by the Fiat investments is that a significant proportion of parts are supplied directly from other Fiat factories.

The above expectations tend to be confirmed by data on Fiat supply firms in the south (Fiat, 1981). For example, at Termoli there are only three Fiat suppliers, none of which are owned locally. Similarly, at Termini Imerese, a total of six firms have been induced by Fiat's investment. Four of these firms are owned locally. In 1978, only 6.6 per cent of Fiat's total expenditure on supplies was destined for firms located in the south (i.e. firms legally registered in the south *and* investments of firms registered outside the south). The report also stated that the whole Fiat group had, in 1980, 453 regular suppliers in the south, of which 420 were locally owned. However, only 42 per cent of the suppliers in the south had an income of over 10 million lire (£5000) per annum. This would suggest that a significant proportion of the southern-owned firms are very small concerns. In terms of the value of trade with Fiat, 7.7 per cent of all the suppliers in the south account for 92 per cent of Fiat's supply expenditure in the south. These 35 major suppliers all have an annual income of over 500 million lire (£250,000). This means that nearly all of Fiat's main suppliers in the south are either branch plants of large national corporations, belong to firms based in the north, or are traditional Fiat suppliers which have also chosen to decentralize into the south.

Therefore it appears that only the small suppliers are southern-owned and the income they receive from Fiat is relatively small. Fiat (1981) explained this thus

The firms which have been induced in the South are characterized by a low degree of ownership, which is explained by backward economic conditions in the South which have reduced the local multiplier effect. However, this ownership pattern is also explained by the productive requirements which are specific to the car industry and by the market structure related to it. (p. 79)

It seems very unlikely that this situation will change in the near future. Indeed, this pessimistic forecast is also endorsed by the above-mentioned Fiat report, which concluded, 'The short-term future of Fiat's supply network in the south seems to be linked, first and foremost, to the process of multi-location taking place in the traditional and important suppliers of Fiat' (p. 81).

In conclusion, then, it would be inaccurate to claim that Fiat's investments in the south rely exclusively on production goods from the north or from other Fiat plants. These goods are also supplied by firms located in the south. What can be said, however, is that these investments, because they occupy a specific and subordinate position within the production process of a multinational company, have not stimulated a process of self-propelling growth in the south. Instead, they have created a supply network in the south which is dominated (in terms of the volume and value of supplies) by a small number of exogenously owned firms. These latter firms are not independent productive units but are, like Fiat investments, units which belong to large manufacturing industries which are themselves engaged in the process of restructuring and spatial decentralization of production. Most of the locally owned firms which have arisen as a result of the Fiat investments are small family enterprises or businesses that are peripheral (in terms of value of trade) suppliers of Fiat. Moreover, they are highly dependent on Fiat and have limited prospects of expansion. Thus, a process of industrial growth, involving large investments in competitive enterprises which are locally owned, has not been generated by Fiat's investments in the south. Indeed, this kind of growth seems an unlikely prospect for the south, if the process of productive restructuring and spatial decentralization within the large Italian manufacturing corporations continues in the same way as it has done in recent years.

Conclusion

This study of Fiat has served to show that although a new era of 'industrialization' in the Italian south began in the early 1970s, it failed to generate productive growth. This is because the new investments in the south were the outcome of a process of restructuring of the Fordist labour process and the spatial decentralization of production within large national (and international) durable commodity manufacturing corporations. As a result, areas of the south have come to be incorporated into a new, intra-firm spatial division of labour in which they occupy a subordinate position. They contain industries which offer predominantly unskilled work and which are unable to stimulate the growth of other locally owned industries which are technologically advanced.

These conditions have wider applicability within Southern Europe for it is not only the Italian south which has experienced such a process of industrialization. Restructuring and internationalization of production in corporations like Ford and Renault has resulted in similar investments in countries like Spain and Portugal (Freyssenet, 1979). Furthermore, this process has not been peculiar to the car industry but has also involved other manufacturing industries with a similar labour process – as illustrated by the decentralization of assembly work within the European electrical engineering industry into Portugal during the 1970s. In all of these cases it is clear that the reasons for, and local effects of, industrial investment are profoundly different from those associated with the industrialization of Northern Europe or North America.

Notes

1 My thanks are due to Jim Lewis, Ray Hudson, John Short, Mick Dunford, Enrico Pugliese, Ada Collida and Abilio Cardoso for their invaluable comments and criticisms on an earlier version of this paper. I am also grateful to Clare Coope for her suggestions on the final draft.

2 This has important consequences for the analysis of spatial growth in general but especially in 'development areas'. Geographers and regional scientists have often tended to relate the growth potential of an industry located in a development area, to the production cycle of the sector (high or low external linkages) or to its technological sophistication. Hence advanced technology investments in a sector with high externalities (e.g. cars), are expected to act as 'growth poles' and to stimulate substantial direct and indirect employment. The real effects of these investments is often disappointing. This incompatibility between expected and real outcomes stems from an initial conceptual error which lies in assuming that spatial growth is defined by the inherent properties

of a particular commodity or the technical composition of the process which produces it. This *'theoretical'* assumption is made on the basis of an *empirical* observation of previous patterns of growth where areas in which competitive industries were located also experience substantial lateral growth. This growth did not occur because of the nature of the product but because this spatial organization (concentration) provided the necessary conditions for profitable production to take place in the industry concerned. The form and nature of 'spatial' growth is determined by the particular structure, organization and requirements of industrial capital in a given historical period. In the present period, the location, in some sectors, of high-technology branch plants in development areas is part of the spatial division of labour *within* a firm. The role that these areas play in this new spatial division of manufacturing activity, with different parts of a production cycle in different areas, is usually that of final assembly work. The problem of conflict between expected and real outcomes does not arise if 'spatial growth' is seen in terms of the different use that individual capitals make of space under different regimes and conditions for profitable production that prevail in different historical periods.

3 In contrast to the 'consensus-based' approach to industrial relations in the USA or West Germany.

4 The process of automation is also associated with the deskilling of the labour force as suggested in Table 7.12.

Table 7.12 *Skill content associated with different forms of technology*

Operations \ Machine tools	Conventional	Transfer machines	Numerically controlled machines
Supply	Skilled/unskilled	Automation and unskilled	Unskilled
Regulation	Hyper-skilled/ skilled	Hyper-skilled/ skilled	Computer and unskilled
Setting up	Skilled/unskilled	Unskilled	Computer and unskilled
Supervision/ control	Skilled	Skilled/unskilled	Hyper-skilled/ skilled

Source: Palloix, 1976.

8

Transnationalization of production, location of industry and the deformation of regional development in peripheral countries: the case of Greece

Marios Nikolinakos

The title of this chapter is indicative of its scope: to investigate the impact of the transnationalization of production, which is the main feature of the present phase of capitalist – and even socialist – development on a world scale[1] on regional development, taking Greece as an exemplary case. In this sense the title itself poses some problems, in particular since 'deformation' implies that some normal process or pattern is being deformed by the said process.

Regional policies are in fact a post-war phenomenon and regional economics a new branch of economics and this is not, of course, accidental. Uneven regional development became a problem for governments after national plans became a fundamental and necessary instrument of promoting economic development, a fact which implied that free market forces, even where they were accepted on principle as cornerstones of the economic system, had to be controlled and directed towards some specific ends, which were formulated as the goals of the whole planning process. Governments and peoples had become conscious by then of the fact that market forces, left to themselves, led to regional economic inequalities, a mechanism analysed initially by Gunnar Myrdal (1963). Since then economic research has penetrated the problem and the state of knowledge is more or less well advanced in this field.[2]

Having all this in mind, one must be rightly struck by the term 'deformation' appearing in the title of this chapter, for deformation is logically understood relative to some normative or real pattern, which is in reality 'deformed'. As a matter of fact, such a pattern does not exist. Equal regional development or balanced development in space or however else one might name such an imaginary pattern does not exist and there is no economic reason why it should. Regional economics has in fact two dimensions: one relating to the mechanisms and conditions of growth and development of a region, which is nothing else but the application of general economic theory to a region,[3] the other relating to the national economy of which the region is only a part. It is this latter case which has raised problems of unequal spatial development, which could not be problems of general economic theory, since the process of economic growth or capital accumulation was thought to take place in a homogeneous, unified space, or better, within a spaceless national economy (see Richardson, 1969; Stillwell, 1978). Regional problems are in fact not economic problems; they are social, political or even demographic problems. If economic science has turned to their analysis, it is in the sense of normative economics; i.e. in the sense of regional policies conceived as objectives and measures to correct regional imbalances (Emanuel, 1972). It follows that whichever pattern of 'equal' economic development may be formulated or conceived it lies outside the sphere of economics.

It must therefore be justly asked by the concerned reader in what sense one speaks of 'deformation of regional development'. The short answer to be given at this point of the argument is that deformation is meant here in terms of some non-economic reasons for balanced regional development; these include both negative aspects of concentrating economic activity in some city or regional centres (e.g. problems of social infrastructure, pollution) and positive aspects expressed in policy goals which go back to moral issues (e.g. that the people should have the right and the possibility to live and work adequately in the place in which they were born and have chosen as the place of their activity), cultural necessities (e.g. the regions where minorities live) or to social, political and even military reasons (e.g. the need to develop some regions for the sake of political balance or for defence reasons). Deformation must therefore be understood in terms of some historically given pattern of equal regional development, historically here being understood as emerging out of concrete power and class relations. Translated into economic terms, this pattern means some minimum socially and politically acceptable degree of inequality between regions in terms of income, social infrastructure and growth.

If uneven regional development is a 'natural' phenomenon of capitalist development, the question arising in this phase of transnationalization of the production process is how far this phenomenon is increased or intensified. In other words, if the valorization of national capital leads inevitably to regional unevenness, how far is this also the result of the valorization of transnational capital? If interregional inequalities are the necessary result of capitalist accumulation,[4] the transnationalization of production through capital either must intensify already existing regional inequalities or create them where they have not so far existed. This is actually the way the problem of regional economic development appears nowadays. If analysis concentrates only on the 'national' variables of the regional 'crisis' which is thought to be connected with the general capitalist crisis, it will fail to grasp the real forces in action which have generated the world capitalist crisis since 1973.[5] If it is true that the general crisis is caused by the difficulties met by capital in the process of its valorization within the framework of national economies, a fact which led it to transnationalize the production process, the regional crisis, so far as it exists, must be connected with this process in two ways: either it is caused by this process or it contributes to its generation. This is the main object of the present investigation.

The theoretical issues

It must be clearly stated that the region does not exist in the logic of capital; nor does it exist in its historical experience. Capital is not interested in developing a region; neither is it concerned whether the accumulation process on a national level is geographically balanced. Capital is interested in making profits and for this reason it chooses to locate in that place which minimizes its costs and maximizes its profits in the long run. Concretely this means that capital primarily locates the units of production where labour is available, the general infrastructure is favourable and usually near to the market, although the development of the means of transport has minimized the importance of this last factor in the post-war period.

All this has been elaborated upon within regional economics in one way or another (Carney, 1980; Damette, 1980; Lipietz, 1980a; Lovering, 1978; Massey, 1978a; Walker, 1978). If it is restated here briefly in a more or less axiomatic way, it is because the statement that capital is not interested in regional development leads logically – and consequently historically – to a second statement; namely that the state intervenes as a corrective and that regional policies are simultaneously contradictory and favourable to the movement of capital. Contradictory, because they aim at discouraging investment in one region by making the conditions of capital valorization in it negative, and aim at encouraging investment in the region they intend to develop by creating positive conditions. To put it bluntly, regional policies run counter to capital's interests in the short run – capital considered as a whole – in the logic of the capitalist system while coping with the long-term interests of capital. For, as has already been mentioned, regional policies are justified when over-development in some regions creates social or environmental problems, or when regions have been 'backwashed' to such an extent that social, political or even ethnic and military problems may be created.

It is evident that the state intervenes when the regional imbalance reaches a degree which is no longer sustainable, socially, politically and to some extent also, economically. In fact, there is no such thing as 'regional crisis', if one understands this term as a break in some functional mechanism. The 'regional crisis' exists mainly as a political one and is, almost exclusively, a crisis of over-development. Over-development in one region actually creates the crisis. Over-development means concentration of economic activity in one city-centre in such a way that labour has become scarce and very expensive, both for the private firm and in terms of increased needs for social infrastructure, that environmental factors (transport, pollution, price of land, ecological difficulties, etc.) have increased the social cost of production to unsustainable heights for capital and that the quality of life has decreased because of the over-concentration of activity. All these factors may exist latently, leading to a 'regional crisis'. This appears as such, however, only when the people living in the region become conscious of the social costs they have to bear and begin to articulate their disagreement on the social (strikes, demonstrations, etc.) as well as on the political level. Capital seeks outlets in other regions only when wages have increased too much and are inflexible downwards, when it begins to bear the social cost of environmental expenses and when labour, besides being scarce, is also very militant. The regional policies of the state aim at facilitating the movement of capital out of the over-developed region.

This analysis leads to three tentative conclusions. *First*, that usually regional policies are initiated primarily by 'push'-factors in over-developed regions and less by 'pull'-factors in underdeveloped regions. *Second*, that regional imbalances are in fact, in this phase of world development, mainly a concern of the developed countries. In the sense of the above analysis, the less developed countries do not face any regional problem, except in the case where they want to anticipate and avoid the negative effects of over-development.[6] In other words, regional policies in less developed countries have a more preventive than corrective character. *Third*, that an overall crisis in capitalist development, such as the current one, aggravates the 'regional crisis'. Hence, regional policies are meant to be a solution to the crisis. Whether they can be successful remains doubtful in view of the transnationalization process.

The internationalization process is the dominating feature of the present phase of development of the world capitalist system. Although there are signs suggesting that even socialist countries are involved in this process, it is advisable for the purpose of the present argument to concentrate on what is going on within the capitalist system. The regional problem as such has been actually created by free market forces and does not exist as a problem of 'crisis' in those countries where central planning in any variant is the main mechanism of the growth and development processes.

The internationalization of production refers to at least the four following developments:

(a) The possibilities of new technologies nowadays enable mass production, which can be absorbed only by a market greater than the national one; the external markets have thus become a constituent part of the market of the individual firm or, to put it in another way, of the national market to which capital is directed.

(b) Inputs, markets and decision-making have been internalized within Transnational Corporations (TNCs); this means that the production process itself has been transnationalized; TNCs operate as one incorporated unit, of which the subsidiaries constitute functional parts.[7]

(c) Investment has been inter- and transnationalized, thus transnationalizing the whole accumulation process itself.

(d) The production process itself has been transnationalized from a technical point of view, in the sense that parts of a final product are produced in different countries.

The transnationalization process is thus not a simple problem of industry location, but a functional aspect of the economic system, both on the national and world level.

The above developments are conditioned to a great extent by fundamental changes of two important variables: science and consumption patterns. Science, at least in the form of basic scientific methods of research, is continuously diffused beyond the national borders, leading to an internationalization of knowledge, while the industrial application of knowledge and further research in particular fields is a matter more of economic possibilities than of knowledge itself. Consumption patterns, on the other hand, have been unified all over the world via the communication systems (TV, tourism, film industry, migration, etc.) creating similar needs and at the same time similar economic and social problems. Besides, as a consequence of the transnationalization process, the labour force, which was thought to be immobile, has been internationalized as well. The great migratory movements in the post-war period, which began with the employment of foreign workers in Western Europe between 1960 and 1973 (pp. 19–21), have afterwards been repeated in the Middle East, Africa, Asia and even Latin America.

Which is the impact of these processes on regional imbalances in the different countries? As already indicated in the introduction, the transnationalization of production through capital must either intensify already existing regional inequalities or create them in cases in which they have not so far existed. A third possibility should be mentioned here: foreign capital might contribute to a decrease of existing regional inequalities in cases in which it is canalized through government regional policies towards regions which have so far been undeveloped.

If left to market forces, capital accumulation will almost inevitably lead to regional inequalities. Since the transnationalization process is nothing else but the spatial expansion of the accumulation process via the movement of capital beyond and over the national borders of states or economies, there is no reason why foreign capital should follow another logic than that explained in Myrdal's (1963) analysis. Capital invests where labour is available and cheap, and infrastructural conditions are favourable. Since labour moves towards urban centres or urbanized regions in which the general infrastructure is available, it is apparent that foreign capital moves generally to the same regions in which national capital has located its production units. From a theoretical point of view, therefore, the first effect of the transnationalization process is expected to be an accentuation of existing regional inequalities within a country.

Foreign monopoly capital in some cases chooses new places to locate its production units, when the government of the recipient state itself creates the necessary infrastructure and guarantees some monopolistic position to the foreign firm. Since labour is abundant in the less developed countries, it is apparent that foreign capital has a great interest in profiting from these favourable conditions. In this case new regional inequalities are created by the penetration of foreign capital, while this very process tends to decrease inequalities in respect to the overconcentrated or overdeveloped regions. Such policies are followed, however, by governments either in the form of special laws on regional development and the respective laws favouring and regulating foreign investment or in the form of special agreements with TNCs (for examples, see Widstrand and Amin, 1975).

It has been stated previously that regional policies are more a concern of the developed than the less developed countries and that their character in the latter ones is more preventive than corrective. In view of the existing situation in many less developed countries with a high degree of urban concentration in metropolitan areas, the above statement might be contested. It might be argued in this respect, that the so-called 'regional crisis' in Western Europe and in North America, which led the EC in the former region to initiate institutions and programmes for regional development as late as 1975, is unimportant compared to the big agglomerations observed almost without exception in all less developed countries around the capital metropolitan centres, accentuating regional inequalities. This is no doubt true, but in our view, it does not change the main argument: regional policies in less developed countries aim not so much at solving problems of over-development and over-concentration in some areas as at promoting development in other regions in order to avoid negative social, political and economic effects. Governments and peoples in less developed countries have recently become aware of the widespread repercussions of a development process concentrated in a few regions; hence the application of regional policies in order to achieve a more balanced management of both social and geographical space. In the developed countries regional policies have been conceived more in the frame of managing the general crisis. In any case, what was concluded above remains true: namely that regional policies are in fact state interventions, expressions of the role of the capitalist state as the ideal collective capitalist and the guarantor of capital valorization.

Historical experience supports the above analysis. In 1971 in Venezuela, 69.6 per cent of foreign capital was concentrated in the central region (axis of Puerto-Cabello-La Guayra). Caracas and its metropolitan area, where development has been concentrated so far, has for this reason been the place to which more than 3 million new migrants moved from neighbouring countries (Colombia, Santo Domingo, Ecuador, Argentina, Uruguay, Chile) since the oil price increases in 1973. The state facilitated the establishment of capital in this region by creating the necessary infrastructure. In two areas in Venezuela, the Central region and the State of Zulia (Maracaibo), which together made 2 per cent of the total surface of the country, were concentrated in 1979 40 per cent of the total population, 70 per cent of the industrial employment and 74 per cent of value added in manufacturing (see Santos, 1980; also Barrios, 1980).

In Brazil, the logic of minimizing production costs leads many TNCs to move out of the central region of São Paulo to establish themselves in the north-east. A similar phenomenon is also observed in Mexico, in particular in the automobiles branch; firms move out of Mexico City to establish themselves either in the north (Saltillo) or at a distance greater than 200 km from Mexico City, for the same reason: namely to profit from lower prices of infrastructural inputs in these new places and exploit a labour force, which qualitatively is not inferior to that available in Mexico City, is willing to work at lower wage rates, is not organized in trade unions and enjoys no legal and social protection (Ikonicoff and Masini, 1981).

Evidence from the behaviour of TNCs in developed countries shows that existing areas of industrial concentration are preferred by foreign firms, since they reduce uncertainty and eliminate unacceptable risks. When they move out of such areas, labour surpluses are a major element in their decision-making. Evidence from developed countries (the United Kingdom, the Netherlands, Belgium, Ireland, the USA) indicates that regional policies have a definite impact on the choice of the location of new plants made by foreign firms (Dunning, 1981).

The case of Greece

The economic development process in post-war Greece bears the main features of the logic and trends analysed in the previous section. This

Fig. 8.1 Regional boundaries in Greece

Table 8.1 *Regional socio-economic indicators*

		Units of Measurement	Eastern continental Greece and islands (excluding Athens)	Central and western Macedonia	Peloponnese and western continental Greece	Thessaly	Eastern Macedonia	Crete	Epirus	Thrace	Islands of Eastern Aegean Sea	Whole of Greece
Population	1977	Thousands	858	1,609	1,245	655	393	457	407	320	320	9,268
Change of population	1961–71	Thousands	17	89	−133	−30	−94.3	−26	−55	−27	−46	381
	1971–7	Thousands	8	134	−38	−5	−22.5	0	−21	−7	−11.5	500
Rate of annual change of population	1961–71	%	0.2	0.62	−0.98	−0.4	−2.02	−0.55	−1.20	−0.78	−1.3	0.44
	1971–7	%	0.1	1.48	−0.50	−0.1	−0.9	0.00	−0.83	−0.45	−0.6	0.93
Rate of urbanization	1977	%	30.0	58.0	30.0	40.0	31.0	37.2	28.0	30.0	29.0	58
Gross Regional Product (GRP) (1970 prices)	1977	Million drachmas	37,400	65,025	40,418	21,020	11,445	14,175	11,373	6,836	8,837	370,583
Rate of change of GRP (1970 prices)	1970–7	%	4.7	7.1	3.8	5.2	3.6	4.7	4.93	2.2	2.8	5.3
Per capita GRP (current prices)	1977	Drachmas	100,000	91,867	77,504	75,177	71,100	74,000	66,900	51,290	63,910	91,335
Rate of change of per capita GRP (current prices)	1970–7	%	18.7	19.6	17.3	19.1	18.8	17.5	19.8	18.6	16.0	17.6
Per capita domestic consumption of electricity	1970	kWh/year	110	147	94	81	79	106	76	48	112	226
	1977	kWh/year	217	374	266	243	245	294	147	165	296	448
Vehicles per 1000 persons	1970		36	40.0	28.6	26.3	25.6	38.5	23.3	18.5	33.3	45.5
	1978		167	111.1	83.3	83.3	83.3	111	76.9	71.4	90.9	125
Telephone sets per 1000 persons	1970			84	60	56	51	67	55	35	82	120
	1977			188	162	174	175	167	153	85	225	245

Source: Centre of Planning and Economic Research, 1981.

second part of the chapter is an attempt to consider the Greek case within this framework of analysis.

Regional inequalities

Table 8.1 gives an overall picture of regional inequalities, excluding Athens, which are large both in the narrower sense of *per capita* gross regional product as well as in the wider sense of economic, social and cultural welfare. It is estimated that *per capita* gross regional product in Athens in 1977 exceeded the corresponding figure for the other regions, with the exception of Thessalonika and the wider region of the capital, by 40 per cent to 100 per cent (see Figure 8.1).

According to statistical data for 1974, 47.8 per cent of industrial activity was concentrated in 'greater Athens'; the region of 'Central and West Macedonia' with 19.2 per cent – of which 13.7 per cent is concentrated in the area of Thessalonika – takes second place. The third most important region in terms of industrialization is the Peloponnese and western continental Greece, which has 8.8 per cent of the industrial activity of the country. The rest, 24.2 per cent of the industrial activity, is dispersed all over the rest of the country. Accordingly, 51.8 per cent of industrial employment was concentrated in the district of Attica (Athens) and 11.7 per cent in Thessalonika (Kintis, 1980). Thirty-five per cent of the population of the country lives in 'greater Athens', in which also was concentrated 65 per cent of all services, 51 per cent of hospital beds, 38 per cent of all physicians, 60 per cent of all students, 58.5 per cent of those employed in industry; 60 per cent of manufacturing output is produced in the same district. The annual growth rate of population in 'greater Athens' is 3.5 per cent, while the rest of the regions show a decrease of their population in the period 1971–7 of between 3 and 5 per cent (Nikolinakos, 1981; Giatrakos, 1980).

These data give an overall picture of the great regional inequalities. The main regional problem of Greece could be thus summed up in the following points:

(a) over-concentration of population and economic activity in the capital of the country (the so-called syndrome of 'hypercephalic-Athens');
(b) a second industrial centre in the north of the country (the district of Thessalonika), which lags behind in relation to the first;
(c) the maintenance of the mainly agricultural character of the economic structure of the rest of the regions and districts;
(d) great inequality expressed in income and welfare between the inhabitants of greater Athens, Thessalonika, some other urban centres on

the one hand – and the inhabitants in the other parts of the country on the other.

During the 1970s some more urban and industrial centres developed (Kavalla, Drama in the north, Volos and Larissa in central Greece, Patras in the Peloponnese, Iraklion in Crete, etc.) which initiated a dispersion of economic activity, which will lead to an economic integration of the whole country. It seems, however, that regional inequalities have so far increased none the less in the post-war period, despite the mentioned trends of decentralizing industry. This fact is demonstrated not only by different indices measuring regional inequality, but also by income distribution among regions, which has deteriorated to the detriment of the majority of regions with the main exception of Athens (Kottis, 1980).

The development pattern

The above developments which could be described as a disintegration process have taken place parallel to a development course which has been to some extent astonishing (see also Commercial Bank of Greece, 1979, 1980; Papaspiliopoulos, 1979; Giannitsis, 1979; Nikolinakos, 1970; Negreponti-Delivanis, 1979; Babanasis and Soulas, 1976; Kanellopoulos, 1980). Between 1960 and 1978 the structure of the gross national product changed as follows:

Table 8.2 *The structure of Greek Gross National Product (%)*

	1960	1978
1 Agriculture	22.8	13.8
2 Industry	25.4	32.7
(manufacturing)	(14.0)	(21.0)
3 Services	50.2	51.0
4 Gross Domestic Product	98.4	97.5
5 Gross National Income	100.0	100.0

The average growth rate of the GNP in the period 1959–77 was 6.3 per cent. The average growth rate of industrial production was 8.3 per cent in the same period. *Per capita* income increased between 1970 and 1977 from US $1000 to US $2285 (current prices) or from US $1070 to US $1465 (in constant 1970 prices). National investment reached 24.7 per cent of national income (averaged over the whole period). Between 1960 and 1978 the pattern of exports also changed radically:

Table 8.3 *The composition of Greek exports (%)*

	1960	1978
Food and beverages	27.6	24.2
Tobacco	34.7	6.2
Raw materials	20.2	4.7
Minerals and ores	8.6	4.9
Industrial goods	3.7	59.0
Miscellaneous	5.2	0.9
Total exports	100.0	100.0

The Greek process of industrialization has been characterized by an important inflow of foreign capital and of technology since there was none to speak of in the country. Furthermore, planning which was formally introduced in the early 1960s has never played any important role, free market forces being the motor of the development process. The state has none the less played a leading role, managing about one-third of gross national product. The strategy of economic development, where there was any, has initially been import substitution, then export promotion of intermediate and final industrial products. Invisibles (receipts from tourism, workers' remittances and shipping) have been a major element in covering the steadily increasing balance of trade deficit, due both to the increase of capital goods needed by the industrialization process and to the increase of consumer goods, which has guaranteed the real increase in the standard of living and has mitigated the effects of inflationary pressures, in particular in the 1970s. Besides, a large wave of emigration in the 1960s 'solved' the unemployment problem, which amounted to 24 per cent of the labour force (unemployment plus under-employment in agriculture) in the early 1960s.

The pattern is well known from many cases in the developing world: a national bourgeoisie, which controls the state completely and makes it an instrument to serve its own interests. The state, as the main mechanism to control social processes and serve the accumulation of capital, becomes bureaucratic, centralized and inefficient. Short-term interests prevail, which makes planning ineffective despite intentions to introduce a long-run perspective for capital. National capital, being small, weak and mainly orientated towards commerce and services, has always pursued short-term solutions. Foreign capital was thus the only possible agent of industrialization and establishing the political system. The Association Agreement with the EC in 1962 was consequently the deliberate policy of the Greek bourgeoisie to lean on foreign capital in general, in order to secure its own valorization in the long term as well as its immediate political survival.

In this sense the model of economic development was itself deformed and deforming. Deformed because it was shaped according to the short-term interests of groups prevailing politically; deforming because of its effects. Agriculture was not used as a strategic variable, but mainly as a 'residual factor'. No serious attempt has ever been undertaken to reorganize and restructure agriculture in order to make it productive and effective. Emigration was the first instrument applied to get rid of the social pressures of the un- and under-employed; industrialization in the capital of the country was the second instrument to promote 'economic development', based on the rules of capitalist accumulation. The agricultural problem was thus left to be solved by the indirect and direct effects of the above two policies.

The regional concentration of population, industry and state activity around Athens was consequently a natural by-product of the above developments, a phenomenon similar to that observed in almost all developing countries.

The role of foreign capital

The role of foreign capital is mentioned here in relation to the transnationalization process in the Greek economy and to the possible effect it might have on uneven regional development.

Regional dispersion has not concerned students who have dealt with foreign investment in Greece (Benas, 1976; Giannitsis, 1971 and 1974; Grigorogiannis, 1975; Papandreou, 1981; Petrochilos, 1979; Roumeliotsis, 1977, 1978). A general conclusion is that foreign capital has behaved as it has in other countries, i.e. it established itself in the region of Athens, where infrastructure was available, for the production of consumer and durable goods. It chose other locations according to the following criteria: (a) accessibility to raw materials (bauxite by Péchiney); (b) labour supply and incentives (this is the case of those foreign firms, who chose the industrial parks in different parts of Greece, like Patras and Kavalla); (c) monopolistic position (the Esso Pappas project in Thessalonika or the long discussed but not realized project at Pylos in the Peloponnese).

Big foreign capital is thus primarily concentrated in the following areas:

- Eleusis and Agii Theodori (near Corinth): of the fifteen biggest plants in Eleusis, eight are foreign owned or have foreign participation (Owens, National Can and Petrogas near the oil refineries of Aspropyrgos and Petrola). At Agii Theodori, Sulphur Hellas and Fulgor have established big plants near the oil refinery of Motor Oil.
- Thessalonika: Esso Pappas (chemicals and oil refinery, etc.), the Japanese firm of Tekossa, Siemens from FR Germany and the Belgian steel plant of North Greece are all located here.
- Itea (Corinth Bay): where Péchiney has built its aluminium plant.

As already indicated some foreign firms have recently chosen the industrial parks near many urban centres, profiting from the incentives given by the Greek government.

Greek industry has in fact developed according to the laws governing its integration into the international division of labour, in particular undertaking the role Western European capital has ascribed to it. All the features of the transnationalization process described in the previous section are present in the Greek case. Foreign capital, by establishing itself in Greece, has been trying, in particular after 1973, to find access to the new markets of the Arab world and Africa. The Greek market being relatively small the big foreign firms have, of necessity, been export orientated, while the transnationalization process within TNCs has been integrating the Greek economy into the internationalized production system (Nikolinakos, 1975a, 1977; Shlaim and Yannopoulos, 1976; Seers *et al.*, 1979; Regul, 1977).

The most illustrative case in this respect is the much-discussed but unrealized big project at Pylos in the South Peloponnese, which included shipyards, a steel plant, a cement works and facilities for the production of engines, as well as some other industries. Two such proposals were made, one by a group of foreign firms among which were the Japanese Ishikawa Jima-Harima Heavy Industries Co. Ltd, Mitsui Co. Ltd and Y.A.R.D., Marcona Inc., the American firms Kaiser Engineers and Constructions Inc., Sulzer Brothers Ltd, Carpaline Export Corporation and the English Air-Products Ltd, which was represented by the Greek shipowner A. M. Karageorgis. The other was made by a group of firms including the Japanese firms Hadocate Inc., Marubeni Inc., Daihatsu Diesel Mfg Co., Japan Radio Co., Hokushin Electric Co., and Seres Shipping Inc. and represented by the Greek shipowner G. P. Livanos. Pylos is very favourably located with respect to the international market of the Mediterranean but lies at the borders of the national market. Since the region is very poor, cheap labour was abundantly available. Moreover, 67 per cent of the working population is employed in agriculture, but only 9 per cent in manufacturing. The project was not realized, being opposed by the local population, which feared pollution, as well as by other capitalist interests (Hadjimichalis and Vaiou-Hadjimichalis, 1980).

If realized this project would have perhaps created a new development pole but would not have promoted a normal regional development, since the project was locally highly concentrated. It is of course debatable whether reducing spatial inequality between the district of Messinia and other districts would be significant for the general social and economic development of the district, since the average values would hide the extremely uneven and unbalanced development between the town of Pylos and the rest of the district, which is mainly agricultural.[8]

To sum up, the internationalization of the Greek productive system through foreign capital does not seem to have greatly influenced the regional pattern of development. If it is true that the industrial core of Thessalonika, the second most important one of the country, was created by the big Esso Pappas investment in the beginning of the 1960s, it is also true that foreign capital established itself mainly where Greek capital had created favourable conditions for its valorization. In this sense it contributed to an increase of regional inequalities. Foreign capital chose other locations outside the two big industrial areas only in very special cases, which so far have not had any important effect in reducing existing regional inequalities.

The deformation of regional development

Regional inequalities can be measured but do not mean anything in normative terms, for there is no economic reason that regional equality – which of course cannot in reality be defined differently than as a socially and politically acceptable degree of regional inequality in terms of income, social infrastructure and growth – should prevail. On the contrary, regional inequality might be completely justified by economic reasons. Regional equality is pursued mainly for reasons other than economic, since the economic logic inherent to capital accumulation creates inequalities. This logic is not to be understood in absolute, abstract terms, but as an historical logic: the logic of capitalist accumulation depends on concrete historical conditions. It is not merely the logic in the head of some intellectual closed up in the abstract world of his study. Deformation of regional development therefore means that some regional imbalances have reached a level which, for social, political, environmental, military or even cultural and, last but not least, ecological reasons, is seen as critical or unacceptable.

The deformation of regional development in the Greek case lies in the big contradiction of concentrating almost 43 per cent of the population and producing almost 50 per cent of GNP in the two areas of Greater Athens and Thessalonika, thus creating big social and political problems there; and depopulating the rest of the regions of the country, thus sentencing them to a steady stagnation.

The problems are pollution and environmental damage, the high social cost of infrastructure, the low quality of life in the two areas which have grown to be the most attractive poles of development, and internal migration. On the other hand, there are vast areas which have remained agricultural and lack the necessary human potential to develop. It is a typical case of internal colonization – Athens being the exploiting centre and the rest of the country being colonized, in the sense that the degree, the structure and the dynamics of its development depend on conditions created by Athens as well as on its will to develop it. The pattern of core and periphery also adequately explains the relation between Athens and Thessalonika and the rest of the regions. The breaking point, which makes the situation socially and politically unacceptable, is the unrest of the population because of the environmental effects of development in Athens and Thessalonika as well as the unrest of the population in the under-developed regions, who have become conscious of their being economically and culturally discriminated against as citizens of their own country.

The Greek regional crisis appears in fact in the blockage of further development in the two areas of Athens and Thessalonika, mainly in the hypercephalic-Athens, but expresses itself mainly on the social and the political level. Large factions of the population have become aware of the detrimental effects of economic development on their quality of life. The famous 'cloud' over Athens – the smog produced by industry, central heating installations and the excessive number of cars circulating in the city – is a potent symbol of the deformed nature of recent Greek development.

Regional policies

It is interesting to notice that the Greek government in power before the elections of October 1981 accepted that up to 1980, when it prepared a regional development programme for the period 1981–5, 'no explicit, comprehensive regional programmes' had been prepared (Centre of Planning and Economic Research, 1981, p. 5; see also Riedel, 1970; Loukakis, 1976). Until 1970 regional development incentives were differentiated in favour of the rest of the country as opposed to Greater Athens (Attica). They were strengthened with Law Decrees 1078/71 and 1377/73 and with Law 289/1976 which was replaced by Law 849/1978 and Law 1116/1981. The country was divided into four groups of regions enjoying priority in their economic development. These attempts have not been very successful however.

The regional programme submitted to the EC authorities (Center of Planning and Economic Research, 1981) mentions these as basic objectives: to reduce internal migration to the minimum necessary and to retain in every region a viable and adequate population; to improve the standard of living in the poorer areas and reduce regional, economic and social inequalities; to preserve a satisfactory level of employment in all regions; the continuation of substantial rates of development in all regions which have been growing at comparatively satisfactory rates; and the acceleration of development in areas with slow growth.

The new socialist government will follow, as expected, its own regional policy. It is interesting to notice, however, that the impact of the accession to the EC upon Greek regional development can hardly be assessed. Both negative and positive effects are expected; it is unknown, however, whether they will balance out finally or whether the positive effects will be stronger (Center of Planning and Economic Research, 1981). The experience within the EC has so far been negative (Commission of the European Communities, 1973; Banco Exterior de Espana, 1979; Mitsovoleas, 1981). In any case the Greek regional problem cannot be solved without far-reaching decentralization of the governmental and administrative apparatus and without a heavy programme of public investment in economic and social infrastructure in regions other than Athens and Thessaloniki. Private capital can follow the stream to the regions only if the economic infrastructure is favourable to its valorization. The solution can be found, however, only if state and co-operative sectors are created which become the main instrument of regional policies and if disincentives are created for private capital in the two overdeveloped regions.

Summary and conclusions

The main argument of the preceding analysis can be summarized in the following three points.

(a) The Greek case is a typical one, similar to experience in many countries. It bears the features of a strong regional deformation, more typical in developing than developed countries.

(b) The transnationalization of the production process, which is the basic characteristic of the international economy in the last quarter of the present century, seems to accentuate regional inequalities in the case of Greece. TNCs there operate naturally where the conditions of capital valorization are favourable, unless they have special reasons to locate their production elsewhere.

(c) In general, capitalist accumulation leads inevitably to regional inequalities and finally to a regional crisis. Regional policies are nothing else but a corrective, aimed at solving the regional crisis. In the Greek case, as elsewhere, they became operative only when the crisis was, so to say, mature. Private capital is generally reluctant to respond to them, unless radical disincentives make capital valorization impossible in the developed regions. At least in the Greek case – although this might be advisable also for other countries in this stage of great capital concentration and monopolization – regional policies could be effective, if state and co-operative sectors could be developed parallel to the private sector, and if state and co-operative plants were located according to a regional economic development plan. Furthermore, decentralization of government and administration are essential prerequisites of an effective regional policy.

Notes

1 An analysis of this process was presented in a paper by the present author at the EADI General Conference, from 11 to 14 November 1981 in Budapest with the title: 'The production of technology and the transnationalization of the production process' (Nikolinakos, 1983).
2 See the most recent publication by John Carney, Ray Hudson and Jim Lewis (eds) (1980b), and the special issue on 'Uneven regional development', *Review of Radical Political Economics*, 10, 3 (Fall 1978), quoted in the following as RRPE.
3 This becomes clear if one considers the geographical space included within the borders of the state of Albania. In the eyes of the Chinese planners it is a tiny region which in fact would have to be incorporated into a larger spatial unit in order to be considered adequately.
4 Some have tried in the frame of Marxian theory to construct a 'Law of Uneven Development', although regional imbalances had not been an issue with which Marx and Engels were concerned. See RRPE, *op. cit.*, p. 3. See further D. Läpple and P. van Hoogstraten, 'Remarks on the spatial structure of capitalist development: the case of the Netherlands', in Carney *et al.*, 1980b pp. 121–3.
5 It is astonishing therefore that the most recent analysis (Carney *et. al.*, 1980a) fails to see the regional problem in an internationalized context. Unequal

regional development is considered within the frame of the 'national' accumulation process, although the crisis is linked with international factors (pp. 21, 25).

6 It is interesting to note that the two main recent publications on regional problems cited in footnote 2 refer to Western Europe and North America. The editors of the volume *Regions in Crisis* speak even of a 'European' Regional Theory (p. 15).

7 We use the term 'transnationalization' in order to denote this internal (within a TNC) and functional character of the internationalization process, while we use 'internationalization' to denote the interdependence created over and beyond the national borders, which has become in fact a necessary, but not necessarily functional, factor. The need for the term 'transnationalization' has become evident since the moment TNCs proceeded from the simply spatial dispersion of their activities, which meant the location of an autonomous production unit in another country producing a final product for the local (national) market, to a functional dispersion of the production process over many countries. In this sense, the different production units were no more autonomous, but parts of the whole production mechanism of the TNC, producing an intermediate product integrated in the production process of final products of the TNC, to be offered on the international market. The first phase was adequately characterized by the term 'internationalization', while 'transnationalization' is relevant for the last present phase.

8 The problem centres on the definition of regions, especially as regards their area. In the recent regional programme of the government it is stated: 'The regional development effort will be distributed in space and as among sectors in such a way that the minimum concentration of effort necessary for effectiveness may be achieved. *An excessive dispersion of activity in the hope of lifting all parts of the country simultaneously cannot be effective*' (Centre of Planning and Economic Research, 1981, p. 22: my italics).

9

Regional variations in the rate of profit in Portuguese industry

João Ferrão

Introduction

Regional uneven development is endemic within the countries of Southern Europe, as several other chapters in this volume demonstrate (for example, Amin, pp. 155–91; Vazquez Barquero and Hebbert, pp. 284–308). Such a conclusion is no less true of Portugal than it is of France, Greece, Italy, Spain or Turkey. There is a considerable theoretical debate as to how such uneven development is to be understood, however. The aim of this chapter is to explore, within a Marxist framework of analysis, the extent to which regional uneven industrial development can be accounted for in terms of regional variations in the rate of profit – profitability being the central driving motor of capitalist production. It is precisely for this reason that in Southern Europe, as elsewhere in the capitalist world, national states have attempted to influence relative levels of profitability in different locations via regional and other policies, in an attempt to discourage industrial development in some areas and encourage it in others. While the analysis is conducted and conclusions drawn specifically with respect to Portugal, then, they have a more general applicability within other countries of Southern Europe in so far as they share a common framework of capitalist production.

In 1971 Portuguese industrialization showed a clear centre-periphery structure. There was an obvious division between the most central areas, especially the cities of Lisbon and Oporto, and the rest of the country, with the former being both already more industrialized and growing more rapidly. This division also affected other aspects of the production process, most notably that which is of greatest interest to capital in general and to each individual capitalist – the availability of high rates of profit.

The existence of differential rates of profit arises from the unequal distribution of the general conditions of capitalist development – both between branches of production and between areas – that affect the processes of extraction and transfer of surplus value. This transfer may be indirect when it involves the transformation of the value of commodities into prices of production and then into market prices, or direct if it depends on fiscal and credit policies, the distribution of profits and the like (Hadjimichalis, 1981). However, there is a common tendency in current Marxist literature to accept that there is no longer an equalization of differential rates of profit in the present phase of the capitalist mode of production since the authors argue that, in a monopolistic period, an 'imperfect competition' develops as part of the structure. Semmler (1982) suggests that in what is regarded as post-Marxist theory of competition and monopoly there are three reasons for this situation: the concentration of production and centralization of capital; increasing limitations on the mobility of capital in industries with high fixed capital investments and, finally, the collusive behaviour of corporations and trusts. According to him, various empirical studies show that, while these factors can act as necessary conditions for differential profitability in some cases, they do not always constitute sufficient or even essential conditions. This shows that the occurrence of high rates of profit does not only result from situations of monopoly but rather from the more general considerations of the specific conditions of production and realization of commodities – especially in relation to productivity, the capital/output ratio, the basic wage levels and the characteristics of growth and demand. In this context several authors have used the concept of the organic composition of capital as the key explanatory variable in analyses which relate the question of regional uneven development to that of accumulation in the industrial sector.[1]

This chapter seeks to establish empirically for the Portuguese case the extent to which the existence of differential rates of profit is due to different processes of the valorization of capital in the competitive and monopolistic phases of the capitalist mode of production, as well as how this relationship is expressed in space. It further seeks to demonstrate that the key variable in this type of analysis is the rate of exploitation rather than the organic composition of capital as is commonly thought. Hence several indicators (organic composition of capital, rate of exploitation, rate of profit, etc.) have been calculated for the complete set of manufacturing industries in fifty-six zones within mainland Portugal in order to present some preliminary conclusions.

A number of limitations, both theoretical and methodological, necessitate a careful reading of the results presented. First, a study of this type

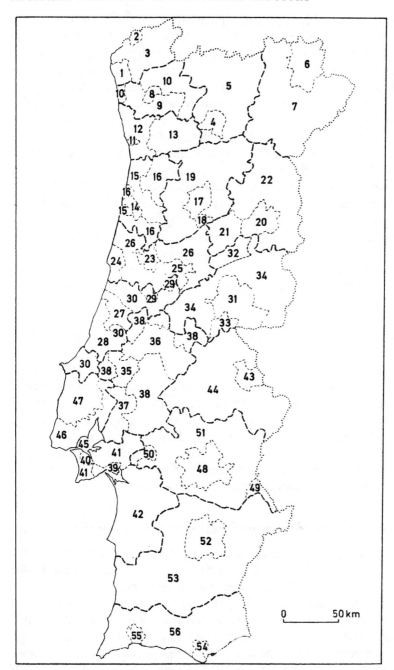

Fig. 9.1 Regional and study area boundaries in Portugal

requires a considerable knowledge of the distribution of the different types of industry – something that is still only partially possible (Matos, 1973; Pereira, 1974; Ministério da Indústria e Tecnología, 1977; Centro de Estudos de Planeamento, 1979) – and it assumes the existence of an overall logic of development common to all the industries in each of the areas studied. Clearly, this kind of approach opens up the possibility of the error of personalizing spaces, as in formulae such as centre versus periphery, and also involves difficult methodological questions about the significance of the pre-established spatial units and the data available.

The definition of the zones resulted from the use of several criteria which sought to ensure maximal internal homogeneity.[2] The primary division was that of the largest local government unit, the *distrito*,[3] each of which was then subdivided by distinguishing the *concelho* of the *distrito* capital and grouping the remaining *concelhos* into one or more sets according to the dominant type of industry and basic character (rural or industrial). These zones are illustrated in Figure 9.1 and summarized in Table 9.1. Even if this procedure is reasonable overall, some doubts must be raised about its usefulness in more complex areas, such as the city of Lisbon or the Lisbon metropolitan area, where the characteristics of existing industrial units, with respect to both age and activity, are far from uniform.

The availability of information poses further problems because of difficulties in relating the classification of official statistics to the concepts used here and also because of the fact that there is only data for one year, 1971.[4] The absence of more recent (or, for that matter, any) comparable data involves the risk of interpreting cyclically determined situations as structurally determined. Finally, there is the problem that the data relate to pre-revolutionary Portugal and the economic and social changes that occurred after 25 April 1974 cannot be analysed in this chapter.

Primary and secondary equalization of rates of profit

Pereira (1974) has calculated the rate of profit for Portuguese industry using the annual statement of accounts of the 226 most important joint stock companies in 1971. He presents two ways of calculating surplus value.[5] The first uses gross profits, calculated by taking total value added and subtracting depreciation, wages and salaries for productive personnel. This result reflects a 'primary equalization' of profits. The second uses net profits, where transfers to the state and interest payments to the banks are deducted from gross profits. Net profits ('secondary equalization'), of course, are what interest the capitalist.

Table 9.1 *Types of industries dominant in each zone*

Distrito	Concelho	Number	Dominant industries in terms of value added
Viana do Castelo	Viana do Castelo	1	Shipbuilding
	Valença	2	Rubber
	Other concelhos	3	Food, wood
Vila Real	Vila Real	4	Drink, food, ceramics
	Other concelhos	5	Drink, ceramics
Bragança	Bragança	6	Food
	Other concelhos	7	Food
Braga	Braga	8	Electrical machinery, textiles, metal products
	Barcelos, Fafe, Guimarães, Vila Nova Famalicão	9	Textiles
	Other concelhos	10	Textiles, wood, ceramics
Porto	Porto	11	Textiles, metal products, publishing, food
	Gondomar, Maia, Matosinhos, Póvoa Varzim, Santo Tirso, Valongo, Vila do Conde, Vila Nova de Gaia	12	Textiles, food, drink
	Other concelhos	13	Furniture, wood
Aveiro	Aveiro	14	Cellulose
	Águeda, Albergaria-a-Velha, Espinho, Estarreja, Fafe, Ílhavo, Ovar, S. João da Madeira	15	Wood, metal products and machines, textiles*
	Other concelhos	16	Drink, shoes, metal products*
Viseu	Viseu	17	Paper, drink, chemical products
	Nelas	18	Basic metals
	Other concelhos	19	Wood, food
Guarda	Guarda	20	Car assembly, textiles
	Gouveia, Manteigas, Seia	21	Textiles
	Other concelhos	22	Drink

(continued)

Table 9.1—*continued*

Distrito	Concelho	Number	Dominant industries in terms of value added
Coimbra	Coimbra	23	Textiles, cement, food
	Figueira da Foz	24	Cellulose, shipbuilding, glass
	Lousã, Góis	25	Textiles, metal products, paper
	Other concelhos	26	Wood, ceramics
Leiria	Leiria	27	Cement, plastic, wood
	Alcobaça, Marinha Grande, Nazaré, Porto de Mós	28	Glass, metal products, ceramics
	Ansião, Castanheira Pera	29	Textiles
	Other concelhos	30	Food, chemical products, ceramics
Castelo Branco	Castelo Branco	31	Textiles, wood, food
	Covilhã	32	Textiles
	Vila Velha Ródão	33	Cellulose
	Other concelhos	34	Wood, resin
Santarém	Santarém	35	Ceramics, wood, food
	Abrantes, Alcanena, Constância, Entroncamento, Tomar, Torres Novas, Vila Nova Barquinha	36	Transport equipment, textile, non-electrical machinery
	Benavente, Cartaxo, Salvaterra Magos	37	Food, non-electrical machinery
	Other concelhos	38	Food, wood
Setúbal	Setúbal	39	Chemical products, cellulose, cement
	Seixal	40	Iron and steel
	Alcochete, Almada, Barreiro, Moita, Montijo	41	Shipbuilding, chemical products
	Other concelhos	42	Food
Portalegre	Portalegre	43	Chemical products
	Other concelhos	44	Food

(continued)

Table 9.1—*continued*

Distrito	Concelho	Number	Dominant industries in terms of value added
Lisboa	Lisboa	45	Food, chemicals, publishing, metal products
	Azambuja, Cascais, Loures, Oeiras, Sintra, Vila Franca de Xira	46	Transport equipment, chemical products, electrical machines
	Other concelhos	47	Metal products, food, ceramics
Évora	Évora	48	Food, electrical machinery
	Mourão	49	Cellulose
	Vendas Novas	50	Car assembly
	Other concelhos	51	Food
Beja	Beja	52	Food, non-electrical machinery
	Other concelhos	53	Food
Faro	Faro	54	Food, wood
	Portimão	55	Food
	Other concelhos	56	Food

* No single dominant type.

In the first case, even though the equalization of rates of profit was not perfect (which would only be the case with perfect sectoral and regional mobility of capital and labour), a close relationship exists between the amounts of invested capital and of surplus value, giving an average rate of profit around 20 per cent. Most of the sectors having rates of profit below 20 per cent were the competitive sectors, linked to industrial capital and dependent upon the banks, whilst those lying above this average value were strongly monopolized and openly linked with national or foreign finance capital. When net profits are used, the split between competitive and monopolistic sectors is accentuated as two distinct levels of profit equalization can be identified – a 13 per cent profit rate for the former and 21 per cent for the latter.

Although Pereira's study is not conducted on a regional basis and deals only with large joint stock companies, these results suggest that there could be a relationship between the monopolized sector with high organic composition of capital, high rates of profit and its location in more central regions, whilst the competitive sector, with low organic composition and lower rates of profit is perhaps located in more peripheral regions. Whether or not such a regional pattern actually existed will be examined empirically below.

Location of manufacturing industry and the territorial division of labour

The pattern of location of Portuguese manufacturing industry is very uneven (Lewis and Williams, 1980, 1982). The industrialized areas (defined in Figure 9.2 using Gross Industrial Product *per capita*) are located along the west coast, from Setúbal to Viana do Castelo, with noticeably higher values around the cities of Oporto (zones 9, 12, 14 and 15) and Lisbon (zones 37, 40, 41, 42 and 46), parts of the distrito of Leiria (27 and 28) and the industrial triangle of Torres Novas-Tomar-Abrantes (36) as well as a few scattered locations. In the interior and in the south, the process of industrialization is less developed, though most of the *distrito* capitals (17, 20, 31, 43, 48, 52 and 54) and *concelhos* with textile industry (21, 32, 25 and 29) stand out, as do *concelhos* having cellulose production (33 and 49), iron and alloy production (18) and fish canning (55) (see Table 9.1 for a list).

In fact, almost all industries in the interior not located in the main cities of the *distritos* are located close to raw materials, energy or water. Thus the following industries are dominant in the interior: food and drink, wood, resin and ceramics, as well as the specific cases of national or export production already mentioned (textiles, pulp and cellulose, iron and alloys, canning). Generally, production of these consumer goods is in small units, supplying local markets (although there are some important exceptions, notably in the food industry).

The *distrito* main towns constitute important regional markets, and even present favourable conditions for location of industries having national or international markets (such as the final stages of broader circuits of production, like Renault in Guarda or Siemens in Evora). They often have favourable conditions for capitalist production, related to break-down of pre-capitalist modes of production and consequent freeing of labour, advantages of agglomeration, greater accessibility, etc.

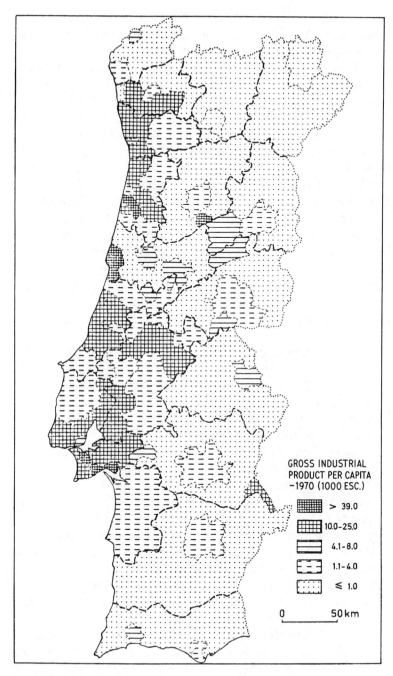

Fig. 9.2 Regional variation in Gross Industrial Product *per capita*

In the coastal belt centred on Lisbon and Oporto, the chemical industry, iron and steel foundries and printing and publishing industries decline in importance with increasing distance from these cities. As they decline, so consumer goods industries – such as textiles, clothing, furniture and foot-wear in the north and the food industries, mechanical products (electrical and otherwise) and metal products – become more significant in both areas, the last two industries particularly in the Lisbon area. These consumer goods are produced in plants of different sizes and generally have both important inter-industry linkages to more centrally located industries such as chemicals and iron and steel. However, they pay lower wages than the capital goods industries and most of the locally available labour is female (and therefore cheaper) because long daily journeys to work are undertaken mainly by males. These consumer goods sectors are strongly infiltrated by foreign capital, such as in the export-orientated industries of textiles, clothing and footwear around Oporto, or in the domestic-market-based industries, which are more important in the Lisbon area. Thus, in both cases, proximity to the two main urban agglomerations is of fundamental importance, both because of accessi-bility to the market and because of centrality at national and international levels.

Outside these two main agglomerations but still in the littoral, is the *distrito* of Leiria (27 and 28), which specializes in non-ferrous minerals (glass and cement), plastics and metal products (tools and ironware). In addition, the industrial triangle of Torres Novas-Tomar-Abrantes (36) produces means of transport, agricultural machinery and a considerable amount of textiles, leather goods and paper. These areas have in common the fact that local, often family, capital dominates, and that production is largely orientated to the domestic market; thus they have a location close to the 'centre of gravity' of the national population.

Finally, mention must be made of the importance of cellulose manu-facture in Aveiro (14), Figueira da Foz (24) and even Setúbal (39), all of which have good harbours. Thus they are much more important than the interior zones of Vila Velha de Ródão (33) and Mourão (49). In this sector heavy investment in fixed capital is necessary, and foreign capital amounts to over 50 per cent of capital invested. The availability of labour and abundant raw materials combined with easy cheap access by sea to the West European market are the main location factors.

The description suggests a strong territorial division of labour in Portugal, a division of which forms the basis of an understanding of regional variations in rates of profit, which in turn imply spatial variations in the labour intensity, rates of exploitation and productivity.

Regional levels of equalization of rates of profit and articulation of different stages of the capitalist mode of production

Figure 9.3 shows the value of organic composition of capital for all industry for each spatial unit used in the analysis.[6] Whilst we might expect falling values of organic composition with increasing distance from the core regions, the following results are found:

- The most industrialized areas (included in the two upper classes of Figure 9.2) usually have average values, though there are some exceptions, such as Lisbon and Oporto which both lie below the national average.
- The capitals of the *distritos* generally have values which lie below the rest of the *distrito*, or at best are at the same level.
- The highest values (>17) are, with a few exceptions, where one or two capital-intensive plants dominate completely (basic industries, such as iron and steel, pulp and cellulose, cement, etc.), and are found in the less industrialized areas of the interior.
- The lowest values (<9 and 9–11) are to be found in some main towns of the *distritos* (Viana do Castelo, Braga, Oporto, Santarém and Lisbon), on the periphery of the more developed areas of the coast (the axis Braga-Oporto-Aveiro and Lisbon) and in *concelhos* with average or high degrees of specialization in traditional sectors (zones 21 and 32 – textiles; 28 – tools and ironware, glass, etc.; 55 – fish canning).

A comparison of Figures 9.3 and 9.4 allows us to draw some conclusions. Regional variations in annual wages per worker are considerable, lying between 14,000 and 56,000 escudos. The spatial units corresponding approximately to the Lisbon metropolitan area stand out clearly and the remaining areas can be divided roughly into two broad regions, the coast and the interior. In the interior, the *distrito* capitals and the textile area of the Serra da Estrela (21 and 32) do, however, stand out from the rest, as do zones 18, 33 and 49.

Whilst not being the sole cause of the regional variations observable in Figure 9.3, the high level of wages per worker is related to the first three results listed. In fact, there is a close, negative, relationship between wage levels and organic composition. Wages are lower in areas with an abundant labour force, caused mainly by the break-up of pre-capitalist modes of production and gradual disintegration of petty commodity production, with a consequent geographical and sectoral migration, accompanied by proletarianization, and passivity in the labour force, with low levels of unionization and skills, and a high percentage of female labour – also

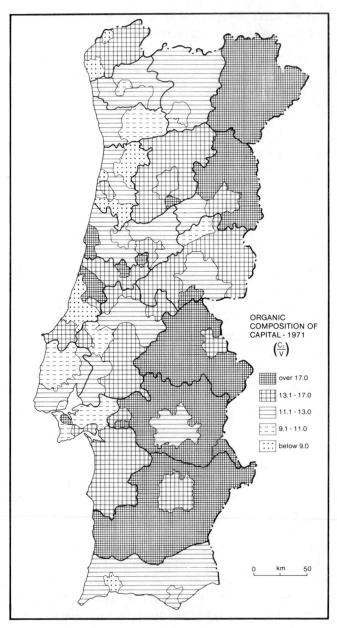

ORGANIC
COMPOSITION OF
CAPITAL - 1971

$$\left(\frac{C_1}{V}\right)$$

over 17.0

13.1 - 17.0

11.1 - 13.0

9.1 - 11.0

below 9.0

0   km   50

Fig. 9.3 Regional variation in organic composition of capital in industry

associated with part-time work and home work. Production units are often small, with a strong family element, having low production costs and strong links with rural life, with low levels of expectation with respect to standards of living and consumption. Thus it is not surprising that high values for organic composition are to be found in those areas which are less industrialized and less developed, in capitalist terms.

It is for the same set of reasons that there is a close positive relationship between levels of industrialization and average levels of wages (Figures 9.2 and 9.4). The higher costs of reproduction of labour even in the main cities of the interior *distritos*, and the larger plant size, facilitating organization of the working classes, is sufficient to create higher wage levels in comparison with surrounding areas.

In the areas where the organic composition of capital is lowest, the negative relationship between this and wage levels is less straightforward. Outside the *distrito* capitals at least, there seem to be two clearly distinct situations: one with a dominance of newer medium-size and small labour-intensive firms (as on the periphery of the Lisbon and Oporto Metropolitan areas, 13, 16 and 47) and one where firms specialize in traditional sectors, with a limited development of fixed capital (32, 28, 55). In some of the main cities of the *distritos* (1, 8, 11, 35 and 45), high wages in certain sectors (shipbuilding, textiles and printing) coupled with the existence of relatively obsolete fixed capital existing in some long-established plants in other sectors may partly explain this relationship.

The negative relationship between values of organic composition and average wages per worker overall permits conjecture concerning the relationship between the organic composition and the rate of exploitation.[7] This relationship can be seen in Figure 9.5. If the relationship was perfect, all points would fall on the same line. This would mean that the rate of profit (S_V/C_I) was equal in all areas – a case of perfect equalization of rates of profit, the surplus value realized by each of the firms in question being apportioned precisely according to the amount of capital invested (C_I).

However, this is not the case. Apart from isolated cases, with a very high organic composition and very low or negative rates of exploitation, to be found in the upper left-hand corner (group C), there is a general grouping around the national average (9.4 per cent).[8] There does, however, seem to be a certain tendency towards an alignment along two distinct axes. If the groups of points lying above and below the average rate of profit are treated separately then very high correlations for each of the groups emerge for the two indicators in question ($^rA = +0.91$ and ($^rB = +0.89$). We would argue that the situation is one of *dual* primary equalization of rates

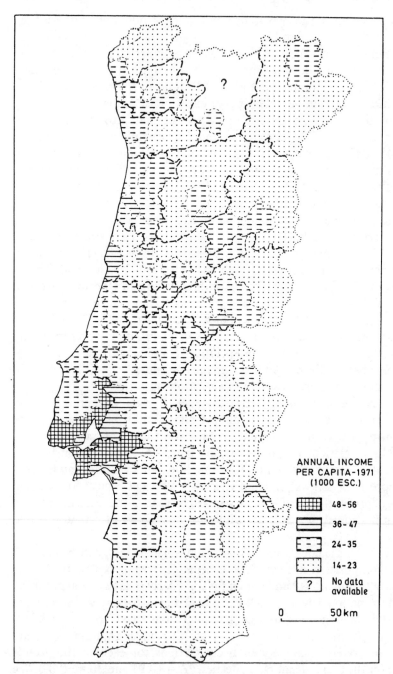

Fig. 9.4 Regional variation in annual average wages for industrial workers

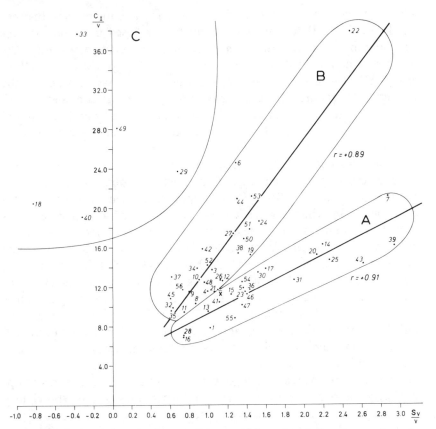

Fig. 9.5 Relationship between organic composition of capital and rate of surplus value by zone

of profit, with a below national average rate for group B (7.5 per cent) and an above national average rate for group A (12.3 per cent). Why do these two different rates of profit exist and what is their significance?

A detailed analysis of Figure 9.5 reveals that, in general, the rate of exploitation (or surplus value) does not increase proportionately with increases in organic composition, growing more slowly and not usually passing the value of 1.6. On the other hand, areas with rates of exploitation higher than this value have a lower organic composition than would be expected on the basis of the trend in the whole graph. If we compare groups A and B, it can be seen that for the same value of organic composition, the higher the rate of exploitation, the higher the rate of profit. Now, as higher values of S_V/V correspond to above average wages, it seems that extraction of relative surplus value dominates in group A, whilst extraction of absolute surplus value dominates in group B. In other words, in group B surplus value extraction is based upon direct over-exploitation of labour, with low salaries, a longer working day (the average number of hours per annum was 2831 per worker compared to 2445 in group A's industries) and harder working conditions. In group A the extraction of surplus value is achieved through intensification of the work process, through creation of better conditions of a physical, social and psychological nature, and increases in productivity due to technical innovation.

If this thesis is correct, then we can hypothesize a situation where unequal exchange is occurring. Emmanuel's unequal exchange in the strict sense (Emmanuel, 1972) is based upon the existence of different rates of exploitation when organic composition is broadly similar. Surplus value is transferred from the less developed sectors or regions to the more developed. This is why Vergopoulos (1978, pp. 112–13) states that 'the existence of backward capitalist branches creates a condition *sine qua non* for the existence and growth of progressive capitalist branches', or 'unequal exchange is an indispensable mechanism, theoretically as well as practically, for sectoral and regional accumulation to progress. The institutionalization of different surplus value, both with respect to rate and mass, is a mechanism which ensures capitalist development in leading sectors, regions and nations'.

It therefore seems reasonable to formulate a new hypothesis to attempt to clarify the relationships between the two groups of areas previously identified, and the stage of development of the capitalist mode of production. At what point does the process of valorization of capital found in the firms dealt within groups B and A, and the transference of surplus value generated, represent the regional articulation of the competitive and monopolistic stages of capitalist development within the manufacturing sector?[9]

Examination of Figure 9.6, showing regional variation in rates of profit (the first two classes corresponding to points included in group A, the following two to group B and the last to group C) permits some clarification of this question. In general, there does seem to be some relationship between the process of industrial concentration and higher rates of profit (Figures 9.2 and 9.6) – though the coast/interior dichotomy is less clear – and there does seem to be an expression of the recent dynamism of industrialization itself. The fact that most of the values above the national average are found on the periphery of the more industrialized areas (Lisbon Metropolitan Area and Oporto-Aveiro-Coimbra axis) and in some *distritos'* capitals in the interior (Viseu, Guarda, Castelo Branco, Portalegre) seems to indicate a growing spatial integration[10] involving the

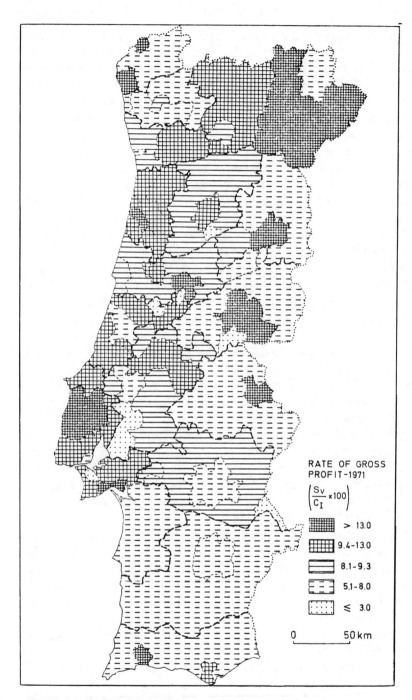

RATE OF GROSS
PROFIT-1971

$$\left(\frac{S_v}{C_I} \times 100\right)$$

> 13.0

9.4–13.0

8.1–9.3

5.1–8.0

≤ 3.0

0   50 km

Fig. 9.6 Regional variation in the rate of gross profit

expansion of the older industrial areas and the main urban agglomerations into more rural areas (areas having the advantages of reasonably low wages and a moderate level of both services and accessibility). On the other hand, the fact that a broad range of values is to be found within the more industrialized areas can be related to differences in the industrial structure within them; in particular between those having a less diversified structure, dominated by the more traditional sectors and even family capital (for example, the textile areas, 9 and 32) and the more advanced areas in capitalist terms. This is the situation when we compare rates of profit in the *distritos* of Oporto and Lisbon. A gradual increase in rate of profit towards the periphery of these *distritos* is to be found ($11 \rightarrow 12 \rightarrow 13$ and $45 \rightarrow 46 \rightarrow 47$) which is more than a simple coincidence and seems to confirm the arguments above concerning the process of industrialization in peripheral rural areas during the 1960s.

Various exceptions remain, however, to be explained. We cannot be sure, for example, whether the high values to be found in the north-eastern *distritos* (5, 7), on the one hand, and the low values of some *distrito* main towns, including Lisbon and Oporto on the other, are due to structural or to cyclical factors, and are thus to be regarded as 'abnormal'.[11] A similar problem arises with regard to the areas grouped in section C of Figure 9.5, where both levels of profit equalization defined cannot be related to the distribution. The two *concelhos* dominated by the iron industry (18 and 40) and the two wood-pulp plants in the interior (33 and 49) show values well above the national average.

Regardless of whether these exceptions result from structural or cyclical causes, they are not serious enough to refute the hypothesis of two different regional levels of primary equalization of profit closely linked to the development of the capitalist mode of production and to the growing integration of Portuguese space, as a result of increasing mobility of bank and finance capital, both national and foreign.

Finally, we must examine the part of the surplus value transferred to the state or the banks from each firm or zone (secondary equalization). The deduction from initial surplus value (S_V) of expenses, such as payment of rates, taxes, and interest (calculating thus S_V') allows us to define an indicator S_V'/S_V, which demonstrates the power of retention of surplus which the group of industries in each territorial unit has.

Whilst the result is not always easy to interpret,[12] it would seem that on the coast, the areas from Setúbal to Leiria, and in the interior, the main towns of *distritos*, have greatest powers of retention. The higher rates of retention often coincide with higher values of S_V/C_I. Thus they reveal an accentuation of inequalities already found,[13] without changing substantially the basic distribution (Figures 9.6 and 9.7).

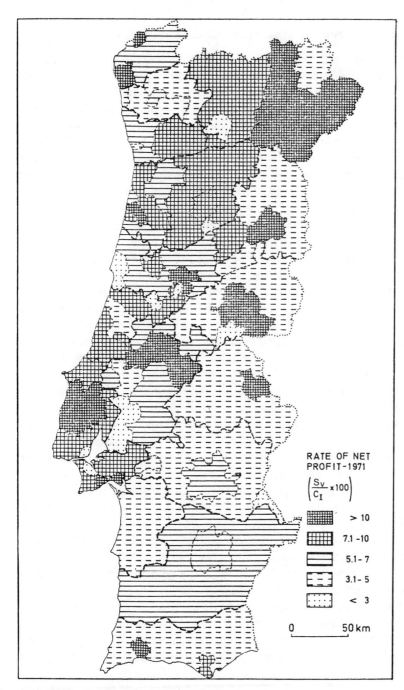

Fig. 9.7 Regional variation in the rate of net profit

Regional and sectoral analysis: similarities and differences

A fuller explanation of the different situations observed so far requires a study of the branches of manufacturing industry carried out in the same way as that for their combination in the 56 zones above. Hence we can distinguish 27 branches using the three-digit version of the Classification of Economic Activities. Their distribution in relation to organic composition of capital and rate of exploitation is shown in Figure 9.8 and shows a clear linear relationship for most of them. Indeed, 16 of the 27 branches can be combined into a single group (1) in which there is a high correlation between the two indices ($r = +0.95$) and the proximity of the Y intercept of the regression line to 0 suggests very similar rates of profit amongst them. This means that, amongst these branches, an increase in capital invested corresponds to a similar increase in retained surplus value. It is thus reasonable to assume a degree of profit equalization for these 16 with an average profit of 9.4 per cent and variation between 8.1 and 13.1 per cent.

However, even if the position of the points referring to branches 19 (other non-metallic mineral products), 23 (non-electrical machinery), 26 (professional and scientific instruments) and 27 (other industries) – those closest to the edges of the group – is due mainly to cyclical factors,[14] the same cannot be said for the remainder. The high rates of profit in the drinks (2), tobacco (3), rubber (15) and other chemical products (13) industries are due to different reasons. If the production of beer is distinguished from that of other drinks and added to 3 and 15, then this set of industries can reasonably be described as being highly concentrated, with heavy participation by finance capital (both national in the cases of beer and tobacco production and foreign in sectors 13 and 15), and producing for protected, or even monopolized, markets.

For those branches with a rate of profit just lower than average – publishing (11), petroleum refining and production of petroleum or coal derivates (14), and iron and steel production (20) – the first case seems to reflect an undervaluation of production rather than any special features of its production process while, in the other two branches, there are heavy fixed capital investments (and thus high amortization costs) as well as a lack of demand for their products in that year.

It is noticeable that average wages well above the national figure (40,000 and 34,000 escudos respectively) are almost entirely associated with branches outside of group 1 (8 out of the 11 cases). This could mean that for those points to the left of the cluster the level of wages has combined in this instance with the sorts of factors just mentioned so as to give low or even negative rates of profit. For those industries located to the right the

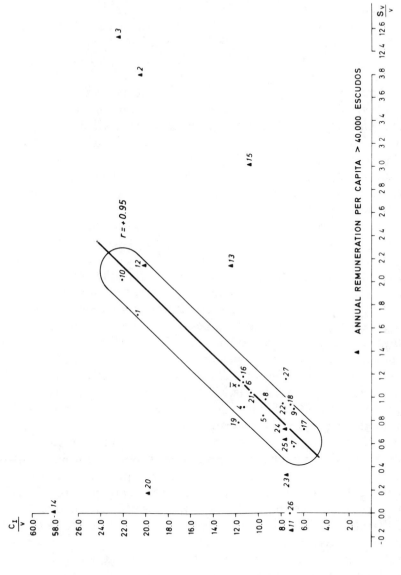

Fig. 9.8 Relationship between organic composition of capital and rate of surplus value (by industrial branch)

level of wages does not seem to cause problems; rather the opposite, for it is in the high wage sectors that the rates of exploitation are highest. As in the preceding analysis of regions, the highest rates of profit are largely based on the extraction of relative surplus value.

The relation between the different variables – organic composition of capital, rate of exploitation, rate of profit and average annual wage – as well as a new variable, the technical composition of capital,[15] in 22 branches[15] is given in Figure 9.9 which draws attention to the 'highly significant' correlations ($p \geq 0.001$). These confirm the extent to which observed rates of profit depend on high rates of exploitation and that these in turn are greatest when the organic and technical compositions of capital are high. The strong correlation between these two means that they can be treated as virtually identical, despite the fact that the level of wages is only strongly correlated ($r = +0.62$) with the latter. As far as this set of branches is concerned, differences in rates of profit between them thus appear to be fundamentally dependent on the extent to which the extraction of relative surplus value is dominant.

However, these conclusions have to be modified when the relationships between the same five variables are examined using the regional framework rather than by branches of production.[16] Thus, while the rate of profit for industries grouped in a zone is higher when the rate of exploitation is higher ($r = +0.50$) this could be the result of two completely different situations. Since there is not a statistically significant correlation between the organic and technical compositions of capital when examined spatially, a particular rate of exploitation could result from the super-exploitation of the workforce through very low wages and long hours or from the intensification of work and increased productivity, even though this may lead to high average wages. These are the two situations identified in the discussion of Figure 9.5 above where two distinct levels of equalization of rate of profit were established.

The statistically significant relationships between the five variables when considered separately for groups A (with relative surplus value extraction dominant) and group B (with absolute surplus value extraction dominant) bears out this interpretation. As regards group A, the correlation structure (summarized in Figure 9.9) is close to that for all branches of industry but in the zones that comprise group B there is less inter-relationship between variables and there is not even a significant correlation ($r = +0.26$) between the rate of profit and rate of exploitation.

The comparison of the results of each of these analyses – by zone and by branch of production – of profit equalization raises the question of their articulation. Is it possible, for example, to claim that the branches of group

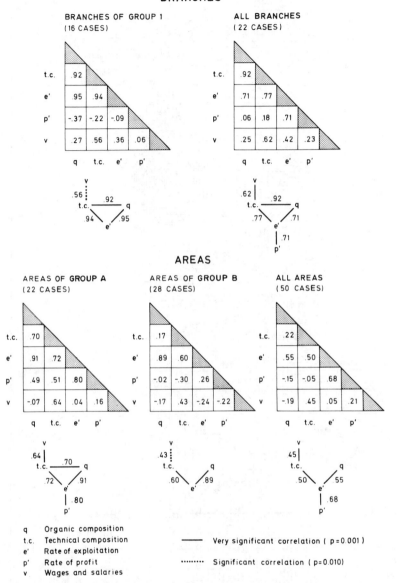

BRANCHES

BRANCHES OF GROUP 1
(16 CASES)

	q	t.c.	e'	p'
t.c.	.92			
e'	.95	.94		
p'	-.37	-.22	-.09	
v	.27	.56	.36	.06

```
        v
     .56 ⋮    .92
      t.c.━━━━━━q
        .94 \  / .95
            e'
```

ALL BRANCHES
(22 CASES)

	q	t.c.	e'	p'
t.c.	.92			
e'	.71	.77		
p'	.06	.18	.71	
v	.25	.62	.42	.23

```
        v
     .62 |    .92
      t.c.━━━━━━q
       .77 \  / .71
           e'
           | .71
           p'
```

AREAS

AREAS OF GROUP A
(22 CASES)

	q	t.c.	e'	p'
t.c.	.70			
e'	.91	.72		
p'	.49	.51	.80	
v	-.07	.64	.04	.16

```
        v
     .64 |    .70
      t.c.━━━━━━q
       .72 \  / .91
           e'
           | .80
           p'
```

AREAS OF GROUP B
(28 CASES)

	q	t.c.	e'	p'
t.c.	.17			
e'	.89	.60		
p'	-.02	-.30	.26	
v	-.17	.43	-.24	-.22

```
        v
     .43 ⋮
      t.c.     q
       .60 \  / .89
           e'
```

ALL AREAS
(50 CASES)

	q	t.c.	e'	p'
t.c.	.22			
e'	.55	.50		
p'	-.15	-.05	.68	
v	-.19	.45	.05	.21

```
        v
     .45 |
      t.c.     q
       .50 \  / .55
           e'
           | .68
           p'
```

q	Organic composition
t.c.	Technical composition
e'	Rate of exploitation
p'	Rate of profit
v	Wages and salaries

——— Very significant correlation (p=0.001)

········ Significant correlation (p=0.010)

Fig. 9.9 Relationships between organic and technical composition of capital, rate of exploitation, rate of profit and average wage levels

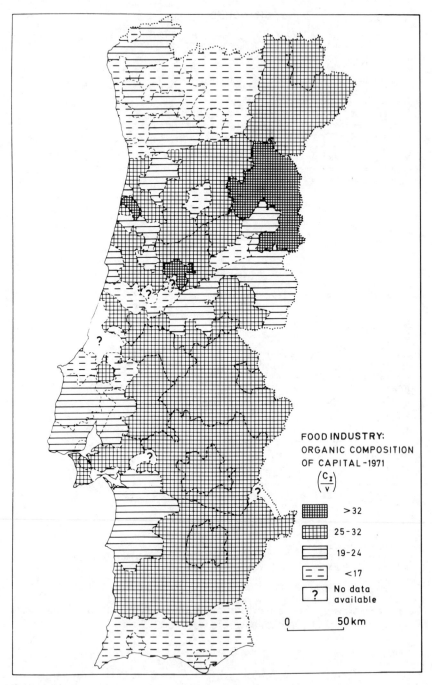

Fig. 9.10 Regional variation in the organic composition of capital in the food industry

1 dominate the zones designated as part of group B or the space to its left in Figure 9.9 or that members of group A dominate to its right? The basic problem is that the significance of the results for each of the zones depend on the degree of internal homogeneity and likewise with the results for the branches. Because internal differences have been submerged by treating industries in combination, it is not possible to link these initial results convincingly. The only way of testing hypotheses of this sort at present is by examining the regional distribution of profitability in each of the 27 branches. Unfortunately, in the majority of these the number of establishments in many of the zones is less than 4 (thus restricting the statistics on them published in the census), so that this kind of more detailed study runs into serious problems. Only the food industry can be seriously subjected to this type of analysis, because it does cover almost all of the country and the existence of some internal differentiation allows us to try to discover the links between this differentiation and its location in particular regions. The food industry has been considered as part of group I but has a relatively distinct position due to its high levels of organic composition and rate of exploitation. However, it does have a rate of profit of 9.6 per cent (when calculated for all the zones unaffected by statistical confidentiality) that is close enough to the average for all industries (9.4 per cent) to suggest comparisons with the preceding analyses and a test of their results.

The high value of organic composition is not only due to the low wages (29,000 escudos per capita compared with the average for industry of 34,000 escudos) but also to the amount of circulating capital – especially in the form of stocks. Indeed, this sector is the one in which circulating capital represents the largest proportion of all constant capital. Figure 9.10 showing the organic composition of capital of the industry does not differ significantly from the pattern for all industries together (Figure 9.3) in terms of relative position of the zones. The most industrialized areas – Lisbon and Oporto – and their surrounds have average or even below average values while the highest values are found particularly in the poorly industrialized *distritos* of the interior where this branch is, almost always, dominant. Yet the earlier pattern with values for the major centres of the *distritos* usually lower than for most, if not all, of the rest of the *distrito* is not so evident, even though the converse is clearly true in all but four cases (Faro, Castelo Branco, Leiria and Aveiro). Likewise when this is compared with the map of rates of profit by region (Figure 9.11), it allows us to confirm several of the points already made.

(a) The zones of above-average rates of profit are largely those with low and very low values of organic composition of capital and are – with a

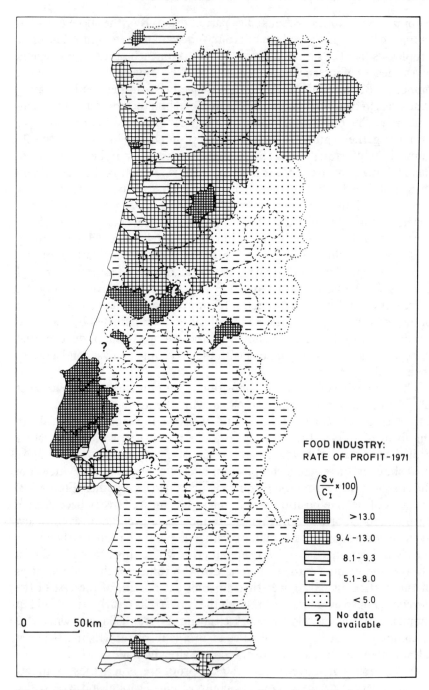

FOOD INDUSTRY:
RATE OF PROFIT-1971

$$\left(\frac{S_v}{C_I} \times 100\right)$$

▦	>13.0
▦	9.4 - 13.0
▤	8.1 - 9.3
▭	5.1 - 8.0
⋮	< 5.0
?	No data available

0   50km

Fig. 9.11 Regional variation in the rate of profit in the food industry

few exceptions such as in the north-east – in the more industrialized parts of the country. This is particularly so in Lisbon and some of the *distrito* capitals (Viana do Castelo, Vila Real, Viseu and Setúbal), areas where the industry was, in part, more organized, productive and commercialized, especially as regards synthetic foods, concentrates and margarine. The high rates of profit, however, come from a higher productivity and intensification of work which does not involve an increase in the value of organic composition of capital. This is much like the situation already described as typical of group A in Figure 9.5 and is also like that of the most advanced branches of group I in Figure 9.8.

(b) Most of the interior of the country has an above-average organic composition of capital while having rates of profit below the national average, a situation which is all the more serious when it is remembered that the food industry is often dominant in these areas. It is close to the type of relationship described for group B in which factories with a traditional and vulnerable productive structure are heavily dependent on the low wages that they pay.

(c) In zones 7, 19 and 26 (the less industrialized parts of Bragança, Viseu and Coimbra *distritos*), there is a meeting of the two extreme positions just described, with average values recorded for both indicators studied. In the first case, this reflects the influence of the agro-industrial complex at Cachão and in the other two cases it seems to be that of better conditions of accessibility than in the bulk of the interior.

The comparison between Figures 9.6 and 9.11, as well as showing the absence of any fundamental differences between the two patterns, suggests that in recent years virtually the only parts of the interior susceptible to more advanced forms of the valorization of capital are the major towns, in large part due to foreign investment.[17] Even considering the possible advantages that the production and commercialization of some industrial products might gain in terms of a lack of direct competition – indeed, almost a monopoly – as a result of isolation and low population totals, the traditional structure of the factories and low purchasing power of the people there are obstacles to the attainment of rates of profit close to the national average. However, this is not a 'natural' result of the characteristics of these areas themselves but rather relates to their role in the general reproduction of capital: that of a reserve of cheap, available labour. Since the role of each part of the country is essentially defined by the most advanced sectors of production, it can be concluded that the survival of these factories in the interior could easily be put into doubt by the imposition of another spatial division of labour as a result of new requirements for the reproduction of finance capital at national and international levels.

It should thus be clear that the regional articulation of different stages of the capitalist mode of production, illustrated by the existence of two levels of profit equalization, is not limited to that of manufacturing industry but rather extends to other sectors and can only be fully understood within an analysis of the whole Portuguese social formation.

A typology of industrial areas in 1971

The previous results allow us to devise a provisional typology of the different areas considered, based on the ways in which they are part of the processes of accumulation and valorization of capital in the industrial sector. Table 9.2 presents the basic categories and these are reviewed briefly below.

I The cities of Lisbon and Oporto

These are primarily associated with high-level management activities which means that a large number of industrial companies have their administrative headquarters there (Gaspar, 1977), ensuring their external relationships but also co-ordinating the growing economic and geographical integration within Portugal. The industrial establishments are quite heterogeneous, being comprised of those branches which are attracted to large-scale service centres – from small warehouses to publishing. Since Lisbon is the capital it is especially important for management functions but the distinction between the two cities in this respect is quantitative rather than qualitative in that it is correct to include them in the same group.

II The metropolitan areas of Lisbon and Oporto (including extensions)

In both cases there is considerable industrialization with above-average growth in 1965–71 and factories affected by economies of scale and agglomeration, but other characteristics are different enough to require a separate treatment. The Lisbon metropolitan area (II.1) is more internally homogeneous and generally is better placed. It appears the prototype of group A in Figure 9.5, with a dominance of relative surplus value and most of the establishments had strong links with finance capital (Instituto Nacional de Estatística, 1970 and 1972; Salgado Matos, 1973; Martins and Chaves Rosa, 1979; and Caixa Geral de Depósitos, 1981). Although only partially developed because of the subordinate position of the Portuguese economy, it is here that most technological research is carried out.

In Oporto metropolitan area and its extensions to the north and south (II.2), the links to finance capital, although important, are not as strong as in Lisbon and the area generally seems to represent a less advanced phase in the valorization of capital. The marked dispersal of settlement combined with factors mentioned above, such as strong links to rural life, limited development of trade unions or the importance of part-time work, has meant the continued survival of types of labour process and lifestyles that the process of industrialization often destroys.

III Areas peripheral to II

Although still little industrialized, these had a rapid percentage increase between 1965 and 1971. Thanks to their location close to the urban and industrial centres of this country, there has been a development of two distinct types of industry – those linked to an intensification of the processing of already existing resources (e.g. food or wood) and those located outside of region II in search of lower wages (especially in the small-scale enterprises found in sectors such as clothing and metal products).

IV Traditional industrial areas of the littoral

These industrial enclaves in largely rural areas were initiated due to their raw materials, energy supplies or transport facilities. Their varying significance and general character illustrates how the viability of traditional sectors has become dependent on the penetration of finance capital. While such areas are usually dominated by industrial capital – and even sometimes family capital – the importance of finance capital is clear from the examples of the leading branches (glass in Marinha Grande, paper in Tomar, Constância, Lousa and Gois) and establishments (e.g. Fabrica Mendes Godinho or Metalúrgica Duarte Ferreira). The principal influence on industrial development in most of this region was its central position in the country as most production was for the internal market.

V Traditional industrial areas of the interior

Although similar in origin to IV these zones are fundamentally different today due to their dependence on family industrial capital and limited diversification (since wool textiles dominate) or mobility. This, linked to

Table 9.2 *Typology of Portuguese industrial areas in 1971*

Type of area	Zones included	Degree of industrialization 1970	Industrial growth 1965–71	Wages per capita 1971	Rate of profit 1971	Rate of exploitation 1971	Organic composition 1971	Technical composition 1971	Notes	Dominant group in terms of profit levels
I Principal metropoles	11, 45	Quite high	Quite low	Quite high	$<\bar{x}$ nat.	Low	Low	Quite high	Dominance of management functions.	B
II Metropolitan areas of I and extensions	II.1: 39, 40, 41, 46	High	Quite high	High	$>\bar{x}$ nat.	Variable	Quite low	High	Strong links to national and international finance capital. Considerable research facilities.	A
	II.2: 9, 12, 15	High	Quite high	Average	Variable	Average	Average	Average	The same as II.1 but less pronounced. Indirect links to international capital over technology and markets.	Both
III Rural areas close to II	13, 16, 30, 37, 47, 50	Average	High	Quite low	$>\bar{x}$ nat.	III$_1$ High III$_2$ Quite low	Low	Quite high	Dominance of industrial capital.	A
IV Old industrial areas in the littoral	25, 28, 29, 36, 55	High	Variable	Average	$>\bar{x}$ nat.	Variable	Variable	Variable	Dominance of industrial capital, sometimes family, but with a significant element of national finance capital in some branches and large firms.	A
V Traditional industrial areas in the interior	21, 32	Quite high	Low	Average	$<\bar{x}$ nat.	Quite low	Quite low	Quite low	Dominance of family industrial capital with local origins and little diversification.	B

(continued)

Table 9.2—continued

Type of area	Zones included	Degree of industrial-ization 1970	Industrial growth 1965–71	Wages per capita 1971	Rate of profit 1971	Rate of exploitation 1971	Organic composition 1971	Technical composition 1971	Notes	Dominant group in terms of profit levels
VI *Distrito* capitals	1, 4, 6, 8, 14, 17, 20, 23, 27, 31, 35, 43, 48, 52, 54	Average	Variable	Average	Variable	Variable	Quite high	Variable	Important foreign direct investment.	Both
VII Rural areas away from II	The rest	Low	Quite low	Low	$\leqslant$ nat.	Quite high	High	Quite high	Dominance of industrial capital.	B

Note: x̄ nat. = national average.

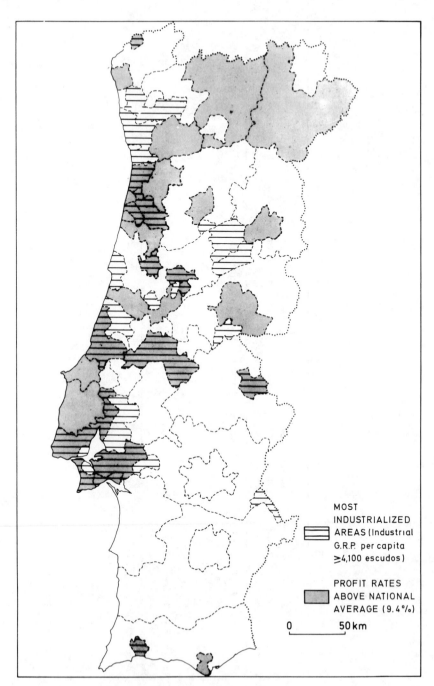

MOST
INDUSTRIALIZED
AREAS (Industrial
G.R.P. per capita
≥4,100 escudos)

PROFIT RATES
ABOVE NATIONAL
AVERAGE (9.4%)

0   50 km

Fig. 9.12 Industrialization and profitability

their poor accessibility, explains the losses that they have had and below-average profitability

VI Distrito capitals

This group also appears to be relatively heterogeneous but clearly provides conditions which attract foreign direct investment: Grundig (Braga); Pextrafil (Viseu), Renault (Guarda), ICI (Portalegre) and Siemens (Évora) are but the best examples. The availability of a cheap labour force is one of the principal advantages, especially for the location of intermediate or final stages of larger production circuits which basically involve unskilled assembly work. Unlike the case above (V), the spatial division of labour that results is more intra-sectoral than inter-sectoral. However, much as this may explain the high rates of profit, there are also considerations such as local markets in their industrialization.

VII Marginal rural areas

With some local exceptions, these have few industrial establishments that are small and in open competition, often underequipped with a heavy dependence on banks and below-average profits. This type of industrialization reflects the limits imposed by the role of these areas in the current spatial division of labour – a labour reserve.

Figure 9.12 combines the extent of industrialization with the location of areas of above-average profit to demonstrate the roles of regional types III and IV in the growing integration of the national space. With the exception of the north-east which has peculiarities already discussed, they are the only ones where there are good rates of profit despite limited industrial development. This is linked to local advantages which facilitate the presence of more advanced forms both in production processes and in the methods of valorizing capital.

Conclusions

The changes since the revolution of 25 April 1974 have altered the situation described above, in some respects quite substantially. A large number of private sector firms are in crisis: the new labour laws (especially the collective wage contracts at a national level which help reduce some regional disparities) and the strengthening of trade unions have encouraged wage rises which threaten the survival of numerous factories which depended on the extraction of absolute surplus value. There were also cases of capital flight and a general reduction in both national and foreign investment. At the same time the nationalization of basic industries such as petroleum refineries, steel, basic chemicals, shipbuilding, cement and cellulose and state intervention in over two hundred firms lead to abandonment by the management, economic sabotage or, quite simply, collapse. Besides, the nationalization of the banks did create opportunities to take indirect control over a number of firms.

Even though I do not have data which allow an empirical investigation of these changes, it is possible to suggest that the inter-regional difference between two levels of profit equalization that were identified above has tended to decline – particularly through the disintegration of group B – giving rise to a more dispersed pattern. It is less easy to know if this lack of profit equalization, which results not only from the internal changes noted but also from the global crisis of capitalism, is temporary or permanent. The future integration of Portugal into the EC will certainly help to resolve this question but it remains to be seen what the cost of this 'necessary' restructuring will be for a large number of factories.

Notes

1 For criticisms of employing organic composition of capital as the central variable see Vergoupolos (1978) and Jensen-Butler (1981).

2 For a criticism of analysis based on predefined areas see Lipietz (1977) and Massey (1978b).

3 Mainland Portugal is divided into 18 *distritos* for administrative purposes, which are further divided into 275 *concelhos*.

4 The information used here only refers to establishments in manufacturing industry with five or more employees which were covered by the latest Industrial Census which took place in 1972 (and refers to December 1971).

5 It is, in fact, apparent surplus value which can be calculated from the data published. This refers to factory prices and is thus already equalized.

6 The organic composition of each of the areas is obtained by dividing the total capital invested – C_I (i.e. the amount of fixed and circulating constant capital together with the total of wages paid) by the total wages of productive workers – v. Productive workers' wages are (following Pereira) the wages paid to the workers together with half of the salaries received by the management, technical and office staff, because it becomes impossible in practice to distinguish the amount earned by those directly involved in the productive process.

7 Calculated by dividing the apparent surplus value S_V – (gross value added less the gross total of depreciation and wages and salaries paid) by the amount of wages and salaries paid to productive personnel – v.

8 This value is lower than Pereira (1974) (20 per cent), as it covers all establishments in manufacturing industry with five or more employees and not only the 226 most important.

9 Without implying their mutual exclusion in geographic space. In reality, there is a predominance of one or the other of the stages.

10 Integration in the sense of Lipietz (1977, 1980a).

11 It is possible to put forward some explanatory hypotheses for certain cases. The predominance of the drinks sector – mineral water and wine – with low levels of investment in zone 5, and the existence of an agro-industrial complex (at Cachão) of much bigger dimension than is usual for rural areas in zone 7, may at least partly explain the high rates of profit found there. At the other extreme, the situation in Lisbon and Oporto may be due to a combination of several factors such as the large number of small firms, the limited replacement of fixed capital in some of the older plants, the higher average wages and the relative importance of the printing industry in this sectoral mix.

12 A high level of retention may, for example, reflect, at one extreme, limited development out of contact with the banking system, and at the other the existence of intense penetration of financial capital and/or strong state protection.

13 S_V/C_I and S_V/C have coefficients of variation of 0.5 and 0.8 respectively.

14 This is not to suggest, however, that the position of each of these branches on the graph is solely due to cyclical factors. For example, the above-average rate of profit in branch 26 is partly due to the presence of the diamond firm Sociedade Portuguesia de Lapidacao de Diamantes.

15 Defined as the sum of fixed and circulating constant capital per worker but not calculated for the anomalous branches 3, 11, 14, 20 and 26.

16 Zones 2, 18, 29, 33, 40 and 49 have been excluded from consideration because of their atypicality.

17 The few scattered cellulose factories are an obvious exception.

10

The rural Languedoc: periphery to 'relictual space'

Nico Kielstra

Introduction

In this chapter I shall try to argue that the concept of 'peripherization', with the meanings usually given to it, is not sufficient to describe the social-economic developments taking place in the Languedoc area in southern France. Similar arguments could probably be set up for various problem areas elsewhere in Southern Europe.

During the last two decades social scientists have used the concept of a 'periphery' in contrast to a 'centre' or 'core' in a rather loose sense whenever they find unequal exchanges on a regional basis. A peripheral region provides cheap products and/or labour to a core region in exchange for more expensive and profitable and/or technologically highly developed products and highly skilled and paid labour. Implicitly, it is usually assumed that the core region has a much more differentiated economic system than a peripheral region and that it controls the flow of capital in the economic system as a whole. As a provider of cheap products and/or labour and a market for more expensive products and labour, a 'periphery' fulfils essential economic functions for a 'centre', though it does not receive a proportionate share in the social and economic benefits produced by the economic system as a whole. The concept of a 'periphery', however one may want to define it exactly, always refers to the integration of an area and its population into a larger economic system.

I shall argue that the Languedoc has played such a peripheral role in the recent past, while in the more remote past it has played a central role in a different economic system. Recently, however, even its peripheral integration in a wider French and Western European economic system has been declining, and the region is moving into a position that cannot adequately be described in terms of the current centre-periphery models.

To describe and analyse such a situation in which the economic integration of an area in a wider economic system is breaking down I shall try to develop the concept of *relictual space*. This term (*zone reliquaire* in French) was, as far as I know, first used by the French geographer Marthelot (1974) in an analysis of the different regional effects of the Algerian agrarian revolution. Marthelot uses the term for agricultural areas where a concentration of agricultural activity into a relatively small number of fairly large and capital-intensive enterprises has not taken place. As a consequence such areas have not been touched by socialist reforms of large agricultural enterprises along collectivist or co-operative lines in countries (like Algeria) where such reforms have taken place. Such *relictual spaces* are typically areas where moderately favourable agricultural conditions led in the pre-industrial period to a relatively dense population of small peasant-owners. Some large landownership may exist, but agricultural profit rates were not sufficiently high to stimulate the further development of large landed properties. Available capital reserves were mainly invested outside the area. Conditions were favourable enough to enable small peasant-owners to modernize their enterprises sufficiently to survive the first period of integration into a nationwide market economy. In the present, however, faced with a highly competitive international market system, the concentration of wholesale activities in the hands of large corporations and high rates of interest on credits, small farmers are no longer able to keep their enterprises economically viable. Even the bigger ones amongst them do not have enough capital reserves to buy up enough land to extend their farms into large-scale capitalist enterprises, while profit rates are too low to attract outside entrepreneurs. Such an area first experiences economic stagnation and then a slow but steady decline, while no new economic activities develop to take the place of the old agriculture. Marthelot mentions Kabylia and the Tunisian Sahel area as examples of such a development in North Africa. I shall argue that the Languedoc (and particularly its wine-growing area) constitutes a French example (Bretagne may be another one). In his brief paper Marthelot says little about the further economic, social and political development that may take place in such relictual spaces. After giving a factual description of developments in the Languedoc I shall attempt some speculations on this point.

'Relictual space' is, like 'periphery', a concept on a fairly high level of abstraction. Regions to which it is applied may show considerable individual differences, while in some borderline cases its application may be a matter of discussion as such. Both concepts can be useful, however, not as shortcuts to a detailed description and analysis, but to focus attention on a specific type of position of a region in a wider economic system.

The economic history of Languedoc

For the sake of simplicity I shall limit my factual presentation to the area of Languedoc proper, i.e. the area that constituted the old province of Languedoc, and which now comprises the *départements* of Gard, Hérault, Aude and Haute-Garonne, the southern parts of the departments of Tarn, Aveyron and Lozère and part (the old county of Foix) of the department Ardèche. The regionalist movement in the area likes to talk in terms of a much larger and more vaguely defined area, the Occitanie, which includes the whole area between the Atlantic and the Italian border and between the northern fringes of the Plateau Central and the Pyrenees with the exception of small Basque- and Catalan-speaking areas in the Pyrenees. The Occitanie is basically an historical linguistic concept: the area where related dialects of the 'langue d'oc' were spoken before French came into general use. It has never constituted an economic or political unit. Statistically, it may be argued that this whole southern part of France scores below average on various indices of prosperity and development.[1] Economic conditions show a wide variety, however. The Languedoc proper is not a homogeneous area either. Outside the urban centres we can distinguish at least three agricultural areas: the wine-growing regions along the coast and in the valleys of the Hérault and the Aude; the wheat-growing plains around Toulouse; and the mountain areas, formerly used for sheep farming and now partly abandoned. The formerly little inhabited narrow coastal strip where large tourist projects have been developed in the last twenty years may count as a fourth economic zone. Before the French Revolution the Languedoc was an administrative unit and a more or less integrated economic whole, however, and economic heterogeneity has increased with time.

Occitan regionalists like to talk about the Cathar heresy and the crusade of the northern French nobility against it in the early thirteenth century, as the period when the possibility of developing an independent southern state was missed. In fact, the Languedoc before the anti-Cathar crusade, in large part under the rule of the counts of Toulouse, was more a neutral buffer zone between the developing kingdoms of France and Aragon than a state. Other embryonic southern states like the duchy of Aquitaine, the kingdom of Provence and the ephemeral Catalan kingdom of Majorca with its capital in Perpignan were not repressed in such a dramatic way, but did not survive either as independent political units. A relative poverty in economic resources compared with the north of France may already then have weakened the southern regions.

Political submission to the kingdom of France did not yet mean economic integration in a national French economy, however. Though modern regionalists have paid relatively little attention to the fact, it can be maintained that in the seventeenth and eighteenth centuries the Languedoc was less part of a French national economic system than of a Mediterranean economic system, and that within this Mediterranean economic system it played a central rather than a peripheral role.[2]

The Languedocian economic system was then based on polyculture (wheat, olives, wine, sheep farming), the products of which were both traded within the region and exported, while sheep farming provided the primary material for a regional, export-orientated drapery industry. The Lower Languedoc is a region of river valleys separated by high limestone plateaus (the *garrigue*, as the local term goes). In the valleys wheat and some other cereals were cultivated on a subsistence basis, while some of the wettest lands were used as water meadows. On the slopes between the valley and the *garrigue* olive orchards and vineyards were planted. These provided for local needs in wine and oil, but also produced an exportable surplus. The *garrigue*, already deforested in prehistory, was used for sheep farming. The wool was sold to draperies in the region. Inland, towards Toulouse, the *garrigue* uplands disappear and the country becomes an uninterrupted high plain. The olive tree disappears in the cooler inland climate, vineyards become more marginal and wheat cultivation more abundant. This is the only area in the Languedoc that ever produced a wheat surplus. To the north and south of the Lower Languedoc and the inland plains we find partly forested mountain ridges. Settlement concentrates in narrow valleys where some agriculture is carried out, but sheep farming on the mountain pastures, sometimes combined with exploitation of the forests, becomes the dominant part of the economy. It was in these areas that wool industries developed in some of the towns in the valleys. The mountain areas also saw some marginal mining activities and a small-scale iron industry in the Ardèche.

Both internal and external trade were stimulated in the second half of the seventeenth century, when the French royal government constructed the new seaport of Sète, while the Canal du Midi, linking the Mediterranean to the lower Garonne river and thus to the Atlantic, was constructed as a combined enterprise by the royal government, the estates of Languedoc (the provincial governing body in which the nobility, the clergy and the main urban centres were represented) and a capitalist entrepreneur from the region. The canal made cheap transportation in bulk possible between the Lower Languedoc and the Toulouse area.

Wheat from the inland plains was now sold to the Lower Languedoc, where local production was only sufficient in good years, while the marginal viticulture in the Toulouse area disappeared in the eighteenth century under the competition of better-quality wines from the Lower Languedoc. Animals (sheep, donkeys, mules, cattle) were bred in the mountain areas and traded with the plains and the Lower Languedoc in exchange for wheat, oil and wine. Some animals were also exported into Spain, but most exports went by sea through the ports of Sète and Marseilles (which held a monopoly on drapery exports).

Wine and spirits (in the seventeenth century also some olive oil) were exported to the coastal cities of Provence, northern Italy, Catalonia, but also directly to Northern Europe. Drapery was exported all over the Mediterranean as far as the Levant. While some wine was being sold to Paris, trade with northern France was kept at a low level by a combination of expensive transportation and high tolls and internal customs duties.

The economic advantage of Languedoc as an export producer over other Mediterranean regions like Italy and Catalonia was probably not due to favourable natural conditions, but to reasonably efficient government and a temporary advance in economic development. At the same time the region was to some degree economically self-supporting and, except in years of crop failure, not very dependent on imports for its basic needs. As a consequence an accumulation of capital took place in the region, which became a capital exporter. Capital exports started as a reaction to political conditions when Protestant merchants fled the religious persecutions under Louis XIV to Switzerland and the Protestant countries of Northern Europe. The emigrants did not return, however, when the persecution of Protestants died down during the eighteenth century. On the contrary, emigration to Paris, where they engaged in large tax farming and national finance, became a standardized final phase in the social ascent of wealthy southern merchant families in the eighteenth century. Such capital export demonstrates the relative prosperity of the Languedoc in that period, but it also shows a basic weakness in the Languedocian economy of the period, which evidently offered few prospects for profitable further expansion.

The central position of the Languedoc in the Mediterranean trade system broke down in the period of the French Revolution and the Napoleonic wars, when British naval dominance in the Mediterranean wrecked French seaborne trade. This loss of export markets did not immediately ruin the regional economy. The economic isolation of France in wartime led to high agricultural prices, and the textile industry changed to cheaper-quality products for the French internal market and especially for the French army. After 1815, however, the region could not reconquer its former export markets, while integration in the French national economic system took place under unfavourable conditions. Though tolls and internal customs duties disappeared (the entry duty of wine into the city of Paris was only lifted in 1861), transportation from the south to Paris and northern France remained slow and expensive. The Mediterranean trade system was at the same time expanded to include cheaper production areas (West Africa for cheap vegetable oils, the Ukraine for cheap wheat). Between 1815 and 1861 France followed in theory a protectionist policy for agricultural products, but the system was never effectively used to protect the farmers. Wholesalers were interested in cheap imported products, and urban industrialists in low food prices to keep wages low, and these interests usually prevailed in political practice.[3]

Commercial wine growing remained economically feasible, and viticulture was extended somewhat, but the development of a nationwide market for wine was still prevented by expensive transportation. French colonization in Algeria since the 1830s created at first a new market for wines from the Languedoc. When French rule was gradually extended to the southern steppe areas of Algeria, however, this started a flow of cheap Algerian wool to the French market, which started the decline of sheep farming in the mountain areas of southern France. The ruin of sheep farming was completed when even larger quantities of cheap Australian wool began to reach the European markets in the 1880s. The mountain areas of Languedoc thus lost their main source of income and a process of depopulation of these mountain areas started, which has continued till the present day.

The textile industry in the Languedoc had been in a bad position from the beginning of the machine age, since it had to bring in coal from a distance. When the Second Empire (1851–70) turned to a free trade policy and withdrew army orders from the southern textile industry in favour of larger and more modern enterprises elsewhere, the old textile industry in Languedoc rapidly disappeared together with many small-scale traditional industries in other rural areas of France. The de-industrialization of the French countryside and the concentration of industrial activities around a few urban centres began in this period.

Agriculture in the coastal plains and valleys of Lower Languedoc and on the high plains of Upper Languedoc was saved by the development of a nationwide railway system in the second half of the nineteenth century, which made cheap transportation in bulk to the consumer centres in the north possible. Commercial wheat growing and mixed agriculture in the Upper Languedoc followed the usual pattern of development in European agriculture: a slow concentration into an ever smaller number of fairly large family enterprises. In the Lower Languedoc a quite different and rather untypical development took place, however.

Because of continuously low wheat prices and the opening up of a rapidly growing consumer market for cheap table wines in northern France, wheat growing was completely abandoned in the Lower Languedoc between 1855 and 1870, and almost all available land came to be used for the monoculture of wine. (A little barley was still grown as horse fodder and a few specialized vegetable growers supplied the local market.) The regional bourgeoisie invested its capital in vineyards and in the wholesale trade in wine. This agricultural specialization went together with the simultaneous decline and final abandonment of almost all other productive activities in the region. The urban centres became commercial and administrative centres for the surrounding wine-growing areas, but developed no important industrial activities of their own.

The period between about 1855 and 1875 is remembered in popular tradition as an unprecedented boom period, but contemporary documents offer a somewhat more modest picture. Crop failures because of plant pests or climatic conditions and rapid price fluctuations caused problems for the winegrowers even then. Agricultural wages remained low, till the agricultural labourers began to constitute effective syndical organizations in 1904.[4] The problem of seasonal unemployment of the agricultural labour force was never solved, till the partial mechanization of viticulture in the 1950s made much of this labour superfluous.

Nevertheless, viticulture was a very labour-intensive form of agriculture and net productivity per hectare was relatively high. This led to the fixation of a previous, pre-modern pattern of landownership and agrarian social structures. Large domains, which had their origin centuries back, survived though not always under the same owners. Small farmers could, however, also survive because of the relatively high productivity per hectare. The gradual concentration of agricultural activities in an ever-smaller number of middle-sized to large enterprises therefore did not take place in the wine-growing area. Even a large number of part-time wine-growers survived. Viticulture offered abundant though rather modestly paid employment and the old social category of part-time small farmers, part-time labourers therefore survived in large numbers.

Between 1876 and 1885, when a plant pest, phylloxera, ruined the French vineyards, large-scale commercial viticulture was started in Algeria. When the vineyards in the Languedoc had recovered from phylloxera in the 1890s, while Algerian viticulture was still rapidly growing (it was the only really profitable agricultural activity for the French colonists in Algeria), viticulture (at least for cheap table wines) was hit by an overproduction crisis that has remained chronic since 1900. This crisis did not lead to a concentration of viticulture in large enterprises, however. Since net profit rates remained low, even large winegrowers could not build up sufficient reserves to enlarge their enterprises. When agricultural wage-labour became more and more expensive during the twentieth century, it became definitely unprofitable to extend an enterprise to a much larger size than could be worked by family labour. If most large domains survived, this was because land became a more or less inflation-proof refuge value for investors in the period of rapid inflation since the First World War, and not because they were very profitable in themselves. The same reason, however, made small landowners reluctant to sell, even if they could no longer work their land themselves. (Such small properties were often rented by agricultural labourers as an additional source of income.) When vineyards came up for sale, they were often not bought by large landowners but as a safe investment for their savings by small entrepreneurs from outside the agricultural sector (shopkeepers, crafts-men, building contractors). This tendency has yet been strengthened in the recent period when rates of interest on loans have become higher than the net profit rates on vineyards. A vineyard may still be a worthwhile investment if it can be bought for cash, but it is completely unprofitable to buy it on credit.

The only part of viticultural activity in which 'economies of scale' have a considerable effect, and in which small winegrowers might be unable to provide the necessary investments, is the process of vinification. This problem had been solved, however, by the foundation of co-operative caves. The first of these were already founded in the first decade of the twentieth century, but a network of them covering all villages was devel-oped in the 1930s. They enable small winegrowers to use modern equip-ment for vinification and storage at a modest investment. In the last decades the co-operatives have also been handling the sale of wine from (small) producers to wholesalers. Only a few per cent of the largest wine-growers still maintain private caves and handle their own sales.

The disappearance of small winegrowers, which had been predicted since the beginning of the twentieth century, has for these reasons not taken place. The whole of viticulture in the Languedoc has, however, since 1900 become strongly dependent on government protection in the form of quality controls, unprofitable use of expensive wine alcohol (instead of cheaper sugar beet alcohol) for industrial purposes by the state alcohol monopoly, a protectionist international trade policy, and since the 1930s a system of controls and restrictions on the national wine market.[5]

When a whole region became dependent on the monoculture of a single market crop, this gave an original stimulus to a hitherto stagnant agricultural economic system, which enabled traditional agrarian structures to survive at a time when a rural exodus began to empty other parts of the French countryside from both its rural bourgeoisie and its rural proletariat, leaving behind only an ever-decreasing number of middle-sized farmers. This was also a form of peripherization, however, making the region dependent on the vagaries of a single commodity market over which it had no control. The overproduction crisis since 1900 came about because of developments outside the Languedoc. Only a national French government, on which the region had only a very limited influence, could provide some degree of protection against the consequences of this overproduction crisis.

Some such government protection came, however, as it did in many similar cases under the Third and Fourth French Republics. The 'rentier mentality' of the ruling French bourgeoisie under the Third and Fourth Republics has often been disapproved of. Their policy of modernizing the French economy and social structure while protecting them as much as possible from foreign competition and influence has, on the whole and in the long run, been moderately successful, however. French economic development was not spectacular, but the country escaped both the long-term economic stagnation and gradual decline of Britain, or the descent into a peripheral international position of, for example, Spain and Italy. The country played no longer a dominant role in Europe, but escaped from the political upheavals of Germany, Italy and Spain. When the Gaullist regime in the 1960s returned to a free market policy and to attempts at international economic expansion, France had both the capital reserves and the modern infrastructures to hold itself amongst the modern world powers.

In the field of agriculture this policy led to the development of a number of potential 'relictual spaces', where traditional agrarian structures survived the first impact of the market economy, but were unable to keep up with the demands of the market in a later stage, when protectionist measures failed or were withdrawn. Protectionist measures had gradually to be taken off when France joined the EC, which forbids most forms of protectionism. The replacement of the neo-liberal regime that had governed France since 1958 by a socialist regime can only make a limited difference. The EC is fundamentally based on a free trade policy between member states and, contrary to their British counterparts, the French socialists have no intention whatsoever of abandoning the EC.

EC free trade regulations were extended to viticulture in 1971, but in the two decades before that date viticulture (and wholesale trading in wine) had already undergone some structural changes which made it more vulnerable. Viticulture was partly mechanized in the 1950s, which led to a sharp decline in the employment of full-time agricultural labourers. At the same time the wholesale trade in wine was taken over from small family enterprises established in the regions of production by large corporations which have their seats near the consumer centres. This too led to some loss of employment in the regions of production. During the same period the gradual growth of the welfare state made working conditions in various forms of urban employment so much more attractive than those in a stagnant, small-scale viticulture, that the young generations began to leave the wine-growing areas of the Lower Languedoc in large numbers. Small-scale viticulture has typically become an affair of elderly small farmers, who reached adulthood during the 1940s and are now in their fifties or early sixties, whose heirs have left. In the next ten or twenty years many of their vineyards will come up for sale or rent and large winegrowers have accumulated too few capital reserves to take them over. For part-time winegrowers who have found non-agricultural employment within the region, wine growing has become less important as an additional source of income. As a consequence they can less easily be mobilized for the defence of viticultural interests than in the past, while the younger generation is becoming reluctant to spend their spare time working their vineyards. In this sector too an increasing offer of vineyards for sale or rent will meet a stagnant or decreasing demand. Even before EC regulations forced France in 1971 to repeal the system of market regulations for wine which should prevent the complete breakdown of wine prices and to open its market for cheap Italian wines, the over-production crisis in viticulture had worsened. The decrease in imports of Algerian wine after Algerian independence in 1962 was offset by a steady decline in average yearly consumption *per capita* in France (from 156 litres in the period 1928–38 to 127 litres in the period 1961–3 and 108·6 litres in 1975). After 1971 the French market was thrown open for cheap Italian wines, and though the imported quantities are relatively small, they help to keep overall wine prices low. A new influx of cheap wine is feared when Spain and Portugal enter the EC.

No economic alternatives for wine growing (and sheep farming in the mountain areas) were found. Fruit and vegetable growing, which can produce as high or higher a yield per hectare than wine, were recommended during the 1950s and early 1960s, but overproduction in this sector soon became even worse than in viticulture and further extension was stopped. This sector too is now faced by the competition of cheap Italian produce. EC agronomists have suggested a transition to soya bean growing, but nobody in the region knows much about the technical or commercial aspects of soya bean growing, while the earlier failure of fruit and vegetable farming has done little to stimulate confidence in official recommendations. Soya bean cultivation would probably only be profitable on large, highly mechanized farms, and nobody has the necessary starting capital to develop these.

In the 1950s there was much talk about 'decentralization' of industry, but this has remained as much an empty slogan in the Languedoc as elsewhere in Western Europe. In the past new industries have sometimes settled in rural areas, because labour was cheap and docile there, while technical qualifications were less important than nowadays. These advantages have disappeared now, and the additional costs of transportation and of attracting skilled labour from other areas effectively discourage industries from settling in remote rural areas. (Special tax advantages which might compensate for these higher costs are forbidden by EC regulations.) Few small and no large private industries have therefore settled in the region. A steel plant in Fos on the Mediterranean coast set up at great expense by the French government, turned out as an economic failure (Bleitrach and Chenu, 1982). During the economic crisis of the second half of the 1970s some of the few existing small industries have even disappeared.

A somewhat more viable economic alternative was the development of tourism. The thinly populated, swampy, mosquito-infected coastal strip of the Languedoc, suffering from strong winds most of the year, was long left out of the development of tourism on the Mediterranean coast. Montpellier, Beziers, Narbonne and Carcassonne began to profit, during the 1960s, from their location on the tourist roads to Spain, but tourists did not stay in the area. In the early 1960s, however, the French government founded a mixed (public and private) syndicate, financed by some investment bankers, to develop the coastal area between Sète and the Spanish border into a tourist zone. This project was successful at least on a superficial level. Some fifteen years later, mosquitoes have been eradicated and a range of new touristic centres have been constructed along the coast which now attract several hundreds of thousands of tourists each summer.

The cultural impact of this large influx of tourists is regarded with mixed feelings by the regional population, but, more important in the present context, the overall economic impact has been less than expected. The projects are financed by outside financiers and most of the profits are consequently not reinvested in the region. Regional building contractors are usually not big enough to participate in the construction. The new tourist centres are at some distance from older centres of population, so that the tourists spend most of their money not in existing shops, restaurants, etc., but in newly established ones in the new centres. Employment in these new centres is strictly seasonal and relatively limited. Most of the new tourist accommodation is in the form of secondary residences for sale or rent, which seems to be the most profitable form of touristic investment for project developers, but also the one that creates least employment. There are some camp sites, but very few hotels. Mass tourism is limited to a narrow coastal strip. Inland tourism has developed on a much more modest scale. Some of the tourists there are emigrants from the region who come to spend their holidays with their parents or other relatives. The outsiders are catered for by some private or municipal camp sites, small private hotels and private houses let for rent during the summer. Most of this tourist accommodation is based on local initiative, but the additional income and employment it creates are insufficient to stop the exodus of young people from the area. Outside project developers begin to infiltrate into the inland mountain areas, where land is cheap, to construct ghetto-like holiday villages there. These create some additional commerce for local shopkeepers, but drive up land prices for local people who want to extend their farms or build new houses. In general one can say that tourism creates additional profits or employment for a small part of the local population, but that it does not create any new stimulus for the declining agriculture and industry in the region. In fact it stimulates the abandonment of agriculture by raising non-agrarian land prices, while it does not create new year-round employment to replace the old agrarian employment. It is feared that a similar development will take place in the viticultural areas when many vineyards will be abandoned there during the next two decades.

The Lower Languedoc is thus losing even its previous peripheral integration into the national French economic system. It is losing its function of producer of cheap agricultural consumer goods to even cheaper foreign competitors. Its only newly acquired socio-economic function as a touristic area cannot create the necessary employment to maintain a stable population even at a lower level than at present. Even the peripheral function of being a breeding ground for cheap migrant labour is disappearing. In the 1970s, in France as elsewhere in the Western world, overall employment has been stagnant or declining, while cheap unskilled labour is recruited from North Africa or some countries in black Africa. In the smaller rural communities an increasing part of the population is becoming *bricoleurs*, exploiting a bit of land of their own, doing an occasional odd job of wage-labour in agriculture or construction or holding part-time jobs in public agencies or the tourist industry and drawing some additional old-age pensions or social security payments. This is not a new way of making a living: the pre-industrial rural semi-proletariat lived that way, and in the viticultural Languedoc with its many part-time agriculturists the tradition has never disappeared. Elderly people have little choice but to go on living this way, and some young people are willing to adopt such a way of life for private reasons of their own. When such a way of life is, however, neither a relic of the past nor a refuge for a small number of dropouts, but the only possible way to survive in a region for an increasing number of its inhabitants, then the economic integration of that region in a wider economic system has evidently failed. There are still some possibilities for outside investment in the Lower Languedoc, in the tourist industry, but these investments hardly need the regional population, nor are they essential for the well-being of the national economy.

The changing social context

The economic decline and gradual depopulation of the region are not in themselves unique. Several, usually mountainous, areas of Western Europe have been largely abandoned by their population in the last 150 years. The rural exodus in many parts of France since the 1850s seems to have caused little social protest in general. City life attracted young people and regional groups often established their own more or less protected socio-economic niche in the new urban environment.[6] Traditional peasant communities disappeared before they had a chance to modernize their way of life and the few farmers who stayed behind knew that they chose for a life of relative social isolation. In the Lower Languedoc, however, labour-intensive viticulture made possible the survival of relatively large and socially heterogeneous rural communities. These modernized their way of life and developed all the amenities that life in a fairly large and prosperous modern village can offer: good public services (schools, public transport, etc.), a well-developed tertiary sector in the field of trade and services and a lively public life organized in a relatively large number of voluntary associations (sports clubs, cultural associations, political parties, etc.). Even for those local people who can survive at a reasonable economic level, depopulation sees the gradual loss of many of these social amenities which they have come to take for granted. Since the 1950s differences in lifestyle and material prosperity between city and countryside have largely disappeared. For those young people who have to leave the countryside now big city life has few new attractions to offer and several disadvantages (high cost of living, loss of social contacts, unattractive suburban habitats, etc.). So both those who have to leave and those who have or prefer to stay now resent the necessity of emigration.

Elsewhere (Kielstra, 1980a,b, 1981) I have argued that this type of development has in the last few decades given rise to a new type of regionalist movement, which is no longer, like earlier regionalist movements, apolitical or conservative, but which tends to ally itself with the radical left. Such a leftist regionalism is a new phenomenon in the French and European political spectrum. Its rise can thus be related to a new type of socio-economic development: the degeneration of peripheries into relictual spaces.

Such a loss of integration into the wider socio-economic system has not only hit regional populations, but also other social categories which cannot be classified as a traditional *Lumpenproletariat*. Amongst these are, for example, relatively highly educated groups of younger people from middle-class origin for whom the entrance into their traditional occupational niches in the academic world and the higher echelons of the state bureaucracy and private enterprises are diminishing. A closer analysis of this group and similar ones would fall outside the scope of this chapter, but they too are joining types of organizations, ecological or anti-nuclear, for example, which fall outside the traditional European political spectrum and come close in their general political orientation and sometimes in their activities to the new leftist regionalist movements.

For some people from this 'alternative' fringe of the Left, Europe's new relictual spaces, particularly Languedoc and Provence which combine a pleasant climate and a beautiful landscape with the facilities of a modern infrastructure, are becoming a kind of promised land where small-scale non-capitalist forms of economic enterprise and new types of community life may be tried out. The largely abandoned mountain areas of Languedoc have in the last ten to fifteen years seen a slow but steady inflow of families or communes of young people who want to return to the land and to practise some alternative form of agriculture (Léger and Hervieu, 1979). Many of such attempts have failed, but some hundreds of these new settlers have managed to establish more or less permanent agricultural enterprises. Such groups, and sympathizers, who have not (yet) settled permanently in the south, often sympathize with the regionalist movement. While they may get along with the young, urban intellectuals of the Occitanist organizations, they are viewed with mistrust by the local rural population. Sheepfarmers and winegrowers are usually not conservatives or puritans, but the economic interests they defend are those of a rational, technologically advanced, market-orientated agriculture, and the type of rural community life they want to maintain is far remote from that of a hippy commune. They may see tourists as a nuisance, but permanent settlers are also rivals for land, cheap housing and scarce agricultural sub-ventions. When hard-pressed to defend their own interests, they may accept the support of all kinds of sympathizers from outside. The dairy farmers of the plateau of Larzac who risked losing their pasture lands to the French army were willing to co-operate with all kinds of wild regional-ist, pacifist or leftist groups, and the struggle for the Larzac plateau became for years a symbol of the regionalist movement. Outside such acute crisis situations, however, new settlers, outside sympathizers and even the wilder young intellectuals from the region itself are received with considerable mistrust. Persons and groups from the counterculture, who want to use the new relictual spaces as a kind of social and economic laboratory for the testing of their ideas, remain as much of an alien element there as the tourist or the military.

According to the 'classical' pattern of economic development the rural population of the Languedoc would now gradually be reduced to a small number of large or middle-sized farmers big enough to survive even under relatively unfavourable market conditions, and a small number of entre-preneurs and employees in the tertiary sector serving both these farmers and the summer tourists. Integration in the larger economic system would thus be restored at a lower level of population, as happened in many French rural areas hit by the rural exodus in the last hundred years. Historical conditions have changed, however. The major weakness of current forms of centre-periphery theory is their lack of attention to the changing historical context. Classical peripheries have been formed when socially backward and economically stagnating areas became integrated into a large economic system in rapid expansion, even when the benefits of that expansion were rather unequally divided. Now, however, the economic growth of the centre is stagnating, probably for a prolonged period, while the new relictual spaces have developed a modern social and cultural infrastructure and a technologically modern market-orientated economic production system. Geographic mobility out of these relictual spaces can offer no economic or social advantages and is strongly resisted.

Trends for the future

It is hard to see any alternative to the gradual decline of these regions within the existing political and socio-economic context. As a consequence regionalist movements are often much divided amongst themselves, since it is almost impossible to formulate any political strategy that is both realistic and protects all the interests of the groups and individuals con-cerned.[7] That does not prevent such movements, however, from acting as pressure groups for the defence of regional interests in specific cases, and they can then often constitute coalitions with other pressure groups with a different orientation, as the example of the plateau of Larzac has shown. Pressure groups are, of course, not a new political phenomenon, but their orientation is changing. In the past social strife was mainly about the division of the benefits of economic growth, while the social transfor-mations brought about by that economic growth might be approved of or regretted by individuals or groups but rarely became the subject of major political action. Now economic growth is stagnating, probably for a long time, but it would be an illusion to think that this would result in a stabiliz-ation of the socio-economic *status quo*. When it is no longer profitable to increase production, private enterprises on all levels will try to raise their profits by a centralization and rationalization of the processes of pro-duction and distribution. This will result in a diminution of overall employment, but also in the specific elimination of the marginal units of production which often constitute the main economic basis of relictual spaces. Since such social transformations will no longer, as in the case of earlier formations of peripheries, be compensated by economic benefits for at least part of the population concerned, they will meet with increasing political opposition. Since such opposition cannot really change macro-economic processes, it will often demand transfer payments from the state to compensate the social consequences of these economic processes. Such transfer payments will have to be financed through an increase of taxation or a decrease in public services for regions and social categories which are least hit by the economic stagnation. This implies the rise of a new type of social opposition between providers and receivers of transfer payments which cuts right through the traditional class oppositions. Institutionalized social organizations (political parties, labour unions, professional organizations, etc.) are usually based on such traditional class oppositions and therefore are little able to deal effectively with these new problems. We can therefore expect, and actually see, the rise of a new network of relatively small and loosely organized pressure groups, co-operating in flexible coalitions to defend the interests of the various regions and social categories concerned.

It is hard to predict how such organizations will develop in the more remote future, but the example of the rise of political parties and labour unions in the nineteenth and early twentieth centuries shows that the establishment of nationwide institutionalized social organizations is a slow process that cannot be completed within a few decades. As long as such a process is not completed, pressure groups have few possibilities of initiating national and international policies of their own, but they may block or retard political decision-making which goes against their interests. For the near future we can therefore expect an increasing blockage of political decision-making and consequently a growing rift between (capitalist) economic development tendencies and the political ability and willingness to create the superstructures necessary for the implementation of these development tendencies. In countries like France where, for historical and geographical reasons, potential relictual spaces are numerous, relictual spaces may become both actual and symbolic focusing points for political strife.

Notes

1 Alcouffe (1979) has attempted this for the Occitanie.
2 On the economy of Languedoc in the seventeenth and eighteenth centuries see, for example, Boissonade (1905), Chaussinand-Nogaret (1970), Dion (1959), Dutil (1911), Frêche (1974), Geraud-Parracha (1955), Marres (1966a,b), Sorre (1913), Trouvé (1818). This bibliography has no pretension of being complete.
3 Concerning economic transformations in Languedoc since the beginning of the nineteenth century see Brunet (1967), Estadas (1953), Marres (1950, 1954), Pech de Laclause (1959), Plandé (1944), Sentou (1948).
4 See Augé-Laribé (1907), Gratton (1971), Passama (1906), Smith (1975).
5 See Bardissa (1976), Barthe (1966), Loubère (1975), Warner (1960).
6 See, for example, Béteille (1978).
7 Touraine and Dubet (1981) have stressed these internal divisions in the Occitanist movement, but without placing them in their larger social and political context. The ethical and methodological aspects of their method of 'sociological intervention', in which the groups studied are confronted with their own internal contradictions, will give rise to considerable discussion.

11

Dependent development in Corsica

Eleonore Kofman

In the aftermath of French decolonization in the 1950s and 1960s, particularly in North Africa, the idea of internal colonialism was adopted by regionalist/nationalist movements and applied to peripheral regions with ethnically distinct populations. It was argued that these regions were economically exploited and culturally subjugated in the same way as France's overseas colonies, where the core collectively discriminated against a culturally distinct people. The closure of the Decazeville mines in 1962 was the first major occasion when this analogy was made (Lafont, 1967, p. 140). This social conflict then developed into the more general issue of regional employment and eventually extended to the role of the regional bourgeoisie and its inability to successfully intercede and deal with the state. Some have seen this conflict as the first occasion when the relationship between local society and the state was called into question (Quéré, 1978, p. 183).

After 1968 most regionalist/nationalist movements incorporated the theme of internal colonialism in their analysis of the relationship between the core and the periphery. The Breton, Occitan and Corsican movements demonstrated not only the effects of past colonialism and policies of national unity, but also the continuing process of economic, social and cultural colonialism carried out by the state and capital, both French and international. They stressed the dispossession by outside interests of the major sectors of the regional economy and the loss of control in decisions affecting the region. The population was now forced to become highly mobile in its search for suitable employment. Menial jobs were often filled by foreign labour, yet the most prestigious occupations were taken up by outsiders, generally from the core regions. Emigration, coupled with a mentality of self-colonization, which devalued regional traditions, thus undermined the cultural identity of the region. (See Figure 11.1.)

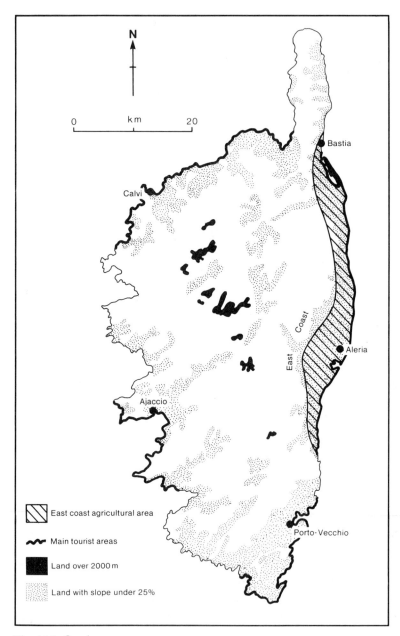

N

Bastia

Calvi

East Coast

Aleria

Ajaccio

Porto-Vecchio

⬛ East coast agricultural area

〜 Main tourist areas

⬛ Land over 2000 m

Land with slope under 25%

Fig. 11.1 Corsica

Furthermore, the regional policies of the Gaullist state had served to integrate more fully the peripheral regions and tighten the hold of the dominant economic and cultural systems. The Occitan and Corsican movements were especially concerned by massive tourist complexes, which did not call upon regional capital, used little local labour, and were only slightly integrated into the regional economy. With the few remaining industries rapidly disappearing, the region was becoming more and more dependent on external capital and goods (Aydalot, 1978).

However, although the internal colonialism thesis drew attention to the underlying rationale of the state's regional development policies, it faced numerous criticisms. Those who had adopted the concept were accused of opportunism and of obscuring the class relations within a region (Alliès, 1976). The comparison with an external colony was also said to mask the nature of the social relations and the role of the bourgeoisie. Moreover, the idea was deemed to be outdated since peripheral regions were no longer solely within the orbit of French capital, but were equally controlled by international capital (Que Faire, 1971). It should also be added that the tendency of nationalist movements, such as the Front de Libération National de la Corse, to concentrate on the colonialism of the state meant that they failed to examine the constitution of the system itself. The region was treated as a homogeneous entity in which social relations are simplified and the consequences of differential modernization neglected (Kofman, 1981).

The distinctiveness of regions such as Corsica, Brittany and areas of Occitanie was not so much the colonial relationship, but the extent to which regional cultures had not been destroyed by national integration, and the impact of the changing relationship between the state and local society in its economic and political links. The increasing penetration of the state together with national and international capital through regional development programmes led, on the one hand, to the creation of spatially and economically dynamic sectors, and, on the other hand, to the decline of less profitable zones. In many cases the latter areas had once supported dense populations and were now ignored by major development projects or had difficulties in adapting to the new national and international economic systems (Reece, 1979).

The injection of massive investment in tourism, industry and the modern, agricultural sector, sometimes in recently cleared areas, has brought about a major distinction between dynamic and stagnant zones in regions where this was previously not so marked. This effect was particularly pronounced because the investment and regional development programmes were so highly concentrated both spatially and sectorally.

This can be clearly seen in the favoured status of the east coast of Corsica and of the coastal sector of Languedoc. Industrial development in the 1960s was also directed towards the modern, highly capital-intensive sectors, with few internal linkages and financed by external enterprises. The best-known example of this type of development was the steel and petrochemical complex of Fos-sur-Mer near Marseilles. Distorted regional economies, arising from capital-intensive industrialization, have also generated social and economic imbalance in regions such as Sardinia where the process of regional rebirth has been represented as neo-colonialism (King, 1977).

The effect of such unbalanced regional development policies is to concentrate regional exports within a few modernized sectors, which are frequently externally controlled, and to create an increased demand from imports, thus 'integrating' more fully the regional to the national economy. In the Mediterranean Basin, mass tourism has often been accorded pride of place in regional development programmes with little consideration for the insertion of tourism into the local economy and culture. The types of industrialization and tourism mentioned above have a tendency to provide little scope for local labour and, hence, are unable to resolve the employment problems which are at the root of much migration of young people. Employment in these regions may also be more seasonal and less secure especially in the tourist and agricultural sectors. Kielstra has mentioned the growth of a *bricolage* lifestyle (Chapter 10, pp. 257–8) in which odd jobs, seasonal work and welfare payments may be combined. The return of retired migrants adds another element to the budget of social transfer payments so that the decline in production of the active population is replaced by a welfare economy.

Possibly one of the most striking examples of a Mediterranean region whose social space has been brusquely dislocated by the introduction of a regional development programme is Corsica. The increased intervention of the state sharpened the social conflicts arising from differential develop-ment and accentuated the dependent relationship with continental France. At the beginning of this process of regional development in the 1950s Corsica could still, to some extent, be regarded as a frontier region of investment opportunities. It also contained a relatively homogeneous population, most of whom spoke Corsican. As regional development made its impact more outsiders were attracted to the island, thereby intro-ducing greater heterogeneity to its society and culture.

Although the differential development and increased dependency of Corsica stands out so strongly, the processes of such a distorted and dependent development can be commonly found in other Mediterranean regions in which the regional economy has been suddenly transformed by a regional development programme. Thus, in the rest of this chapter, I shall first outline the principal orientations and strategies of regional development policies since their initial implementation in 1957 and then examine the way in which these policies accentuated a highly differentiated and dependent form of development, which not only affected Corsicans, but the entire population of the island.

Political and economic integration of Corsica

Corsica only became part of France in 1768 after being ceded by the Genoese. In the nineteenth century it was treated as a colony with special customs regulations and several unsuccessful attempts to settle colonists as in Algeria (Demailly, 1978, pp. 96–9). A law, passed in 1818, taxed non-agricultural exports from Corsica and exempted French imports. It was modified in 1835 when raw materials, such as oil, silk and iron, were also exempted from duty, but was not completely abolished until 1912. The embryonic industrialization, lasting from about 1835 to 1870, could not, in the end, compete with other colonial investments and the penetration of French products (Demailly, 1978, pp. 98–100). The one activity which did attract French interest and capital was the production of ewes' milk for Roquefort as from the 1890s (Renucci, 1974, p. 206).

Its most exploitable resource was, in fact, its population, for with the demise of industries, particularly in the north, and the competition from external products, the rate of emigration accelerated from 1890. Rural Corsica, with 220,000 inhabitants in 1881, had no more than 60,000 in 1962 (Renucci, 1974, p. 108). Many of these immigrants were to play an integral part in France's own colonialism in the army and administration (Labro, 1977, p. 45).

By the 1954 Census the population had declined to 191,000 inhabitants from over 300,000 at the end of the nineteenth century. It was economically the poorest region in France, based on an index of *per capita* income of 38 compared with 166 for Paris (ibid., p. 52). The salaried population had dropped from 14,000 in 1931 to 4000 in 1959 (FRC, 1971, p. 20). Its main exports consisted of wood and related products and asbestos, both of them without any value added. Such was the demographic and economic situation at the outset of the first regional development plan in 1957.

Regional development policies

The *Plan d'Action Régionale* (1957) aimed to raise the *per capita* income of the island and to encourage integrated development that would take off from two key sectors, that of a modernized agriculture and mass tourism. It was envisaged, however, that the interior would also benefit from development programmes and that the agricultural sector would be backed up by small-scale industries processing raw materials. In order to implement the project in the two key sectors mixed public companies were set up – SOMIVAC (Société de la Mise en Valeur de la Corse) for agricultural development and SETCO (Société pour l' Équipement Touristique de la Corse) for tourism. The planners saw Corsica as a region of great potential but one which would require a dynamic population from outside the island.

Right from the start tourism was judged to be the best candidate as the main development activity since it possessed a high multiplier effect. It was hoped that Corsica could become the second Côte d'Azur. The agricultural development of the east coast, now malaria-free, would be based principally on cereal cultivation. It was considered that only high-quality wines should be encouraged and the rest be strictly limited, if not got rid of altogether. The objectives of this plan were not translated into concrete developments, for several major social and political changes intervened in the years immediately following its publication.

First, the Fourth Republic was replaced in 1958 by the much less generous Fifth Republic which initially saw Corsica in strategic military terms rather than as a region of opportunities. Of course, later, Corsica did come to provide a region where international and national capital could reap sizeable economic rewards. Still, what was important for the future of the development programmes was that Corsica received far less from the governments of the Fifth Republic than it had under the Fourth. Secondly, the loss of Algeria in 1962 meant that almost a million repatriates had to be resettled in a short period. Although figures vary, it is estimated that about 15,000 repatriates arrived in Corsica from the three North African countries from 1962 to 1966 and that the majority settled on the east coast or Ajaccio and Bastia (Pastorelli, 1971, p. 21).

These two radical, political changes put an end to any form of integrated development for the influx of population and the financial reductions left SOMIVAC and SETCO only able to develop a few limited areas and to be interested in quick solutions with a minimum of cost and a maximum of return in a short period. The lack of finance during the early stages of development was particularly serious for over 80 per cent went to investment in hydraulic equipment, leaving little for land development. The group to have financial resources were the repatriates who benefited from cheap loans, but they also needed to invest in a crop with quick returns. Hence the east coast came to specialize overwhelmingly in the production of ordinary wines and to resemble in parts the Algeria the repatriates had left. The lucrative coastal areas attracted investment which resulted in soaring land prices. From 1953 to 1971 the value of land planted in vines rose over five times and that of wooded land twenty-five times (Perrier, 1975, p. 24).

The interior was neglected in favour of the more financially rewarding coastal zones. The traditional symbiosis, expressed by the transhumance of the shepherd, was broken for the coastal areas were withdrawn from communal use and turned over to agricultural uses and tourist developments. Wine increasingly dominated exports and the interior had fewer products to offer so that an unbalanced, export-orientated agricultural economy was created. Other aspects of the Plan such as cheaper transport, the provision of basic agricultural education and services and the development of small industrial plants, were forgotten.

By the mid-1960s the state began to elaborate a new development strategy in which it tried to incorporate the modernizing élites and, at the same time, pacify the traditional élites. This was the period of massive projects and of principles of functional hierarchies and growth poles. For Corsica, the first concrete expression of this strategy was the *Schéma d'Aménagement* prepared in 1971 by the Mission Interministérielle in Corsica. Again, as in 1957 tourism presented the most attractive option, but this time its potential was calculated exactly in terms of beach and hotel capacity. The higher of the two estimates of 2,210,000 tourists per year would have inundated Corsica with ten times its population (209,000 at the 1968 Census), and this mainly during the short summer season. So, although the document speaks of a 'controlled development which would not destroy the originality of the island . . . and respect its natural and human characteristics' (DATAR, 1972, p. 17), it fails to work out the implications of its proposals or to consider problems of commercialization for the agricultural sector. The continued emphasis on a narrow, export-orientated economy and the growth of tourism without integrated development could only lead to an increase in the consumption of goods. This is exactly what happened for the rapid expansion of tourism in the 1970s resulted in an even more pronounced imbalance between exports and imports.

As we shall also see, the employment generated from tourism was low, especially in the large complexes. These were often separate from existing settlements and could only function during a limited season. An example of such an ambitious scheme was the SETCO project at Pinia on the east coast. In 1972 a proposal for a 20,000-bed complex on 400 ha. was put before Corsican *conseillers généraux*. The size of the scheme led to an outcry and reinforced the antipathy towards the tourist orientations of the 1971 *Schéma*. There was also much evidence of speculation and appropriation of coastal sites by multinationals and powerful French interests (Labro, 1977, pp. 65–7).

Nor were scandals lacking in the agricultural sector where new regulations were introduced for the production of wine (chapitalization) in 1971. It was no longer permitted to raise the alcoholic content of wine by more than 2°. The scandals which arose from its abuses, especially among the repatriates, a good number of whom were large landowners with their own wine cellars, and the difficulties of marketing the vast quantities of ordinary wines, were to bring about the events of Aléria in 1975. The irony was that while all possible means were used to persuade southern French growers to abandon this type of viticulture, dispensations were granted to Corsican growers. From 1963 to 1972, 895 applications to plant 10,866 ha. of vines were granted (Holohan-Dressler, 1981, p. 138). As late as 1972 a ministerial edict gave permission for the planting of an additional 3,000 ha., an increase of 11 per cent of the area under cultivation (Perrier, 1975, p. 29).

Popular protests against the malpractices of wine production and commercialization, the decline of the interior, the tourist orientation of the *Schéma* and environmental pollution (*boues rouges*) forced the government to abandon the *Schéma* in 1975. It has been pointed out, however, that the studies and plans which put the general orientation of the *Schéma* into practice were never discarded even after the *Charte de Développement Économique de la Corse* was adopted in 1975 (Poncet, 1977, pp. 72–3). For the first time some of the conflicts arising from too rapid and unbalanced development were admitted officially. Overall, despite the programmes for the renovation of the interior, small-scale industries and greater opportunities for the education and employment of the young, some of the fundamental problems of Corsican development have not been comprehensively tackled. For example, the perennial problem of high transport costs led to lower prices for passengers and for large-scale exporters, but no help was forthcoming for those exporting small quantities. The effect of the new development has simply been to modify some of the excesses of the previous development, while leaving the economy as fragile and externally dependent as before.

Admittedly, in recent years, special programmes have been set up for interior rural areas and financial assistance increased. Thus two acts of legislation in 1974 and 1975 classified areas as *zone de montagne*. Since 1974 IRAM (Intervention pour la Renaissance Agricole de la Montagne), operated by the SOMIVAC, has turned 8632 ha. to farming at a cost of

Table 11.1 *Regional budget in Corsica, 1976–80 (million francs)*

	1976	1978	1980
Education and training	19.1	48.9	39.3
Urban development	13.5	18.3	22.2
Rural development	69.9	84.7	111.7
Transport and telecommunications	125.8	160.7	191.1
Economic action	14.3	19.3	19.1
Total*	257.1	376.3	430.8

* The total includes other expenditure on cultural and social activities, health and general administrative services.

Source: Etablissement Public Régional Corse, 1980.

75 million francs (SOMIVAC, 1981). In 1977 a SAFER (Société d'Aménagement Foncier et d'Éstablissement Rural) was finally established after being demanded for a number of years by the agricultural federations. Criticism of these rural renovation programmes has focused on the inadequate sums allocated to the interior compared to the coastal areas, the uncoordinated efforts of the various organizations and the continued centralization of decision-making.

The response of the state was to pour vast sums of money into the improvement of infrastructure and proliferate small-scale plans and regional organizations. What has been termed a *politique de comptable* strategy was most evident each time Giscard d'Estaing visited Corsica, as in June 1978 (De Barrin, 1980). Thus in 1980, despite budgetary constraints, 376.3 million francs were set aside for infrastructural development. Furthermore, the regionalized budget in the seventh Plan showed a steady increase in spending, with a maximum of 466 million francs in 1979. Table 11.1 indicates the principal sectors to have benefited.

The transformation of the Corsican economy and the value of state financial transfers increased household consumption (15 per cent per annum) and income *per capita* (20 per cent per annum). These average figures do not indicate changes in the major urban centres and the interior or the various socio-economic groups. Tables 11.2 and 11.3 outline the increases in *per capita* income and the semi-public and private sector.

These increases were, nevertheless, at the expense of massive debts accumulated in the key sectors of the economy which, in turn, have necessitated the further intervention of the state to mitigate the effects of uneven development and a fragile economy. The population then becomes

Table 11.2 Per capita *income in Corsica and France (thousand francs)*

	Corsica	France
1965	5,290	7,940
1968	6,500	9,930
1970	7,630	12,100
1973	10,000	—

Source: Holohan-Dressler, 1981.

Table 11.3 *Salaries in the semi-public and private sector*

	Corsica	*France*	*% difference*
1968	9,540	13,150	27
1979	33,640	44,570	23

Source: Etablissement Public Régional Corse, 1980.

more dependent on the state for financial transfers which maintain the existing social and political system in which the role of the class is to mediate the intervention of the state in the region.

Dependent development

The main protagonists in the transformation of Corsica from a traditional, relatively self-sufficient economy to a modern, dependent economy have been the repatriates, national and international capital, the clans and the state. The repatriates, as we have seen, were instrumental in the development of a mechanized, export-orientated agriculture. They also played a part in the modernization of commerce which in the late 1950s was still composed of thousands of small concerns and very few large ones (Holohan-Dressler, 1981, p. 75). They injected a dynamic element into Corsican society and were outside the traditional social networks based on the clans. The wealthier ones, who had already invested in Corsica before 1962, had access to national capital. In general the repatriates were given cheap loans and favourable conditions for investment by the state. Their presence was not so noticeable in the tourist sector where it was national and international capital that appropriated and developed extensive areas in the coast – Rothschild, Banque de Suez, Paribas (*U Ribombu*, 1981, no. 17, p. 6). In other sectors, Corsica's expanding market provided many opportunities for banks, insurance companies and supermarket chains. For example, in 1966 there were 5 banks with 16 branches; in 1973 there were 9 banks with 42 branches, mainly in Ajaccio and Bastia.

It was thus the repatriates and large companies that supplied much of the private investment capital since Corsica did not have a real regional bourgeoisie. The inability of the bourgeoisie to constitute itself as a dominant class was due to its successive dependence upon Pisa and Genoa, to which capital flowed, and the tradition of communal land in the pastoral economy (Demailly, 1978, p. 103). The power of the clans emanated from the system of clientelism rather than on the possession of financial resources. The contribution of the clans to Corsica's dependency was partly through the operation of the patron/client network in emigration and, later on, with the expansion of the welfare state and planning, the distribution of social transfers and management of land use. However, the rapid pace of development left them unable to intercede successfully on behalf of their traditional clientele.

Apart from the increasing reliance of the Corsican economy on the state during the past two decades, the administrative reforms carried out in the name of efficiency and better management have also consolidated state power in the periphery (Grémion, 1976). Thus the diffusion of central power in the region and the massive financial handouts brought about greater integration of the periphery and added another dimension of dependency.

In the first stage of regional development, which could be said to have ended in the early to mid-1970s with the rejection of the *Schéma*, the state concentrated on the modernization and opening up of two key sectors whose growth firmly linked the Corsican economy to national and international markets and capital. Once this economic integration had been set in motion, the modified development programme, as expressed in the *Charte*, did little more than distribute slightly more equally financial assistance between Corsicans and non-Corsicans and the interior and the coast. Although the population decline was stopped, the population was still extremely dependent upon continental France for its higher education needs and employment opportunities and, therefore, forced to emigrate.

Thus, in order to evaluate the impact of regional development policies on the level of regional dependency, it is necessary to examine not only changes in the key economic sectors which link the region to the national economy, but also the ability of the region to provide suitable opportunities for its population. Other aspects, such as the level of state transfers to the region and the extent to which decisions are made else-where, could also be considered. However, for practical reasons I shall focus on the main economic changes and their consequences on the degree of dependency. But before embarking on a detailed examination of the structure of the economy, I shall outline the principal characteristics of the population during the past two decades.

The population decline was finally reversed in the 1960s due to the immigration of repatriates and foreign labour. In 1962 there were 176,160 inhabitants, in 1968 209,780 inhabitants and in 1975 227,425 inhabitants. This increase of 29 per cent was accompanied by a much larger increase in the foreign population who, in 1962, had numbered 6860, and in 1975 30,090. The composition of the active population also changed with a substantial decrease in the number of farmers by 42 per cent from 1962 to 1975. This was accompanied by a steep rise in the number of farm labourers (81 per cent) due to the development of the east coast. During this period the building sector and public works and services increased by 129 per cent and 81 per cent. Altogether 30,000 jobs were created.

Structure of the economy

Agriculture

From 1955 to the agricultural census in 1979 the number of farms declined from 12,279 to 7035. The decline was greatest in the mountainous areas and among small holdings. At the same time the proportion of farms over 50 ha. rose from 2 per cent in 1955 to 6 per cent in 1970 and 8 per cent in 1979 (INSEE, 1981, p. 23). The displacement to the coast and the creation of large holdings have been associated with concentration on export crops and neglect of grazing. The latter constantly declines in the twentieth century, reaching its lowest levels in the early 1970s. Table 11.4 outlines the changes in agricultural production from 1955 to 1978.

The expansion of viticulture was the means of penetration of modern capitalist agriculture on the east coast. In 1959, 5537 ha. produced from 140,000 to 180,000 hectolitres of wine, the production of which did not yield substantial profits. Only one property covered almost 100 ha. (Renucci, 1974, p. 349). By 1970 there were almost 30,000 ha. with 21 farms of over 100 ha. The largest belonged to outside capital and non-residents and employed vast numbers of North African labourers. From the enormous factory-like cellars almost the entire production was exported. Finally, there was little contact with the region (ibid., 1974, p. 325). The distri-bution of the small- and medium-sized production was controlled by

Table 11.4 *Agricultural production*

	1955	1962	1973	1978
Vegetable				
Wine (thousand hectolitres)	160	231	2,100	1,908
Clementines (quintals)	1	24	113	275
Herds (thousand head)				
Cattle	37	45	30	43
Pigs	40	42	24	49
Sheep	217	180	130	131
Goats	145	70	35	46

Source: Salkanazov and Vienot, 1980, p. 29.

wine merchants and outside capital. Relatively little was bottled locally, for this was less profitable. Of the 4448 hectolitres bottled locally in 1973, most was done by small-scale artisanal units (Holohan-Dressler, 1981, p. 143). Two sectors could be distinguished, one producing ordinary, cheap wines that were largely exported and passed through the hands of the repatriates and outside capital, the other, a quality production in Corsican hands.

Since 1976 about 7,000 ha. of vines have been uprooted, leaving 23,840 ha. (Service Régional de Statistique Agricole, April 1981). Thirty-two holdings are over 100 ha. and incorporate roughly a quarter of the area under cultivation (INSEE, 1980, p. 23). The contribution of wine to total agricultural production has also declined from the high level of 63 per cent (59 per cent ordinary wine) in 1973, although it is still well above the third it formed in 1963.

Citrus fruit, the other modern agricultural sector, also expanded rapidly, especially from 1966 to 1968. The production of wine and citrus fruits consisted of 60 per cent of total agricultural production in 1978. Most of this sector is composed of clementines, which have not been entirely successful, due to problems of climate fluctuations and marketing difficulties. As in the wine sector, debts were also a major problem, for in the early stages the authorities were often slow in responding to needs and in attributing the appropriate loans.

Clearing and destoning the land was an expensive process, as was the cost of hydraulic works. In more recent years the increase in the cost of labour, inputs such as fertilizers, machinery, etc., have not been matched by prices. Furthermore, it is claimed that Corsican farmers must bear higher costs than their Mediterranean competitors (Holohan-Dressler, 1981, p. 194). Thus in 1972 the accumulated debts among winegrowers amounted to 600 million francs or twice the value of the annual agricultural product. The moratorium on debts which came into force in 1973 did not apply to 30 per cent of the winegrowers and was of most benefit to the repatriates and the least in debt (ibid., 1981). In fact, in 1974, 85 per cent of the loans to agriculture was short-term and inappropriate to the needs of the growers.

The export orientation of these two sectors and the decline of the interior have lessened the ability of Corsica to feed itself and its tourists. For example, in 1964 Corsica produced 11.7 per cent of its meat production; in 1971 only 2.7 per cent (Perrier, 1975, p. 33). With the upturn in production in the mid-1970s Corsica now imports 84 per cent of the meat consumed and 90 per cent of milk from continental France (*U Ribombu*, 1981, no. 17, p. 4). A number of factors have caused the abandonment of grazing. Basically, the pastoral system itself collapsed so that the community no longer fully supported the life of the shepherds, while much of the lowland pasture was given over to crop growing. The disappearance of an integral agriculture in the interior, the extension of the *maquis* and the constant fires have depleted the amount of forage crops. Thus the shepherds have had to have increasing recourse to the market to ensure the survival of their herds. This can be seen in the quantity of straw and hay imported, which increased from 1258 quintals in 1967 to 15,623 quintals in 1973, decreasing to 2028 quintals in 1977 (Pernet, 1978, p. 79).

Much of the production of ewes' milk is delivered to the *Sociétés Roquefort* which in 1962 took 86,000 hectolitres out of 98,000. This has now declined to 52,000 hectolitres out of an estimated production of 100,000 hectolitres in 1980 (Service Régional de Statistique Agricole, 1980, no. 2). Corsica's share of the total quantity of milk collected by Roquefort fell from 7.6 per cent in 1974 to 6 per cent in 1980. The price paid to Corsican producers has been consequently lower than that of those in the Aveyron. The 30 centimes difference is supposed to cover transport costs, although it has been calculated by FDSEA (Fédération Départementale des Syndicates d'Exploitants Agricoles) that the cost of transport only accounted for a third of the difference (Demailly, 1978, p. 110). The future of this production is uncertain for Roquefort has announced that it is completely withdrawing from Corsica without even giving the agreed two years' notice.

It can be seen from this brief survey of agriculture that the dependence of Corsica on continental France for its foodstuffs was the result of the development of two export products and the collapse of an integrated pastoral system. It is unrealistic to think that one could return to the traditional systems, but it is possible to revive production which has been neglected and hence revert to a more integrated system. This is the proposed plan for the production of charcuterie based on increased chestnut production. Only about 2200 ha. are now maintained out of 25,000 ha. due to a great extent to the lack of manpower in the interior (Service Régional de Statistique Agricole, 1981, no. 1). The expansion of market gardening is currently being considered for much of the island's needs are imported by five large wholesalers. As is also evident in the replacement of imported building materials, there is much resistance from continental exporters and transporters.

Industry

Every major planning document mentions the lack of industry apart from building and public works. In 1966 there were just under 1000 industrial establishments, in 1979 just over 1000. During this period the number of agricultural and food processing plants rose from 334 to 421 (Salkanazov and Vienot, 1980, p. 30). Throughout the period of rapid growth the industrial sector has remained stable, barely increasing by 14 per cent in employment from 4,320 in 1962 to 4,930. On the other hand, building and public works was one of the fastest-growing sectors and accounts for two-thirds of the secondary sector.

This period was typified by industrial closures and failures. In 1949 there was still the mining of asbestos, which produced 30 per cent of the national needs, a fish canning factory, tobacco, wood and cork. In the early to mid-1960s all these activities, with the exception of the JOB tobacco factory at Bastia, closed down. The Casamozza canning factory shut down in 1971 after only three months' operation. Other initiatives to set up industrial production for local needs have been blocked by continental interests, as in the case of cement where the local market would certainly support a cement works (Holohan-Dressler, 1981, p. 157).

Industrial grants were not effective. Between 1970 and 1973 five subsidies were granted and an industrial bureau set up at the Mission Régionale. However, by 1975 this office had only received 12 applications creating 350 jobs. One of the few industrial establishments to have succeeded was a Corsican firm (Femenia) that manufactures grape-harvesting machines. Since 1973 it has had difficulties in developing a machine for scrub clearance. Compounded with the inability to market a new machine, its continental partner and distributor (SCPA) now wants to pull out because of declining sales of the existing machinery. The new machine would have permitted Femenia to have continued an orientation towards the Corsican market. This example also highlights the limited nature of industrial assistance in regional development policies which are concerned more with creation of employment than with technological advance (*U Ribombu*, 1981, no. 9, p. 2).

The absence of even a limited industrial base processing primary products and producing inputs for this sector thus completes the total dependence on imports and raises the cost of living which, in turn, makes any Corsican product more expensive. The internal market is left open for continental producers. An examination of imports and exports will show the deterioration in Corsica's balance of trade in relation to continental France.

Imports and exports

Since 1962 the volume and composition of imports and exports have totally altered with the effect that Corsica has become inextricably linked with continental France through its increase in consumption and need to export its own agricultural products. In 1963 Corsica exported 22,500 tons of asbestos and 30,000 tons of wood and related products (Salkanazov and Vienot, 1980, p. 28). In 1965 it still exported 3000 tons of products of animal origin which by 1974 had fallen to 1355 tons (Poncet, 1977, p. 42). By now wine dominated the export sector (Table 11.5). While exports doubled from 1962 to 1978 imports rose even faster in response to the increasing number of tourists. In 1974 the ratio of exports to imports fluctuated around 27 per cent; by 1978, a bad year for exports, it had descended to 20 per cent, rising the following year to 22 per cent. The general pattern has been that of a substantial variation in amount exported and a constant progression of imports. Table 11.5 indicates the composition of imports and exports in 1974 and 1979.

The trends in the next few years will most likely be similar to those of the past. Exports will tend to vary due to climatic fluctuations and marketing difficulties. The most striking feature is the absence of products with any value added which will certainly persist. In contrast the volume of imports will follow the increase in tourist numbers which are continuing to grow every year.

Tourism

Tourism has figured in every development plan, but unlike the industrial sector it has become a booming activity, expanding spectacularly from

Table 11.5 *Composition of imports and exports*

	1974	1979
Imports (tons)		
Construction material	282,000	273,900
Hydrocarbons	275,000	345,900
Food products	151,000	168,656
Fertilizers	19,000	27,302
Others	160,000	176,900
Total	887,000	992,700
Exports (tons)		
Wood and cork	21,900	9,200
Citrus fruits	10,700	27,200
Wine	182,100	153,300
Animal origin	1,350	1,200
Other	21,170	27,200
Total	237,000	218,600

Sources: Préfecture de la Région Française, 1974.
Direction Régionale de l'Équipement, 1980.

130,000 tourists in 1960 to 512,000 in 1970 and 1,277,000 in 1980. This has represented an annual growth rate of 9 per cent in recent years with a greater increase among foreigners than French. Tourist revenue has increased from 136 million francs in 1965 to 1500 million francs in 1978. However, tourism is an activity which is heavily concentrated on the coast (eight out of ten tourists) and in the summer months (55 per cent in July and August). There is little evidence of any major change in this pattern (Salkanazov and Vienot, 1980, p. 31).

The principal question is the value of tourism for the Corsican economy and employment. Much of the financial benefits accrue to outside capital since Corsican participation in the large-scale coastal developments has been slight. A high proportion of tourist expenditure does not remain in Corsica, for one could almost say that the goods and food required by tourists come in with them. Twice as much meat, milk, drinks and flour are imported in summer (ibid.). Ninety per cent of the building materials are also imported.

As for employment, the menial jobs and management positions are occupied by outsiders. In 1974 only 28 per cent of salaried employees in hotels were Corsicans, 43 per cent French from the mainland and 29 per cent foreigners (INSEE, 1979, no. 15, p. 14). In addition, much of the employment is seasonal, thus generating partial unemployment and unstable conditions conducive to continued emigration. The new tourist complexes outside urban centres find it unprofitable to stay open all the year round. This only occurs in traditional family hotels.

Not only has international tourism reinforced Corsica's dependence on imports and outside capital, but it has also not helped in resolving its employment problems. The need to surround tourism with activities which feed into it has become obvious. The failure of SETCO in fostering this type of development and the fact that it gave assistance solely to the private sector led to it being disbanded in 1977. Its most contested development involved a proposed 20,000 bed complex covering 400 ha. at Pinia on the east coast. This scheme illustrated the carrot and stick approach, whereby local authorities were offered employment (2000 jobs) in return for massive public finance (Labro, 1977, p. 68). In many coastal communes considerable investment has to be borne by the resident population for an activity which only takes place during a few months of the year. It has been estimated that 60 per cent of the state's investment is linked directly or indirectly to tourism (Poncet, 1977, p. 81). Furthermore, such a complex would have certainly employed mainly outside labour.

Employment

The figure of 30,000 jobs created from 1962 to 1975 is frequently quoted to demonstrate Corsica's economic progress, but a closer examination of this statistic would reveal that many of these jobs have not been taken up by Corsicans and therefore would not have served to stem emigration. Many of the unskilled jobs, such as farm labouring, employ foreigners (Italians and North Africans). Corsica has the highest percentage of foreign workers in France due partly to the type of development it has undergone. Immigrants constitute 48 per cent of those in agriculture, 83 per cent of farm labourers and 57 per cent of those in the building sector (INSEE, 1979, no. 14, p. 15). Obviously a large number of the jobs generated during the period of rapid expansion went to immigrants, for they accounted for 70 per cent of the population increase between 1968 and 1975. In 1962 there were 7000, in 1968 8000, and in 1975 30,000, according to the census.

At the other end of the job market, many positions were occupied by continental French. It has been argued that 78 per cent of the higher echelons in banking, 60 per cent of SOMIVAC and the Electricity Board (EDF) and 40 per cent in the administration were filled by non-Corsicans (Sanguinetti, 1979, p. 57). Sanguinetti also suggested that 80 per cent of the jobs created from 1962 to 1975 were in the hands of foreigners (including continental French and repatriates). It is likely that there has been some Corsification of employment in the past few years, since SOMIVAC boasted in the late 1970s that 87 per cent of its 213 staff were Corsican or related to Corsicans (SOMIVAC, 1979).

The most telling statistic of Corsica's fragile employment structure is the level of unemployment which is about 1 per cent higher than the French average. In 1978 it was 6 per cent, in 1979 7 per cent and in 1980 8.4 per cent. A breakdown of this figure shows much higher percentages amongst the young men and women. In 1979, 4.6 per cent of men were unemployed, 17.5 per cent of women and 21.2 per cent of young people under 25 years (INSEE, 1980, *Bilan de l'Emploi*).

What has altered in the past decade is the attitude of young people towards emigration. The recurrent theme among regionalists and nationalists of 'vivre et travailler au pays' appears to have made major inroads so that young people are much less willing to accept work outside of Corsica. According to a survey carried out among young, unemployed Corsicans, 70 per cent of those in rural areas and 78 per cent in Ajaccio and Bastia would not accept work outside of Corsica. This compares with a French average of 48 per cent for those who would leave their region. Just over half said they would be willing to accept a less qualified job if it were based in their canton. Unfortunately the survey has limited application since it only questioned the unemployed who were still in Corsica. One does not know for how long those who were forced to emigrate in order to obtain a suitable job had stayed in Corsica while unemployed. It should be remembered that not only is the rate of unemployment higher in Corsica, it also lasts for a longer period and frequently takes the form of alternating periods of work and unemployment, due primarily to the seasonal nature of the tourist industry.

Regional development policies have not solved Corsica's employment problems because they have not been concerned with providing suitable opportunities for the young, including the necessary educational institutions for their training. At present there is still no agricultural secondary school. Tertiary education could only be obtained on the mainland and thus weighed heavily in the family budget. This meant that despite rapid economic growth, dependence on the mainland for suitable employment and professional training continued.

Emigration

Until 1962 the population declined due to the large contingent of emigrants after the Second World War. From 1954 23,220 people left Corsica and only 6320 immigrated, leaving a deficit of 16,900. In the following period from 1962 to 1968, the number of emigrants fell to 17,144 while the number of immigrants rose sharply to 14,920, a loss of 2224 persons. Finally in the last intercensal period (1968–75), 23,285 persons left and 28,660 entered. However, although for the first time there was a positive balance, a breakdown of the statistics reveals a more complex situation. During this period 8905 born in Corsica left for France, but only 7345 of those born there returned, leaving a deficit of 1560 persons (INSEE, 1980, no. 20, p. 18). It is very likely that many of those returning were doing so upon retirement and that those leaving were the young and active. Since the last census the rate of emigration is thought to have decreased, although this may well have resulted in the young accepting less rewarding or seasonal work. Furthermore, unemployment in France would have also had a deterrent effect on those willing to leave Corsica in search of work.

Emigration constitutes cultural as well as economic dependence for it necessitates a rupture with Corsican society, a break which cannot be assumed to be felt only by those of Corsican origin. Little is known about the attitudes and integration of the children of the repatriates. It should also be remembered that about a quarter of the repatriates were actually born there and that many of them left for the North African colonies from 1920 to 1955 (Renucci, 1974, p. 284). The appeal of the popular, regionalist slogan 'vivre et travailler au pays' reflects the omission of a narrowly ethnic bias.

In effect the importance of the Corsican/non-Corsican distinction diminished during the second decade of the regional development policies when the modernized sectors began to suffer from the external dependence on highly competitive and unreliable markets. The average repatriate as well as the Corsican farmer had to return to the state to liquidate debts and extend loans. Tourism is the one constant growth industry, the value of its output now double that of agriculture and triple that of the building and public works sector (DATAR, 1981, p. 5). Yet the large tourist complexes on the coast are mainly externally controlled.

To associate cultural position with economic class, or in other words Hechter's (1975) cultural division of labour, is to obscure the social conflicts in contemporary Corsican society. The non-Corsican population is far more heterogeneous than is allowed for in internal colonialism theory. It includes poorly paid immigrant workers, repatriates of different classes and higher-level civil servants, who are only temporarily resident in the island. It is far more the clans who, in much autonomist literature and in the discussion about the proposed *statut particulier* for Corsica, are considered the key social agents in the maintenance of a dependent society and mode of development. Despite their inability to defuse social conflicts and to satisfy the demands of the modernizing elites, the clans have retained control, for the most part of local and regional political bodies. Through these bodies they were able to push through or veto planning decisions. For example, the *Conseil Général* actually accepted, with reservations, the *Schéma* which was rejected by the unions because of its disproportionate emphasis on tourism. More recently (1980), the *Schéma d'Aménagement du Littoral* was adopted by the *Conseil Général de Haute Corse* but not accepted by the *Conseil Général de la Corse du Sud* due to the excessive restrictions it imposed (*U Ribombu*, 1981, no. 17, p. 6). The bipartmentalization of Corsica in 1975 meant that the two clans could be played off against each other and yet kept content within their respective territories. The massive injection of resources, especially during the past decade, has ensured that the clans have preserved an important role in the allocation of resources from the core to the periphery.

The clans have thus acquiesced in a regional development programme whose main impact was to create a consumer society at the expense of an unstable and vulnerable productive structure and a deeper degree of dependency upon external markets for imports and exports and the financial assistance of the state. This process has caused so much damage to the productive capacity of the island that the modification of the past decade and the increasing level of financial aid are patently insufficient to secure a more balanced and less dependent development.

Regional development programmes in Corsica and other similar Mediterranean regions have not only opened up new investment frontiers and promoted a greater degree of distorted and destabilized economies through the increased transfer of welfare payments. However, the allocation of welfare payments and, in general, the process of planning itself, have served to reinforce the power of the established local social and political forces. Where dependent and uneven development leads to marked spatial and social inequalities, the authority of the local élite may be challenged in its ability to negotiate and bargain with the state by regionalist and nationalist movements representing disadvantaged groups. The response in any given region in Southern Europe to the impact of dependent development will be related to the specific intervention of the state, the level of economic and social development and the configuration of regional, social and political forces.

12

Spain: economy and state in transition

Antonio Vazquez Barquero and Michael Hebbert[1]

The relationship between national and regional development has two aspects. One is economic, namely, the manner in which changes in a nation's structure of production affect the character and relative prosperity of the regions which compose it. Historically, the rapid process of industrialization of the economies of the Mediterranean basin, and the narrowing of the gap which separates them from the advanced economies of Northern Europe, has everywhere involved a widening of the internal gap between their constituent regions, making regional underdevelopment a price of national development.

The second aspect is political. Though political/bureaucratic decisions about the territorial incidence of taxation and public expenditure are not the principal cause of regional inequalities they are an important means of alleviating or exacerbating them. All modern states perform a certain redistributive or compensatory role through public service provision, but some go much further in allocating resources explicitly towards the end of inter-regional equalization. The greater the degree of political leverage enjoyed by regional interests, whether through formal or informal channels, the more regions will compete to ensure a favourable spatial pattern of transfer payments via taxation, public expenditure and governmental action. Satisfying these regional claims may have its price in reduced national development.

Acute conflicts between priorities of national and regional development can be seen as the transitional economies of the Mediterranean basin face the problem of adjustment to the new international division of labour. While national governments are preoccupied with closing the external gap between themselves and the advanced economies, and maintaining their precarious lead over the newly industrializing countries, they are also subjected to quite contradictory pressures generated by the internal gap between advanced and backward regions. Many observers note how integration of the world economy has been associated with a resurgence of localist sentiment and a weakening of the nation state (e.g. Cameron, 1981). It is not clear how we should interpret this conjuncture. Should we, with Papandreou (1972) and Friedmann and Weaver (1979), view political regionalism as the first step towards a reconstruction of the international economic order? Or should we follow the more pessimistic interpretation of Hobsbawm (1977) or Poulantzas (1975), who attribute regional fragmentation to the success of multinational enterprise in breaking down such political safeguards as national sovereignty affords to non-capitalist interests?

We shall pursue the question by looking at Spain, the nation which perhaps best exemplifies the complex political as well as economic dimensions of regionalism. It does so for the historical accident that the onset of and adjustment to the economic crisis have happened to coincide in Spain with the critical transition from dictatorship to democracy including the creation of a new system of autonomous regions (Figure 12.1). The relations between these two parallel processes of economic and political adjustment merit attention, not only because they are central to an understanding of modern Spain, but also for the light they shed upon wider issues of national and regional development which were the object of the Durham conference (described in the Preface).

The structure of this chapter is simple: first, we discuss the economic crisis, next the crisis of the polity. The third and final section attempts an analysis.

The crisis of the economy

After just over a decade of expansion the performance of the Spanish economy deteriorated sharply in 1973–4. The crisis was precipitated by the OPEC price rises, but it had already been in the making as the model of development on which the country had made its transition to industrialism lost its vitality because of changes on world markets and because of internal contradictions. We shall first sketch the main features of this crisis, then discuss the ways out of it.

After the oil shock of 1973–4 the rate of growth of the Spanish economy has switched abruptly from being one of the highest to one of the lowest in Europe. Between 1961 and 1974 GDP had grown at a cumulative annual rate of 7.0 per cent. Between 1975 and 1978 the growth rate was 2.3 per

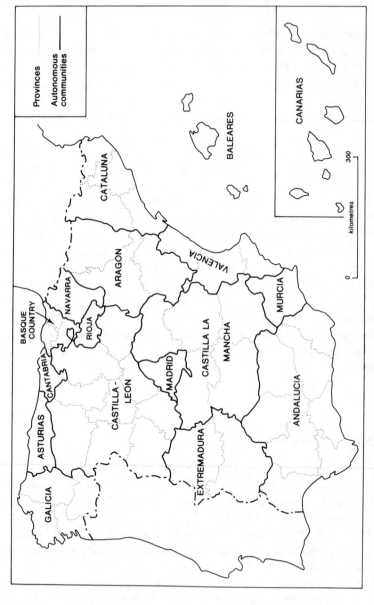

Fig. 12.1 Regional division of Spain under the 1978 constitution

cent, falling to 1.1 per cent in the period 1979 to 1983. Industrial production, construction excluded, is virtually stagnant, with 0.6 per cent growth during the same period, and private fixed asset formation has fallen uninterruptedly. The crisis shows itself also in the shortening of the duration of the business cycle from four years, until 1975, to two. The recessions have got deeper and more frequent against a background of sustained inflation. Price increases have been a traditional mechanism for recovering profits in the Spanish economy, especially in the industries with a high degree of oligopoly (i.e. the most dynamic sectors in the transition process). Between 1953 and 1975 consumer prices rose at a cumulative annual rate of 7.5 per cent, with increases of more than 10 per cent in 1957, 1958, 1965 and 1973 onwards. But inflation averaged 17.8 per cent per annum between 1974 and 1980 as enterprises shifted on to prices, i.e. the product market, the losses sustained on the factor market through increases in wages and salaries, social security contributions and real energy costs. The consumer price index rose to a peak of 26.4 per cent in 1977, though tight money policies and high interest rates have pulled it back to a steady 14.3 per cent in the period 1979–83.

The unemployment total has grown steadily since the onset of the crisis, numbering 2,710,400 people in September 1984. The Spanish economy has historically displayed a limited capacity to absorb labour. Not only did net emigration amount to 11.5 per cent of the active labour force in the period 1950–73 (EEC, 1978, p. 141) but the activity rate actually declined during the period of economic expansion from 38.1 per cent in 1960 to 37.5 per cent in 1975. The crisis has worsened the employment problem. The steepening decline in the activity rate (35.4 per cent in the last quarter of 1983) expresses an absolute fall of 4 per cent in the number of jobs between 1974 and 1980 in which time the national population has increased by 5.5 per cent, partly by return migration from the now depressed economies of Northern Europe. In 1980–1 alone employment fell by a further 3.2 per cent, bringing the level of unemployment to 14.6 per cent with significantly higher rates in the industrial areas of northern Spain (see Figure 12.2). Though the apparent growth of the unenumerated black economy during the 1970s casts some doubt on the exactness of employment and production statistics, there can be no doubting the gravity of the crisis on both fronts. Quite apart from the human costs of unemployment, its impact via social security transfers has been felt increasingly at a macroeconomic level as a significant factor behind the public sector deficit, which widened from 218,674 million pesetas in 1979 (1.7 per cent of GDP) to 1,340,700 million pesetas in 1983 (5.9 per cent of GDP).

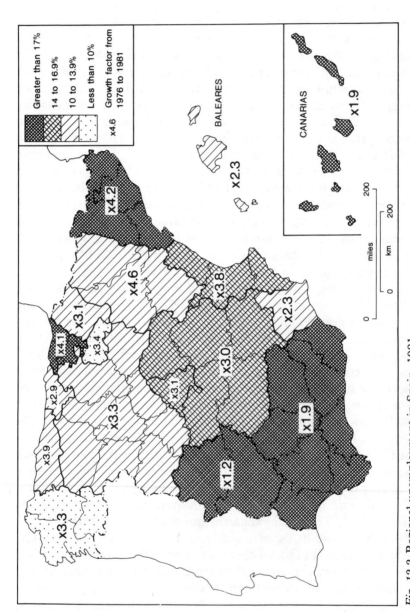

Fig. 12.2 Regional unemployment in Spain, 1981

Source: Instituto Nacional de Estatística, *Encuesta de Población Activa.*

The difficulties of the Spanish economy stem from its relatively un-favourable industrial structure. The economic crisis has, as it were, held up the structural changes which would enable Spain to finish off its industrial revolution, its transition from an economy based on agriculture to one based on industry and services (Vazquez Barquero, 1980). The pattern of ownership is still fragmented, with more than a million enter-prises and a long tail of small-scale, first-order establishments – typical of a transitional economy – which operate on a traditional basis with very limited capital and low productivity (Fuá, 1980). Only protectionism enables certain weaker sectors to survive, while the dynamic and export earning industries are located in precisely the sectors where supply most exceeds demand on world markets, the manufacturing staples of older industrial economies such as Britain which are now being eroded by keen competition from newly industrializing nations. Unlike Britain, however, Spain has no strength in the more technologically advanced sectors to offset her decline in steel, shipping, chemicals, cars or textiles (OECD, 1981, p. 11).

Industry in general suffers from a problem of poor profitability. Various indirect indicators show the scale of the problem. One is the preponder-ance of wages and salaries as a proportion of GDP; from an average of 57 per cent over 1954–75 it rose to 64.5 per cent in 1977, reflecting the temporary release of the labour market from political control after the end of the dictatorship, declining to 61.4 over 1977–83 as a result of rising unemployment and political restraints on collective bargaining. Another is the trend of profit margins; on one estimate, profits over the period 1961 to 1978 decreased at a cumulative annual rate of 2.7 per cent, with a slight rise towards the end of the decade. Whereas agriculture and the traditional industries were afflicted by low profits throughout the 1960s, since 1970 it has been the basic problem for the propulsive growth industries. Being less able to finance its own requirements, business has been forced increas-ingly to seek credit from financial institutions, and particularly the power-ful oligopoly of the seven big banks. Banking is the only sector to have strengthened its profit position throughout the period of crisis, assisted by monetary restriction and high interest rates. But the Spanish banking system remains, in any comparative perspective, relatively antiquated and inflexible in structure, and unresponsive to changing demands for credit within the economy. The big banks have prevented competition from new financial intermediaries, and this, combined with a liberalization of inter-national movements of capital, explains in part the increasing recourse to international financing and the consequent growth of Spain's external debt.

Turning now to the external aspect of the crisis, we see a balance of payments deficit of $2.5 billion in every year since 1973, 1978–9 excepted. A basic element of the crisis is Spain's inability to generate a sufficient external surplus to maintain its industrialization, that is to say, to finance the capital goods and import the new technologies needed for a restructuring of the economy. During the 1960s the country enjoyed a favourable balance less because of the competitiveness of Spanish products on world markets than because of tourist expenditure, emigrant remittances and direct foreign investments, notably in property. Since 1970 it has been particularly vulnerable because around 70 per cent of its primary energy sources are imported, as against the OECD average of 36 per cent, the national oil bill rising from $6.75 billion to $12 billion in 1979–80 alone. Besides the unfavourable terms of trade, Spain's dependence on international finance has already been noted. In 1983 the external debt stood at $29.4 billion, and interest payments, mostly to private lenders, equalled a fifth of exports of goods and services. Moreover, the net balance of overseas direct investment reached $1507 million in 1980, as the multinationals strengthened their holdings both on some sectors in crisis (the motor industry, chemicals and tourism) and in such expanding sectors as agrobusiness, consumer durables and banking, where the monopoly of the national bourgeoisie has for the first time been breached (MacMillion, 1981, pp. 294–8). In the geo-economic maps of the multinationals, Spain, bridgehead for Africa, is favourably situated in the medium term despite the growing importance of the newly industrializing countries (Lawlor, 1975). But this makes their presence all the more threatening for national industry competing from a position of dependence upon external technology.

So much for the general dimensions of the crisis of the economy. What of the government's response? The fact that the world slump coincided with the end of the dictatorship and with the attendant problems of political and constitutional reconstruction, no doubt helps to explain the rather passive and agnostic attitude of Spanish governments in the face of the country's economic decline, and the serious delay in recognizing that energy price rises were not just 'conjunctural' but constituted a permanent and major shift in world markets requiring a coherent structural adjustment (OECD, 1981, pp. 5–29; Tamames, 1980, pp. 478–89).

The point of departure for the longer-term economic strategy must be increased integration into the international economic system through membership of the EC. The process of opening up of the economy which began in the 1960s has yet to be completed. There are still numerous relics of protectionism, and Spain's overall foreign trade ratio (i.e. the average value of exports and imports of goods and services in relation to GDP) is still relatively low despite the economy's apparent vulnerability to external fluctuations (OECD, 1981, p. 7). Integration will, it is hoped, promote recovery in three ways: by increasing competition and so productivity, by attracting in the foreign investment which is needed for restructuring, and by opening up new markets. Quite the opposite can be argued from a perspective of dependency theory, but the concept of an alternative reconstruction strategy based upon closure and self-reliance enjoys little support. The harsh experience of autarky under the dictatorship and the historical association between isolationism and authoritarian rule perhaps explains why, in sharp contrast to Latin America, the *dependista* approach has generally not been felt to offer an adequate analysis of Spanish problems. Debate about the economic crisis centres therefore around the appropriate strategy for integration, and the extent to which the adjustment of the economy should be planned, or guided spontaneously by market forces.

Historically, the Spanish economy has always been characterized by a high level of state intervention (Tamames, 1980). If we may speak of Britain and the United States as examples of *competitive capitalism*, then Spain exemplifies the more typical Southern European model of *assisted capitalism*. Industrialization has from the outset been promoted under state patronage through protectionism, transfers and business subsidies as well as a strong presence of state control in the basic industrial sector, complementing rather than competing with private manufacturing industry. Under Franco, assistance was managed autocratically through 'personal relationships' between the regime and the industrial and financial bourgeoisies. The return of democracy has opened up controversy about the mechanisms of assistance to the productive system. Two basic positions can be distinguished within the spectrum of constitutional political opinion. One seeks to shift Spain towards a purer form of competitive capitalism. This solution has support from some political forces of the centre-right, from multinational interests and from a new business élite eager to exploit its comparative advantage over traditional industrialists; it also enjoys an intellectual attraction among the liberal professions. But a Thatcherist or Reaganite programme would in the Spanish context imply a rupture of truly revolutionary proportions, and there is no evidence that, under democracy, such a project could command the required political backing. Certainly the traditional bourgeoisie shows no inclination towards it, as the representatives of big business in the Spanish Confederation of Business Organizations (CEOE) have demonstrated in their resistance to the modest liberalization reforms pursued by UCD governments. This leaves, as the only viable alternative, the maintenance of a model of assisted capitalism in which the mechanisms of state involvement inherited from the Franco era are progressively brought under social control. The nature of this control is, of course, the central problem for negotiation and compromise between democratic forces and the bourgeoisie in contemporary Spain. Its outcome will depend largely upon the reconstruction of the country's system of government, to which we turn in the second section of this chapter.

The crisis of the polity

Spain's transition from dictatorship to constitutional order and political pluralism, brilliantly analysed by Giner in Chapter 13, has been a two-stage process. In the immediate aftermath of the dictatorship the apex of the Francoist system was broken, not by a revolution, but by a consensual and negotiated transition to constitutional democracy. When the constitution entered into force in 1978 there commenced the major stage of renewal of the political and administrative systems. This involved the creation of a completely new tier of government: the autonomous region, and adjustments at all other tiers. It is a necessarily long and complex process which will continue for many years and is charged with conflict, as basic cleavages of regional and class interest, submerged in the consensual process of drafting the constitution, resurface through the process of implementing it. The constitution was based upon three cardinal principles: regional autonomy, inter-regional solidarity and national unity, which are complementary in logic and have the support of all political forces bar a very small minority of ultra-right conservatives and 'independentist' nationalists. But agreement in principle allows considerable scope for disagreement over the weight to be given to each in practice. In this section we first describe the process of decentralization that was initiated in 1978, then focus on its continuing unresolved aspects. For as Ursula Hicks has observed (1978, p. 12), designing a decentralized state organization is a task which few nations get right at the first shot. We might expect this to be particularly in Spain which is, in Professor Blondel's words, 'the classic case of a country locked into a permanent state of crisis because of the conflict between centre and periphery' (1981, p. 319).

The relevant provisions of the 1978 Constitution were contained in Title VIII, 'Concerning the Territorial Organization of the State', which attempted to restore to the Basque, Catalan and Galician regions the autonomy which they had briefly enjoyed under the Republican Constitution of 1931, while also satisfying a more general demand for territorial self-determination on the part of areas of emigration, rural poverty and economic dependency which has been 'backwashed' during the expansion of the 1960s. At the least, this economic periphery was anxious to prevent the Basque Country and Catalonia from obtaining a privileged political status which would compound their advantages as leading areas of the industrialized zone. More positively, there was optimism that political decentralization could be the starting point for economic recovery, an assumption to which we return below. The constitution provided for a new subnational tier of regional governments, the so-called autonomous communities or *autonomías*, with a wide range of powers in the fields of transport, employment, housing, welfare, planning, agriculture, fisheries, police, etc. They were to have their own political assemblies and it was intended from the outset that this should be a *political* decentralization and not merely a *functional* one (for such distinctions see Smith, 1980, ch. 9; Hayward, 1969; Kofman, 1981; and Morell Ocana, 1974, pp. 117ff.).

However, to have a regional decentralization you must have regions. With the exception of Catalonia, the Basque country and Galicia, the regions of Spain were new artifacts, with sometimes ambiguous historical precedents in the medieval kingdoms. The constitution did not attempt to define a map of their boundaries or determine a cut and dried set of powers and responsibilities. Instead, it devised a loose set of procedures whereby the ethnic regions could move rapidly towards obtaining a statute of autonomy while other units, based upon voluntary groupings of existing provinces, would establish themselves provisionally and attain autonomy by slower stages.

This permissive approach produced an uneven map of autonomous communities in terms of their geographical scale and an exceptionally confused administrative position, with sixteen subnational governments all negotiating separately with the centre for their own package of powers, each working to a separate timetable for devolution. Encouraged perhaps by low turn-out rates in some of the regional referenda, the Democratic Centre Union (UCD) government seems during 1979–80 to have pursued a line of passive neglect, not directly blocking the devolution process but rather stifling it through administrative inertia and shortage of funds. But this dangerous strategy was abandoned after the attempted military coup of 23 February 1981, which served as a reminder to national political leaders that if they did not untangle the regional problem ultra-right elements in the armed forces might take it upon themselves to cut the Gordian knot.

At once the UCD government and the socialist (PSOE) opposition took steps to speed up constitutional reform. In July 1981 they agreed upon an important series of measures which established in detail the fiscal basis of the autonomous communities, and fixed a uniform timetable for the devolution process whereby in 1983 all regions should have achieved a position of formal autonomy, with their own statutes, executives and assemblies, for which elections should be held simultaneously early in that year. Thus the crisis of the polity, this still incomplete process of transition from an authoritarian to a democratic system of government, changed in character during 1981. Until then the principal uncertainties had been on basic questions of institutional design which the constitution left unresolved: what the regions should be, how financed and with what powers. Since the UCD-PSOE agreements and subsequent legislation the blueprint is more clear: a scheme of general devolution containing features of both unitary and federal models, with the powers of the new regions standardized (or, to use the term borrowed from the EC vocabulary, 'harmonized') so far as is possible given their great differences in size and character, in order to ensure a decentralization of the central state apparatus *pari passu* with the build-up of the new level of government. The UCD government prior to October 1982 was politically too weak to implement this blueprint, but the substantial PSOE victories, first in national and then local elections in 1982–3, created the necessary conditions for the decentralization process to be effectively co-ordinated and programmed for the first time. The PSOE government has been criticized for that 'mania for uniformity' which J. S. Mill observed in continental legislatures (1910, p. 375). Its general blueprint has been vigorously challenged by the ethnic nationalist minority parties, who see in harmonization only a reduction to the lowest common denominator of the new, weak regions, and an erosion of the substantial autonomy already won by Catalonia and the Basque country and enshrined in their statutes (Ariño Ortiz, 1981). In so far as one may still speak of a crisis of the polity (and crisis is an overworked word in the Spanish political vocabulary), it is this continuing problem of assimilating the two powerful autonomous communities, with their strong sense of nationhood, into a general decentralization of the state.

The period of political transition will not be over until the complete set of regions have their powers and resources together with routine working relationships between each other and the centre – the work of another decade or more. Given the failure of so many previous episodes of liberal reform in Spanish history, and particularly those involving any element of political decentralization, it is opportune to consider the prospects for this critical process of transition to a new model of the polity, the so-called *Estado de las Autonomías*, or 'State of the Autonomies'. Put simply, the risks are that there will be insufficient decentralization on the executive side, and too much on the political. We discuss these in turn.

The Spanish civil service is traditionally centralist (Medhurst, 1973) and remains, with the army, one of the last unreconstructed power blocks of the old regime (Arango, 1978, ch. 9; Baena del Alcázar and García Madaria, 1979), presenting perhaps the most serious obstacle to the achievement of the decentralized state model of the 1978 Constitution. Nevertheless, in the Basque country and Catalonia substantial transfers of personnel, plant and resources took place between 1979 and 1982. For example, the Catalan government had a payroll of no fewer than 74,599 personnel at the end of 1982, all but 4 per cent of whom had been devolved from the control of Madrid. The incoming PSOE government at once took steps to speed up the devolution process and bring all regions to an equivalent level by the end of 1984. Though this was a substantial achievement, it still touched only the field services of the main ministries. Teachers, road menders, nurses, market supervisors, vets, industrial inspectors, foresters and other grass-roots public employees have been transferred to regional control, but their former headquarters staff remain so far undepleted in Madrid. In this respect at least the experience of Spain's autonomous regions has matched that of their earlier Italian counterparts (Freddi, 1980).

The philosophy of Felipe Gonzalez' Socialist Party, in opposition as well as in government, has been that regionalization must be accompanied by a reduction of headquarters staff, both for administrative efficiency and for economic reasons to which we return below, and that this will only be achieved if blocks of powers are transferred simultaneously to all regions at once instead of being negotiated bilaterally on a region-by-region basis, as was done in the case of the Basque country and Catalonia. New sectoral transfer commissions, one for each ministry, have been created to achieve this. The advanced regions have refused to participate in them on the basis that the sectoral approach will tend to produce a less generous transfer of powers, because it will be dominated by an unholy alliance of weak regions with small executive capacity and strong ministries with an overriding functional orientation. Besides, neither the Basque country nor Catalonia are interested in being involved in a mere sectoral deconcentration within the Spanish civil service. They seek to build up separate executives with their own linguistic requirements, recruitment and career structures. Whatever the attractions of this from the perspective of Bilbao or Barcelona it poses undeniable problems for regionalization as a whole. The unity of the civil service, with possibilities of personnel movement from one part of the country to another, is of critical importance if bureaucracy is not to be duplicated, and if the PSOE government is to achieve the difficult mission of reforming the central administration.

If the bureaucratic problem is to disperse real decision-making capacity to the regions in line with their considerable formal powers, the political problem is to maintain the centrality of the major Spanish parties (Blondel, 1981). The prospects for democracy will depend upon the evolution of the various political groupings, and particularly on the relative salience of class-based versus territorial conflict within the party system (Lasuén Sancho, 1981). It is evident from comparative political analysis that competition between nationwide parties based upon class or other kinds of social cleavage tends to perform an integrative function within a national political system, whereas competition between parties concentrating their claims to support in particular regions is inherently unstable (Lipset and Rokkan, 1967; Rose and Urwin, 1975; Smith, 1980). The problem with the regional party is that it flourishes upon a sense of territorial grievance, while smooth centre-regional relations within a decentralized framework will tend over time to erode away its political constituency. Hence the distinctively intractable character of inter-territorial conflict, especially where it has an ethnic or linguistic dimension (Barry, 1975). In the last resort the threat of secession or some equally direct challenge to authority is never far from the surface, since a dominant regional party already meets one of the two defining attributes of the independent state: it has an identifiable territory it wishes to govern, and all it lacks is lawful recognition of its claim for sovereignty.

Party political activity has been legal in Spain for less than a decade, and the Francoist legacy of depoliticization can still be seen in the instability of the party system (McDonough et al., 1981). Nevertheless, a notable feature of the new political scene was the strong regionalist current, not only in the ethnic nationalist regions of the Basque country and Catalonia, but in other regions where territorial identification had not hitherto been a source of political cleavage. It was manifested both in the growth of regionalist parties and in a recurrent problem of local discipline within the national mass parties. García Cotarelo (1981), in his analysis of 'The crisis of political parties in Spain', outlined the bleak possibility that the Spanish political parties could wholly disintegrate on geographical lines, leaving 'a central parliament whose authority would not extend beyond the provincial limits of the country's capital while the provinces themselves would be ruled by another set of political institutions'. The growth of Andalusian nationalism in the late 1970s was particularly disturbing from this point of view, since it seemed to some observers to presage 'a contagion of regionalism' which would spread throughout Spain as a political reflex to the progressive creation of autonomous regional governments. Building a regional party, Blondel forecast, 'will seem increasingly to be the only way to obtain advantage (and especially financial advantage), equal to those obtained by the regions which have already acquired a significant amount of autonomy' (1981, p. 331). In the event, developments during 1981–2 failed to bear out this pessimistic view of the correlation between governmental decentralization and political fragmentation. In the regional elections in Galicia in October 1981 and Andalusia in May 1982 the national mass parties regained ground from the territorial minorities. The painful disintegration of the centre-right UCD was matched by growing success of the hard-right Popular Alliance (AP), an unwelcome development in all respects save this: that AP used the regional governments as the stepping-stone towards consolidating its position in the national arena, acquiring *en route* a newfound, if weak, commitment to regional autonomy. Above all, the PSOE victories in the general election of October 1982 and local elections of May 1983 gave the socialists control of all large cities and nearly all regional governments as well as of the centre. Only in the Basque country and Catalonia did nationalist parties retain a significant presence. The statesmanlike qualities of the Gonzalez government will be fully tested by the problem of maintaining working relations with the strong regions which it does not control, while getting the majority of weak ones of its own colour properly established.

To summarize: the critical issue in Spain's continuing transition back to democracy is no longer what the formal design of the system should be, but whether the necessary accompanying developments in bureaucratic and political organization can be achieved. As we shall now try to show, the future prospects both for administrative reform and for maintaining an integrative political system may be significantly affected by measures taken on the economic front.

How the crises interlock

In the previous two sections we have described the crises of the economy and the polity, both of them essentially crises of transition from one model to another. The way out of the economic crisis is through policies for commercial and sectoral adjustment which promote external integration and managed reflation. The way out of the political crisis is through generalization of regional autonomy. In our last section we will put these two desiderata together and ask how they match up. Are they complementary or contradictory? Will the creation of the 'state of the autonomies' help or hinder the management of the economic adjustment? How compatible is political decentralization with bringing the Spanish model of assisted capitalism under democratic control?

To put our discussion into perspective we should first recall that the creation of the state of the *autonomías* is not *the* most important political development from the point of view of the performance of the Spanish economy. Labour and social policy have a much more immediate bearing upon economic performance, and it is quite possible to give a detailed analysis of the crisis (as, for example, OECD, 1981; Ministerio de Economía, 1979; or Liebermann, 1982), without making any reference at all to the reform of subnational levels of government. Even if the reverse is not quite true, nevertheless it is clear that the politics of regionalism in Spain owe as much to linguistic, cultural and historical factors as they do to the structural problems of the economy. But, as we shall argue, the two crises are related and it is instructive to study this relation, particularly in so far as it takes the form of a vicious circle in which economic disorders contribute to unstable central-regional relations, which in turn impede national economic management.

The economic consequences of regionalization can be considered on two levels. First is the question of the direct overhead costs of establishing a new tier of government. Ever since January 1980, when the executive committee of the UCD first decided to slow down the pace of the devolution process, the economic crisis has been cited as justification for proceeding cautiously. Though the price may well be judged to be worth paying, there is no denying that, in any political system, the creation of new governments is inherently expensive. The impact of the limited decentralization so far achieved may already be detected as one factor behind the rapidly growing public sector deficit (OECD, 1982a). Salvador Giner reminds us in Chapter 13 that clientelism is still an important feature of Spanish and other Southern European public administrations. A decentralized state apparatus may be all the more liable to overloading by parasitic personnel, particularly in the context of what Enrico Pugliese calls the *dependent assisted economy* of backward areas (see Chapter 5; also Graziani and Pugliese, 1979, ch. 3; Wade, 1980). So far, the multiplication of regional governments in both advanced and backward areas has outstripped the transfer of functions, and many observers have commented unfavourably on the apparent 'intoxication with power' of regional politicians who have surrounded themselves by the trappings of sovereignty in inverse proportion to their executive responsibilities (Ariño Ortiz, 1981, p. 102; Ferrando Badia, 1980, pp. 288–9). The philosophy of the PSOE government is clear: that to avoid a costly multiplication of functions, there must be a physical transfer of bureaucracy from centre to region to match the devolution of functions, and that the regions should themselves make use – in so far as possible – of the existing administrative resources of the provinces. On the face of it, these seem sound principles. But they take little account of the political tension existing between tiers of government and the administration's powers of resistance to undesired change. Even on the most generous assumptions, devolution will involve a considerable increase in unproductive expenditure at a moment of growing public sector deficit.

Granted that decentralization involves certain costs, these may of course be offset by the benefits of a more efficient and responsive system of government than the previous monolithic Madrid bureaucracy. Many have pointed to the administrative conservatism and inefficiency of the dictatorship, which contributed to the exhaustion of growth even before the economy had felt the impact of the OPEC price rises. Just as all the reviews that were made of Francoist regional policy commented that the policies would work better if local decision-makers had greater autonomy (Buttler, 1975; Richardson, 1975), so contemporary commentators argue the inherently greater efficiency of decentralized governments, because they can tailor their services to match local needs and preferences, because of their capacity for inter-departmental planning and coordination, and because of their superior resources of information and informal influence. The danger, in this interpretation (for which see Quintas Seoane, 1981, or the comprehensive theoretical review of Lázaro Araujo, 1979), lies not with too much devolution but with an insufficiently drastic reorganization of the existing administrative structure. And this case for decentralization might be thought to grow proportionately stronger at a time of austerity in public expenditure: the smaller the total of public expenditure, the greater the case for leaving regional governments a free hand to allocate it where it will yield the maximum social return. The higher overhead costs of a decentralized system may be offset in this interpretation by improved performance and accountability.

But this leads us back to the second and weightier aspect of the economic consequences of regionalization, namely the new fields of substantive conflict which it opens up, both horizontally, as between regions, and vertically between region and centre. For the remainder of this chapter we discuss the character of such conflicts and the means for their democratic resolution.

By way of introduction, we must see how the constitution defines the division of labour between state and regions in the field of economic policy (for this topic see García de Enterria, 1980; Tornos, 1979, 1981).

Comparative study of federal systems of government indicates that, what-ever the degree of political decentralization, the exigencies of modern state-hood require that certain indivisible functions should reside at the centre, namely the responsibility for external relations and defence, and for the maintaining of the value of the currency, the unity of the national market, and the common rights of citizenship. It is to ensure this hierarchy of functions that legislative supremacy ultimately lies in the capital. The constitution of 1978 follows this principle, though not without some ambiguities which have attracted much comment. While it gives the Madrid government exclusive responsibility for national matters, it explicitly sets up a counter-principle of exclusive and unimpugnable regional sovereignty in regional matters. The decentralist spirit of the constitution can be seen in its comparatively generous approach towards the devolution of economic power – comparative, that is, to the Italian Constitution of 1947 or to most federal systems with the possible exception of Canada (Muñoz Machado, 1980). The autonomous regions are granted 'financial autonomy for the development and exercising of their powers in conformity with the [two] principles, of coordination with the State Treasury, and of solidarity among all Spaniards'. Financial autonomy was described in the preamble to the subsequent regional finance law as 'the ability of the autonomous communities to decide both the structure and the level of provision of public services'. As we shall see, the Catalan and Basque statutes and the conduct of the autonomous governments to date have inclined towards a broader rather than a narrower interpretation of these words, reflecting the regions' consti-tutional responsibility (under article 148.13) for the general promotion of economic activity within their areas. Their potential powers for this extend appreciably further than, say, those of the Italian regions, and include powers over industry and labour, banking and credit, and certain forms of price control, as well as infrastructure investment. They certainly do not correspond with the textbook allocations of national and local functions in fiscal theory (Lázaro Araujo, 1979; Ariño Ortiz, 1981).

The newly established regional governments have been encouraged by the crisis to build up their claims to legitimacy on the prospect of using their powers to the full in pursuit of the two economic planning objectives – not necessarily complementary, as Torres Bernier (1980) observes – of boosting employment and improving the structural mix of their regions. Regional economic initiatives get equal prominence in the backward rural regions such as Andalucia, where a consciousness of underdevelopment and relative deprivation has been the principal stimulus to the new regionalism, and in the traditional industrial regions of Catalonia and the

Basque country (Hebbert, 1982a). As we noted earlier, the older industrial areas have had, since 1975, the fastest growing unemployment rates in Spain, and by 1981 their level of unemployment was equalling or exceeding that of the poorest rural regions – and this is mainly urban unemployment, which readily finds organized political expression. Two further important factors stand out in the relatively rich core regions. The first is the problem of the infrastructure deficits which they inherited from the Franco years. The basis of the 1960s boom was very rapid expansion of the productive base with a minimal level of investment in non-productive infrastructure, a short-term strategy which is now, in the medium term, producing a serious problem of delayed demand for social capital in the major urban centres. That is also where we find the largest concentration of ageing industrial plant, the most pressing claims for capital investment and the closest involvement of the industrial bourgeoisie in the politics of regionalism. Not for the first time in Spanish history, their conflict with the state bureaucracy and the financial bourgeoisie in Madrid finds expression in territorial politics.

The essence of regional autonomy in both richer and poorer areas is the promise which it holds for economic recovery. This theme dominates the speeches of regional politicians, and the groundwork for regional economic planning attracts much of the resources of their executives. As yet the work has mainly been at a preliminary stage, but the experience of the relatively well-established Basque and Catalan governments indicates the kind of initiatives which we can expect to appear elsewhere as regional governments attempt to put into operation a 'bottom-up' planning of development in their areas (Arino Ortiz, 1981; Muñoz Machado, 1980). The spread of measures is typical of the stronger type of regional development agency with general-purpose powers in modern Europe (Yuill, 1983), and includes external promotion, traditional infrastructure measures such as the development of advance factory sites, management advice and aid with technical development, financial programmes, utilizing, so far as legal powers permit, funds of provincial or regional savings banks to supplement the resources available to regional governments for industrial aid, and much more ambitiously, regional-level industrial restructuring policies operated at the three-digit level (i.e. dealing with groups of firms in quite specialized sub-sectors) in the interstices of the national government's industrial modernization plan.

Alongside its developmental programmes, the wealthy government of the Basque country has a straightforward programme of current expenditure on unemployment relief in minor public works, which in the financial year 1982–3 was estimated to have created 20,000 jobs. It also operated an employment premium, granting an average of 300,000 pesetas to firms for each net extra industrial job created. During 1982, over 1000 grants were made on this basis. (For details of the Basque and Catalan economic initiatives, see Gobierno Vasco, 1983; Oller i Campañ, 1981; Bassa, 1982.)

In the early days of the autonomous regions, the emphasis given to economic policy by regional politicians alarmed some commentators, who suggested that the new governments might, within the relatively permissive framework of the constitution, experiment with extreme protectionist measures which could break the unity of the national market. (See particularly the views of the business community in Circulo de Empresarios, 1979.) The eminent constitutionalist García de Enterria, introducing his book on this topic (1980, p. 19), expressed his foreboding at the tendency of regionalist groups to expound proposals

> to stimulate their autonomous communities with completely exclusive, separate and different economic policies from those reigning in the rest of the country. This singularity on occasions extends to actual systems of economic and social planning alongside those provided for in the Constitution. Other times they talk about applying rules to prohibit the 'export' of capital generated by the citizens of the Community to benefit investments located in another, local monetary policies, covering savings and credit, separate industrial relations systems, and of course, wholly original taxation systems separate from the national exchequer. These proposals seem to flourish among political groups in their schemes for the regions. It is not difficult to foresee that an immediate consequence of this type of action, if it happened to be implemented, would be an outbreak of economic rivalry between regions, which would promptly struggle to attract investments and revenue, force unproductive or simply inconvenient elements to emigrate, and get benefits while shedding costs onto neighbours. The reestablishment of internal customs would add the finishing touch to the complete break-up of the national market.

No doubt the exaggerated tone of much of the autonomist literature in the post-Franco years (for a convenient summary of which see Bernal Martin, 1977) contributed to such disquieting speculation, with its echoes of the abortive federalism of the First Republic of 1873 which collapsed almost instantaneously into anarchic localism. However, the early years of the 1978 regionalism have shown no tendency to follow the same path. With one or two exceptions, to which we return below, the initiatives of the autonomous regions have been perfectly compatible with the integrity of the national economy, as may be supposed from their resemblance to initiatives promoted by regional tiers in many other European countries. The threat of protectionism, which may have had some relevance at an earlier stage of economic development when political regions did correspond to functional entities with a certain level of economic closure, has none in modern Spain, with its high level of business concentration, its integrated national market, its nationally determined wage rates, and above all its web of transfer-payments via public sector and welfare services. Though some regions, notably the Basque country and Catalonia, employ the rhetoric of economic nationalism, in practice the conduct of their governments has quite comfortably accommodated to the role of a territorial pressure group and implementation agency *within* a national framework.

Nothing demonstrates this better than the only consistent element of national economic policy during the period covered by this paper, namely, the industrial restructuring plans for sectors worst hit by the crisis. Since the legal base for intervention was established in the 1981 Law on Industrial Reconversion, plans have been implemented to support the rationalization of various sectors, among them special steels, textiles, automobile electrical parts, and shipbuilding. Both Basque and Catalan governments have Departments of Industry with their own policies and instruments to reorganize old industries and stimulate new ones, each with substantial annual investment budgets of (in 1982) about 3000 million pesetas. No serious conflicts have been generated by the operation of industrial policy on two tiers. On the contrary, the centre–region division of labour has evolved much on the lines envisaged by the constitution. The Spanish government initiates sectoral plans (and carries the political costs, sometimes heavy, of their implementation). A region participates in preparing the plans wherever it has more than 10 per cent of the employment in the sector concerned. It then both shares the implementation of the resulting national plan, and complements it with whatever rationalization schemes it may have of its own for ancillary sectors (Gobierno Vasco, 1983, pp. 119–29). The successful operation of a multi-tier industrial programme in the leading regions offers an encouraging precedent. Policymakers are aware that the ability to operate such programmes will become doubly important after accession to the EC.

As indicated above, not all aspects of the decentralization have gone as smoothly as industrial policy. First, there have been conflicts over the administrative transfer of certain aspects of economic policy. In the Basque country, for example, one of the most difficult and protracted of all the transfer negotiations was that over industrial research and development. Secondly, there have been some conflicts over the subsequent initiatives of regional governments. Here again, the most important examples are from the Basque country. Of the many regional laws which have been challenged by the state, two are in the field of economic policy: one established new forms of public intervention over haulage contractors in the Basque country, the other bestowed on the Basque government the right to regulate savings banks within the region. Both cases went before the Constitutional Tribunal which, as in any federal or quasi-federal system (Sawer, 1969), is now playing a crucial role in demarcating the respective scope of regional autonomy and central control. The tribunal's rulings make interesting reading for its careful discussion of the concept of the unity of the national market and of the extent to which this unity is compatible with independent regional initiative. Both rulings were broadly favourable to the Basque government while reaffirming the underlying principles of market integrity and the responsibility of the state to guarantee it. They lend weight to our argument that the vertical coordination of economic policy between centre and regions may prove less problematic than was initially feared by Garcia de Enterria and other commentators.

Apart from the degree of economic independence from the centre to be enjoyed by the governments of the autonomous communities, the other major question concerns their mutual obligations to each other. Though the gap between rich and poor regions has narrowed marginally in the present depression, it still remains wide, as Figure 12.3 shows (Hebbert, 1982a). Once again, we may use Pugliese's concept of the *subsidized* economy to characterize the deep-rooted dependence of central and southern Spain on the redistributive role of government via transfer payments and preferential investments (see Mochon Morcillo, 1980, for an attempt to quantify these subsidies in the case of Andalusia). Regionalization clearly requires changes in the mechanisms of redistribution. It also highlights and politicizes the distributive outcomes.

There is a clear polarization of views on the question of 'solidarity'. The poorer regions perceive themselves as dependent and exploited. They argue that they have helped to build up the prosperity of Spanish manufacturing by supplying labour, capital and resources, and that in a relatively closed and protected economy they have provided a reserved preferential market for domestic industry. They justify inter-regional compensation as a counterbalance to the northward drain of private capital labour and resources, and as a safeguard against 'an explosive situation whereby the underdeveloped regions become aware that national unity simply ensures their insolidary exploitation by the more industrialized regions' (Javaloys, 1978, p. 23). The Basques and Catalans, for their

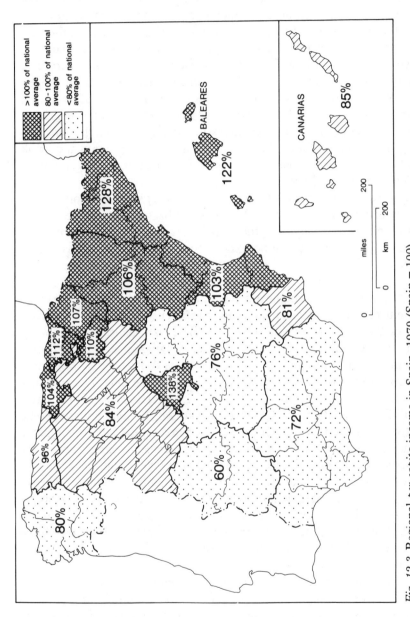

Fig. 12.3 Regional *per capita* income in Spain, 1979 (Spain = 100)

Source: Banco de Bilbao (1982), *Renta Nacional de España y su Distribución Provincial 1979*

part, have traditionally perceived the rest of Spain as a drag on their own dynamism. They attack the shallow-rootedness of the new *autonomías* and the cynicism of the central state which allowed them to proliferate. They argue that the urbanized regions are in no position to subsidize the rural periphery, now that they have to cope with the problems of economic recovery on top of the deficits of social facilities and infrastructure inherited from the boom of the 1960s. And they also point to the dependence of the entire Spanish economy upon the prosperity of its leading regions. Such contrasted perceptions of the solidarity issue, which are deeply embedded in popular attitudes in the regions (García Ferrando, 1978), have produced a high degree of political confrontation and brinkmanship over the financial arrangements for the autonomous communities (Quintas Seoane, 1981).

The constitution, in setting up the system of regional autonomy, made explicit provision for horizontal cross-subsidization in the interests of what it called 'solidarity', i.e. the principle that in a more decentralized system of taxation and public expenditure, the richer regions should compensate the poorer not merely to the degree necessary to ensure a basic minimum level of public services throughout Spain – a normal provision in federal systems – but in the much greater degree required for 'the establishment of a just and adequate economic balance between the different areas of Spanish territory' (Article 138, I). This constitutional commitment to use public investment in order to guarantee inter-territorial economic equilibrium is, as López Nieto and Fernandez Rodriguez observe (1981, pp. 208–18), unique in comparative law. The principal mechanism for giving effect to it is an 'Interterritorial Compensation Fund' (FCI), already in 1982 a substantial kitty of 180,000 million pesetas (say £1000 million), i.e. 30 per cent of budgeted capital investment net of defence expenditure. Every region of Spain gets something from it, but the distribution, made according to a weighted combination of the four factors of *per capita* income, out-migration, unemployment and surface area – with special increment for the islands – provides 15,782 pesetas per inhabitant of Extremadura, the poorest region, and only 2235 *per capita* in the Madrid region. These transfers must be dedicated to projects of infrastructure, public works, irrigation, housing, social facilities and improvement of the rural habitat.

Here is a new conception of regional economic policy, and one which involves evident risks that investment may be scattered through areas which for lack of entrepreneurial capacity or the absence of markets are not capable of sustained economic growth, implying an opportunity cost to the economy as a whole. Even a relative improvement in the position of less developed areas may – in the context of highly competitive world markets – be purchased only by a weakening of development potential at the level of the state (Lasuén Sancho, 1981). In this context it is interesting to note that the annual allocations in the Interterritorial Compensation Fund have been strongly criticized on the grounds that they are not actually as redistributive as they appear to be, but involve merely a relabelling of existing expenditures of central government departments. Nevertheless, inter-regional transfer payments of this sort have a high degree of political visibility. Whatever the actual redistributive effect of the solidarity principle, there is no doubt that it has – ironically – been one of the most divisive issues in the process of regionalization (Linares Martín, 1981).

No doubt these horizontal conflicts have tended to accentuate the latent localism within the Spanish political system, as Linares Martín (1981, p. 88) has argued, though the alarming vision of a fragmentation of the party system on territorial lines was happily dispelled by political developments during 1982–3. It is clear that the circumstances of the economic crisis do make the political adjustment appreciably more difficult than it would be in a period of expansion. And by a vicious circle, political uncertainty about the decentralization process is itself a factor making for business uncertainty and a poor investment climate.

So we return to our central theme: the relation between the economic and political dimensions of change in modern Spain. MacMillion (1981) has characterized them pessimistically as an economic process of *international integration* and a political process of *intranational disintegration*, arguing that penetration of multinational enterprise can only deepen the regional disequilibrium of the Spanish economy, and with it, the territorial cleavages in the political system. The country is trapped, in this interpretation, in a vicious circle whereby a territorially divided state is cumulatively less and less able to present a countervailing force against international economic forces, which in turn progressively aggravate its internal divisions. (John Carney offers the same argument at a more general level in Carney, 1980, pp. 54–5.)

This chapter has offered a less catastrophic interpretation of the change now occurring. Though the polity is in crisis, it is not a crisis of *disintegration* but of transition to a new constitutional model based upon political *decentralization*. Far from weakening the state's capacity to plan and stimulate economic recovery, decentralization is vital to it. The exhaustion of growth in Franco's years was linked inextricably with the concentration of power in a top-heavy and unresponsive institutional system. Conversely, the most innovative developments in economic policy at present can be found at the regional and municipal levels.

Nevertheless it remains true – despite the delusions of some romantic nationalists (e.g. Busquet and Vidal, 1980, p. 110) – that the commanding heights of the economy are to be found in Madrid, and are accessible, if at all, only to intervention by the Spanish state. Bottom-up planning within a dependent economy offers no prospect of success unless monetary, credit and trade factors are running in its favour. Decentralized policy may perversely impede national economic adjustment, by multiplying political and legal checks upon state action, by enlarging the bureaucracy, by scattering investment. The problem is to establish a stable institutional framework that combines local autonomy without depleting the sovereignty of the centre over those aspects of economic policy which of their nature must fall, in even the most decentralized system, to a central government whose jurisdiction is coterminous with the relatively closed boundaries of the national economy. In the European context the Federal Republic of Germany provides a conspicuously successful model (Johnson, 1979).

The constitution laid the basis for such a system, though not without some ambiguities which may or may not be resolved through the current legislation on the harmonization of central and regional governments. Conflicts over issues affecting the balance of power between centre and regions and between rich and poor regions will continue throughout the long transitional period until the constitutional model of the State of the Autonomies becomes fully established. The path of economic and political adjustment may be obscure in parts but the destination, we have argued, is now clear, and not unpromising.

Note

1 The authors are grateful to Javier Alfonso Gil for his comments on an earlier draft, and to Toni Tulla and Dolores Garcia-Ramon for a good discussion at the Durham Conference: but responsibility for the content of this paper is the author's alone.

13

Political economy, legitimation and the state in Southern Europe[1]

Salvador Giner

Introduction

Until recently, the countries of Southern Europe have often been seen as standing half-way between the fully developed capitalist industrialized nations and the areas much farther removed from the historical centres of initial modernization. Their belated and, no doubt, incomplete passage from an economically and politically peripheral (or, more accurately, semi-peripheral) position in the world capitalist division of labour into a far more central one has put these societies in a relatively difficult situation from the point of view of analysis.[2] Compounding this difficulty is the fact that some cities and regions in this part of Europe have had for a long time domestic bourgeoisies with a fully 'modern' and 'Western' outlook and, hence, they did not, in any correct sense of the word, 'import' capitalism or the industrial mode of production. They are societies which have always been European in many a substantial sense, save to the unperceptive minds of travellers from the north in search of exoticism. In fact, two of them became the metropolis of vast and enduring empires, thus actively participating in the consolidation of what was to become the modern Eurocentric system of international economic interdependence. (By contrast, another one, Greece, has not only never been an imperial power in modern times but was itself a part, until 1821, of the Ottoman Empire.)

These societies have been subject to the ambiguities, strains and endemic polarizations generated by the simultaneous presence of a number of contradictory trends, uneven stages of economic development and, in some cases, highly heterogeneous ethnic, class and cultural components. The most diverse and apparently irreconcilable trends vigorously asserted themselves within their boundaries: cultural universalism and local and kinship bonds of patronage; religious legitimation of public institutions and militant secularism; classless and doctrinaire political commitments and uncompromisingly class-bound ideologies; dependent industrialization through foreign capitalist investment and a very substantial degree of national capitalism, later followed by state capitalist intervention. For this reason Southern European societies could (and still can) not be easily ranked along any of the several conventional and imaginary continua, or axes, often used (perhaps quite carelessly) for the rough classification of societies, such as those exemplified by the familiar dichotomies backwardness v. modernity, pre-industrial capitalism v. advanced capitalism, traditionalistic fatalism v. enterprising individualism, non-scientific, religious mentality v. rationalism and a scientifically minded attitude. The confrontation of these conflicting forces in the northern rim of the Mediterranean, the strife and strains they have continuously generated and the successive undemocratic solutions that have frequently been reached at the political level give the region – in spite of its striking internal variations – an unmistakable commonality and distinctiveness within the larger framework of European society.

This distinctiveness, together with certain historical continuities and a common geopolitical and economic location on Europe's southern flank allows the analyst to advance a number of cautious and limited generalizations. In this chapter I propose to make and substantiate such generalizations by analysing some important aspects of the class and power structures resulting from the cleavages and many-sided confrontations which characterize Southern Europe – by which I mean only Greece, Italy, Portugal and Spain – as the basis for a macro-sociological explanation of social change in the region. This must be done historically with the help of a periodization appropriate to all four societies in question. I thus hope to show that their troubled national histories possess a much higher degree of consistency than is often thought to be the case. The fact that certain general patterns, cutting across countries and states, do emerge, belies the image of haphazard instability, volatility and unpredictability so often held by observers of Europe's southern world.

The recognition of these historical and structural patterns does not mean that all northern Mediterranean societies can be made to fit one single Procrustean bed, only that they exhibit a number of interesting common traits with respect to their historical evolution, predominant modes of political domination, the form and the tempo of their economic development (or stagnation, as the case may be) and systems of class relations. By comparing them and looking at their common traits as much as at their divergencies, we will be in a better position to know not only why these countries are economically late developers, but also why they began to improve their status at a given moment in their recent history or, more accurately, why they have not done even better. Unfortunately, the very scope of the analysis, together with the limited length of this chapter, will not allow me to go into the details of every particular historical event in each country.

As a heuristic device the entire historical process in Southern Europe since the early nineteenth century can be sub-divided into four distinct periods, separated by three modes of transition. The ensuing discussion will show their remarkable degree of overlap and synchronicity. More important for our argument than the relative synchronicity of the stages of change, however, is their sequential and episodic similarity across all the societies examined. The four phases are the following.

Oligarchic rule and extreme popular exclusion

The immediate breakdown of the four *ancien régimes* allowed exceptional popular participation in wars of liberation and independence, linked to ephemeral moments of radical liberal access to power. Yet these events were soon harnessed by the oligarchic monopoly of the state and the systematic exclusion of the subordinate classes from any form of participation in the political sphere by means of a restricted franchise and frequent military intervention. (The longest-lasting case seems to have been Greece where court and *tzakia* control by notables lasted from 1820 to 1869.) This type of domination was made possible by the small scale of the local industrial bourgeoisies, the nature of international capitalist penetration based largely on foreign dealings with state officials and foreign loans and the vastness of the rural population. Nevertheless, in this period certain parliamentary processes and a limited opposition were established.

Bourgeois consolidation and continued popular exclusion

At one point the façade of parliamentary institutions created in Phase I began to be used by rising commercial, rural and industrial bourgeoisies allied to 'respectable' middle classes everywhere. The latter often rallied to incipient modern (so-called 'mass') parties. Popular exclusion and lack of lower class representation (persecution of trade unions, rigged elections, etc.) allowed the creation of 'turning' bourgeois regimes with governments which rotated between conservatives and liberals. Between them, they tightly controlled the small sphere of 'legitimate' political activity. Thus efforts by Venizelists in Greece, Giolittists in Italy,

Mauraists in Spain, and other similar movements towards 'national regeneration' from within the established order were doomed by their incapacity or unwillingness to incorporate the peasantry, the proletariat and other popular forces. Exceptions to this form of class and political exclusion at the end of the period, however, produced the de-radicalization of some socialist parties where they were accepted as legitimate participants, but this did little to alter the overall conservative nature of the regimes. The transition to the next phase occurred when the political order of such monarchist, parliamentary and thoroughly bourgeois hegemonic regimes failed to achieve two aims: (a) the successful incorporation (or, alternatively, neutralization and control) of the growing radical extraparliamentary opposition, and (b) the successful implantation of a privately financed imperialist state. This latter aspect of the phenomenon was illustrated by the Italian defeat in Abyssinia (1895), the Portuguese humiliation in Angola and Mozambique (1896 rebellion), the Spanish colonial disaster (Spanish-American War, 1898), and later, the Greek holocaust in Asia Minor (1922).

Fascist and fascistoid military dictatorships

The transition to this period came with the 'disorders' bred by the on-slaughts of the excluded and persecuted radical bourgeoisies and their allies against the old ruling groups, now in disarray largely because of their own political failures. In a number of cases the latter managed to bring about quasi-revolutionary republican regimes but, as a response to their serious challenge, law-and-order militaristic or militarily consolidated reactionary coalitions came to power. They set about to complement the endemic shortcomings of private capital accumulation with state intervention. Thus, despite the cultural archaism of some of the dictatorships (Italian fascism was certainly more of a novelty) modernization from above continued everywhere. The civil freedoms precariously allowed to exist under Phase II as part of its basic arrangements were now abolished.

Constitutional order within advanced capitalist corporatism

The exhaustion of the dictatorial praxis was caused by the continued rise of the middle classes, further urbanization and depeasantization, secularization, working class opposition, state capitalism and the international penetration of the economy. A series of crises, some of them linked to military defeats and adventurism, others to a renewed upsurge of popular and democratic forces, brought about the end of the dictatorships and the present parliamentary democratic regimes in Southern Europe. Although the radical rhetoric of the left has been kept alive, its virtually unprecedented political inclusion has come in exchange for its almost complete abandonment of revolutionary pretensions. Class distinctions and economic exclusion based on the relative permanence of the inherited social inequality are accepted by the left-wing opposition as a compensation for its incorporation into the legitimate sphere of political life. Thus, general moderation in respect to the traditional political demands of the radicals and a commitment to a minimum of welfare state policies by the conservatives form the basis of a new consensus. Yet, given the region's inherited political culture, the levels of ideological dissent, extremism of every kind, including both nihilism and maximalism, continue to be higher, by contrast, than they are in certain other European societies, though much lower than those prevalent earlier in it. Given the nature of international tensions today, however, it is not prudent to predict that these phenomena will continue to diminish. Meanwhile, all this is taking place with the full participation of these societies in the development of contemporary 'corporatist' tendencies in the economy. In all countries concerned a tripartite process of agreement between government, the employers and the trade unions has become an important feature of their economic life, whereas several of the other features often attributed to contemporary corporatism have also taken root. In this sense it is now possible to speak, albeit very tentatively, of a limited degree of 'convergence' with the arrangements prevalent elsewhere in the west.

The rise of capitalism in late developing societies

The political and intellectual history of Southern Europe in modern times cannot be explained without the anguished self-consciousness of the members of certain élite groups – from enlightened ministers of *ancien régime* governments to bourgeois reformers and educators – about the problem of relative backwardness. Their practical initiatives to put an end to it have ranged from notable improvements in education, health and transportation to the most foolish imperialist adventurism, from patient and skilful introduction of tolerance and liberalism to hurried and crude recourse to reactionary dictatorship for the violent, involuntary, accumulation of private and state capital. The Southern European preoccupation with what was seen as its endemic *backwardness* and the avid search for ways to overcome it did not appear suddenly, as did the related concept of *underdevelopment* when it burst out in the midst of ex-colonial countries in the twentieth century.[3] Ironically, theories of underdevelopment and economic dependence were later extended to the Southern European region, despite the fact that the evolution of their economies and political life has been very different from that of the so-called Third World.

Having witnessed the emergence and consolidation of certain social structures and cultural innovations which were to transform, in due course, the face of the European world, the peoples of the northern Mediterranean rim suffered a sharp and profound reversal in their fortunes towards the end of the Renaissance. Though the prosperity of the entire European Atlantic seaboard affected Castile and Portugal through their ports at Seville and Lisbon, the fortunes of the great patrician republics – the imperial cities of Barcelona and Venice – suffered irreparable damage under Ottoman expansion, not to speak of the entire Byzantine Greek world, which entirely fell within the power of the Porte. For example, Catalonia, Barcelona's hinterland, had become by the Renaissance one of the most advanced areas in Europe (Wallerstein, 1974, p. 101).[4] Subsequently excluded from trading with the overseas colonies of the Spanish monarchy, Catalans had hardly any choice but retrenchment and occasional revolts against the crown. Commercial stagnation combined with agricultural decline in the southern half of Europe, precisely when momentous innovations were taking place in these fields elsewhere on the same continent.[5]

The industrial revolution began in those countries (first in England, followed by Belgium) which had earlier experienced certain very far-reaching and unprecedented innovations in agriculture. Whereas the majority of European farmers were subsistence peasants living on small-holdings (or on large *latifundia* in certain areas of Southern Europe), the situation in the Low Countries and Great Britain had already begun to change in the sixteenth century. There a profound agricultural revolution had produced a capitalist, commercialized, and highly efficient farming system by 1800. This, no doubt, enhanced the further development of non-agricultural capitalism. In England, the existence of coal and iron ore, side by side, provided a special encouragement to industrialization. By contrast, the Mediterranean countries were immensely poor in natural resources. Thus, Italian industrialization throughout the nineteenth century, especially in the development of its non-textile industries, went hand in hand with the costly importation of coal. Because of the low quality of its coal, up to the eve of the First World War, Spain had to be supplied by the United Kingdom with well over 40 per cent of its coal and coke needs (Cafagna, 1975; Fontana and Nadal, 1975). Given the technological knowledge, specific resources and consumer needs of those times, Southern Europe was poor both in relative and in absolute terms.

The formidable rise of industrial and financial capitalism in North-western Europe, followed by intense international competition between its national powers in search of new markets and areas of influence, had very serious consequences for the incipient development of bourgeois industrial society in its southern semi-periphery. The seeds of the latter had been planted much earlier, and were unmistakably to be found in Catalonia, Lombardy, Piedmont and Oporto, as well as in the far-flung merchant classes of the Greek nation. Yet massive advanced capitalist intervention in the guise of both political interference and the *diktat* of much more powerful foreign buyers and sellers imposed two forms of constraint.

In certain cases, such as Portugal and Greece, early promises of development were frustrated. Thus, Greek efforts to create a textile and shipbuilding industry floundered already before the 1821 war of independence against the Turks (Mouzelis, 1978, p. 4). On the other hand, Pombal's eighteenth-century reforms in Portugal had their obvious built-in limitations, but they might have ultimately led the country into non-agricultural growth and modernization, had Portugal not been forced to become a client nation with a client empire under British tutelage in order to survive as a relatively independent state. In the larger societies, Italy and Spain, there occurred less a complete destruction of autochthonous possibilities for capitalist development than a special process of subordinate development. I use the term special because, in the first place, competition and dissension among the great powers (and the private companies and finance institutions operating from them) often slackened foreign surveillance and allowed for important bursts of non-dependent economic development in both countries, leading to the consolidation of national capitalist industries. In the second place, their national bourgeoisies, sheltered behind weak and inefficient but nevertheless somewhat effective states, managed to build up their strength by creating markets in their own territories. This also allowed them to enter the international arena when conditions were favourable. The consolidation of this pattern occurred in Italy during the expansion of 1878–89, when the 'leap forward' from textiles – silk, cotton, wool – to railway machinery and engineering opened the way for full transformation in the first decade of the twentieth century with the establishment of chemicals, light and heavy machinery, and hydroelectric plants. The meagre participation of foreign capital over the period (the years 1889–96 witnessed a serious international depression) only emphasized this point. A similar phenomenon occurred in Spain, though it lagged behind in both time and consequence. The same diversification from textiles to chemicals, iron and steel and hydroelectric power, occurred there. Although it began in the years before the First World War, the process gathered momentum under the advantageous conditions for export enjoyed by the non-belligerent economies during the conflict (Cafagna, 1975; Fontana and Nadal, 1975, pp. 460–73).[6]

The belated rise of industrial capitalism in Southern Europe before and during the First World War was only the most visible trace of a deeper current, with a much longer past: the qualitative transformation of all the economies in question into commercial, market economies, with wage payments for labour, proletarianization, and capital accumulation – often, of course, 'primitive' capital accumulation. The initial defeat of the industrial revolution in some parts (Portugal, Greece) and its circumscribed success in others (Italy, Spain) meant that capitalism had to confine itself for a long time to the commercial and property spheres. To oversimplify this complex issue: the societies of the south had long ceased to be pre-capitalist, but their new-found capitalism became stunted – its transition to industrialism systematically blocked by the forces that have been described and others that will be analysed below. What happened was not so much that these countries were 'late joiners' to the capitalist industrial transformation, but rather that their bourgeoisies had failed in their efforts to be among the 'first comers'.

The peripheral state and the path towards reactionary despotism

When Southern Europe entered the post-Napoleonic era, its political map was extremely varied. Yet important common traits and developments may be discerned. Despite a number of initial reforms begun (save in Greece) under the auspices of the *ancien régime*, nineteenth-century efforts to continue the process met with very stiff resistance and counter-attacks which drew their strength from the still massive pre-capitalist component of those societies. Liberal and reformist forces managed to reach power and introduce modernizing innovations only precariously and during very brief periods, usually when the traditionalist ruling classes were caught off their guard. On the whole, the liberal bourgeoisie managed to continue furthering capitalism only at the price of its continual alliance with the most backward-looking elements in the society. They thereby forsook some of the civic and political facets of the liberal creed to which they claimed adherence. In exchange, the initially anti-capitalist stance of the upper classes of the surviving *ancien régime* was largely abandoned, though their own view of profit maximization remained rather peculiar in a number of cases. The seigneurial ethos of the great rural landlords of

Sicily and Andalucia is a typical example of this survival and a paradoxical one at that, since feudal ties were themselves very weakly defined in Southern Europe. Defeudalization took the lines of least resistance, as shown by the forcible sale of church lands and properties in the middle and latter part of the nineteenth century.

With some variations, the process was everywhere similar. Thus, throughout the 1808–1914 period the Iberian bourgeoisies were too small and weak for their aspirations of economic and political supremacy. In Portugal, compromise with an immobilist and patriarchal establishment was their lasting option. Moreover, the Portuguese ruling classes were also forced to accept 'free exchange' by their British ally, thus dooming all chances for the development of a substantial national industry (Cabral, 1976, 1979).[7] The far larger and more complicated Spanish society offered somewhat greater possibilities. Yet the Catalan bourgeoisie and, later, the Basque, were rooted on ethnically and economically very distinct and limited grounds. Their ability to control the huge, cumbersome, remote and, as they saw it, archaic state apparatus in Madrid soon became problematic. As a consequence, significant sectors of the Catalan bourgeoisie soon began to appreciate the attractiveness of regionalism and, later, to engage in a persistent demand for home rule (Nadal, 1975). Eventually, both bourgeoisies would settle for a protectionism which allowed them to enjoy unmolested the exploitation of the Spanish market (including the remaining overseas possessions) for their own industries. Tariff protection, however, reinforced the familistic structure of Catalan capitalism and, by eliminating competition, made industrial renewal and innovation less necessary (Izard, 1978),[8] thus widening the serious gap which existed between industry in Spain and in the more advanced areas abroad.

The reverse situation obtained in Italy at the time of the Unification. Whereas the Catalans possessed a relatively advanced society which was subordinated to a larger pre-industrial political unit, the Piedmontese, Lombards and Ligurians formed the nucleus from which a modern state structure was being erected. The northern Italian élites were also, initially, the élites of the new state. Yet, the rapid inclusion of backward areas of large demographic weight meant a rapid loss of their control over the emergent public administration. The new state provided vast and relatively more attractive opportunities for employment for the urban non-industrial middle classes from the dismantled Papal states and the Kingdom of the Two Sicilies. Moreover, clientelist favouritism and electoral manipulation helped to inflate the ranks of officialdom. This last phenomenon, of course, was not restricted to Italy. Greece, for instance, suffered from even greater bureaucratic inflation as soon as the nation acquired an independent state (Mouzelis, 1978, pp. 16–17). What is significant in every case is that, no matter where the initiative to reform or build the state came from, the result was similar. The very circumscribed or hardly existent industrial sector combined with the needs of an aspirant modern state and oligarchic democracy. This led to the overloading of the public administration by parasitical personnel. This has remained a feature of Southern Europe down to its present day.

During its early stages, the modern state did not itself engage in production, save perhaps as a subsidiary to entrepreneurs for whom certain functionally necessary investments were not yet or no longer profitable. Certainly, the states of Southern Europe were at the time in no position to engage in subsidizing production. Under the new conditions, earlier traditions of state investment – Venice had had the earliest and the longest lasting state industry of any European polity – were of no avail. Yet, when they finally did, in the twentieth century, they did so with a vengeance, often under the auspices of fascistic autarkic economic policies. However, until such a time arrived, the chief service they rendered to their industrial bourgeoisies was an inconsistent protectionism, some public works and police and army protection. Economic protectionism was not restricted to tariffs against foreign manufacturers for privileged contracts, for local suppliers also played a very important role. Even this happened very late and haphazardly, and only after convoluted and protracted political battles within the ruling classes. For example, the introduction of the protective tariff in Italy only occurred in 1887. The endemic financial weakness of the national treasuries forced governments to accept foreign investment as a solution. Even admitting that this might have had some beneficial effects on the standard of living of the people directly affected by it, it could never by itself help create an independent and fully advanced economy, on a par with those from whence investment came. (The United States was also at the time dependent on foreign capital, but national capital formation was intense, and did not have to struggle against pre-capitalist or 'primitive' capitalist forces, once the Civil War was over.) Nevertheless, there were different degrees of success in the bourgeois 'nationalization' of capital investment: Italy was most effective in developing a strong capitalist class; Spain came nearest; Portugal lacked one and Greece possessed an absentee merchant bourgeois class. All this raises a number of important questions in the economic history of international development, dependence and arrested development which still remain unresolved.[9]

The long road to fascistic and semi-fascistic autarky was paved with the frustrations of a chronic dependence on foreign powers. The hegemonic classes of the Southern European countries up to the rise of the inter-war dictatorships were plagued by their own ideology of international free trade among unequal nations which they tried to make compatible with certain doses of protectionism. They were undermined by the free trade interests of their own agricultural exporters and by those of their government officials, so often open to foreign pressures and bribery. Foreign investments poured into the countries without regard to specific needs of their populations and profits were repatriated without substantial reinvestments in the host country. Very often and for a very long period of time, great mineral wealth was exploited by foreign companies at ridiculously low tax rates. The governments were too ill-equipped both ideologically and technically to face the implications of such dependence. Often, during the crucial early stages of the new era, their attention was absorbed with a deadly struggle with backward hinterlands (brigandage in Greece, Carlist warbands in Spain) and their resources were wasted by an incompetent officialdom. One can hardly wonder why they did not act otherwise: loans were often raised abroad, not to modernize or to industrialize, but simply to put down such awkward rebellions. In contrast with, say, Prussia, poised to lead the final transformation of Germany into a great industrial power and without serious internal dissensions (at least, not after 1848), the political leaders of the Southern European countries were usually not in a position to see beyond their immediate, pressing and often bewildering concerns. To compound all this, international threats and competition were very different from each other in Southern, Central and Northern Europe, being least favourable − given the nature of their economy − for the southerners.

Until the outbreak of the First World War substantially changed the political frame of reference for so many countries, the universe in which these Southern ruling classes moved was certainly non-totalitarian. Their model for national aggrandizement, industrialization and progress was embodied in the great parliamentary democracies, especially Great Britain. Alternative 'routes to modernity' were, of course, being devised, of which the political formulas of Bismarckian Germany and Meiji Japan are now the best known, but such a solution to the problem through 'modernization from above' was not yet understood as a 'model' by Southern Europeans − however much military and banking institutions might have been copied. The implications of the 'initially liberal' nature of state control and class inequality for the political order of the south were interesting. In the very early stages, when pre-industrial and/or *ancien régime*-based upper strata were still very powerful, they attempted to rule according to an overtly atavistic system of semi-feudal privilege. The set of oligarchic families crowding around the Greek throne (the *tzakia*, as they were known) and literally owning and running the Greek state is perhaps the ultimate example of this phenomenon. The *tzakia* even managed to survive the sweeping 1864 electoral reforms by a form of vote control (Tsoucalas, 1969). Its Spanish counterpart was the institution of political bossism known as *caciquismo*. Although it would be an overtly simplistic view of any Mediterranean country to describe it as dominated by a handful of families, at least in one case, Portugal, the role of oligarchic lineages and family *coteries* in the power structure of the state played a vital role until very recently. According to some authors the small Portuguese nepotistic oligarchy developed a symbiotic relationship with Salazarism and its power actually increased as time went on, reinforcing its strength in the regime's most typical institutions.[10] The opposite seems to be the case, however, for the Southern European world – even in Portugal – soon grew too complicated for the maintenance of such primitive arrangements as pivots of the political order (Schmitter, 1979).

The most accomplished, lasting, and characteristic political formula arrived at in these societies before the rise of fascism involved the accommodation of the then paradigmatic 'North-western' European pattern of liberal-democratic bourgeois government to their own backward environments. It found its clearest expression in Giolittian Italy (1878–1914) and Restoration Spain (1876–1923) but it could, almost as well, describe the Greece of Venizelos after 1910, and long periods of Portuguese 'republicanism' from 1822 to 1926. It is essential, however, not to regard these regimes as they so often have been, as mere aberrations of some ideal European model – an ideal which existed only in the realm of liberal political theory. Rather, they were the specific forms which liberal/conservative class domination took under the socio-structural, economic and cultural circumstances of the south. The specific elements of the Southern European hegemonic political formula for that age could perhaps, very sketchily, be described as follows.

Restrictive parliamentarianism

This was based on a limited, albeit expanding, degree of class pluralism. The incorporated political class was drawn, almost exclusively, from the upper and upper middle classes. Recruitment from other social classes into the 'legitimate' political class could occur only after individuals had been safely separated from their social origins through their integration into one of the three main recognized vertical corporations: the church, the army or the civil service. The stability (and instability) of such a highly conservative political order was underpinned by the actual and promised extent of the franchise. Barriers to its expansion were erected, as elsewhere, on the basis of literacy, property ownership, and so forth. Their demolition, however, was too slow and erratic for the efficient assimilation or neutralization of certain strategically located, hostile sectors of the society. As a consequence, a radicalization of lower middle-class intellectuals ensued. Elsewhere, disappointment and bitter scepticism grew – often connected with the growing urban proletariat and the increasingly commercialized peasantry. The real crisis often came when the ruling classes, trapped in their own intransigent ultra-conservative ideologies, ran out of concessions. It is true, however, that some leaders (notably Giolitti) were hardly ever ideologically trapped and that they were notably open to making such concessions.

The liberal creed

The ultimate sanction of the political order of that period was not autocracy in any of its known guises. Thus, even military dictators often issued their proclamations (*pronunciamientos*) by presenting themselves only as emergency saviours of a 'monarchic-liberal' order. Nor was it the application of sheer physical coercion. It was the liberal creed, usually in its conservative version, but also occasionally and uneasily combined with more radical (often anticlerical) and doctrinaire ideologies. In fact, the latter version, known often as 'radicalism', frequently functioned as the accepted opposition. The split into two distinctive forms of liberalism, or rather, of capitalist bourgeois ideology, did not, however, involve a drastic cleavage in political life. In fact, the distinction became less and less intense as time went on. We find the roots of this split at the very beginning of the period – for instance, in the juxtaposition of Mazzini's Young Italy Movement (which was secular, republican and democratic) and Cavour's constitutionalism (ready to find a role for the monarchy and an accommodation with the church). The Greek *dichasmos*, or schism, between Monarchists and Venizelists (after 1916) is another example. The virulence of the struggles between the two branches of the accepted political spectrum should not blind us to the fact of their complementarity and shared dominance within the political arena. The problem, which led much later to the ultimate breakdown of the system, was the inability of both wings (more glaring in the case of the radicals) to encompass, co-opt or otherwise integrate the vast sections of the civil society which fell outside the class-bound liberal creed. Unlike the Social Democrats in Northern and Central Europe, anarchists, socialists and other system challenging movements – left and right – in the South were never offered the chance of entering into a real and lasting compromise, save perhaps in Italy in 1910 and 1911. In that country, however, the chance was ruined by the Libyan war: once again the effects of colonialism upon the internal affairs of these countries appear as highly disruptive. In a word, the radical opposition, by and large, was constantly kept beyond the pale and led to some form of final confrontation.

Societal 'dualism'

Under such circumstances, reform and modernization occurred through an exceedingly slow process of accommodation between the interests of the ruling classes and the pressures from below. The former included the maintenance of low wages, the avoidance of agrarian reform whenever possible, and the advantageous private participation in state-sponsored projects through loans, etc. The latter included, of course, the workers' movement, middle-class revolutionary intellectuals and academic and peasant unrest. This built-in lag in responsiveness explains the enormous volume of accumulated contradictions in which Southern European societies found themselves on the eve of fascism. On the one hand, some essential structural changes had not taken place at all, such as the agrarian reform.[11] (Save in areas where external factors had forced it upon the government, such as the influx of citizens through wars, as in Greece. In 1917 Venizelos was able to break up the large Thessalian *latifundia*, or *chiftliks*, and, subsequently, the 1922 Asia Minor *débâcle* put further pressure on land occupation and distribution among the people.) On the other, there had arisen a sizeable industrial sector, with its urban proletariat and a small but growing middle class: little or no effort was made to meet their demands. In the specific sense of these cleavages – but not in the sense that there were 'two' societies and 'two' economic orders in each country – the Southern European region possessed a degree of dualism.[12]

The utopian element

In this social and political context, impossible dreams of national aggrandizement were nourished. Governing élites of the Southern countries spoke a language and manipulated the symbols of belligerent expansionism or imperialism – often as a means of detracting attention from their failure to implement domestic reform. Let me hasten to say that realistic (and materialistic) bourgeois imperialist aims were also present, for example, in the Spanish mining interests in the Riffian wars in Morocco, the Portuguese share, however meagre, of the economic exploitation of the country's own vast overseas territories, the desire of Italian industrialists to possess greater markets for an economy that was beginning to be quite substantial in world terms by the turn of the century. These must all loom large in the explanation of imperialist expansionism. The fact remains, however, that only hurt pride, not political calculation, could have inspired the Spaniards to send their antiquated and feeble fleet against the American aggressors in the Caribbean and in the Philippines in 1898. Other cases, such as the Greek Anatolian adventure (posthumously defined as 'folly' by Greek critics) may have been objectively less foolish in the sense that it was perhaps reasonable at the time to assume the extreme weakness of the Turks, especially after they had been so thoroughly routed in the First World War. The uneasy success of Italian expansion in Africa may also weaken claims that Southern imperialism was utopian. Yet, only a perception of national realities in terms of ethnocentric European ideological distortion can help us understand the behaviour of governments which refused to improve their internal markets, raise the educational level of their peoples, and even promote further capital accumulation in their own economies and instead embarked on disastrous wars in hopeless emulation of the Great Powers – even if that emulation sometimes served the immediate purpose of diverting popular discontent from the much graver social issues of the day.

The inner contradictions of each one of these basic components – limited parliamentarianism, restricted and divided liberalism, stunted reformism and utopian imperialism – irrevocably led these societies towards a very specific form of class despotism – namely, fascist and/or *fascistisant* dictatorship. This occurred when the social transformations created under the aegis of the above 'paternalistic' political order became too much at odds with it. A new solution had to be found that would, on the one hand, allow the continued legitimation of the inherited system of inequality, foster the widespread aim of national aggrandizement, and further capitalist industrialization while, on the other, successfully destroying the revolutionary movements of the left which had begun to challenge seriously the existing order. Such a solution was found and imposed through various forms of violence at somewhat different points in time. Its triumph meant the end of the old liberal bourgeois order as well as a redefinition of the political and economic functions of the state. It meant, also, the demise of the revolutionary path to modernization in Southern Europe.

'Fascism' and class domination

The question of the precise nature of fascism is a puzzling one. No less confusing is the question of 'how fascist' Italy, Spain and the other Mediterranean countries really were (Woolf, 1968). Fascism *in abstracto* possesses a series of characteristics which can only be found in varying degrees of intensity in the area analysed here. 'Pure' fascism entails a political cult to one single chief; a mode of class domination closely related to single party control of the society; very extreme nationalism; the systematic neutralization of the opposition, up to and including its physical extermination; autarchic economic policies linked to state enterprise; the myth of ethnic, national or cultural superiority; extreme anti-communism and the reduction of all opposition to communism; imperialism; political paranoia. In real life, however, this construct appears as part and parcel of a larger political universe in which other, less explicit, structures of power and inequality play a considerable role.

Not only the degree of 'fascistization' but also the kind of fascist experience varied considerably from society to society. In the Mediterranean area, the nearest thing to the fascist ideal type was, of course, Mussolini's regime. It dominated Italy from 1922 to 1943. Some observers may claim that only Italy was fascist as it was the only country with a popular, charismatic leader. This ignores the perhaps unpalatable fact that Franco and Salazar were as popular and, indeed, cherished, in several substantial sections of their countries as was Mussolini. One could even argue that they were more 'legitimate', for they were rather more closely identified with certain mentalities and deeply engrained class attitudes than Mussolini, who was committed to a party and a movement. Others may claim that authentically 'fascist' economic policies of national autarky were carried out in only two out of the four countries. Despite these and other differences, the other Mediterranean dictatorial regimes came quite close to the Italian formula, especially at certain stages of their history. They were Salazarism in Portugal (1926–74) and Francoism in Spain (1936–76). The Greek Metaxas regime (1936–40) shared important characteristics with the others and certainly the outspokenly fascist beliefs of that dictator himself firmly placed the country within the sphere of European Mediterranean 'fascism'. Moreover, certain other regimes in the area, either preceding or succeeding the hard-core fascist periods just mentioned – for example, the Primo de Rivera dictatorship in Spain (1923–31) and the Colonels' dictatorship in Greece (1967–74) – were perhaps less completely fascist, but they can be analysed as either starting or completing the historical process. For Southern Europe must be viewed as a whole, rather than as a number of discrete and unrelated instances of praetorian right-wing rule. The fascist or *fascistisant* solution in that part of the world must be understood as an essentially 'long wave' counter-revolutionary phenomenon.[13]

All these societies passed through at least one variety of that kind of solution and did so under relatively similar historical conditions. Basically, fascist and semi-fascist dictatorships appeared when the traditional political formulae of bourgeois parliamentary domination began to break down. The crises came to a head at different times after the First World War, though earlier 'warnings' of what was coming could be detected (e.g. the Barcelona insurrection of 1909 and Lisbon insurrection and proclamation of the republic in 1910). They occurred when the pressures of increasingly radical and revolutionary movements combined with serious setbacks in the economy. Both became all the more serious because important structural transformations had previously taken place in the societies concerned. These were beginning to be felt by political orders which were becoming quite unsuited to cope with such new demands and forms of political action. It was then that the several varieties of modern despotism which go under the generic name of 'fascism' came to the rescue. This new order possessed the following characteristics.[14]

A specific mode of class domination

In Southern Europe the form of reactionary despotism that may be defined as 'fascist' or that adopted certain forms of 'fascist state corporatism' was essentially a mode of class domination brought about by a right-wing political coalition.[15] Regimes which followed its pattern invariably claimed to represent everyone's interests – hence their frequent recourse to populistic nationalism for the control of the collective means of emotional production[16] – but from the start they were deliberately entrusted with the preservation of the interests of a reactionary coalition. Usually they paved the way for further capital accumulation and the development of capitalism in accordance with the wishes of the ruling classes, though this aspect of the situation soon ran into difficulties when confronted by other, equally important, imperatives.

At any rate, these regimes neutralized the working classes and other threatening groups (such as dissident intellectuals and students) so that internal peace was assured. With the notable exception of Italy the reactionary coalition – landowners, industrialists, financiers – controlled the state through the army, whose highest echelons were amply rewarded, although the concrete mode of articulation between ruling groups varied from

country to country. Thus, the key office of chief of state was taken over by
the military in Spain and Greece, though Portugal's dictatorial head of
government was a civilian. In Italy, intense militarization of the Fascist
Party largely made up for the less prominent weight its army had in the
general arrangements of the fascist dictatorship. In Greece, the right-wing
forces went through a long and tortuous path of coalition formation: the
1936 Metaxas dictatorship suppressed and temporarily superseded the
dichasmos between the radical, middle-class Venizelists and the Monarchists, but the two sides were not really reconciled until confronted with
their common enemy in the Civil War, at the earliest. Full reconciliation
took place in the 1970s, under a new dictatorship, as well as under the
pressures of considerable social change and the relentless passage of time.
By then, however, the Colonels' dictatorship was approaching matters
quite differently. Their government went out of its way to woo the established bourgeoisie and the 'unreliable' sections of the armed forces – the
Navy and Air Force – but was notoriously unsuccessful in welding the
ruling classes into one firm reactionary coalition. This major structural
weakness allowed the notables of the right-wing parties, whose democratic
credentials were more than doubtful, to convert to democracy and come to
power in 1974. For the first time they shed the accepted double-standards
of Greek pseudo-democratic rule: government under a liberal constitution
with the help of a set of illiberal and thoroughly repressive unconsti-
tutional laws, forming a 'para-constitutional order' in themselves.

These reactionary coalitions assured the centralized control of the
political and administrative apparatus in its intermediate and lower rungs
through a *Dienstklasse* or 'service class' (Renner, 1953; Archer and Giner,
1977) drawn from a relatively wide spectrum of population. The easy
recruitment and loyalty of this 'class' were assured by the backward or
semi-developed nature of the economy: job security, a steady income and
health and medical advantages were even more highly valued in Southern
Europe than farther north. This arrangement also helped consolidate the
alliance of the rulers with the middle classes.

These regimes combined, therefore, traditional forms of class domination
with a tight control of the public administration, an effective distribution of
state rewards and a fairly adequate neutralization of the subordinate classes,
not necessarily involving political mobilization. This means that they can
neither be seen as mere reflections of a mode of production (or, even, a
reflection of an articulation of modes of production into a complex whole)
nor as mere tools of the ruling classes. Each despotic regime may be, of
course, partly a 'tool' of that nature, but the vested interests of the
institutions and corporations on which it has to rely become themselves

constraints at the level of domination, i.e. limitations on power and orientations for policy stemming from the make-up of the regime itself. For these reasons modern despotic regimes and their states are among the most important structuring agents of the societies over which they rule. Once established they generate and maintain certain patterns of opportunity, occupation, and inequality which cannot be explained solely by the mere presence of inherited class structures nor by the dynamics of market trends, capital accumulation and other aspects of the economy. Nevertheless, their capacity to reshape the social structure is less than that of genuine totalitarian states. In fact, in the latter, the party is the central institution of power, privilege and class, whereas in the former (when it exists) it is secondary to the ruling class coalition. This is the reason why modern despotisms can more easily dismantle their party, police and 'trade-union' façades and give way to other, historically or economically, more adequate political arrangements, including, of course, parliamentarian democracy.

Restricted ideological sphere and limited political pluralism

In so far as a coalition of different classes differentially but firmly represents each one of them at the centres of political power, it is to be expected that the officially sanctioned ideological spectrum will also include ideological components drawn from each class. Likewise, the official ideological amalgam will explicitly exclude the ideologies and values of all the subordinate classes and outlawed parties and movements, although some rhetorical and symbolic concessions may have to be made to 'democracy', the 'common good' and other altruistic notions. This exclusion will entail a sustained and virulent propagandist attack on one main culprit (and its 'allies') whose progress is said to have been arrested by the establishment of the dictatorship. The culprit is usually 'communism', invariably not only the permanent scapegoat of reactionary despotism but also the convenient label attached to any liberal, socialist, separatist, or simply democratic opponents of the regime. In Southern Europe, communism tended to be singled out as the source of all evils even when it was non-existent (e.g. the Greek *Idionym* of 1929, or Special Law for the Security of the Social Regime) as a real internal menace, or when it was only one force – often a small one – among others on the left, as in Portugal before 1933.

The Southern dictatorships possessed a syncretic ideological substratum, ranging from fascism to ultramontane monarchical legitimism from which the dictator and the ruling clique could choose at every political juncture. In fact, one of the main tasks of the chief of state was to establish the successive adequate balances within the amalgam and to emphasize each one of its aspects according to time and place. One of the most arduous was to produce a convincing doctrine by reconciling the essentially reactionary nature of the regime with officially acknowledged rhetorical expressions of support for the subordinate classes.

A very limited, but qualitatively highly important, degree of political pluralism corresponds to all this. It was restricted to the ruling classes, to factions and movements of the reactionary coalition, and was made extensive to the employees of the regime's political police, propaganda personnel, single-party members, high civil servants, sympathizers among the local notables, and so forth – though these also had to show the highest degree of discipline and subservience to the chief of state at all times.

Coercion and state control through the service classes

The victorious reactionary coalition inherited the state administration, but in order to govern set up a large number of new institutions for repression, economic development, welfare and education. A traditional straightforward military-bourgeois dictatorship could no longer be successfully implemented given the new conditions of economic complexity and mass aspiration characteristic of the post-war period.

Associations and movements not sanctioned by the government were outlawed, excluded, or suffered tight surveillance on the part of the forces of repression and manipulation. Non-organized individuals and persons not stigmatized by their past political activity – a majority of the population – were left alone in the enjoyment of their property, the carrying out of their private lives – their search for employment, their expression of religious belief, and their adherence to cultural norms. Cautious non-interference with vast areas of social life thus became the hallmark of modern dictatorial regimes in Southern Europe, coupled with a keen protection and encouragement of recognized 'apolitical' institutions such as the established national church and other associations devoted to the control of the means of emotional production, especially those geared towards popular distraction and national patriotism.

State power was thus implemented through service classes. They legitimated the regimes and its members were given, in return, the intermediate rungs in the diverse chains of authority. Part of the personnel in these 'classes' did not directly belong to the state apparatus. Such was the case of the religious legitimizers of the traditional order upheld by the reactionary government: Catholic priests and Greek Orthodox popes.[17] At any rate, given the ultimately non-totalitarian nature of these states, the service classes did not interfere with everyday life in civil society. Surveillance and, especially, the use of institutionalized violence – political terror, torture, arbitrary imprisonment – tended to be selective, that is, to be applied only to suspects and 'trouble makers', real or potential.[18] The political formula of the fascist or *fascistisant* regimes in the Mediterranean inherited and incorporated the 'live and let live' tenet of traditional despotism as a very essential unwritten rule of their existence.

Political co-optation and passive obedience

Under such circumstances recruitment into the sphere of state employment tended to be more pragmatic than ideological, especially after the phase of regime consolidation was over. Members of the service classes – mayors of towns, high and middling civil servants, university professors – were asked to express allegiance to the official doctrine, yet what was decisive was their personal loyalty to the chief or arbiter of the reactionary coalition and their explicit promise not to question the legitimacy of the dominant political arrangements.

This sort of allegiance found its counterpart in the selective form of repression pointed out above. This blocked the access to political participation for the perennial *classes dangereuses* – workers, students – and aggravated discrimination against ethnic, religious and national minorities, but it also avoided the unnecessary harassment of well-behaved and law-abiding citizens. Tight control of the mass media and the strict censorship of public opinion made these tasks easier. Yet it is important to stress that the entire repressive apparatus of the state was geared towards obtaining the passive obedience of the subordinate majority rather than, as already indicated, its active mobilization. Large-scale militancy, even in favour of the regime, was avoided. Public occasions of multitudinous support were often arranged on special occasions, but tended to be as orderly and ritualized as possible. Obviously, in so far as the Italian regime was far more fascist than the other three, this last characteristic, low popular mobilization, did not apply. However, as many observers have pointed out, the mobilization and penetration of the civil society by the *Partito Fascisto* did not go as far as that of the Nazi Party and declined considerably after the late 1930s. Moreover, the Italian Fascist Party, in a country without the tradition of praetorian right-wing rule such as existed in the Greek and Iberian peninsulas, filled many of the functions carried out by the Portuguese, Spanish and Greek armies in their respective societies. Its martial role was therefore even more prominent than, say, that of the Spanish Falange. Likewise, the Italian party can also be seen as part of a reactionary coalition of the kind described above. This broke down after Stalingrad and the Allied invasion of Sicily. That such a coalition was still not ready for a switch to pluralist democracy is shown by Badoglio's immediate prohibition of all political parties after the deposition of Mussolini in 1942. Yet, under Allied pressure and with Communist support for constitutional rule (Togliatti's *svolta di Salerno* in 1943), Italy became the first northern Mediterranean country to enter the parliamentarian camp on a relatively solid basis.

Cultural legitimation in the Southern polities

It seems appropriate, at this juncture, to look briefly into some important issues involving the cultural legitimation of power and authority in the Southern European countries. I have so far treated culture as unproblematic, concentrating on class domination and sheer political control in the context of a period of rapid economic transformation. This could give the impression that my entire argument is committed to a vision of culture as a mere by-product of other, supposedly objective, realities. The political economy and the structure of a society may remain the best starting points in any macro-sociological analysis but, if taken alone, they fail to explain the success or failure of a political order.

I have already referred to the failure of the Enlightenment to erode significantly the inherited traditional world and its culture, both in the Iberian peninsula and in Italy. Greece, of course, in this period remained utterly beyond the pale of that great European current. Interestingly enough, the participation of these countries in the Enlightenment itself was quite considerable, but the tensions and confrontations unleashed by the Napoleonic wars and their aftermath put an end to the orderly, and in so many ways, spectacular evolutionary path initiated by them during the eighteenth century. A final and most remarkable effort at modernization without chaos and generalized revolutionary and counter-revolutionary violence was the Spanish Cortes at Cadiz in 1812. The constitution elaborated and proclaimed there was destined to have wide international repercussions, not least in the Mediterranean world. It inspired the Portuguese Constitution of 1822 after the Oporto 1820 revolution, the Neapolitan rising of 1820 and the Piedmontese rising and Constitution of 1821.

The immense resilience of the cultural edifice built by the Counter-Reformation was certainly not confined to religious and clerical support for the interests of backward-looking ruling classes, essential as that was for the subsequent politics of reaction. Such classes were interested in the maintenance of, say, slavery, for that was vital to the plantation economy and seigneurial domination overseas, but were less united as to whether obscurantist policies were to be pursued in higher education, and even less in agreement with respect to the new emerging forms of capital accumulation. Extreme conservatism had a popular (and later, populistic) basis in regions with a profoundly pious agricultural population. This might have been less so in more 'pagan' areas such as Sicily, or 'dechristianized' ones such as Andalucia, both *latifundia* regions with uprooted rural proletariats, but the areas where legitimist slogans of 'God, Altar, Throne' were to triumph were deeply committed to ancient pieties. Their mode of distinguishing between the sacred and the profane and of defining the relationship of both to earthly authority had not been much affected by secularization. They were rather violently and suddenly confronted, if not with 'satanic mills' – though these were not entirely unknown – at least with 'satanic powers', i.e. with liberal, atheistic, and masonic governments, intent on undermining the ultimate unity of earthly power and holiness. That must be understood in order to grasp the historical bitterness and virulence of the religious/secular tension, and the non-class components of confessional parties and political allegiances in all the countries concerned. Thus religious allegiance continues to be a factor in contemporary political alignments in varying degrees according to country and region.[19]

The degradation of the tensions between the sacred and the secular into a ruthless confrontation of clericalism and anti-clericalism seemed inevitable in the absence of Protestantism which had found a solution for the creative reconciliation of the two in Northern Europe. In Italy the Carbonari, for example, were immediately forced to take a conspirational stance against institutions which embodied a religiously sanctioned legitimacy for the immense majority of the population. Later still, Vatican resistance to the political unification of Italy not only exacerbated the confrontation, but created a rift between two primordial, *Gemeinschaftlich* levels of the collective consciousness: national loyalty and religious identification. In other countries, such as Ireland and Poland, these forces went (and still go) together. In Southern Europe their unity has been essential for the collective identity of the Basque people, and the same can be said of the Greeks, at least for as long as the Ottoman yoke had not been overthrown. In the case of the latter though, the early antagonism of the Orthodox Church hierarchy to the war of liberation also made the rift inevitable, despite important differences between the nature of anti-clericalism in the eastern and western Mediterranean.

A chance to heal the wounds of the liberal/traditionalist cleavage which rent asunder and largely paralysed the Mediterranean countries was missed during the late decades of the nineteenth century up to 1914, when the rule of conservative liberalism and limited constitutionalism prevailed throughout the region. This happened because a thoroughly cynical political culture had grown amongst the political class and had spread scepticism and apathy in the electorate. Perhaps no other outcome could have been expected from the inherited structure of class domination, the difficulties encountered by industrial and financial capitalism and the virulence of the radical opposition, which had so many reasons to be aggressive and so few reasons to expect understanding from the rulers and their allies. This institutionalized cynicism penetrated the Portuguese *rotavismo*, or alternation in power between Regenerators (conservatives) and Progressives (liberals) during the 1861–89 period. It was embedded in the same rotation between similar parties during the Spanish Restoration, linked there as in Portugal to *caciquismo* and other undemocratic forms of vote control. It found its supreme example in Italian *trasformismo*, the practice whereby cabinets were set up without regard for the party affiliations or political principles of their members. For the sake of office, politicians would abandon their electoral mandate altogether (Kolinsky, 1974). Meanwhile, in Greece, there had arisen the semblance of a two-party system. It lasted for much of the twenty years after 1883. When the 'alternating', modernizing governments led by Charilaos Trikoupis were in power during that period they managed to carry out significant reforms, with the support of business interests in the country. In all countries, however, if reforms from above were sometimes notable[20] they never managed to do away with the nefarious practices of the closed parliamentary system and its narrow dedication to the class interests it served.

In the long run all this would prove fatal for the prospects of democracy. The liberal intelligentsia itself began to desert the basic creed of enlightened, orderly and progressive democracy. Thus Costa in Spain began to veer towards a technocratic theory of government and of economic reform, while Pareto in Italy elaborated, in bitter disappointment, a theory of political élites which severed all links with progressive liberalism. It is not accidental that both authors have been seen by some as ideological forerunners of fascism. At any rate, the weakening of the liberal moral fibre, caught between denial of the legitimacy of the state on the one side (so forcefully expressed by the substantial anarchist movement of Southern Europe, among other forces), and unflagging resistance to cultural change by the traditionalists on the other, was a decisive factor in the ultimate triumph of the fascist doctrine in all its varieties. Commendably, some analysts have pointed out that despotism or fascism were not fatally destined to take over the government and that democratic regimes, even in those countries, did not necessarily have to break down (Linz, 1978). While strongly sympathizing with the importance they grant to skilful strategies and democratic statesmanship over structural determinants, one is bound to reach quite pessimistic conclusions about the real possibilities of liberal republicanism in the area for the period in question. It was only after further economic development and changes in the class structure had transformed the situation almost beyond recognition that parliamentarian democracy was to be given a much more solid chance.

The cultural polarization represented by the dichotomy of religious traditionalism v. liberal radicalism entailed more opposing sets of attitudes than are explicit to its two terms. It encompassed, for instance, opposing attitudes towards industrialization, the spread of literacy and the conception of social justice and public welfare. The latter stemmed, for some, from Christian charity, while for others it was to be based on philanthropy and the natural duties of the state. Polarization created in these countries, as well as in others such as France, a duality and a cleavage that consumed energies and paralysed minds. The great Andalusian poet Antonio Machado was right when he warned every Spaniard who came into the world that, whichever camp he was born into, the 'other half' of his fatherland was bound to 'freeze his heart'. An appalling Civil War (1936–9) fought over these two irreconcilable modes of legitimation soon proved him right. The same could be said of situations elsewhere, *mutatis mutandis*. The terror generated by the Portuguese PIDE, the Metaxas police, the fascist thugs, was directly linked to the Manichaean paranoia bred by extreme cultural polarization. This, needless to say, was also true of the political terror of the left, for instance, in those areas in Greece and in Spain dominated by Stalinist Communists during their respective civil wars.

The ideological 'solutions' arrived at by the fascist or ultra-nationalist forces to cope with this fatal cultural cleavage merit some attention. By and large they consisted of an amalgam of historical myths, racist doctrines, sublimations of imperial frustrations and inherited pseudoscientific theories about society. Wrong and ridiculous as they may seem today, as they indeed already were when they were first put forward, they were used in a manner that led, quite inevitably, to their own exhaustion by dint of a sheer *reductio ad absurdum*. Random examples of this motley collection might include the 'theory' advanced by a Portuguese myth-monger in 1914 that his countrymen were neither *homini europeii*, nor specimens of *homo mediterranensis* but rather the far superior members of an imaginary *homo atlanticus* race. Such ideas would later become marginal to Salazarist pragmatism, but a thoroughly distorted view of the 'Christian civilizing mission of the Lusitanian nation' was not. A daydream akin to this formed an essential element in the rhetoric of *Hispanidad* ideology under Francoism. The Greek *megali idea* which had evolved out of the anxieties, illusions and frustrations of the early panhellenic liberation movement was likewise appropriated by the right and conveniently distorted by it out of all recognition. Italian fascist notions of Roman empire and *civiltà* are too well known to need discussion here. In all these cases no regard whatsoever was paid to the glaring contradictions of the ideology. Cultural dissonance would have reached an unprecedented pitch had the thoroughly sceptical populations of the ancient Mediterranean ever fallen, as so many Germans did, for such official nonsense. Thus the Greek colonels, in the late 1960s, claimed that they were synthesizing the (essentially contradictory) values of ancient Hellas and later Byzantium (Sardinha, 1914; Clogg and Yanno-poulos, 1972, p. 143).[21] Their relatively short dictatorship, which in so many practical ways completed the unpalatable tasks initiated by the earlier Metaxas regime, floundered amidst general indifference and universal derision. This may speak well of the Greek people's sense of humour (though derision was not absent from the other Mediterranean peoples either), but it was largely made possible by the 'lateness' with which the colonels had come to power. By this time the cultural and ideo-logical situation had already profoundly changed everywhere in the West, including Mediterranean Europe.

The manner in which each fascist ideology – each extreme right-wing formulation and justification of the reactionary social order – collapsed dif-fered from country to country. Defeat, either in war or by virtue of foolish adventurism, brought the ideology into eventual total disrepute in Italy (1943) and Greece (1974). In Spain it was eroded, very slowly, by the regime's own policies, especially after 1959 when the Opus Dei began to dis-place certain old-fashioned clericalist and falangist sectors from power and led the country into pragmatic neo-capitalist policies by repealing the autarkic economic policies in force until then. By the time the dictator died in 1975, the official ideology of the regime had practically evaporated. As for Salazar, he was the wisest of the fascistoid leaders. He saw from the begin-ning the dangers of real 'modernity' for the stability of his own rule and quite successfully kept the population as ignorant as possible of the vain entice-ments of the industrial, technologically advanced and secularized world.

The ultimate failure of this syncretic fascist culture by its own *reductio ad absurdum* was spectacular and nowhere more so than in the 'fascist-clericalist' Spanish regime, where seminaries began to empty and church attendance perilously declined under its very aegis and despite its active protection of the official religion. Worse than that, a powerful oppositional movement arose from the early 1960s onwards from the ranks of the church, led by Christian left-wingers. A limited 'back to the church' movement may be foreseeable there, as was perceptible in Greece in the 1970s.[22] However, perhaps such events may have more to do with wider modern cultural fluctuations in the West and elsewhere than with a true renaissance of the now embattled older sources of religious legitimation.

As for the oppositional or radical side of the traditional cultural cleavage, its basis shifted from one sector of the political challengers to another. Thus, once liberalism lost all its credibility as an opposition movement (if not as a plausible framework for peaceful coexistence and pluralism), socialism and communism took over the radical legacy of militant secularism and anticlericalism. Therefore, the politico-cultural mix described above was not lost, but rather re-cast into the terms of newly emerging ideologies. The question today, however, is to establish whether it has been merely redefined after decades of post-Second World War prosperity, urbanization, labour migration, growing international interdependence, and the inroads of the new hedonism and consumerism, or whether it is now really on the wane. Although one may agree with many observers that in Southern Europe a relatively new 'alternative' subculture has arisen linked to the several socialist and communist parties, one should be wary of attributing to it the aggressive and antagonistic qualities such divisions once possessed. Accommodation with church, Christianity and with the liberal, lay (non-collectivistic) subcultures has gone a very long way everywhere – even if nostalgic or extremist groups, for instance, are still easily identifiable here and there. Enrico Berlinguer's launching in 1973 of the theme of an 'historic compromise' may have been part of his party's momentary political and cultural strategy just as his and Santiago Carrillo's later profession of faith in 'Eurocommunism' may be considered as passing phases of the partisan struggle. Nevertheless, there is little doubt that the commitments implicit in such policies – the social-democratic maintenance of welfare capitalism, the open acceptance of political pluralism, etc. – imply, if not a 'waning of opposition' as some have suggested (cf. Tarrow, 1979), at least a serious weakening of the deepest split in the traditional political culture, and a reinforcement from the left of a consensual civil legitimation.

It is perhaps in this light that some forms of extremist militancy – from political terrorism to acute forms of 'extraparliamentary' opposition – can be best understood, especially in Italy and in Spain, in the 1970s and early 1980s. In fact the creation of terrorist groups, extremist militant movements and parties may be linked to the weakening of the inherited cleavage between the two cultures of legitimation. In turn, every act of violence forges a greater degree of unity among all parliamentary parties. Witness the massive support for democratic parliamentarianism and law and order, generated by the assassination of Prime Minister Aldo Moro in 1978, and stemming from the Communist Party of Italy. At another level the tactics of the ETA, the military branch of the Basque separatist movement, may be seen as uniting, rather than weakening the ties among the most diverse parties of Spain, forcing them to find a common political culture in establishing the rules of the political game. This is something which was certainly absent there before 1936.

Polarities and cleavages in the cultural universe of Southern Europe are not restricted to the confrontation of conservative consensus and radical challenge. There are those which arise from the mosaic-like character of national cultures. Apart from the linguistic-ethnic pluralism of the Iberian Peninsula, the usual distinction between north and south Italy, accepted by the most acute and demanding critics, appears as paradigmatic. It may also be applied, albeit with quite different implications, to Portugal, north and south of the Tejo, although to the Portuguese themselves, the Lusitanian cultural world often seems to divide elsewhere, perhaps on the banks of the Mondego at Coimbra. These distinctions do not always find parallels nor do they correspond to the more questionable economic dualism of the societies concerned. Marxists are right when they reject the notion of the 'dual economy' as it has often been applied to Italy or Spain. While it is true that in some areas of those countries rudimentary agricultural and simple commodity production predominated while others were quite advanced industrially, it is misleading to conceive of them as separate parts of the same economy. Once the national capitalist market was created, the entire economic system and its different class and inequality patterns became linked into one single and evidently complex 'social formation' with mutually dependent elements. That does not contradict the fact that two (or several) discontinuous cultural, social and productive worlds now coexist under the same state and the same macro-economy. On the contrary, it is clearly the case that the traditional sector – often made up of small, family-owned firms, with relatively low productivity – is very frequently complementary to the more advanced, modern sector, is supported by it and is, therefore, not necessarily threatened by it.[23]

Other socio-structural cleavages, which are also largely cultural in nature, are to be found in all these countries on a local and regional basis. One of the most important is the gap, indeed often the abyss, between the highly civilized city and its immediate, very backward, rural hinterland. Naples comes quickly to mind. This has been a fundamental feature of all these societies for many centuries, perhaps millennia (Caro Baroja, 1963, 1966). It would therefore be foolish to assume that these varied and practically timeless features of traditional Southern cultural anthropology have had little or no effect upon the troubled history of despotism and democracy in Mediterranean Europe. Nor are they likely to change easily in the near future.[24]

From despotism to pluralist politics

Two paradoxical developments led the dictatorships of Southern Europe towards a more pluralistic social order and on to an infinitely more democratic situation: (1) the exhaustion of traditionalist-legitimation *via* the fascist ideology, and (2) the transformation of the structure of the economy produced, to a considerable extent, by the policies of the dictatorships themselves. In turn, the process was made possible by the essentially nontotalitarian nature of the system of class domination.

The stresses and strains brought about by the birth of industrial society – before, during and after the First World War – within the framework of the reactionary structure described earlier, bred a revolutionary opposition rather than a merely radical one. Significant efforts to integrate moderate socialism into the established political system failed in the end under the two-pronged attack of revolutionary movements and reactionary or fascist repression. That was the story from the time of the Turin factory occupations during the *Biennio rosso* (1919–20), which led to the formation of a revolutionary party by Gramsci and his colleagues, to the crushing defeat of socialists, communists, and anarchists by the Francoist forces in 1939. Until such time as moderate socialism (either as social democracy or Eurocommunism) was allowed a recognized and assured place in the polity, the dominant regime was quite simply reactionary despotism.

The reactionary regimes of twentieth-century Southern Europe were wedded to the state apparatus in a novel way. They employed it to complement the weak efforts of private capital in the task of large-scale capital accumulation, massive industrialization, increased urbanization, and so forth. The ruthless methods they used to accomplish these ends are well known and were hinted at above in the model of modern despotic regimes. With the partial exception of the 'old-fashioned' pre-Keynesianism of Salazarist economics, the other Mediterranean dictatorships actively engaged in state capitalist expansion and state capitalist monopoly production. Under the aegis of national autarky, Italy and Spain developed vast state industrial holdings, such as the Istituto per la Ricostruzione

Industriale (IRI, set up in 1933) and the Instituto Nacional de Industria (INI, established in 1941), which subsequent democratic regimes have not attempted to dismantle. The origins of this trend were far from being strictly 'fascist' or explicitly calculated. In Italy, for example, they can be found in purely remedial public interventions brought about by the dislocations of the 1929 economic crisis.[25] For their part, successive Greek governments have shown strong interventionist tendencies, especially through the banks (whose powers and share of the economy are as considerable as, if not more than, in Spain) and have included an enormous public investment programme. After some early friction and tensions with areas in the private sector, the publicly owned legacy of the defunct fascist state has blended easily with the new forms of Western advanced capitalism. It functions today, as does state industry elsewhere, as part and parcel of the system. Thus the state may absorb 'lame ducks', take over deficitiary but 'necessary' industrial, financial and commercial activities, and sometimes even run profitable public companies, ranging from airlines to civil engineering. After the appearance of massive foreign investment in the 1960s (and even earlier in Italy) spearheaded by multinational enterprise, the role of the state shifted to that of a general coordinator of the economy, guaranteeing its smooth functioning, the easy repatriation of foreign capitals and its close integration into the capitalist core.

International conditions after Yalta and 1945 entailed the exclusion of socialist and of state socialist development in the four countries. That meant that their states, whether dictatorial (Spain, Portugal), parliamentary (Italy) or of the right-wing, anti-communist, so-called 'guided democracy' type (Greece), had no option other than opening themselves up to foreign capital investment by providing stability and low wages. They sheltered a 'liberal' economy within an illiberal polity. Foreign investors did not have to contend with unruly or defiant trade unions and striking workers in the three poorest countries where labour was cheapest. In Greece, stability also meant that Greek diaspora capital could be finally enticed back on a considerable scale, along with other foreign investment. As all these countries entered the 1970s, resistance to foreign capitalist penetration declined to almost nothing. There was but a short-lived exception in the case of Portugal after the revolution of 1974, and it ended with the stabilization plan of 1978 when the economy returned to producing a surplus and international confidence was restored (cf. Schmitt, 1981). Greece's entry into the European Community in 1981 has meant that only the Iberian countries are still out. As they are both now actively engaged in entering it, they have been also engaged in a not always easy process of adjustment (i.e. liberalization) of their economic institutions to the standards prevailing among the Ten, even if, in some cases, that implied dismantling and privatizing certain highly profitable state monopolies (such as CAMPSA, the Spanish petroleum state monopoly).

Exaggerated notions about dependent development and 'economic colonialism' in Southern Europe must, however, be avoided. For one thing it is far from clear that all significant national industries and enterprises are or will soon be subordinate to foreign capital. Italy, of course, already has its own important locally based multinationals, and some industries elsewhere in Southern Europe, for instance in Spain, are quite internationally competitive. Furthermore, foreign trade expansion of Spanish and Greek companies (let alone Italian) is not rare, though its scope is still comparatively limited. Part of this expansion, such as that of the Spanish aircraft industry, tends to be at least partially linked in less visible ways to Northern European firms.[26] All this may be a sign that the final entry of the Southern European region into the core areas from the semi-periphery to which they so far belonged has also entailed lasting and significant changes in the international division of labour (pp. 16–50). For instance, labour migrations from Southern to Northern Europe (cf. Giner and Salcedo, 1978) have declined after 1973 and German, French, American and other industries have begun to set up factories in the South, where labour *in situ* is cheaper, the workforce is now sufficiently skilled, and the infrastructure (motorways, telecommunications, etc.) is as good as can be desired. Thus, the 'shift to core' has not necessarily meant economic independence, but a much greater subordination to the international corporate economy. The national industrial bourgeoisies, having first seen their power relatively circumscribed by the rise of state economic power, are now rapidly selling many of their industrial possessions to foreign corporate bidders, when they are not going into joint ventures with foreign 'partners'. Under the new circumstances they are losing very rapidly the role of economic protagonists they once shared with state enterprise.[27] One of the main consequences of this shift in the heretofore paramount position of the traditional bourgeoisies is the vastly increased importance of new pressure groups, parties, unions and other organizations linked to different sectors of the economy, which were formerly excluded from power. This has meant the rise of popular (even populistic) opposition parties with considerable leverage in parliament and government circles, but also the rise of new corporate groups, such as the technocratic 'state bourgeoisies' and financial-industrial conglomerates with their own new interests to foster.

The collapse of the dictatorial ideology, coupled with the abovementioned changes in the structure of capitalism, has finally opened the gates for a kind of 'pluralist' politics which comes much closer to the North-western European model, though it is still different in several important ways. Thus, parties of notables, endowed with an eminently syncretic ideology and out to colonize the state, are common on both the political centre and right (di Palma, 1977). Except for Greece since 1981, they became, in fact, the ruling parties. The metamorphosis of the old reactionary political class into a democratic 'party' representing centre, right and non-socialist opinion was made possible, as hinted earlier on, by the class composition of the non-totalitarian despotic regimes that came before. This seems to apply equally well to Karamanlis' *Nea Demokratia* and to Suárez's (and later, Calvo Sotelo's) *Unión de Centro Democrático*. Their electoral platforms presented noticeable class, factional and ideological similarities. After a brief period of praetorian-socialist rule in Portugal, the 1979 and 1980 victories of Sá Carneiro's conservative coalition (later led by Pinto Balsemão) seemed to herald the relative convergence of the other three Mediterranean governments with the formula established in Italy after 1948, which allowed continuous Christian Democratic domination for a very long period. Yet, events soon took an unexpected turn: the formation of a coalition government in Italy including the socialists and their conquest of the premiership through Bettino Craxi and PASOK's triumph at the polls in Greece in 1981 were followed by the 1982 socialist victory in Spain and the rise of Mário Soares to the Portuguese premiership. This seemed to indicate that the traditional left-wing opposition was finally being allowed to govern in the region and carry out its reforms in peace by conservative forces no longer bent on barring it from power at any cost and by any means at its disposal.

Nowhere in these four countries did the transition from dictatorship to a modern democracy occur through revolution. Instead there has been, in all cases, a significant measure of 'democratization from above' (di Palma, 1977) even if that was not precisely desired by the dictators themselves, nor by many of their successors. In Italy the transition was initiated by a democratic domestic force but was precipitated and made effective by foreign invasion. Allied intervention also dashed the revolutionary aspirations of partisans and left-wingers in the 1948 electoral defeat of the Popular Front. In Spain serious plans for a 'democratic rupture' with the dictatorial past harboured by anti-Franco forces as late as 1977 were rendered inappropriate or unnecessary by certain strategically placed groups within the regime which were inclined to make concessions. These groups were, in turn, helped by the remarkable willingness shown by most outlawed opposition leaders to compromise and embark on consensual politics. A genuinely revolutionary break with the past did not even take place in Portugal, where the initial clamour for justice against the over-thrown regime played such a prominent role in the 1974 coup and where a socialist programme of reforms became eventually incorporated into the Constitution. One of the reasons for this was that the military coup was conspiratorially prepared and executed only by military officers who themselves were of several political persuasions (Schmitter, 1976).[28] It did not initially involve any significant participation by radical civilian politi-cal forces. In spite of early stages when the left, torn though it was between Leninist and majority socialist tactics, was given an historic opportunity, conservative and moderate forces were allowed to regroup and come back into their own, though this time under constitutional rule by army officers. In Portugal, like three decades earlier in Italy, the international military, political and economic order of the West would have made any serious attempts at abrupt social or political structural change, not only highly costly in every sense, but ultimately very unlikely to succeed.

The narrowness of the choices which have faced all political formations involved at these crucial moments of transition (government élite, oppo-sition parties – legal and otherwise – army officers, democratic move-ments, and so on) has led some observers to believe that a 'consociational' model of democracy and parliamentarianism ought to emerge, at least in some of these countries. Supposing, for the sake of argument, that consociationalism does exist in some polities such as the Netherlands (which is also subject to much dispute), it seems rather problematic to me that it will ever happen in Southern Europe. 'Consociationalism' (Lijphart, 1968, 1977), or compromise and agreement between the several élites capable of controlling their respective followers and concerned about establishing a common course of action to avoid polarization, confrontation and other mutually destructive strategies, can only occur when all are equally free, proportionately rewarded, and equally concerned about safeguarding democracy. In Southern Europe, by contrast, almost all the forces present were obliged to enter into mutual agreements and concessions leading to constitutional rule *under powerful surveillance from above and/or outside*. In every case there were certain internal and/or external arbiters of the situation which imposed the limits and conditions of the transition. They did that in a clearly asymmetrical way, in a manner congruent with the existing structures of class, power and privilege. To assume, therefore, that the transition to democracy in countries such as Spain has been consociational and that this may lead the way eventually to some majoritarian form of democracy may be mistaken. Rather the contrary could be the case, as Italian politics demonstrate. From the *apertura a sinistra* of 1962 to the *compromesso storico* of 1973

strategies were inspired, one could argue, by a desire to compromise con-
sociationally for the sake of maintaining democratic rule, yet they
occurred after, not before, sweeping concessions and mutual guarantees
were forced upon all 'contracting' actors during the crucial years of 1943
and 1948. Likewise in Greece one party, Karamanlis' New Democracy,
imposed the constitution upon the other political forces, without
substantial negotiation with them. The Portuguese case, with the military
coup of 1974, hardly needs mentioning.

Be all that as it may, the result of the transition process[29] has been that –
apart from the rise of new political, trade union and other institutions
linked to parliamentary and constitutional democracy – the inherited
patterns of class domination and social inequality have been respected by
the new system of political praxis. This is, after all, the same system that
predominates elsewhere in Western Europe.

Between freedom and corporatism

The final obsolescence and rejection of the dictatorial solution for the
political order in Europe's southern region is a particularly significant
event, not only because of its intrinsic importance, but also because of the
historical moment at which it has occurred. Thus the new European
parliamentary democracies have not joined the liberal world of yesteryear,
but rather the new post-liberal universe of today. This is based on a technologically advanced, politically competitive, and organizationally corporate society. The corporate society can be characterized, in the West, on
the one hand, by a measure of political pluralism, civil rights and democratic representation, but on the other by the constant growth of large
formal organizations at all levels: the state, first and foremost, but also
trade unions, employers' and professionals' associations, political parties,
multinational corporations, financial institutions, welfare agencies, and so
forth.[30] It is also a society where class conflict, market trends, and personal
and collective social integration are practically always mediated by the
presence of the all-pervading 'corporations': they are redefined, filtered
and governed by them. Political power, market prices, sectional interests,
military duties, nationalist movements, working class demands, even
religious beliefs are all mediated by corporate institutions and groups.
Such society, therefore, cannot be defined only in terms of state intervention in the economy, and much less in terms of any resemblance to the
so-called 'corporate states' which once emerged precisely in Southern
Europe. Mussolini's and Salazar's 'corporatist' orders were shams:[31] their

harmonious blueprints hid much harsher and imperfect realities. Therefore they ought not to be confused with the new phenomenon.

Southern Europe's entry into the 'corporate world' has also occurred
when its standards of living, income distribution, levels of urbanization,
literacy, health, and so many other indicators have either reached Northern European standards or, as is more often the case, are relentlessly
approaching them. Is it necessary to give here the familiar data on income
per capita, automobiles per 100 inhabitants, and such like? The gulf
between Sicily and Franconia is still very great, and so is the one between
Andalucia and the English Midlands, or Thessaly and Jutland, but the
significant point is that it is narrowing. To speak more accurately, what is
now being bridged is the gap between the industrialized and developing
areas of the South and the corresponding areas in the North, as well as that
which exists between the underdeveloped and poor areas of the South and
those which are underdeveloped, depressed or even undergoing de-
industrialization in the North of Europe. By all international criteria,
Southern Europe has now ceased to be a part of the periphery, or even of
the semi-periphery of the capitalist world economy.[32]

The acknowledgement of these important facts, however, ought not to
lead into simplistic assumptions about the 'convergence' between Northern and Southern European societies. For one thing the historical path
followed by the former was by and large grounded on strong and prosperous civil societies. Despite the growth of the state and the recent development of corporatism their internal equilibrium and order still largely
depends on the strong living traditions of their civil societies. In the
South, by contrast, civil society was always much weaker. As a consequence the region as a whole reached the 'corporatist order' through a
very different historical path, full of strife, stalemates and confrontations.
For another, the 'advanced', industrialized, welfare-state capitalist core
has been enlarged to cover Southern Europe without diluting its class
structures, local cultures, patronage systems and other features into one
single wider social system. These features may not have remained intact
under recent urbanization and industrialization processes – quite the
contrary is the case – but the repercussions have produced structural
results which differ widely from those generated in the North. Even the
very expansion of the capitalist core further South has not forced the main
centres of political and economic decision-making to shift to other places.
Societal and geopolitical inequality in participation and influence in such
spheres continues unabated. In other words, while there has occurred
much integration (even some 'convergence') at the level of corporate
organization between European nations, there has hardly been any at the

level of class, community, privilege and local power. In these areas, the Mediterranean societies of Europe continue to possess their own distinctiveness.[33] So much so that trans-national generalizations among southern societies are difficult and often highly problematic. The disparities at this level between, say, Sicily and Andalucia are immense, as are the overall social structures of each of these countries. Even if they were linked to different stages in the development of capitalism, it would be impossible to plot them along some simple continuum. Italy would certainly appear ahead of the other three, followed by Spain and then perhaps by Greece with Portugal in last place but this would be a futile exercise, as large areas of Italy – Calabria, Basilicata – appear to many observers as true enclaves of archaism. At the opposite pole, we encounter advanced industrial areas in places like Thessalonika (Nikolinakos in this volume, pp. 201–5) or Setúbal (Ferrão in this volume, pp. 238–9) – enclaves of exactly the opposite kind, surrounded still by a large hinterland of simple commodity production, lower acquisitive power, small-scale family business, and so on. Likewise in at least two countries, Italy and Spain, industry is no longer concentrated upon its traditional regions but far more widely spread. If 'enclave' capitalism has long been gone, 'enclave' industrialism is now following suit.

The pluralistic corporate societies of the West to which the Southern European countries are now, more than ever, linked, are neither totalitarian nor monolithic. Increasing monopolies and oligopolies in the economic sphere and the constant expansion of the state apparatus and bureaucracy are wedded to a great number of competing parties, political formations, public opinion institutions and autonomous and semi-autonomous bodies. New trends towards further corporateness and bureaucratization can also be detected. They were intensified by the energy crisis and the recession that gripped the Western world after 1973, precisely at the moment when three out of the four countries discussed here found again their place in its midst as parliamentary democracies. These developments are particularly relevant for the ultimate consequences socialism may have in the area. By 1983, the four Southern European countries, as well as France, had come under either socialist-majority governments or under coalition governments headed by a socialist premier. Yet they were all treading with varying degrees of care in the implementation of their originally quite radical programmes. Some, like the Greek, the French and the Portuguese socialists tried in different ways to live up to the revolutionary promises first made by at least implementing some parts of their programmes. Others, having been elected partly on a promise of moderation, found it more expedient to engage in sensible, 'non ideological' reformism, such as industrial reconversion, financial restraint and fiscal soundness. This was the Spaniards' case. The control of public expenditure and fiscal reform was also the chief preoccupation of the Italians, while the Portuguese were once more forced to yield to the exigencies of their own economic difficulties. Fortunately, the initial economic setbacks of the French socialist government had forewarned other 'sun-belt' socialists about the costs of structural reforms in times of high unemployment, fiscal penury and economic stagnation.

There appears to be no reason, however, why socialism in Southern Europe must be confined to the achievement of minor tasks. In fact, the lingering backwardness of the region affords its supporters a unique opportunity to legitimize their rule and to make a lasting contribution to the prosperity and progress of their countries. In them, administrative and educational reform and regional devolution, for instance, can hardly be considered minor events. The mere consolidation of democracy through the peaceful access to power and effective rule of socialist governments in all these countries is in itself a unique achievement, and a measure of the extent to which the political world of Southern Europe has changed. However the shift from the original promises of structural change to a more circumscribed emphasis on the 'moralization' and the 'modernization' of the inherited world poses interesting questions. What will happen to the socialist parties when this necessary and preliminary part of their project has been accomplished? For how long can they legitimize their rule on this basis alone?

Here the question of corporatism – the widespread organization of interest groups of all sorts into large corporate bodies – rears its head once again. In a pluralist corporate society socialism must come to terms with big business, but also with big labour – the latter often under communist or non-socialist control – as well as with a powerful and traditional state machinery. To this, in places such as Greece and Spain, the army must be added, and in some senses the church as well.[34] This, together with the persistence of regional imbalances and traditional arrangements, and institutions of patronage and protection – which in some cases, as in Italy, include criminal networks – confers upon the corporatism of the region its distinctiveness and sets the constraints within which any democratically elected government must operate. Therefore the conglomeration of all these forces is bound to establish notable constraints upon the socialist effort. At any rate it has already forced a displacement of its immediate goals from revolution to the rationalization and modernization of the existing society. This is due not only to fears of a violent reaction by the right-wing opposition and its powerful reactionary allies, but is also the consequence of far-reaching changes in the very texture of those societies: a much greater density in the sphere of organized interest representation has brought with it in Southern Europe a world that tends to preclude violent confrontations and ideological maximalism. The institutionalization of the negotiated resolution of conflicts imposed by corporatism represents a final break with the past. The advent of modern times cast those societies into a mould of oppression and fruitless rebellion. Their strife-torn past will not repeat itself. Civil discord and violence, if it comes, will stem from different sources of discontent.

The uncertainties of the Western world as a whole are now also the uncertainties of Southern Europe. Therefore, this exploration into its recent and contemporary political evolution and its cultural and political underpinnings must also end on a note of uncertainty. None of the specific ills of the South can any longer be isolated from the larger whole of which they are now a part. In the same manner that the 'dual economy' soon ceased to exist at the national level, the European 'dual economy' (North and South) has in a sense also ceased to exist through national, supranational and international integration and mutual dependence.[35] Vast Northern European (as well as American, Japanese and Arab) economic interests are now involved in the South – from simple house ownership to large industrial investment. The weight of the South is no longer limited to providing a workforce for the North, as it seemed it was destined to be during the 1950s and 1960s: its political and economic strengths are already being felt within the North. Besides this increased interdependence, other trends have created a more common framework of problems for all countries, North and South: a sharp drop in productive investment in the 1970s and beyond; the rise of comprehensive welfare programmes and its effects on individual competitiveness and trade union strategies; the further development of corporatist, interest politics, linked or not, to the state; the continued growth of government; the limits to East–West military *détente*. These harsh facts have pulled all Western European societies further together, not apart. They have now thus ceased to be islands, if indeed they ever were.

Notes

1 I am very grateful to Professors Maurizio Cotta (University of Sienna), John Macdonald (Chelsea College, London), Edward Melefakis (Columbia University) and Nicos Mouzelis (London School of Economics) for commenting on this chapter. Special thanks are due to Professor Philippe Schmitter (University of Chicago) for his helpful and thorough criticisms and suggestions.

2 The sociological distinction between centre and periphery originates with

Shils (1975) and has been recast in *Marxistisant* guise by Wallerstein (1979). Another significant development of the notion is to be found in Galtung (1979). In this chapter I make use of the distinction put forward by these authors, and especially of Wallerstein's notion of the 'semi-periphery'. At one point the entry of the Southern European countries into the advanced, wealthier and industrialized centre is described as a 'shift to core', borrowing an expression from Wallerstein. In the present European context, Galtung's concept of the 'inner periphery' (or 'outer centre') seems particularly appropriate. Other than this I am not committed to their more general, and different, views. For a brief discussion of Wallerstein's notion of the semi-periphery as it may be applied to Southern Europe, see Bailey *et al.* (1981). For a 'centre-periphery' discussion of the relationship between the state and civil society which largely applies to the area examined in this essay up to the time of its final integration into the Western economic and political order, cf. Vergopoulos (1983).

3 The notion of a 'backward society' (*société arriérée*) linked as it is to traditional ideas about progress was driven out, for a number of reasons, by the ideologically more acceptable concept of 'underdevelopment'. In Spain (and its former colonies) it is embodied in the abundant literature on *atraso*. The Italian Risorgimento cannot be understood without it. Cf. Cattaneo's (1961) radical liberalism and the efforts made by him to modernize his country.

4 Ironically, subsequent events led to the restoration of a 'medieval' society in Catalonia: by freezing feudalism the Catalans attempted to preserve their liberties and privileges. See Mackay (1977) and Giner (1980).

5 There were, of course, exceptions to this general decline, such as Venice's remarkable capacity for survival and even continued prosperity, or the development of a Greek merchant bourgeoisie under new masters. On the retrenchment and decline of the area, see Braudel (1966).

6 The economic crises that ensued when the war was over did not destroy the industrial basis thus created.

7 The phenomenon of the transition to capitalism without industrial expansion or a quantitative growth of commodities has been explored for one Mediterranean country in the eighteenth century by Vilar (1962) which Cabral quotes (1976, pp. ix–x). What happened, then, during the pre-First World War period was that the capitalist economy ceased to be circumscribed to areas such as Catalonia and Piedmont. Yet its expansion did not always necessarily mean 'growth' and 'industrialization'. Cf. also Pereira (1974).

8 Protectionism of course, does not necessarily have to result in the sclerosis of capitalism. Protectionism in the USA had different consequences.

9 For instance, according to Jordi Nadal and other historians foreign ownership of Spanish firms robbed the country of an industrial take-off. While vastly profitable to foreign investors their concerns in Spain had a detrimental effect upon Spanish development. Harvey (1982) has attempted to qualify such charges in his study of the Rio Tinto copper mines, but he has not refuted them altogether.

10 'By the 1960s a circle of twenty families – multimillionaires all – virtually controlled the system of pre-Revolutionary Portugal' – Gallagher (1979, p. 396).

11 On the political importance of the lack of agrarian reform for the breakdown of parliamentary democracy in the area, see Malefakis (1970) and Sevilla (1979).

12 On the precise nature of structural dualism in Southern Europe, see the discussion below on pp. 336–7.

13 This issue has its parallel in the important, if often neglected, question of how revolutionary (in the 'proper' sense of the word) fascism really was. Since, by definition, fascism appears as an essentially counter-revolutionary force most observers have neglected its transformation potential. It is also a most unpalatable issue. For a rigorous approach to the problem, however, see de Felice (1970).

14 The following model was elaborated first in an essay by Sevilla and Giner. It was refined with the help of Pérez Yruela (Giner and Pérez Yruela, 1979) and appears in a more extended English version in Giner and Sevilla (1980).

15 'Reactionary coalition', as in Barrington Moore (1973, p. 436ff.).

16 The term 'means of emotional production' is borrowed from Collins' discussion of the manipulation of the materials and techniques used to stage rituals producing strong emotional bonds – as well as bonds of obedience, I would add (see Collins, 1975, pp. 58–9).

17 With further industrialization and secularization the Spanish church began to divide and to become ideologically much more heterogeneous (see Hermet, 1981).

18 On the crucial importance of selective repression for the maintenance of Salazarism see Gallagher (1979), where he adduces evidence for the class nature of that repression. In the light of Gallagher's discussion, the description of Salazar's rule (or indeed Franco's or Metaxas') as a dictatorship of the bourgeoisie seems in order and cannot be considered as a 'leftist' oversimplification. By the same token the 'extermination of the enemy' ethos of these Manichaean regimes cannot be forgotten. For the grim data on the Spanish case, see Reig Tapia (1979). For a development of the concept of despotic coercion, cf. Jackson et al. (1978). In this paper, the label 'coercive authoritarianism' is applied to regimes mostly in certain 'Third World' states which I would call despotic. The authors relate dependence on rich nations to internal violence and political distortions. Although what seems to apply to a much more developed Southern Europe can hardly be extended without modifications to Latin America or (much less so) to Africa, similitudes in certain areas are important enough to invite comparison.

19 'Non-class' does not mean that correlations between religion and class cannot be found for, in a great number of cases, the contrary is the case. Yet the exceptions are too abundant and the effects and sources of religious affiliation too varied for their reduction to class and for class analysis to be meaningful. On the other hand, to affirm that 'religion is a more important factor than

social class' in accounting for the 'moderate and conservative choices of voters', may appear as too strong a statement. See Linz (1979). The moderate choices of the Southern European left (linked to Social Democratic and moderate Eurocommunist parties) cannot certainly be attributed to that. It was when the church was used to 'delegitimize' socialism and communism and ban them (often with threats of excommunication) that these movements were most radical. But this raises other issues.

20 Cf. the 'regeneration' politics of the conservative premier Maura as analysed by Punset (1979).

21 It is curious, however, how while in opposition in the 1970s, the modern left-wing, anti-Common Market, patriotic, 'Third World' orientated socialist Pasok party in Greece showed subtle connections with these feelings which went deeper than its mere 'panhellenic' name may suggest.

22 On the limited Greek Orthodox revival (foundation of new monasteries and convents, etc.), see *The Times*, 11 December 1979, p. v of special supplement on Greece, by Archimandrite K. Ware.

23 The importance of the traditional sector and its integration into the modern economy, not only in Italy, but elsewhere in modern societies, has been emphasized by Berger and Piore (1980). Their use of the term 'dualism' refers to the existence, side by side, of different forms of economic activity which are nevertheless integrated at another level. They do not claim that there are two economies, separated in every sense (a view rejected in this essay) but rather that there is segmentation of one single economy.

24 Again, Naples seems the paradigmatic city in this respect. About the permanence of its sociocultural features, see Barzini (1980). Of course, a less 'culturalist' and fatalistic view can be taken of Neapolitan resilience to 'modernization', political corruption, and other phenomena, as shown in Allum (1968).

25 For an analysis of the place of the Italian IRI within the economic and political structures of fascism, cf. Maraffi (1980). Maraffi emphasizes both the 'remedial' character of state intervention and the 'enclave nature' of public enterprise within the economic order of fascism. The same, *mutatis mutandis*, applies to Spain.

26 A major Eurasian manufacturing aircraft deal took place in 1979 between Spain's CASA and Indonesia's Nurtanio. CASA's successful Aviocar plane is to be developed in a bigger version. Yet both American Northrop and German Messerschmitt partly own CASA. In turn the latter has a 4 per cent share in the Airbus international jetliner.

27 That does not mean they are powerless or that their respective confederations of managers and industry owners are unimportant. Yet, employers' organizations are increasingly channelling the interests of large corporations into the general economy.

28 Schmitter's analysis of the fall of the regime largely in terms of factors inside it deserves much attention. His emphasis on the relative autonomy of the state as a source of weakness, rather than of strength, is most relevant as a cure for

excessive emphasis on the congruence that 'ought to exist' between social structure and regime. As Schmitter emphasizes, alternative strategies could have been followed by the government which might have led in a different direction avoiding the ultimate outcome of the 1974 events. For a relatively similar stress on the 'autonomy' of political actors, see Mouzelis (1978), where limits are established to class determination of government policy.

29 In this chapter I have refrained from any detailed consideration of some of the sub-processes which can be distinguished within the general process of transition to democracy, such as regime liberalization, dictatorial recrudescence ('backlash'), democratization, and so forth. For a critical account of the analytical problems involved in such sub-processes, together with a model of the transition patterns, cf. Schmitter (1981).

30 For a detailed view of the corporate society and a critical account of theory about it, see Giner and Pérez Yruela (1979).

31 However, some observers seem to believe they were not shams: cf. Wiarda (1977).

32 The 1979 $25 Million World Bank loan to Greece for reforestation and agricultural development is the last one to be given in view of Greece's advanced stage of development.

33 Patterns of social inequality and class analysis may have been the stance from which the main problems have been approached in this essay, but I have refrained from a detailed account of them, in order to gain in clarity. Although the sources are abundant, the reader may find the following useful, in so far as they have been used to underpin my arguments: Cutileiro (1971); Mouzelis (1978); Archer and Giner (1977); Giner (1978); Sylos Labini (1974); Acquaviva and Santuccio (1976); finally a most useful list of sources is to be found in Diamandouros (1979). For a further development of these ideas, cf. Giner (1984); also in Pridham (1984).

34 For a more detailed account of corporatism in one Mediterranean country, cf. Giner and Sevilla (1984).

35 The rise of a 'southern question' on a European scale rather than on a national one was pointed out above. It is not incompatible – on the contrary – with these wider trends. Cf. Nikolinakos (1975b).

Bibliography

Abadan-Unat, N. (1964) *Bati almanya' daki türk işçileri ve sorunlari*, Ankara, State Planning Organization.

Abadan-Unat, N. (1974) 'Turkish external migration and social mobility', in Benedict, P. *et al.* (eds) *Turkey: Geographic and Social Perspectives*, Leiden, Brill, 362–402.

Abadan-Unat, N. (ed.) (1976) *Turkish Workers in Europe, 1960–75*, Leiden, Brill.

Abadan-Unat, N. (1979) 'Die politischen der Türkischen migration im In- und Ausland', *Orient*, 17–32.

Abadan-Unat, N., Keleş, R., Penninx, R., van Renselaar, H., van Velzen, L. and Yenisey, L. (1976) *Migration and Development: A Study of the Effects of International Labour Migration on Boğazliyan District*, Ankara, Institute of Housing, Urban and Regional Development and the Faculty of Political Science, Ankara University and NUFFIC/ IMWOO.

Accornero, A. and Andriani, S. (eds) (1979) *Gli anni 70 nel Mezzogiorno*, Bari, De Donato.

Aceves, J. B. and Douglass, W. A. (eds) (1976) *The Changing Faces of Rural Spain*, New York, Schenkman.

Acquaviva, S. S. and Santuccio, M. (1976) *Social Structure in Italy*, London, Martin Robertson.

Adler, S. (1981) 'A Turkish conundrum: emigration, politics and development, 1961–80', *World Employment Programme Working Paper*, no. 52.

Aglietta, M. (1979) *A Theory of Capitalist Regulation – the U.S. Experience*, London, New Left Books.

Aker, A. (1972) *İşçi göçü*, Istanbul, Sander.

Akre, J. E. (1975) 'Turkish administrative structures and the migrant worker: toward greater government support and participation', in Abadan Unat, N. (ed.) *Turkish Workers in Europe, 1960–75*, Leiden, Brill.

Alcouffe, A. (1979) 'Occitanie, une économie soumise', in Alcouffe, A., Lagarde, P. and Lafont, R. *Pour l'Occitanie*, Toulouse, Privat.

Alliès, P. (1976) 'Question nationale et question régionale', *Critique*, 10, 1–18.

Allum, P. (1968) 'Ecologio politica di Napoli', in Dogan, M. and Petracca, O. M. (eds) *Partiti politici e strutture sociali in Italia*, Milan, Comunità, 491–542.

Alquati, R. (1975) *Sulla FIAT e altri scritti*, Milan.

Andrikopolou Kafkala, E., Hermanns, H., Kafkalas, G. and Napoli, O. (1982) 'Regional structure of Thraki, industrialization, regional labour markets and productive investment by remigrants in a peripheral region: the case of Thraki in northern Greece', Project Report 3, University of Thessalonika.

Arango, E. R. (1978) *The Spanish Political System – Franco's Legacy*, Boulder, Colorado, Westview Press.

Arcangeli, F., Borzaga, C. and Goglio, S. (1980) 'Patterns of peripheral development in Italian regions', *Papers of the Regional Science Association*, 44, 19–34.

Archer, M. A. and Giner, S. (eds) (1977) *Contemporary Europe: Class, Status and Power*, London, Weidenfeld & Nicolson.

Archibugi, F. (1978) 'Capitalist planning in question', in Holland, S. (ed.) *Beyond Capitalist Planning*, Oxford, Blackwell, 49–68.

Ardagh, J. (1982) *France in the 1980s*, Harmondsworth, Penguin.

Aresvik, O. (1975) *The Agricultural Development of Turkey*, New York, Praeger.

Ariño Ortiz, G. (1981) 'El estado de las autonomías – realidad política, interpretación jurídica', in Acosta España, R. *et al. La España de las autonomías*, Madrid, Espasa-Calpe.

Atalay, M. E. (1976) 'Ausländsbeschäftigung und insbes. die Rück-kehrgrade der türkischen Arbeitnehmer', in *Materialien zum Projektbereich 'Ausländische Arbeiter'*, no. 14, Bonn, 107–15.

Augé-Laribé, M. (1907) *Le problème agraire du socialisme. La viticulture industrielle du Midi de la France*, Paris, Giard & Brière.

Aydalot, P. (1978) 'L'aménagement du territoire en France: une tentative de bilan', *Espace Géographique*, 17, 245–53.

Azmaz, A. (1980) *Migration of Turkish 'Gastarbeiters' of Rural Origin and the Contribution to Development in Turkey*, Saarbrücken, Verlag Breiterbach.

Babanasis, S. and Soulas, K. (1976) *Greece in the Periphery of the Developed Countries*, Athens (in Greek).

Baena del Alcázar, M. and García Madaria, J. M. (1979) 'Elite franquista y burocracia en las Cortes actuales', *Sistema*, 28, 3–50.

Bagnasco, A. (1977) *Tre Italie. La problematica territoriale dello sviluppo italiano*, Bologna, Il Mulino.

Bagnasco, A. (1982) 'Economia e società della piccola impresa', in Goglio, S. (ed.) *Italia: centri e periferie*, Milan, Angeli, 84–98.

Bailey, A. M. *et al.* (1981) 'The anthropology of southern Europe: towards an integrated explanatory framework', *Critique of Anthropology*, 16, 4, 56–62.

Baklanoff, E. N. (1978) *The Economic Transformation of Spain and Portugal*, New York, Praeger.

Balassa, B. (1981) *The Newly Industrializing Countries in the World Economy*, Oxford, Pergamon.

Banco Exterior de España (1979) *La economía de la comunidad económica europea*, Madrid.

Baran, P. (1957) *The Political Economy of Growth*, New York, Monthly Review Press.

Bardissa, J. (1976) *Cent Ans de guerre du vin*, Paris, Tema-Editions.

Barrington Moore, J. (1973) *Social Origins of Dictatorship and Democracy*, Harmondsworth, Penguin.

Barrios, S. (1980) 'Les inégalités régionales dans le Venezuela actuel', *Revue Tiers Monde*, XXI, 84, 749–59.

Barry, B. (1975) 'Political accommodation and consociational democracy', *British Journal of Political Science*, 5, 477–505.

Barthe, R. (1966) 'Economie et politique viticoles de la France (1950–1965)', 2 vols, Ph.D. thesis, University of Montpellier.

Bartoloni, P. and Meloni, B. (eds) (1978) *L'azienda contadina*, Turin, Rosemberge e Sellier.

Barzini, L. (1980) 'Una grande calamità', *New York Review of Books*, 7 February, 43–5.

Bassa, J. (1982) 'CIDEM: un ajut a l'empresa catalana', *Revista de Economía Industrial*, 174, 51–4.

Baučić, I. (1972) *The Effects of Emigration from Yugoslavia and the Problems of Returning Migrant Workers*, The Hague, Nijhoff.

Baučić, I. (1974) 'Yugoslavia as a country of emigration', *Options Méditerranées*, 22, 5–66.

Baučić, I. (1979) 'Possible positive effects on external migration on the development of Mediterranean sending countries', paper to International Migration Conference, Como.

Baucić, I. and Maravić, Z. (1971) *Vracanje i zaposljavange vanyskih migranata za SR Hrvatske*, Zagreb, Radovi Instituta za Geografiju Sveucilista u Zagrebu, Bd. 10.

Benas, D. (1976) *The Invasion of Foreign Capital into Greece*, Athens (in Greek).

Benelbas, F. (1981) *Economia agraria de Catalunya*, Barcelona, Ketres.

Bennett, B. C. (1979) 'Migration and rural community viability in Central Dalmatia (Croatia), Yugoslavia', *Papers in Anthropology*, 20, 1, 75–83.

Berberoglu, B. (1980) 'State capitalism and industrialisation in Turkey', *Development and Change*, 11.

Berger, S. and Piore, M. J. (1980) *Dualism and Discontinuity in Industrial Societies*, New York, Cambridge University Press.

Bernal Martin, S. (1977) *Segovia y el regionalismo*, Segovia, Nueva Imprenta Gabel.

Béteille, R. (1978) *Rouergue, terre d'éxode*, Paris, Hachette.

Birks, J. S. and Sinclair, C. A. (1982) 'The socio-economic determination of intra-regional migration', in ECWA, *International Migration in the Arab World*, vol. 1, Beirut, United Nations Economic Commission for Western Asia.

Bleitrach, A. and Chenu, D. (1982) 'Regional planning – regulation or deepening of social contradictions? The example of Fos-sur-Mer and the Marseilles metropolitan region', in Hudson, R. and Lewis, J. (eds) *Regional Planning in Europe*, London, Pion, 148–78.

Blondel, J. (1981) 'Political integration and the role of political parties: the case of Spain', in Torswick, P. *Mobilization, Centre–Periphery Structures and Nation Building*, Bergen, Universitets forlaget.

Boccella, N. (1982) *Il Mezzogiorno sussidiato*, Milan, Angeli.

Bogdanov, V. (1979) *Devolution*, Oxford, Oxford University Press.

Böhning, W. R. (1974) 'The economic effects of the employment of foreign workers with special reference to the labour markets of Western Europe's post-industrial countries', in Böhning, W. R. and Maillat, D. *The Effects of the Employment of Foreign Workers*, Paris, OECD, 41–123.

Böhning, W. R. (1975a) 'Some thoughts on emigration from the Mediterranean Basin', *International Labour Review*, 111, 251–77.

Böhning, W. R. (1975b) 'Mediterranean workers in western Europe: effects on home countries and countries of employment', *World Employment Programme Working Paper*, no. 2, Geneva, International Labour Organization.

Böhning, W. R. (1976) 'Migration and policy: a rejoinder to Keith Griffin', in Böhning, W. R. 'Basic aspects of migration from poor to rich countries: facts, problems, policies', *World Employment Programme Working Paper*, no. 6, Geneva, International Labour Organization.

Böhning, W. R. (1979) 'International migration in western Europe: reflections on the last five years', *International Labour Review*, 118, 401–4.

Boissevain, J. (1977) 'Tourism and development in Malta', *Development and Change*, 8.

Boissevain, J. (1979) 'Tourism and the European periphery', in Seers, D. *et al.* (eds) *Underdeveloped Europe*, Brighton, Harvester Press.

Boissonade, P. (1905) 'La production et le commerce des céréales, des vins et des eaux de vie en Languedoc dans la seconde moitié du XVIIe siècle', *Annales du Midi*, 17, 329–60.

Bonazzi, G. (1975) *In una fabbrica di motori*, Milan.

Borzaga, C. (1982) 'Lo sviluppo regionale italiano durante gli '70', in Goglio, S. (ed.) *Italia: centri e periferie*, Milan, Angeli, 19–43.

Borzaga, C. and Goglio, S. (1981) 'Economic development and regional imbalance: the case of Italy, 1945–1976', *Dunelm Translations*, 6, University of Durham, Department of Geography.

Boura, I. M., Jacinto, R. M. M., Lewis, J. R. and Williams, A. M. (1984) 'The economic impact of returned emigrants', in Comissão de Coordenação da Região Centro, *Emigração e Retorno na Região Centro*, Coimbra, CCRC.

Bourquelot, F. (1976) 'Les salaires agricoles en France', doctoral thesis, Paris, Ecole Pratique des Hautes Etudes.

Bovenkerk, F. (1974a) *Migration des travailleurs, retours au pays et cooperation au développement*, REMPLOD Project, 1.

Bovenkerk, F. (1974b) *The Sociology of Return Migration: A Bibliographic Essay*, The Hague, Nijhoff.

Braña, J., Buesa, M. and Molero, J. (1982) 'State aid, power groups and industrialisation policy in Spain 1970–7', paper presented to the Conference on National and Regional Development in the Mediterranean Basin, Durham, 13–17 April.

Brandes, S. M. (1976) 'The impact of emigration on a Castilian mountain village', in Aceves, J. B. and Douglass, W. A. (eds) *The Changing Faces of Rural Spain*, Cambridge, Mass., Schenkman.

Braudel, F. (1966) *La Méditerranée et le monde méditerranéen à l'époque de Philippe II*, 2 vols, Paris, A. Colin.

Braverman, H. (1974) *Labor and Monopoly Capital*, New York, Monthly Review Press.

Brettell, C. B. (1979) 'Emigrar para voltar: a Portuguese ideology of return migration', *Papers in Anthropology*, 20, 1, 1–20.

Brunet, J. M., Busom, I., Esteñbanell, E., Gratacos, A., Grifoll, J. and Sogues, J. (1980) *L'agricultura catalana: estudi economic*, Barcelona, Banca Catalana and Fundació Bofill.

Brunet, R. (1967) 'Mutations du XIXe problèmes du XXe siècles', in Wolff, P. (ed.) *Histoire du Languedoc*, Toulouse, Privat.

Brusco, S. (1982) 'The Emilian model: productive decentralisation and social integration', *Cambridge Journal of Economics*, 6, 167–84.

Brusco, S. and Sabel, C. (1981) 'Artisan production and economic growth', in Wilkinson, F. (ed.) *The Dynamics of Labour Market Segmentation*, New York, Academic Press.

Bulutoğlu, K. (1980) *Bunalim ve çikiş*, Istanbul, Tekin.

Busquet, P. and Vidal, C. (1980) *Le Pays Basque et sa liberté*, Paris, Editions de Sycomore.

Butera, F. (1980) 'La questione dell'organizzazione del lavoro in Italia', *Quaderni di Rassegna Sindacale*, 83, 154–71.

Buttler, F. (1975) *Growth Pole Theory and Economic Development*, Lexington, Mass., Saxon House.

Cabral, M. V. (1976) *O desenvolvimento do capitalismo em Portugal no século XIX*, Lisbon, A. Regra do Jogo.

Cabral, M. V. (1979) *Portugal na alvorada do século XX*, Lisbon, A. Regra do Jogo.

Cafagna, L. (1975) 'Italy 1830–1914', in Cipolla, C. M. (ed.) *The Emergence of Industrial Societies, Part I*, London, Fontana.

Caixa Geral de Depósitos (1981) *As principais empresas em Portugal*, Lisbon, CGD.

Caldo, C. (1982) 'The effects of African migrants on labour markets in Italy and Sicily', paper presented to the Conference on National and Regional Development in the Mediterranean Basin, Durham, 13–17 April.

Cameron, D. (ed.) (1981) *Regionalism and Supranationalism*, London, Policy Studies Institute.

Carney, J. (1980) 'Regions in crisis: accumulation, regional problems and crisis formation', in Carney, J. *et al.* (eds) *Regions in Crisis*, London, Croom Helm, 28–59.

Carney, J., Hudson, R. and Lewis, J. (1980a) 'New perspectives in European regional theory: some introductory remarks', in Carney, J. *et al.* (eds) *Regions in Crisis*, London, Croom Helm, 15–27.

Carney, J., Hudson, R. and Lewis, J. (eds) (1980b) *Regions in Crisis*, London, Croom Helm.

Caro Baroja, J. (1963) 'The city and the country', in Pitt-Rivers, J. (ed.) *Mediterranean Countrymen*, Paris, Mouton.

Caro Baroja, J. (1966) *La ciudad y el campo*, Barcelona/Madrid, Alfaquara.

Carr, R. (1980) *Modern Spain, 1875–1980*, Oxford, Oxford University Press.

Carter, F. (1981) 'Greece', in Clout, H. D. (ed.) *Regional Development in Western Europe*, Chichester, Wiley, 389–402.

Cassinis, U. (1963) 'Le migrazioni alla rovescia', *Nord e Sud*, 38 (99), 41–6.

Cassinis, U. (1968) 'Emigrazione e industrializzazione del Mezzogiorno: per una politica del rientro', *Studi Emigrazione*, 5, 13, 513–36.

Castellano, L. *et al.* (1978) *La fabbrica nel sud: il mercato del lavoro a Cassino dopo l'insediamento FIAT*, Cosenza.

Castillo, J. (1980) *La emigración española en la encrucijada*, Madrid, Centro de Investigaciónes Sociológicas.

Catalano, F. (1980) *Fiat e sindacato nella crisi economica*, Milan.

Cattaneo, G. (1961) *La società umana*, Milan, Mondadori.

Centre of Planning and Economic Research (1981) *Regional Development Programme of Greece, 1981–5*, Athens.

Centro de Estudos de Planeamento (1979) *Localização do emprego industrial*, Lisbon, Estudos Urbanos e Regionais.

Cerase, F. P. (1967) 'A study of Italian migrants returning from the USA', *International Migration Review*, 1, 3, 67–74.

Cerase, F. P. (1974) 'Expectations and reality: a case study of return migration from the United States to Southern Italy', *International Migration Review*, 8, 2, 245–62.

Cerase, F. P. (1979) 'Italy', in Kubat, D. (ed.) *The Politics of Migration Policies*, New York, Center for Migration Studies, 233–45.

Chaussinand-Nogaret, G. (1970) *Les financiers du Languedoc au XVIIIe siècle*, Paris, SEVPEN.

Chayanov, A. V. (1966) *The Theory of Peasant Economy*, edited and introduced by Kerblay, B., Thorner, D. and Smith, R. E. I., Homewood, Ill., Irwin.

Christodoulou, D. (1976) 'Portugal's agrarian reform', *Land Reform*, 2.

Ciaccio, C. C. (1978) 'Tourisme et Mezzogiorno', *Méditerranée*, 33, 59–65.

Ciafaloni, F. (1981) 'Il sindacato del dopo-FIAT', *Unità Proletaria*, 1–2, 131–5.

Ciborra, C. (1979) 'L'automazione nell'industria dell'auto', *Sapere*, January, 19–30.

Cinanni, P. (1979) *Emigration und Imperialismus zur Problematik der Arbeitsemigraten*, Munich, Verlagskooperative Trikont.

Círculo de Empresarios (1979) 'Las autonomías: la concepción autonomista del nuevo orden constitucional y su incidencia sobre la economía', Madrid, Círculo de Empresarios.

Clark, J. R. (1975) 'Residential patterns and social integration of Turks in Cologne', in Krane, R. E. (ed.) *Manpower Mobility and Cultural Boundaries*, Leiden, Brill, 61–76.

Clogg, R. and Yannopoulos, G. (eds) (1972) *Greece under Military Rule*, London, Secker & Warburg.

Cockcroft, J. D., Frank, A. G. and Johnson, D. L. (1972) *Dependence and Underdevelopment*, New York, Anchor Books.

Collidá, A. (1978) *Mezzogiorno, lavoro, sussidi*, Milan, Angeli.

Collins, G. B. (1983) 'Trans-atlantic linkage: a case study of Epataliori, Greek Macedonia, and its New England connections', University of Durham, unpublished M.A. thesis.

Collins, R. (1975) *Conflict Sociology*, New York, Academic Press.

Comito, V. (1980) 'Note sul settore della robotica a sullo sviluppo della robotica e dell'elettronica nel settore automobilistico', mimeo.

Commercial Bank of Greece (1979) 'Developments of the Greek economy: the 1970s', *Economic Bulletin*, 102, 5–12 (in Greek).

Commercial Bank of Greece (1980) 'The development of the Greek economy since the Association with the EEC', *Economic Bulletin*, 106, 8–18 (in Greek).

Commission of the European Communities (1973) *Regional Problems in the Enlarged Community*, COM (73) 550 Final, Brussels.

Commission of the European Communities (1975) *Stocktaking of the Common Agricultural Policy*, COM (75), 100, Brussels.

Commission of the European Communities (1978) *The Economic Implications of Demographic Change in the European Community: 1975–1995, Parts 1–3*, Directorate General for Economic and Financial Affairs, Brussels.

Commission of the European Communities (1980a) *Reflections on the Common Agricultural Policy*, COM (80), 800 Brussels.

Commission of the European Communities (1980b) *The Agricultural Situation in the Community 1980 Report*, Brussels.

Commission of the European Communities (1981) *The Situation of the Agricultural Markets 1980*, COM (81) 58 Final, Brussels.

Commission of the European Communities (1982) *The Agricultural Situation in the Community 1982 Report*, Brussels.

Cornelisen, A. (1976) *Women of the Shadows*, London, Macmillan.

Coulet, L. (1978) 'La fabrique diffuse en Emilie-Romagne', *Méditerranée*, 4, 13–25.

Courlet, C. (1980) 'L'Espagne: une économie semi-industrialisée', *Peuples Méditerranéens*, 11, 103–21.

Cuadrado Roura, J. R. (1981), 'Los flujos financieros interregionales', in

Acosta España, R. *et al.* (eds) *La España de las autonomías*, Madrid, Espasa-Calpe.

Cuadrado Roura, J. R., Granados, V. and Aurioles, J. (1983) 'Technological dependency in a Mediterranean economy: the case of Spain', in Gillespie, A. (ed.) *London Papers in Regional Science, 12*, London, Pion, 118–31.

Cuisenier, J. (ed.) (1963) *Problèmes du développement économique dans les pays méditerranéens*, The Hague and Paris, Maison des Sciences de l'Homme, Mouton.

Cutileiro, J. (1971) *A Portuguese Rural Society*, Oxford, Clarendon Press.

D'Aloia, G. (1980) 'Conflittualità e microconflittualità in una fabbrica del sud – un introduzione', *Quaderni di Rassegna Sindacale*, 84/5, 153–7.

Damette, F. (1980) 'The regional framework of monopoly exploitation: new problems and trends', in Carney, J. *et al.* (eds) *Regions in Crisis*, London, Croom Helm, 76–92.

Danielson, M. N. and Keleş, R. (1980) 'Urbanization and income distribution in Turkey', in Ozbudun, E. and Ulusan, A. (eds) *The Political Economy of Income Distribution in Turkey*, New York, Holmes & Meier.

DATAR (1972) 'Schema d'aménagement du territoire', *Travaux et Recherches de Prospective, No. 32*, Paris.

DATAR (1981) *Notes sur les actions de la mission interministérielle. Bilan d'activité de la mission interministérielle d'aménagement et d'équipement de la Corse*, Ajaccio.

De Barrin, J. (1980) 'La politique de comptable', *Le Monde*, 24 April, 12.

Del Monte, A. and Giannola, A. (1978) *Il Mezzogiorno nell'economia italiana*, Bologna.

Del Monte, A. and Roffa, M. (eds) (1977) *Tecnologia e decentramento produttivo*, Turin.

Demailly, S. (1978) 'La Corse en dépendance: éléments pour une réflexion retro-prospective', *Peuples Méditerranéens*, 3, 89–112.

Diamandouros, N. (1979) 'Southern Europe: an introductory bibliographic essay', Athens, Centre for Mediterranean and Arab Studies, mimeo.

Di Leo, R. (1959) *I Braccianti non servono*, Turin, Einaudi.

Di Leo, R. (1976) 'Review of Tarrow's Mezzogiorno, PCI e contadini', in *Quaderni di Rassegna Sindacale*.

Dina, A. (1980a) 'Crisi Fiat: si discute il modo di lavorare degli anni 80', *Classe*, XI, 18, 23–9.

Dina, A. (1980b) 'Come cambia l'operaio alla Fiat', *Inchiesta*, X (48), 72–5.

Dion, R. (1959) *Histoire de la vigne et du vin en France des origines au XIXe siècle*, Paris, s.e.

Direction Régionale de l'Equipement (1980) *Corse 79, statistiques régionales et commentaires*, Ajaccio.

Donolo, C. (1980) 'Social change and the transformation of the state in Italy', in Scase, R. (ed.) *The State in Western Europe*, London, Croom Helm, 164–96.

DPT (1973) *Kalkinmada öncelikle yörelerii tespiti ve bu yörelerdeki teşvik tedbirleri*, Ankara.

DPT (1979) *4. Beş yillik kalkinma plani, 1979–1983* (The Fourth Five Year Development Plan), Ankara.

Drewe, P., Van der Knaap, G. A., Mik, G. and Rodgers, H. M. (1975) 'Segregation in Rotterdam', *Tijdschrift voor Economische en Sociale Geographie*, 66, 4, 204–16.

Drury, M. P. (1982) 'Population movements in Greece: changing responses to internal and external stimuli, 1951–81', paper presented to the IBG annual conference, Southampton, 8 January.

Dumas, D. (1982) 'Le commerce de detail dans une grande station touristique balnéaire espagnole: Benidorm', *Annales de Géographie*, 506, 480–9.

Dunning, J. H. (1981) *International Production and the Multinational Enterprise*, London, Allen & Unwin.

Dutil, L. (1911) *L'Etat économique du Languedoc à la fin de l'ancien régime (1750–1789)*, Paris, Hachette.

Ecevit, Z. H. (1981) 'International labour migration in the Middle East and North Africa: trends, effects and policies', in Kritz, M. M., Keely, C. B. and Tomasi, S. M. (eds) *Global Trends in Migration*, New York, Center for Migration Studies.

Edwards, A. (1979) *The Newly Industrialising Countries and their Impact on Western Manufacturing*, vols 1 and 2, London, Economist Intelligence Unit Ltd.

Edwards, R. C., Gordon, D. and Reich, M. (1982) 'Segmented work: divided workers', in Edwards, R., Reich, M. and Weisskopf, T. (eds) *The Capitalist System*, Cambridge, Cambridge University Press.

Edwards, R. C., Reich, M. and Gordon, D. (1975) *Labour Market Segmentation*, Lexington, Mass., Lexington Books.

Emanuel, A. (1972) *Issues of Regional Policies*, Paris, OECD.

Emmanuel, A. (1972) *Unequal Exchange*, London, New Left Books.

Eraydin, A. (1981) 'Foreign investment, international labour migration and the Turkish economy', in Hamilton, F. E. I and Linge, G. R. J. (eds) *Spatial Analysis: Industry and the Industrial Environment*, vol. II, Chichester, Wiley.

Ertuna, Özcan (1976) *Planli dönemde toplam mevduat ve toplam kredilerin bölgelere dağilimi* (The Distribution of Total Deposits and Total Credits in the Planned Development Period), Ankara, SPO.

Estadas, J. (1953) 'Evolution du marché viticole et du commerce des vins depuis 1850', Ph.D. thesis, University of Montpellier.

Etablissement Public Régional Corse (1975) *Charte du développement économique de la Corse*, Ajaccio.

Etablissement Public Régional Corse (1980) *La Corse.*

European Economic Community (1978) 'FRESCO: economic and sectoral problems connected with enlargement', Brussels, mimeo.

Eurostat (1980) *Review 1970–9*, Luxemburg, Statistical Office of the European Communities.

Eurostat (1983) *Yearbook of Regional Statistics*, Luxemburg, Statistical Office of the European Communities.

de Felice, R. (1970) *Le interpretazioni del facismo*, Bari, Laterza.

Fennell, R. (1979) *The Common Agricultural Policy of the European Community*, London, Granada.

Ferrando Badia, J. (1980) 'Las comunidades preautonómicas', *Revista de Estudios Regionales*, Extraordinary vol. II, 'Las autonomías', 203–39.

Ferrão, J. M. M. (1979) *Interacção regional e divisão territorial do trabalho*, Lisbon, Centro de Estudos Geográficos.

Ferraris, P. (1978) *La contraddizione meridionale*, Turin.

Ferraris, P. (1981) 'La Fiat nell'anno della svolta', *Inchiesta*, XI (49–50), 19–26.

Fiat (1979a) 'Relazioni di bilancio delle imprese', Turin, mimeo.

Fiat (1979b) 'Gli interventi di riorganizzazione del lavoro operaio nel settore auto, 1971–8', Turin, mimeo.

Fiat (1980a) *FIAT Auto*, Turin.

Fiat (1980b) 'Documentazione per la commissione di studio – problemi settore auto', Turin, mimeo.

Fiat (1981) *La Fiat nel Mezzogiorno–l'esperienza degli stabilimenti automobilistici*, Turin.

Fielding, A. J. (1975) 'Internal migration in western Europe', in Kosínski, L. A. and Prothero, R. M. (eds) *People on the Move: Studies on Internal Migration*, London, Methuen, 237–54.

Fontana, J. and Nadal, J. (1975) 'Spain 1914–70', in Cipolla, C. M. (ed.) *Contemporary Economies*, Part II, London, Fontana.

Fonte, M. and Furnari, M. (1975) 'L'occupazione precaria in agricoltura in Italia e nel Mezzogiorno', *Rassegna Economica.*

Food and Agricultural Organisation (1977) *Prix des produits et de certains moyens de production en Europe et en Amérique Latine, 1975–6*, New York, FAO.

Food and Agricultural Organisation (1981) *Production Yearbook*, New York, FAO.

Frank, A. G. (1970) *Latin America: Underdevelopment or Revolution*, New York, Monthly Review Press.

Frêche, G. (1974) *Toulouse et la région Midi-Pyrénées au siècle des lumières vers 1670–1789*, Toulouse, Cujas.

Freddi, G. (1980) 'Regional devolution, administrative decentralisation and bureaucratic performance in Italy', *Policy and Politics*, 8, 4, 383–98.

Freyssenet, M. (1979) *Division du travail et mobilisation quotidienne de la main-d'œuvre – le cas de Renault et Fiat*, Paris.

Friedland, W. H., Barton, A. and Tomas, R. J. C. (1980) *Manufacturing Green Gold*. Davis University of California, Research Monograph No. 15, Department of Applied Behavioural Sciences.

Friedland, W. H. and Nelkin, D. (1981) *Migrant Labour*, Cambridge, Cambridge University Press.

Friedmann, J. and Weaver, C. (1979) *Territory and Function*, London, Edward Arnold.

Fröbel, F., Heinrichs, J. and Kreye, O. (1980) *The New International Division of Labour*, Cambridge, Cambridge University Press.

Front Régionaliste Corse (FRC) (1971) *Main Basse sur une île*, Paris, Editions Martineau.

Fuá, G. (1980) *Problems of Lagged Development in OECD Europe: A Study of Six Countries*, Paris, OECD.

Furnari, M. (1977) 'Articolazione sociale e territoriale dell'occupazione agricola in Italia', *Rivista di Economia Agraria*, 1.

Furtado, C. (1971) *Development and Underdevelopment*, Berkeley, University of California Press.

Gallagher, T. (1979) 'Controlled repression in Salazar's Portugal', *Journal of Contemporary History*, 14.

Gallagher, T. (1983) *Portugal: A Twentieth Century Interpretation*, Manchester, Manchester University Press.

Galtung, J. (1971) 'A structural theory of imperialism', *Journal of Peace Research*, 8.

Galtung, J. (1979) 'On the last 2,500 years in western history', in Burke, P. (ed.) *The New Cambridge Modern History*, New York, Cambridge University Press, 318–61.

Ganguly, P. (1982) 'Small firms in manufacturing', *British Business*, 19 November.

García Cotarelo, R. (1981) 'The crisis of political parties in Spain', *European Journal of Political Research*, 9, 2, 215–18.

García de Enterria, E. (1980) *La distribución de las competencias económicas entre el poder central y las autonomías territoriales en el derecho comparado y en la constitución española*, Madrid, Instituto de Estudios Económicos.

García Ferrando, M. (1978) 'La conciencia regional en España de nuestros días', in Asociación Española de Economía y Sociologìa Agrarias, *La política agraria y la cuestión regional en España*, Madrid, Instituto de Relaciones Agrarias.

Garcia-Ramon, M. D. (1975) 'El muestreo territorial aplicado a la actividad agrícola', *Document d'Analisi Territorial*, 1, 42–65.

Garcia-Ramon, M. D. (1979) 'Une interprétation du paysage agraire: le cadre théorique et sa vérification empirique', *Brouillons Dupont*, 4, 5–14.

Garofoli, G. (1981) 'Lo sviluppo delle "aree periferiche" nell'economia italiania degli anni settanta', *L'Industria-Rivista di Economia e Politica Industriale*, 3, 391–404.

Garofoli, G. (1982) 'Areas of specialised production and small firms in Europe', paper read to the Conference on National and Regional Development in the Mediterranean Basin, Durham, 13–17 April.

Garofoli, G. (1983a) 'Sviluppo periferiche e sistemi produttivi locali: il caso della Lombardia', *Economia Marche*, 1, 2, 227–39.

Garofoli, G. (1983b) *Industrializzazione diffusa in Lombardia*, Milan, Franco Angeli Editore.

Garofoli, G. (1983c) 'Uneven regional development and industrial restructuring: the Italian pattern in the 1970s', paper presented to the Conference on European Integration, Naxos, 31 August–2 September.

Gaspar, J. (1977) 'A localização das sedes das principais sociedades em Portugal', *Finisterra*, 12.

Gaspar, J. (1984) 'Urbanisation', in Williams, A. M. (ed.) *The Transformation of Southern Europe*, London, Harper & Row, 208–35.

Geipel, R. (1982) *Disaster and Reconstruction*, London, Allen & Unwin.

Geraud-Parracha, G. (1955) *Le Commerce des vins et des eaux-de-vie en Languedoc sous l'ancien régime*, thèse de la Faculté de Droit, Montpellier.

Giannitsis, T. (1971) 'Foreign owned enterprises in Greek manufacturing', Athens, mimeo.

Giannitsis, T. (1974) *Private Ausländskapitalien im Industrialisierungsprozess Griechenlands (1953 bis 1970)*, Berlin, Diss.

Giannitsis, T. (1979) 'Problems of Greek development', in *Oikonomia Kai Koinonia*, 1, 26–45.

Giannitsis, T. (1983) *Greek Industry*, Athens, Gutenberg (in Greek).

Giannola, A. (1982) 'Industrializzazione, dualismo e dipendenza economica del Mezzogiorno negli anni '70', *Economia Italiana*, 1, 65–90.

Gianotti, R. (1979) *Trent'anni di lotte alla Fiat (1948–78)*, Bari.

Giatrakos, N. G. (1980) *The Greek Regional Problem*, Athens (in Greek).

Gigliobianco, A. and Salvati, M. (1980) *Il maggio e l'autunno: la risposta di due borghesie*, Bologna.

Giner, S. (1978) 'La estructura social de España', in López Piña, A. (ed.) *Poder y clases sociales*, Madrid, Tecnos.

Giner, S. (1980) *The Social Structure of Catalonia*, Sheffield, Sheffield University Press (2nd edn, 1984).

Giner, S. (1984) 'Southern European socialism in transition', *West European Politics*, 7, 2, 138–57.

Giner, S. and Pérez Yruela, M. (1979) *La sociedad corporativa*, Madrid, CIS.

Giner, S. and Salcedo, J. (1978) 'Migrant workers in the European social structures', in Archer, M. S. and Giner, S. (eds) *Contemporary Europe*, London, Routledge & Kegan Paul, 94–123.

Giner, S. and Sevilla, E. (1980) 'From despotism to parliamentarianism: class domination and political order in the Spanish state', in Scase, R. (ed.) *The State in Western Europe*, London, Croom Helm, 197–229.

Giner, S. and Sevilla, E. (1984) 'From corporatism to corporatism: the political transition in Spain', in Williams, A. (ed.) *Southern Europe Transformed*, London, Harper & Row, 113–41.

Gitmez, A. S. (1977) *Göçmen işçilerin dönüşleri*, Ankara, ODTÜ.

Gitmez, A. S. (1979) *Dış göç öyküsü*, Ankara, ODTÜ.

Gitmez, A. S. (1981) *Göçmen işçilerin dönüsü*, Ankara, ODTÜ.

Gmelch, G. (1980) 'Return migration', *Annual Review of Anthropology*, 9, 135–59.

Gobierno Vasco (1983) *Informe económico-financiero*, Vitoria, Departmento de Economia y Hacienda.

Goglio, S. (ed.) (1982) *Italia: centri e periferie*, Milan, Franco Angeli.

Gökdere, A. (1978) *Yabanci ülkelere isgucu akimi ve türk ekonomisi üzerine etkisi*, Ankara, T. Iş. Bankasi.

Gor, M. (1976) 'Die Situation der Türkischen Arbeiter in der Bundesrepublik und nach ihrer Rückkehr in die Turkei', in *Materialien zum Projektbereich 'Ausländische Arbeiter'*, no. 15, Bonn, 239–55.

Gough, I. (1979) *The Political Economy of the Welfare State*, London, Macmillan.

Granados, V. (1984) 'Small firms and rural industrialization in Spain', in Hudson, R. (ed.) *Small Firms and Regional Development*, Copenhagen,

Institute for Transport, Tourism and Regional Economy, Publication 39.

Granados, V. and Aurioles, J. (1982) 'Limitations on regional policies in the context of the new international (and interregional) division of labour', paper read to the Conference on National and Regional Development in the Mediterranean Basin, Durham, 13–17 April.

Gratton, Ph. (1971) *Les Luttes de classes dans les campagnes*, Paris, Anthropos.

Graziani, A. and Pugliese, E. (eds) (1979) *Investimenti e disoccupazione nel Mezzogiorno*, Bologna, Il Mulino.

Graziosi, A. (1979) *La ristrutturazione nelle grandi fabbriche, 1973–6*, Milan.

Grémion, P. (1976) *Le Pouvoir périphérique*, Paris, Seuil.

Griffin, K. (1976) 'On the emigration of the peasantry', *World Development*, 4, 353–61.

Grigorogiannis, A. (1975) *Foreign Capital in Greece*, Athens (in Greek).

Guidi, G. *et al.* (1974) *FIAT-struttura aziendale e organizzazione dello sfruttamento*, Milan.

Gurisatti, P. and Nardin, G. (1983) 'Piccole imprese: integrazione o concorrenza', *Strumenti*, 2, 51–72.

Habermas, J. (1979) *Communication and the Evolution of Society*, London, Heinemann.

Hadjimichalis, C. (1981) 'The geographical transfer of value', Ph.D. thesis, University of California, Los Angeles.

Hadjimichalis, C. and Vaiou-Hadjimichalis, P. (1980) 'Penetration of multinational capital into backward regions: a policy analysis in Greece', *Peuples Méditerranéens*, 10.

Hale, W. (1981) *The Political and Economic Development of Turkey*, London, Croom Helm.

Hamilton, F. E. and Linge, G. J. R. (1981) 'International industrial systems', in Hamilton, F. E. and Linge, G. J. R. (eds) *Spatial Analysis Industry and the Industrial Environment*, Vol. II: *International Industrial Systems*, Chichester, Wiley, 1–117.

Harrison, B. (1979) 'Welfare payments and the reproduction of low wage workers and secondary jobs', *Review of Radical Political Economics*, XI, 2.

Harrison, M. (1977) 'The peasant mode of production in the work of A. V. Chayanor', *Journal of Peasant Studies*, 4, 4, 323–36.

Harvey, C. E. (1982), *The Rio Tinto Company: An Economic History of a Leading International Mining Concern, 1873–1954*, London, Alison Hodge.

Harvey, D. W. (1982) *The Limits to Capital*, Oxford, Blackwell.

Hayward, J. S. (1969) 'From functional regionalism to functional representation: the battle of Brittany', *Political Studies*, 17, 48–75.

Hebbert, M. (1982a) 'Regional policy in Spain', *Geoforum*, 13, 2.

Hebbert, M. (1982b) 'Births and deaths of regional planning agencies', *Environment and Planning*, Series B, 4, 2.

Hebbert, M. and Alonso Teixidor, L. F. (1982), 'Regional planning in Spain and the transition to democracy', in Hudson, R. and Lewis, J. (eds) *Regional Planning in Europe*, London, Pion, 7–34.

Hechter, M. (1975) *Internal Colonialism: the Celtic Fringe in British National Development*, London, Routledge & Kegan Paul.

Heinemeijer, W. F. *et al.* (1977) *Partir pour rester*, The Hague, REMPLOD.

Hermet, G. (1981) *Les Catholiques dans l'Espagne franquiste*, Paris, Fondation Nationale des Sciences Politiques.

Hicks, U. K. (1978) *Federalism, Failure and Success*, London, Macmillan.

Hobsbawm, E. J. (1977) 'On the break-up of Britain', *New Left Review*, 105.

Holohan-Dressler, W. (1981) *Développement économique et mouvement autonomiste: le cas de la Corse*, vol. II, Grenoble, Institut de Recherche Economique et de Planification.

Hudson, R. (1983a) 'Capital accumulation and chemicals production in western Europe in the post-war period', *Environment and Planning A*, 15, 105–22.

Hudson, R. (1983b) 'Regional labour reserves and industrialisation in the EEC', *Area*, 15, 223–30.

Hudson, R. and Lewis, J. (1982a) 'The regional problem in an enlarged European community', paper read to the Annual Conference of the Institute of British Geographers, Southampton, 8 January.

Hudson, R. and Lewis, J. (eds) (1982b) *Regional Planning in Europe*, London, Pion.

Hudson, R. and Lewis, J. (1984) 'Capital accumulation: the industrialization of southern Europe', in Williams, A. (ed.) *Southern Europe Transformed*, London, Harper & Row, 179–207.

Hull, C. (1980) 'France', in Yuill, D., Allen, K. and Hull, C. (eds) *Regional Policy in the European Community*, London, Croom Helm, 52–81.

Hümmer, P. and Soysal, M. (1979) 'Investitionsverhalten ausländischer Arbeitnehmer in ihrem Heimatland. Die Türkei als Beispiel', *Geographische Rundschau*, 315–18.

Hytten, E. and Marchioni, M. (1970) *Industrializzazione senza sviluppo. Gela: una storia meridionale*, Milan.

Ikonicoff, M. and Masini, J. (1981) '1978–81 trois années de recherche: état de la question, perspectives d'avenir', paper presented to the EADI Conference, Budapest.

Ileri, M. (1975) 'Türkei: Bilanz fünfzehnjähriger Arbeitskraftewanderung Rückblick und Vorschau', *Orient*, 132–46.

INSEE (1977–81) *Economie corse*, Ajaccio.

INSEE (1980) 'Bilan de l'emploi: 1979 Corse', *Les Dossiers d'Economie Corse*, I.

Instituto Nacional de Estatística (1970) *Principais sociedades*, Lisbon, INE.

Instituto Nacional de Estatística (1972) *Principais sociedades*, Lisbon, INE.

Ioakimidis, P. C. (1984) 'Greece', in Williams, A. (ed.) *Southern Europe Transformed*, London, Harper & Row, 33–60.

İşletmeler Bakanligi, T. C. (1979) *Halk girisimleri anket sonuclari*, Ankara.

Istituto di Studi sulle Relazioni Industriali (1980) *Dati sulla industria automobilistica*, Rome, ISRI.

Izard, M. (1978) *El segle XIX: burgeses i proletaris*, Barcelona, Dopesa.

Jackson, S., Russet, B., Snidal, D. and Sylvan, D. (1978) 'Conflict and coercion in dependent states', *Journal of Conflict Resolution*, 22, 4.

Javaloys, J. G. (1978) *La autonomía regional: ¿solución o problema?* Madrid, Ediciones ICE.

Jensen-Butler, C. (1981) 'Capital accumulation, regional development and the role of the state', *University of Aarhus, Geographical Institute, Working Paper*, no. XX.

Johnson, N. (1979) 'Some effects of decentralization in the FDR', in Sharpe, L. (ed.) *Decentralist Trends in Western Democracies*, London, Sage.

Jones, A. (1981) 'The EEC's mediterranean policy', University of Durham, unpublished M.A. thesis.

Jones, A. (1984) 'Agriculture: organization, reform and the EEC', in Williams, A. (ed.) *Southern Europe Transformed?* London, Harper & Row, 236–67.

de Kadt, E. (ed.) (1981) *Tourism: Passport to Development?* Oxford, Oxford University Press.

Kafkalas, G. (1984) 'Small firms and the development of a peripheral region: the case of Thraki, Greece', in Hudson, R. (ed.) *Small Firms and Regional Development*, Copenhagen, Institute for Transport, Tourism and Regional Economy, Publication 39.

Kallweit, M. and Kudat, A. (1976) *Rückwanderung ausländischer Arbeiter:*

Zwangsweise oder freiwillig?, Berlin, International Institute für vergleichende Gesellschaftsforschung Berlin, Pre-Print Series P–76–5.

Kanellopoulos, A. (1980) *The Economy between Yesterday and Tomorrow*, Athens (in Greek).

Karpat, K. H. (1976) *The Gecekondu: Rural Migration and Urbanization*, Cambridge, Cambridge University Press.

Kautsky, K. (1970) *La cuestión agraria*, Paris, Ruedo Ibérico.

Kayser, B. (1970) *Manpower and Labour Markets*, Paris, OECD.

Kayser, B. (1977) 'European migrations: the new pattern', *International Migration Review*, 11.

Keleş, R. (1973) *Urbanization in Turkey*, New York, Ford Foundation.

Keleş, R. (1976) 'Regional development and migratory labour', in Abadan-Unat, N. *et al. Migration and Development*, Ankara, Institute of Housing.

Kielstra, N. O. (1980a) 'Economic marginalization and the revival of Occitan regionalism', *Euromed Working Paper*, No. 16, Amsterdam, Anthropological-Sociological Center.

Kielstra, N. O. (1980b) 'The Languedoc: positive and negative definitions of a region and a culture', Paper presented to the Conference of Europeanists, Washington, DC, 23–5 October.

Kielstra, N. O. (1981) 'Economic marginalization and the disillusions of the Left: the case of Occitan regionalism', Paper presented to the Symposium on the Social Anthropology of Europe at the IUAES Intercongress, Amsterdam, 23–4 April.

Kindleberger, C. P. (1965) *Economic Development*, 2nd edn, New York, McGraw-Hill.

Kindleberger, C. P. *et al.* (1978) *Migrations, croissance et développement*, Paris, OECD.

King, R. L. (1973) *Land Reform: The Italian Experience*, London, Butterworth.

King, R. L. (1976) 'Long-range migration patterns within the EEC: an Italian case study', in Lee, R. and Ogden, P. E. (eds) *Economy and Society in the EEC*, Westmead, Saxon House, 108–25.

King, R. L. (1977) 'Recent industrialisation in Sardinia: re-birth or neo-colonialism?', *Erdkunde*, 31, 87–122.

King, R. L. (1979) 'Return migration: a review of some case studies from Southern Europe', *Mediterranean Studies*, 1, 2, 3–30.

King, R. L. (1980) 'The Maltese migration cycle: perspectives on return', *Oxford Polytechnic Discussion Papers in Geography*, no. 13, Oxford.

King, R. L. (1981) 'Italy', in Clout, H. D. (ed.) *Regional Development in Western Europe*, Chichester, Wiley, 119–50.

King, R. L. (1984) 'Emigration, return migration and internal migration', in Williams, A. (ed.) *Southern Europe Transformed*, London, Harper & Row, 145–78.

King, R. L. and Strachan, A. J. (1980) 'The effects of return migration on a Gozitan Village', *Human Organisation*, 39, 2, 175–9.

Kintis, A. A. (1980) 'Regional industrial development of Greece and the effects of EEC entry', *Problems of Regional Economic Development*, 54–5 (in Greek).

Koelstra, R. W. (1978) *Au Travail dans la périphérie*, IMWOO, NUFFIC.

Koelstra, R. W. and Tieleman, H. J. (1977) *Développement ou migration?*, IMWOO/NUFFIC.

Kofman, E. (1981) 'Functional regionalism and alternative regional development programmes in Corsica', *Regional Studies*, 15, 173–81.

Kofman, E. (1982) 'Differential modernisation, social conflicts and ethno-regionalism in Corsica', *Ethnic and Racial Studies*, 5, 300–12.

Kolinsky, M. (1974) *Continuity and Change in European Society*, London, Croom Helm.

Kottis, G. Ch. (1980) *Industrial Decentralisation and Regional Development*, Athens (in Greek).

Krane, R. E. (1975) 'Effects of international migration upon occupational mobility, acculturation and the labour market in Turkey', in Krane, R. E. (ed.) *Manpower Mobility across Cultural Boundaries*, Leiden, Brill, 161–204.

Krane, R. E. (ed.) (1979) *International Labour Migration in Europe*, New York, Praeger.

Kudat, A., Ozkan, Y. and Oncü, Y. (1975) *Yurtdisina isgücu göcünün yöresel boyutlari*, Berlin.

Labro, M. (1977) *La Question corse*, Paris, Editions Entente.

Lafont, R. (1967) *La Révolution régionaliste*, Paris, Gallimard.

Läpple, D. and van Hoogstraten, P. (1980) 'Remarks on the spatial structure of capitalist development: the case of the Netherlands', in Carney, J. *et al.* (eds) *Regions in Crisis*, London, Croom Helm, 117–66.

Lasuén Sancho, J. R. and Pastor Bodmer, A. (1981) 'Perspectivas regionales de España', in Acosta España, R. *et al. La España de las autonomías*, Madrid, Espasa.

Lawlor, T. (1975) 'Foreign investment in Franco's Spain', *Iberian Studies*, IV, 1, 21–30.

Lázaro Araujo, L. (1979) 'Sector público, decentralización y autonomías en la constitución española de 1978', *Revista de Estudios Regionales*, 4, 17–66.

Leal, L. J., Leguina, J., Naredo, J. M. and Tarrafeta, L. (1975) *La agricultura en el desarrollo capitalista español (1940–70)*, Madrid, Siglo XXI.

Léger, D. and Hervieu, B. (1979) *Le Retour à la nature. 'Au Fond de la forêt ... l'Etat'*, Paris, Editions du Seuil.

Leontidou-Emmanuel, L. (1981) 'Working class and land allocation: the urban history of Athens, 1880–1980', Ph.D. thesis, London School of Economics and Political Science.

Lewis, J. R. and Williams, A. M. (1981) 'Regional uneven development on the European periphery: the case of Portugal, 1950–78', *Tijdschrift voor Economische en Sociale geographie*, LXXII, 2, 81–98.

Lewis, J. R. and Williams, A. M. (1982) 'Desenvolvimento regional desequilibrado em Portugal: situação actual e impacto provável de adesão a CCE', *Desenvolvimento Regional*, 14–15.

Lewis, J. R. and Williams, A. M. (1984) 'International labour migration and regional uneven development in contemporary Portugal', in *City and Region* (forthcoming).

Liebermann, S. (1982) *The Contemporary Spanish Economy – A Historical Perspective*, London, Allen & Unwin.

Lienau, C. (1977) 'Geographische Aspekte der Gastarbeiter wanderungen Zwischen Mittelmeerlandern und europäischen Industrielandem mit einer Bibliographie', in Rother, K. (ed.) *Activ- und Passivraume im mediterranen Südeuropa*, Düsseldorf, Düsseldorfer Geography Schriften 7.

Lijphart, A. (1968) *The Politics of Accommodation Pluralism and Democracy in the Netherlands*, University of California Press.

Lijphart, A. (1977) *Democracy in Plural Societies: A Comparative Exploration*, New Haven, Yale University Press.

Linares Martín de Rosales, J. (1981) *Régimen financiero de las comunidades Autónomas Españolas*, Aragon, Diputación General.

Linz, J. J. (1978) 'Crisis, breakdown and reequilibration', in Linz, J. J. and Stepan, A. (eds) *The Breakdown of Democratic Regimes*, Part I, Baltimore, Johns Hopkins University Press.

Linz, J. J. (1979) 'Europe's southern frontier: evolving trends towards what?', *Daedalus*, 108.

Lipietz, A. (1977) *Le Capital et son espace*, Paris, François Maspero.

Lipietz, A. (1980a) 'The structuration of space, the problem of land, and spatial policy', in Carney, J. *et al.* (eds) *Regions in Crisis*, London, Croom Helm, 60–75.

Lipietz, A. (1980b) 'Inter-regional polarization and the tertiarization of society', *Papers, Regional Science Association*, 44, 3–18.

Lipset, S. M. and Rokkan, S. (1967) *Party Systems and Voter Alignments*, New York, Free Press.

Livi Bacci, M. (1972) 'The countries of emigration', in Livi Bacci, M. (ed.) 'Demographic and social patterns of emigration from Southern European countries', *Serie Ricerche Empiriche*, No. 7, Florence, Università di Firenze Dipartimento Statistico–Matematico, 7–123.

López Nieto, A. and Fernández Rodriguez, F. (1981) 'La solidaridad y el desarrollo regional en la constitución y en la LOFCA', in Acosta España, R. *et al. La España de las autonomías*, Madrid, Espasa.

Lopreato, J. (1967) *Peasants No More*, San Francisco, Chandler.

Loubère, L. (1975) 'Vins et politique en Bas-Languedoc, 1848 à 1914', *Droit et gauche de 1709 à nos jours. Actes du colloque de Montpellier, 9–10 juin 1973*, Montpellier, Centre de l'Histoire Contemporaine du Languedoc Méditerranéen et du Roussillon.

Loukakis, P. (1976) *Regionale Strukturprobleme in Griechenland unter Berücksichtigung des wachsenden Industrialisierungsprozesses*, Aachen.

Loukissas, P. J. (1977) 'Tourism and environment in conflict: the case of the Greek isle of Mykonos', *Studies of the Third World*, 105–32.

Lovering, J. (1978) 'The theory of the "internal colony" and the political economy of Wales', in *Radical Review of Political Economics*, 10, 3, 55–67.

Lutz, V. (1961) 'Some structural aspects of the southern problem: the complementarity of emigration and industrialisation', *Banca Nazionale del Lavoro Quarterly Review*, 14, 367–402.

McDonough, P., López, Pina A. and Barnes, S. (1981) 'The Spanish public in political transition', *British Journal of Political Science*, 11, 1, 49–79.

Mackay, A. (1977) *Spain in the Middle Ages*, London, Macmillan.

MacKerron, G. and Rush, H. J. (1976) 'Agriculture in the EEC: taking stock', *Food Policy*, 1, 4, 286–300.

MacMillion, C. W. (1981) 'International integration and international disintegration', *Comparative Politics*, 13, 33, 291–312.

McWilliams, C. (1972) *Factories in the Fields*, Santa Barbara, Perigrine Smith.

Majoral, R. (1977) 'The consequences of depopulation in the Western Pyrenees of Catalonia', *Iberian Studies*, 6, 24–33.

Malefakis, E. (1970) *Agrarian Reform and Peasant Revolution in Spain*, New Haven, Yale University Press.

Mandel, E. (1978) *The Second Slump*, London, New Left Books.

Maraffi, M. (1980) 'State/economy relationships: the case of Italian public enterprise', *British Journal of Sociology*, XXXI, 4, 507–24.

Margalef, J. (1979) *El tarragones, estructura económica: expansió industrial i desiquilibris territorials*, Barcelona, Caixa d'Estalvis de Catalunya.

Marres, P. (1950) *La Vigne et le vin en France*, Paris, Armand Colin.

Marres, P. (1954) 'La Modernisation de l'économie du Bas-Languedoc et des Cevennes méridionales', *Bulletin de la Société Languedocienne de Géographie*, 2e série, XXV, 2, 117–60.

Marres, P. (1966a) 'Le Languedoc méditerranéen aux XVIIe et XVIIIe siècles', *Annales de l'Institut d'Etudes Occitanes*, 412, 151–6.

Marres, P. (1966b) 'L'Amélioration des Liaisons routières entre le Bas-Languedoc et la Montagne au XVIIIe siècle', *Annales de l'Institut d'Etudes Occitanes*, 412, 179–86.

Marthelot, P. (1974) 'Réflexions sur certaines conséquences de la révolution agraire en Algérie, *Maghreb-Machrek*, 65, 32–5.

Martins, M. B. and Chaves Rosa, J. (1979) *O grupo estado*, Lisbon, Edições Jornal Expresso.

Massey, D. (1978a) 'Capital and locational change: the UK electrical engineering and electronic industries', in *Radical Review of Political Economics*, 10, 3, 39–54.

Massey, D. (1978b) 'Regionalism: some current issues', *Capital and Class*, 6, 106–25.

Matos, L. S. (1973) *Investimentos estrangeiros em Portugal*, Lisbon, Seara Nova.

Medhurst, K. N. (1977) *The Basques and the Catalans*, London, Minority Rights Group.

Merigo, E. (1982) 'Spain', in Boltho, A. (ed.) *The European Economy: Growth and Crisis*, Oxford, Oxford University Press.

Merrett, C. R. (1981) 'Petrochemicals in Japan and Western Europe', *Barclays Review* (November), 83–7.

Mik, G. and Verkoren-Hemelaar, N. (1976) 'Segregation in the Netherlands and Turkish migration', in Abadan-Unat, N. (ed.) *Turkish Workers in Europe, 1960–75*, Leiden, Brill, 253–83.

Mill, J. S. (1910) *Utilitarianism, On Liberty, Representative Government*, London, Everyman.

Ministerio de Economía (1979) *Programa a medio plazo para la economía española*, Madrid.

Ministério da Indústria e Tecnologia (1977) *Plano a médio prazo 1977–80: Diagnóstico de situação e estratégia de desenvolvimento da energia e das indústrias extractivas e transformadoras*, Lisbon, Imprensa Nacional.

Ministero Industria, Commercio e Artigianato (1980a) *Programma finalizzato – industria automobilistica*, Rome.

Ministero Industria, Commercio e Artigianato (1980b) *Analisi preliminare dell' industria automobilistica italiana*, Rome.

Mishalani, P., Robert, A., Stevens, S. and Weston, A. (1981) 'The pyramid of privilege', in Stevens, C. (ed.) *The EEC and the Third World: A Survey*, vol. 1, London, Hodder & Stoughton, 60–82.

Mitsovoleas, T. (1981) 'Greek entry will accentuate regional inequalities in the Community', *Epsilon*, 13, 44–8.

Mochón Morcillo, F. (1980) 'Análisis de algunos flujos económicos a la luz de las autonomías con especial referencia al caso andaluz', *Revista de Estudios Regionales*, 4, extraordinary vol. II, 444–64.

Molle, W., with van Holst, B. and Smit, H. C. (1980) *Regional Disparity and Economic Development in the European Community*, Farnborough, Saxon House.

Morell Ocaña, L. (1974) 'La administración local', in Fraga Iribarne *et al.* (eds) *La España de los años 70*, vol. III, Madrid, Editorial Moneda y Crédito.

Mori, A. (1961) 'Osservazioni sull'emigrazione vitalizia nell'Italia meridionale', *Bollettino della Società Geografica Italiana*, Series 9, 2, 4–6, 234–47.

Mottura, G. (1980) 'Appunti sulla questione agraria in Italia tra gli anni '30 a gli anni '50', *Agricoltura e Società*, 1.

Mottura, G. and Pugliese, E. (1972) 'Observations on some characteristics of Italian emigration in the last fifteen years', *International Review of Community Development*, 27/8, 3–19.

Mottura, G. and Pugliese, E. (1975) *Agricoltura Mezzogiorno: mercato del lavoro*, Bologna, Il Mulino.

Mouzelis, N. (1978) *Modern Greece: Facets of Underdevelopment*, London, Macmillan.

Muñoz, J., Boldan, S. and Serrano, A. (1980) 'The growing dependence of Spanish industrialization on foreign investment', in Seers, D., Schaffer, B. and Kiljunen, M.-L. (eds) *Underdeveloped Europe*, Brighton, Harvester Press.

Muñoz Machado, S. (1980) 'La cuestión en la Constitución Española', in García de Enterría, E. (ed.) *La distribución económicas entre el poder central y las autonomías territoriales en el Derecho Comparado y en la Constitución Española*, Madrid, Instituto de Estudios Económicos, chapter V.

Munro, J. M. (1974) 'Migration in Turkey', *Economic Development and Cultural Change*, 22, 634–53.

Murolo, A. (1982) 'The Greek economy: the role of transnationals and the EEC', *Mezzogiorno di Europa*, 2.

Murray, F. (1983) 'The decentralization of production – the decline of the mass collective worker', *Capital and Class*, 19, 74–99.

Musto, S. (1982) 'Enlargement and the structures of Western Europe', in

Seers, D. and Vaitsos, C. (eds) *The Second Enlargement of the EEC: The Integration of Unequal Partners*, London, Macmillan.

Myrdal, G. (1957) *Rich Land and Poor*, New York, Harper & Row.

Myrdal, G. (1963) *Economic Theory and Underdeveloped Regions*, London, Methuen.

Nadal, J. (1975) *El fracaso de la revolución industrial en España, 1814–1913*, Barcelona, Ariel.

Nairn, T. (1977) *The Break-Up of Britain: Crisis and Neo-Nationalism*, London, New Left Books.

Naylon, J. (1981) 'Iberia', in Clout, H. D. (ed.) *Regional Development in Western Europe*, Chichester, Wiley, 359–88.

Negreponti-Delivanis, M. (1979) *Analysis of the Greek Economy*, Athens (in Greek).

Newbigin, M. L. (1924) *The Mediterranean Lands*, London, Christophers.

Newland, K. (1979) 'International migration: the search for work', *Worldwatch Paper*, no. 33, 6–8.

Nikolinakos, M. (1970) 'Materialien zur Kapitalistischen Entwicklung in Griechenland', *Das Argument*, 57, 340–74.

Nikolinakos, M. (1973) 'The contradictions of capitalist development in Greece: labour shortages and emigration', *Studi Emigrazione*, 30, 222–35.

Nikolinakos, M. (1974) 'The concept of the "European South" and the north-south problem in Europe', Preprint Series, No. 75–14, Berlin, Science Centre.

Nikolinakos, M. (1975a) 'Wanderungsbewegungen, Investitionen und Handelsbeziehungen zwischen Regionen verschiedenen Entwicklungsgrades unter spätkapitalistischen Bedingungen. Der Fall Mittelmeer', in Leggewie, C. and Nikolinakos, M. (eds) *Europäische Peripherie Die Dritte Welt*, Sonderheft, Meisenheim am Glan.

Nikolinakos, M. (1975b) 'Il concetto di "Sud Europa": Il problema Nord–Sud e il Mediterraneo', *Quaderni Mediterranei*, 1, 53–72.

Nikolinakos, M. (1977) *Die Arbeitsteilung zwischen EG and Mittelmeer: Zur Frage des Industrialisierungsprozesses in den Mittelmeerländern*, Berlin, Science Centre.

Nikolinakos, M. (1981) 'The problem of regional development in the context of the EEC', *Epsilon*, 10, 80–3 (in Greek).

Nikolinakos, M. (1983) 'The production of technology and the transnationalisation of the production process', Working Paper, 3, EADI, Tilburg.

O'Connor, J. (1973) 'Political parties and capitalist development', *Kapitalstate*, 6.

O'Flanagan, T. P. (1980) 'Agrarian structures in north-west Iberia: responses and their implications for development', *Geoforum*, 11, 2, 157–69.

Oller i Compañ, V. (1981) 'La política industrial en Cataluña', *Información Comercial Española*, March, 53–7.

Organization for Economic Cooperation and Development (1967) *Emigrant Workers Returning to the Home Country*, Paris, OECD.

Organization for Economic Cooperation and Development (1981) *Economic Survey: Spain*, Paris, OECD.

Organization for Economic Cooperation and Development (1982a) *Economic Survey: Spain*, Paris, OECD.

Organization for Economic Cooperation and Development (1982b) *Economic Survey: Sweden*, Paris, OECD.

Organization for Economic Cooperation and Development (1982c) *Tourism Policy and International Tourism*, Paris, OECD.

Organization for Economic Cooperation and Development (1983) 'The economic and social role of local-level employment initiatives', paper presented to the conference on Rural Entrepreneurial Capacities, Senigalia.

Orlando, G. (1983) 'L'inpatto sull'agricultura vista da un economista agrario', in Fuá, G. and Zacchia, C. (eds) *Industrializzazione senza fralture*, Bologna, Il Mulino.

Özkan, U. (1975) *Stabilisierungstaktor oder revolutionäres Potential? (Politische Sozialisation der türkischen Gastarbeiter)*, Berlin, International Institute für vergleichende Gesellschaftsforschung Berlin, Preprint Series P75–1.

Paine, S. (1974) *Exporting Workers: The Turkish Case*, Cambridge, Department of Applied Economics, Occasional Paper no. 41.

Paine, S. (1979) 'Replacement of the west European migrant labour system by investment in the European periphery', in Seers, D., Schaffer, B. and Kiljunen, M. (eds) *Underdeveloped Europe*, Hassocks, Harvester Press, 65–95.

Palloix, C. (1976) 'The labour process: from Fordism to neo-Fordism', in Conference of Socialist Economists (CSE) *The Labour Process and Class Strategies*, London, CSE Books.

di Palma, G. (1977) 'Italia, Portogallo, Spagna: Ipotesi su tre reginii alla prova', *Prospettive Settanta*, III, 1, 44–8.

Papageorgious, C. L. (1973) *Regional Employment in Greece*, Athens, National Centre of Social Research.

Papandreou, A. (1972) *Paternalistic Capitalism*, Minnesota, University of Minnesota Press.

Papandreou, V. (1981) *Multinational Enterprises and Developing Countries: the Case of Greece*, Athens (in Greek).

Papaspiliopoulos, S. (1979) 'The Greek economy, 1962–78', in *Evropaiki Koinotita* (June), 14–15 (in Greek).

Parodi, M. (1977) 'Les Multinationales en Provence – Alpes – Côte d'Azur', *Peuples Méditerranéens*, 1.

Passama, P. (1906) *Condition des ouvriers agricoles dans le Minervois*, Paris, Giarde Brière.

Pastorelli, L. (1971) 'L'implantation des français d'Afrique du Nord dans les capitales corses', in University of Nice, *L'Implantation en Corse des Français d'Afrique du Nord*, vol. I, Nice.

Pearce, D. (1981) *Tourist Development*, Harlow, Longman.

Pearce, J. (1981) 'The Common Agricultural Policy', *Chatham House Papers*, no. 13, London, Royal Institute of International Affairs.

Pearce, J. (1982) 'Reform of the Common Agricultural Policy and the Third World', in Stevens, C. (ed.) *EEC and the Third World: A Survey*, London, Hodder & Stoughton, 47–63.

Pech de Laclause, J. (1959) 'La Vigne dans les Basses-Corbières depuis le XVIIIe siècle', Toulouse, thèse, Centre d'Edition Autonome, Amicale Sciences-Po.

Pennacchi, L. (1979) 'Il Caso Fiat nella crisi dell'industria internazionale dell'auto', *Politica e Economia*, 6, 51–70.

Penninx, R. and van Renselaar, H. (1978) *A Fortune in Small Change*, The Hague, REMPLOD.

Pereira, J. M. (1974) *Indústria, ideologia e quotidiano*, Lisbon, Edições Afrontamento.

Pérez Yruela, M. and Sánchez, A. (1981) 'La recogida de las aceitunas' al bien común', *Sociología del Trabajo*.

Pernet, F. (1978) 'Quelques questions exemplaires a propos du pastoralisme corse', *Peuples Méditerranéens*, 2, 73–85.

Perrier, E. (1975) *Corse, les raisons de la colère*, Paris, Editions Sociales.

Pescetto, G. *et al.* (1980) *La ristrutturazione dell'auto nei componenti e la posizione del Fiat*, Turin.

Petrochilos, G. S. (1979) 'Foreign direct investment in the Greek economy', *Lanchester Polytechnic, Discussion Paper*, no. 28.

Pizzorno, A. (ed.) (1974–8) *Lotte operaie e sindacato in Italia (1968–72)*, 6 vols, Bologna.

Plandé, R. (1944) *Géographie et histoire du département de l'Aude*, Grenoble, Editions Françaises Nouvelles.

Podbielski, G. (1981) 'The Common Agricultural Policy and the Mezzogiorno', *Journal of Common Market Studies*, 19, 333–50.

Poncet, E. (1977) 'La Corse', *Les Cahiers de l'Institut de Formation, de Recherche et de Promotion*, 8.

Portes, A. (1978) 'Migration and underdevelopment', *Politics and Society*, 8, 1.

Porto, M. C. L. (1984) 'Portugal – twenty years of change', in Williams, A. (ed.) *Southern Europe Transformed*, London, Harper & Row.

Poulantzas, N. (1975) *Classes in Contemporary Capitalism*, London, New Left Books.

Power, J. (1978) *Western Europe's Migrant Workers*, 2nd edn, London, Minority Rights Group.

Pridham, G. (1984) *The New Mediterranean Democracies: Regime Transition in Spain, Greece and Portugal*, London, Cass. (Also to be published in *West European Politics*, 7, 2.)

Prodi, R. (1980) 'Una cura per l'auto', *Mondo Economico* (19 April), 73–9.

Punset, R. (1979) 'Maura y el maurismo: perspectiva histórica de la revolución desde arriba', *Sistema*, 33, 29–41.

Que Faire (1971) *Colonialisme intérieur et minorités nationales*, 8/9.

Quéré, L. (1978) *Jeux Interdits á la frontière*, Paris, Editions Anthropos.

Quintas Seoane, J. R. (1981) 'El hecho autonómico y el desarrollo Regional', in Acosta España, R. *et al. La España de las autonomías*, Madrid, Espasa Calpe.

Reece, J. (1979) 'Internal colonialism: the case of Brittany', *Ethnic and Racial Studies*, 2, 3, 275–92.

Regul, R. (ed.) (1977) *Die Europäischen Gemeinschaften und die Mittelmeerlände*, Baden-Baden.

Reig Tapia, A. (1979) 'Consideraciones metodológicas para el estudio de la represión franquista en al guerra civil', *Sistema*, 33, 99–128.

Renner, K. (1953) *Wandlungen der Modernen Gesellschaft*, Vienna.

Renucci, J. (1974) *Corse traditionnelle et Corse nouvelle*, Lyon, Audin Imprimeurs.

Revelli, M. (1982) 'Defeat at Fiat', *Capital and Class*, 16, 95–108.

Review of Radical Political Economics (1978) 'Uneven regional development', Special Issue, 10, 3.

Reyneri, E. (1979) *La Catena migratoria*, Bologna, Il Mulino.

Rhoades, R. E. (1978) 'Intra-European return migration and rural development: lessons from the Spanish case', *Human Organisation*, 37, 2, 136–47.

Rhoades, R. E. (1979) 'From caves to main street: return migration and the transformation of a Spanish village', *Papers in Anthropology*, 20, 1, 57–74.

Richardson, H. W. (1969) *Elements of Regional Economics*, Harmondsworth, Penguin.

Richardson, H. W. (1975) *Regional Development Policy and Planning in Spain*, Farnborough, Saxon House.

Riedel, J. (1970) *Kritische Untersuchung über die regionale Wirtschaftsplanung in Griechenland*, Munich.

Rist, R. C. (1978) *Guest Workers in Germany*, New York, Praeger.

Ritter, G. (1972) 'Landflucht und Stadtewachen in der Türkei', *Erdkunde*, 26, 177–96.

Ronzani, S. (1980) 'Regional incentives in Italy', in Yuill, D. *et al.* (eds) *Regional Policy in the European Community*, London, Croom Helm, 134–56.

Rose, R. and Urwin, D. W. (1975) *Regional Differentiation and Political Unity in Western Nations*, London, Sage.

Roumeliotsis, P. B. (1977) *Direct Foreign Investment and the National Economy: The Case of Greece*, Athens, Centre for Planning and Economic Research (in Greek).

Roumeliotsis, P. B. (1978) *Multinational Enterprises and Transfer Pricing*, Athens (in Greek).

Rullani, E. (1983) 'L'economia periferica di fronte ad una nuova fase dello sviluppo: ri-progettare il "modello" veneto', *Strumenti*, 1, 45–56.

Saenz de Buruaga, G. (1981) 'Hacia una nueva política regional en España', in Acosta España, R. *et al. La España de las autonomías*, Madrid, Espasa Calpe.

Salkanazov, N. and Vienot, A. (1980) 'La Corse en mutation', *Economie et Statistique*, 123, 23–34.

Salt, J. (1981) 'International labour migration in Western Europe: a geographical review', in Kritz, M. M., Keely, C. B. and Tomasi, S. M. (eds) *Global Trends in Migration*, New York, Center for Migration Studies.

Salt, J. and Clout, H. (eds) (1976) *Migration in Post-War Europe*, Oxford, Oxford University Press.

Sanguinetti, A. (1979) *Procès de Jacobins*, Paris, Grasset.

Sanli, İ., Ünal, Y. and Kilinçaslan, I. (1976) *Internal Migration and Metropolitan Development in Turkey*, Istanbul.

Santos, M. (1975) *L'Espace partagé*, Paris, Th. Genin; (1979) *The Shared Space*, London and New York, Methuen.

Santos, M. (1977) 'Underdevelopment, geography and planning', *Antipode*, 9, 3, 86–98.

Santos, M. (1980) 'Société et espace transnationalises dans le Venezuala actuel', *Revue Tiers Monde*, XXI, 84, 709–20.

Sardinha, A. (1914) *O valor da raca*, Lisbon.

Sawer, G. R. (1969) *Modern Federalism*, London, C. & A. Watts.

Schiller, G. (1972) 'Strukturprobleme der europäischen Arbeitskraftemobilitaet', in Salowsky, H. and Schiller, G. (eds) *Ursachen und Auswirkungen der Ausländerbeschäftigung*, Cologne.

Schmitt, H. O. (1981) *Economic Stabilisation and Growth in Portugal*, Washington, DC, International Monetary Fund.

Schmitter, P. C. (1976) 'Liberation by golpe: retrospective thoughts on the demise of authoritarian rule in Portugal', *Armed Forces and Society*, 2, 1, 5–33.

Schmitter, P. C. (1979) 'The "Régime d'exception" that became the rule: forty eight years of authoritarian domination in Portugal', in Graham, S. L. and Makler, H. M. (eds) *Contemporary Portugal: The Revolution and its Antecedents*, Austin, University of Texas Press.

Schmitter, P. C. (1981) 'The transition from authoritarian rule to democracy in modernizing societies: can Germany's proposition (and pessimism) be reversed?', paper presented at the Conference on Transactions from Authoritarianism and Prospects for Democracy in Latin America and Southern Europe, Woodrow Wilson Centre, Washington DC, mimeo.

Schrettenbrunner, H. (1970) *Bevolkerungs- und sozialgeographische Untersuchung einer Fremdarbeitergemeinde Kalabriens*, WGI Berichte zur Regionalforschung.

Seers, D. and Vaitsos, C. (eds) (1982) *The Second Enlargement of the EEC*, London, Macmillan.

Seers, D., Schaffer, B. and Kiljunen, M. L. (eds) (1979) *Underdeveloped Europe: Studies in Core-Periphery Relations*, Brighton, Harvester Press.

Semmler, W. (1982) 'Competition, monopoly and differentials of profit rates: theoretical considerations and empirical evidence', *Review of Radical Political Economics*, 13, 4, 39–52.

Sentou, J. (1948) 'Les Facteurs de la révolution agricole dans le Narbonnais', *France méridionale et pays ibériques. Mélanges géographiques offerts en hommage à M. Daniel Faucher*, 2 vols, Toulouse, Editions toulousaines de l'Ingénieur, vol. II, 651–66.

Service Régional de Statistique Agricole (1980–1) *Bulletin statistique agricole*, Ajaccio.

Servolin, C. (1972) 'L'absorption de l'agriculture dans la mode de production capitaliste', in Tavernier, Y., Gervais, M. and Servolin, C. (eds) *L'univers politique des paysans dans la France contemporaine*, Paris, Libraire Armand Colin and Fondation Nationale des Sciences Politiques, 41–77.

Sevilla, E. (1979) *La evolución del campesinado en España*, Barcelona, Península.

Shils, E. (1975) *Center and Periphery*, Chicago, University of Chicago Press.

Shlaim, A. and Yannopoulos, G. N. (eds) (1976) *The EEC and the Mediterranean Countries*, Cambridge, Cambridge University Press.

Signorelli, A. (1980) 'Regional policies in Italy for migrant workers returning home', in Grillo, R. D. (ed.) *Nation and State in Europe: Anthropological Perspectives*, London, Academic Press, 89–103.

Silva, F. and Grillo, M. (1980) 'Costi, produttività e prezzi nell'industria dell'auto', *Politica ed Economia*, XI, 2, 49–56.

Silva, M., Amaro, R. R., Clausse, G., Conim, C., Matos, M., Pisco, M., Seruya, L. M. (1984) *Retorno, emigração e desenvolvimento regional em Portugal*, Lisbon, Instituto de Estudos para o Desenvolvimento.

Slater, M. (1984) 'Italy – surviving into the 1980s', in Williams, A. (ed.) *Southern Europe Transformed?*, London, Harper & Row.

Smith, G. R. (1980) *Politics in Western Europe – a Comparative Perspective*, London, Heinemann.

Smith, J. H. (1975) 'Work routine and social structure in a French village: Cruzy in the nineteenth century', *Journal of Interdisciplinary History*, 5, 3, 357–82.

Solinas, G. (1982) 'Labour market segmentation and workers' careers: the case of the Italian knitwear industry', *Cambridge Journal of Economics*, 6, 331–52.

SOMIVAC (1979) 'Jean Risterucci parle de la Somivac cette mal-aimée', *Revue d'Information, Somivac*, 92.

SOMIVAC (1981) *La Somivac*, unpublished report, Bastia.

SOPEMI (Continuous Reporting System on Migration), various dates, *Annual Reports*, Paris, Organization for Economic Cooperation and Development Directorate.

Sorre, M. (1913) *Etude critique des sources de l'histoire de la viticulture et du commerce des vins et eaux-de-vie en Bas-Languedoc au XVIIIe siècle*, Montpellier, Imprimerie Roumégons et Déhan.

Sotelo, I. (1981) 'La fragilidad de la democracia', *El País*, 22, iv, 81.

State Institute of Statistics (1977) *Census of Population: Social and Economic Characteristics of the Population 1970*, publication number 756, Ankara.

State Institute of Statistics (1979) *Income Distribution and Consumption Expenditures in Rural Areas*, publication number 881, Ankara.

Stathakis, G. (1984) 'Industrial development and the regional problem: the case of Greece', University of Newcastle, unpublished Ph.D. thesis.

Statistiches Bundesamt (1973) *Allgemeine Statistik des Auslandes Lander-berichte, Turkei, 1972*, Stuttgart and Mainz.

Statistiches Bundesamt (1979) *Statistik des Auslandes Landerkurzbericht Turkei, 1979*, Stuttgart and Mainz.

Stefanelli, R. (1969) *I Braccianti: Venti anni lotte*, Naples, ESI.

Stillwell, F. J. B. (1978) 'Competing analyses of the spatial aspects of capitalist development', *Review of Radical Political Economics*, 10, 3, 18–27.

Strachan, A. J. and King, R. L. (1982) 'Emigration and return migration in southern Italy: a multivariate, cluster and map analysis', *Leicester University Geography Department Occasional Paper*, no. 9, Leicester.

Swamy, G. (1981) 'International migrant workers' remittances', World Bank Staff Working Paper 481, Washington, DC, World Bank.

Sylos Labini, P. (1974) *Saggio sulle classi sociale*, Bari, Laterza.

Tamames, R. (1980) *Introducción a la economía española*, 3rd edn, Madrid, Alianza Editorial.

Tapinos, G. (1974) *L'Economie des migrations internationales*, Paris, Armand Colin.

Tarrow, S. (1979) 'Italy in 1978: where everybody governs, does anybody govern?', in Denitch, B. (ed.) *Legitimation of Regimes*, London, Sage, 229–48.

Taylor, F. W. (1911) 'The principles of scientific management', reprinted in Taylor, F. W. (1964) *Scientific Management*, New York, Harper & Row.

Taylor, R. (1980) *Implications for the Southern Mediterranean Countries of the Second Enlargement of the European Community*, Brussels, Europe Information.

Toepfer, H. (1980) 'Mobilität und Investitionsverhalten Türkischer Gastarbeiter nach der Remigration', *Erdkunde*, 34, 206–14.

Toepfer, H. (1981) 'Regionale und Sektorale Kapitalströme als Folgeerscheinung der Remigration türkischer Arbeitskrafte aus Westeuropa', *Erdkunde*, 35.

Toepfer, H. and Sviçmez, V. (1979) 'Sektorale und regionale Mobilität von Rückwanderern in die Türkei', *Orient*, 20, 92–107.

Tolan, B. (1972) *Türkiye de iller itibariyle sosyo-ekonomik gelişmislik endeksi* (Socio-economic Development Indices of Turkish Provinces), Ankara, SPO.

Tornos, J. (1979) 'La intervención de las Communidas Autónomas en la Economía', *Revista Española de Derecho Administrativo*, 21, 221–39.

Tornos, J. (1981) 'El proceso de distribución de las competencías económicas y la necesaria unidad de la política económica', *Revista Española de Derecho Administrativo*, 29, 319–28.

Torres Bernier, E. (1980) 'Relaciones entre política económica estatal y regional', *Revista de Estudios Regionales*, extraordinary vol. II, 'Las Autonomías', 371–86.

Touraine, A. and Dubet, F. (1981) *Le pays contre l'Etat. Luttes occitanes*, Paris, Editions du Seuil.

Trebous, M. (1970) *Migration and Development: The Case of Algeria*, Paris.

Trouvé, Baron (1818) *Etats de Languedoc et département de l'Aude*, vol. II, 'Description générale et statistique du département de l'Aude', Paris, Didot.

Tsoucalas, C. (1969) *The Greek Tragedy*, Harmondsworth, Penguin.

Tsoukalis, L. (1981) *The European Community and its Mediterranean Enlargement*, London, Allen & Unwin.

Tümertekin, E. (1968) *Internal Migration in Turkey*, Istanbul, Geographical Institute of Istanbul University.

Tümertekin, E. (1970–1) 'Gradual internal migration in Turkey', *Review of the Geographical Institute of the University of Istanbul*, 13, 157–69.

Turkish State Planning Organization (1983) *A Report on Rural Entrepreneurial Activities*, presented to the Conference on Rural Entrepreneurial Capacities, Senigalia, 7–10 June.

Unger, K. (1983) *Die Rückkehr der Arbeitsmigraiten*, Saarbrucken, Verlag Breiterback.

U. Ribombu (1981) nos 17 and 19.

van Renselaar, H. and van Velzen, L. (1976) 'Public and private initiatives aimed at using external labour migration for development', in Abadan-Unat, N. *et al. Migration and Development*, Ankara.

van Velzen, L. (1977) *Peripheral Production in Kayseri, Turkey*, Ankara, Ajans-Türk Press.

van Velzen, L. and Penninx, R. (1977) *A Contribution to the Theory of International Labor Migration: The Export of Manpower from a Rural District in Central Turkey*, REMPLOD Project, IMWOO, NUFFIC.

Vázquez Barquero, A. (1980) 'Los países de la Europa del sur ante la nueva revolución industrial', *Papeles de la Economía Española*, 5, 100–19.

Vázquez Barquero, A. (1983) 'Industrialization in rural areas: the Spanish case', paper presented to the conference on Rural Entrepreneurial Capacities, Senigalia.

Vergopoulos, K. (1978) 'Capitalismo disforme', in Amin, S. and Vergopoulos, K. *A Questão camponesa e o capitalismo*, Lisbon, A Regra da Jogo.

Vergopoulos, K. (1983) 'L'état dans le capitalisme périphérique', *Revue du Tiers Monde*, XXIV, 93, 34–52.

Verlaque, C. (1981) 'Patterns and levels of port-industrialisation in the western Mediterranean', in Hoyle, B. S. and Pinder, D. A. (eds) *City-port Industrialisation and Regional Development*, Oxford, Pergamon.

Vigorelli, P. (1969) 'Returning migrants re-employed in Italian industry', *Migration News*, 18, 2, 3–13.

Vilar, P. (1962) *La Catalogne dans l'Espagne moderne*, Paris, SEVPEN.

Wade, R. (1980) 'The Italian state and the underdevelopment of south Italy', in Grillo, R. *Nation and State in Europe*, London, Academic Press.

Walker, R. A. (1980) 'Two sources of uneven development under advanced capitalism: spatial differentiation and capital mobility', in *Radical Review of Political Economics*, 10, 3, 28–38.

Wallerstein, I. (1974) *The Modern World System*, New York, Academic Press.

Wallerstein, I. (1979) *The Capitalist World Economy*, New York, Cambridge University Press.

Ward's Automative Yearbook (1980) Detroit, Ward's Communications, Inc.

Warner, Ch. K. (1960) *The Winegrowers of France and the Government since 1875*, New York, Columbia University Press.

Watson, M. (1978) 'A critique of development from above, the lessons of French and Dutch experience of nationally defined regional policy', *Public Administration*, 56, 457–81.

Wiarda, H. J. (1977) *Corporatism and Development: The Portuguese Experience*, Amherst, MIT Press.

Widstrand, C. and Amin, S. (eds) (1975) *Multinational Firms in Africa*, Uppsala.

Woolf, S. J. (ed.) (1968) *The Nature of Fascism*, London, Weidenfeld & Nicolson.

World Bank (1982) *World Development Report, 1982*, Oxford, Oxford University Press.

World Bank (1983) *World Development Report 1983*, Oxford, Oxford University Press.

Wynn, M. (ed.) (1984) *Housing in Europe*, London, Croom Helm.

Yuill, D. (ed.) (1983) *Regional Development Agencies in Europe*, Aldershot, Gower.

Zacchia, C. (1983) 'Summary of case studies', in Fuá, G. *et al. Rural Industrialisation in the North-East and the Center*, presented to the Conference on Rural Entrepreneurial Capacities, Senigalia, 7–10 June.

Zangheri, R. (ed.) (1959) *Le Lotte agrarie in Italia*, Milan, Feltrinelli.
Zingaro, R. (1969) 'Re-integration of returnees in Andria', *Migration News*, 18, 2, 19–22.

Name index

Place index

Subject index

accessibility, 30, 123, 218, 243; to EC markets, 31, 33, 37; to export markets, 42–3, 51; to markets, 40, 205, 218–20; to national markets, 36
activity rates, 13, 287
'agrarian question', 125–6
agricultural: change, 26–33, 140–54; day labourers, 114, 180; fertilizers, 28–9, 149–53, 275; internal segmentation of, 138; reform, 323; working class, 123–39
agriculture, 5, 7, 10–12, 18, 23, 26–33, 78–87, 89–90, 92–3, 96–7, 101–3, 114–15, 121, 123–39, 248–56, 268–9, 274–7; casual workers in, 112, 133, 136; family farming, 27, 140–54, 188; fragmentation within farms, 29, 57; *latifundia*, 26–9, 104, 314, 322, 331; mechanization, 26, 132–9, 149–51, 255, 272; *minifundia*, 26–9, 77; part-time, 26–7, 139, 151, 252, 258; productivity, 57; regional specialization of, 29, 50–2, 140–54, 252–6; seasonal workers in, 133, 137, 139, 151, 153
ancien régime, 311, 313, 316–17, 319
artisanal production, 111, 118, 120, 273
asymmetric growth, 55–6, 74
autarky, 39, 291, 318, 324, 337
automation, 161, 168, 170–3; and deskilling, 187, 191

balance of payments, 5–6, 9, 36, 203, 290
balanced growth, 54–5, 74
banking, 44, 71–3, 217, 244, 273, 289–90, 300, 319, 338; bank deposits, 73

bourgeoisie, 11, 134, 265, 309, 311–12, 315–18, 339, 348; national, 290, 315–16, 339; petty, 12; regional, 252, 263, 273
branch plants, 156–7, 161, 170, 178, 180, 187–9
building industry, 87–99

capital, 2, 43, 54–5, 67–8, 76–7, 85, 89, 102, 117, 120–1, 144, 273, 279, 289; accumulation, 1–2, 16–17, 73, 79, 87, 98–9, 148, 154, 167–8, 170, 193–5, 197, 203–4, 206, 209, 226, 240, 247, 250, 255, 312–13, 316, 323–7, 331, 337; centralization of, 212; circulating capital, 235, 244–5; finance, 217, 228, 230, 240–1, 244, 315, 332; fixed, 41–2, 155, 212, 220, 230, 244–5; foreign, 10, 47–8, 197, 203–6, 220, 265, 268, 272, 338–9; forms of organization, 35, 38–43; hypermobility of, 17; indigenous, 30, 225, 228; industrial, 190, 217; investment, 92–3; investment of returned migrants, 65–74, 87–99, 120–1, 144, 273, 279, monopoly, 197; movements of, 10, 25–50, 53, 96–7, 250; multinational, 30, 35, 38–40, 42–3, 136, 189, 270, 285, 290–1, 306, 338–9; organic composition of, 155–7, 212, 218, 221–3, 230, 232, 235, 237, 244; technical composition of, 232; valorization of, 193–4, 198, 204, 206, 208–9, 212, 226, 237, 240–1, 243
capitalism, 1–2, 16–17, 308–9, 313–16, 332, 339, 344, 347; assisted, 291–2, 298;